AMERICAN HIGHER EDUCATION: A DOCUMENTARY HISTORY

American
Higher
Education

A DOCUMENTARY HISTORY

Edited by RICHARD HOFSTADTER and WILSON SMITH

VOLUME I

THE UNIVERSITY OF CHICAGO PRESS

V

Library of Congress Catalog Card Number: 61-15935

The University of Chicago Press, Chicago & London
The University of Toronto Press, Toronto 5, Canada

© 1961 by The University of Chicago. Published 1961
Composed and printed by The University of Chicago Press
Chicago, Illinois, U.S.A.

To

C. VANN WOODWARD

PREFACE

THIS BOOK HAS BEEN prepared to meet the need for an anthology of discussion about American higher education throughout our history. We are living in an age of heightened educational criticism and increasing interest in the educational past. There is every reason to believe that among general students of American history a minor boom in studying the history of education is beginning that will eventually fill many of the gaps in our present knowledge.

Those whose main interest is in the history of higher education have had to work thus far without some of the elementary tools available in many other fields. Students of the history of law and the Constitution have innumerable handbooks of cases and materials; students of labor can turn to the immensely helpful volumes of the *Documentary History of American Industrial Society* brought out by John R. Commons and his associates many years ago and recently reprinted; those interested in political or social history can find collection after collection of speeches, polemics, travelers' accounts, descriptions, and other firsthand materials. But for those who wish to read in the original materials, too often missing from even the larger college or university libraries, or to find in a single place a representation of the major trends and essential controversies in American higher education, there is no handbook and no help.

To be sure, Edward C. Elliott and M. M. Chambers brought together in one volume in 1934 the charters of many colleges and universities; but such texts, however useful for reference, make sodden reading, like most statutes and charters, and in any case can tell us only a small part

of what we want to know. Edgar W. Knight and Clifton L. Hall in
1951 prepared an interesting book, *Readings in American Educational
History,* but, since it embraces all levels of the educational system, its
coverage of higher education is severely limited. Knight's five-volume
Documentary History of Education in the South (1949–53) is of course
confined to one region, and its broad coverage of various educational
levels again compelled the editor to restrict his materials on colleges
and universities even within the South. The reader who wants to get
from original materials an over-all view of the development of higher
education—its institutions, their systems of government, curriculum,
conditions of faculty organization, academic freedom, educational controversies—must resort to hundreds of scattered works. There has been
no central sourcebook to satisfy this important area of curiosity, to
serve the purposes of teachers, or to stimulate research. There is not
a single work, for instance, that reprints the main argument of the
famous Yale Report of 1828, probably the most important educational
document written in America before the Civil War. Nor is there any
that gathers together the primary educational statements by the great
founders of the American universities in the last decades of the nineteenth century: Charles William Eliot, Andrew D. White, and Daniel
Coit Gilman.

Our working assumption has been that the major outlines of the history of our colleges and universities could be captured in one readable
source volume. Readability was an important criterion—and one sur-
prisingly easy to fulfil. It is commonly felt that education is an interesting and important field in which there is an immense mass of un-
interesting and unimportant writing. But those whose impressions of
educational literature have been formed mainly by exposure to the
work of compilers of dreary textbooks in educational psychology or
educational administration may tend to forget that it is a field that has
also excited the concern of such great men as Locke and Rousseau,
Jefferson and Newman. It is gratifying to go back over the history of
American education, especially before the field became intensely professional, and to find that the educational writings of Jefferson, Cooper,
Lindsley, Wayland, Ruggles, Tappan, Ticknor, White, Gilman,
Veblen, and Hutchins are full of spirit and savor and that they can
be read with pleasure. We have found it desirable, for the sake of
illustration and information, to include a limited number of documents like early college charters and rules that provide a necessary

structure for our history. But, for the most part, these pages constitute a sampler of three hundred years of a rich literature of educational discussion and controversy.

We have not tried to account in depth for every aspect of the history of higher education. We have left professional schools and academic professional organizations alone in order to give an adequate account of undergraduate colleges and the universities—the main stem of higher education. Since student life has been the subject of so many histories and anthologies, we have felt free to portray it only incidentally and by indirection. There is a large legal literature in the field of American education history which we have not tried to represent, except for the Dartmouth College case. In this respect the reader can be helped by the volumes compiled by M. M. Chambers, with E. C. Elliott, *The Colleges and the Courts* (1936–52). We have recognized that in the fullest sense it is impossible to compile a documentary history of American higher education, just as it would be impossible to compile a documentary history of law and politics: the sources are too many, too vast, and, often, like many trustees' minutes, altogether inaccessible. Consequently, we have restricted our collection chiefly to printed sources.

We hope that our collection will be found to have the merit of good documentary collections in other fields—which is not the merit of comprehensiveness but of being representative, informative, interesting, and serviceable. We have tried to portray with reasonable consistency the nature and structure of colleges and universities for the first three centuries of their existence: the diffusion of the educational system throughout the country; the problems created by sectarian affiliations; the character and functions of presidents and trustees; the evolution of curricular controversies and educational ideals; the institutional position and role of the professor and the conditions of professorial life; the development of academic freedom.

We hope, too, that these readings will be useful to students from varied fields. For these documents touch not merely upon teaching and research but also upon some central aspects of American life and character—upon our religion and politics, our social and intellectual aspirations, our very creativity and our failures as a people. Not only will they serve the social or intellectual historian or the sociologist who may find provocative materials here for tracing the rise of comparative institutions; they can also instruct all educators with or without portfolio who may hope to find in the history of our higher institutions a story that illustrates the character and pace of some significant changes in American history.

We gratefully acknowledge the assistance of those who helped us in preparing the manuscript for publication. An initial grant of funds to begin typing the documents was made in 1958 by the University Research Committee of Princeton University. Thereafter our expenses were met by a generous grant from the Committee on the Role of Education in American History. Walter P. Metzger advised us on the areas of interest to be represented in the documents. Without the enthusiastic efforts of graduate students in American history at the Johns Hopkins University, who proofread the typescript, the volume would have taken much longer to complete. Those who helped in this way were Lynn Parsons, James McPherson, Owen Edwards, James Crooks, and Travis Crosby.

For indispensable assistance in putting the book through the press we are grateful to Gerald Stearn.

CONTENTS TO VOLUME I

Part two

THE COLLEGIATE SYSTEM IN THE
EIGHTEENTH CENTURY

Part three

THE NATION, THE STATES,
AND THE SECTS

Part Four

Part Five

FREEDOM AND REPRESSION IN THE
OLD-TIME COLLEGE

Part I

FROM THE BEGINNINGS

TO THE

GREAT AWAKENING

O<small>NE OF THE</small> most impressive things about the Puritan community of Massachusetts Bay was the rapidity with which it took steps to found a college and propagate learning. The first recorded appeal for a college, that of John Eliot (Doc. 1), dates from 1633; and as early as 1636, when the little community perched on the edge of a howling wilderness hardly numbered 10,000, Harvard was legally established by an act of the General Court. Instruction began in 1638, and bodies of laws governing the conduct of the student body (Doc. 3) survive from the 1640's. In 1650 the General Court devised for the college the charter (Doc. 4) under which it is governed to this day.

It is still commonly believed that Harvard and the other early colleges were established as theological seminaries, with the sole object of rearing a ministry. One authority for this notion is the early appeal for funds, *New England's First Fruits* (Doc. 2), in which the unknown author speaks of the community's dread of leaving "an illiterate Ministery to the Churches when our present Ministers shall lie in the Dust." There can be no doubt that the maintenance of the Puritan tradition of a learned ministry was an important object, but one can hardly make a greater error than to imagine that our modern conceptions of specialized and professional education were meaningful to the Puritan founders. A theological seminary had no more meaning for them than an engineering school. They did not distinguish sharply between secular and theological learning; and they believed that the collegiate education proper for a minister should be the same as for an educated layman. They expected that the early colleges would produce not only ministers but Christian gentlemen who would be civic leaders.

Harvard's charter referred to the purpose of "the advancement of all good literature arts and Sciences" and to "the education of the English & Indian Youth of this Country in knowledge: and godliness." Cotton Mather, in his charming history of the college (Doc. 5), adverts to the need for "a succession of a learned and able ministry," but also emphasizes the role of the college simply as "a nursery for . . . men." The first charter in 1701 under which Yale was temporarily governed spoke of the school as one in which the youth of Connecticut would be instructed in the arts and sciences so as to be "fitted for Publick employment both in Church & Civil State." The charter upon which Yale settled as its instrument of government in 1745 (Doc. 11) repeated in its opening lines this dual statement of purpose.

William and Mary, which was the second college to be called into being by its charter of 1693 (Doc. 9), was in fact the third to offer collegiate instruction; for Yale had been graduating classes for some time before the Virginia college finally installed the faculty provided for in its charter to teach at this level. William and Mary's charter expresses the hope that it will educate ministers, but also that it will raise the youth "in good Letters and Manners" and propagate Christianity among "the Western Indians." The destruction of many of its records by fire has obscured much of its early history, but its statutes survive from 1727 (Doc. 10).

In practically every respect the first American colleges attempted to duplicate the conditions of the colleges of the ancient universities of England with which their founders were familiar. They were residential colleges in the English fashion; they carried on with the classical curriculum; their bodies of rules (Docs. 3, 10, 12) were patterned, almost verbatim in the earliest days, from the customs of Cambridge or Oxford. They aimed at the formation of Christian character, as well as the furtherance of learning. The Harvard statutes admonished the scholars not to "frequent the company and society of such men as lead an ungirt and dissolute life." The Yale statutes were very explicit in their condemnation of the student's "Disobedient or Contumacious or Refractory Carriage towards his Superiours, Fighting, Striking, Quarreling, Challenging, Turbulent Words or Behaviour, Drunkenness, Uncleaness, Lacivious Words or Actions, wearing woman's Apparel," and a list of further crimes warranting punishments ranging from fines to expulsion.

In one important respect it proved to be impossible to reproduce the conditions of the old English and European universities. The academic institution in America ceased practically from the very beginning to be a body of self-governing scholars and fell under the control of non-resident laymen. The European universities had been founded by groups of mature scholars; the American colleges were founded by their communities; and since they did not soon develop the mature scholars possessed from the beginning by their European predecessors but were staffed instead for generations mainly by young and transient tutors, the community leaders were reluctant to drop their reins of control. From the first this reluctance was manifested in the constitution of Harvard by the creation of a board of Overseers, consisting of six magistrates and six ministers, a body which, somewhat expanded in 1642, was the sole governing agent of the college until the granting of the charter of 1650. That charter created an additional body, the Corporation, to be composed of the president, the treasurer, and five fellows; the Corporation was given a large share of the powers of government and jurisdiction over the practices prevailing in Harvard since 1636. But the Overseers continued for a long time to govern in accordance with custom and not with the terms of the charter. Finally, the Corporation itself began to turn into a non-resident body—whereupon near the end of the eighteenth century the powers of government did gravitate into its hands. A momentous protest was made in 1721–23 against the drift toward making the Corporation a non-resident body by excluding from it newly appointed college tutors. As a consequence of a factional fight in the province, two tutors, Nicholas Sever and William Welsteed, attempted in effect to restore as much as possible of the tradition of resident self-government by laying claim to membership in the Corporation on the ground that the charter of 1650 had meant to make fellows of all teaching officers. This interpretation, argued at some length by Sever (Doc. 7), was very likely correct, so far as the intent behind the 1650 charter was concerned. But it ran against now long-standing college usage and was formidably opposed by President Leverett (Doc. 8), who had the backing of the governor. This last serious effort to re-create the conditions of self-government was a failure.

A further source of difficulty was that of keeping the colleges orthodox, a problem brought home to the Overseers as early as 1653, when President Henry Dunster fell into the snares of heresy by opposing infant baptism and was forced out of his post (Doc. 6). By and large the early colleges were set up to propagate the orthodoxies of their denominations and communities, and not even Dunster had denied the propriety of this goal. But when the churches were riven into factions by the enthusiasms of the Great Awakenings, the question arose which side should have proprietorship in a college, or whether it should be shared by both. Those who were moved by the enthusiasm of the Awakenings felt that the established clergy had grown cold and that the religious slackness of the community had penetrated the colleges. Such charges were leveled against Harvard and Yale by the Great Awakener, George Whitefield, during one of his evangelizing trips to the colonies, and they led to a heated controversy (Docs. 13, 14, 15) in 1745. The effects of unauthorized enthusiastic preachers upon the minds of undergraduates also became an issue at Yale in 1745, when two students attended Separatist church services with their parents while at home on vacation. Rector Clap and his faculty stoutly upheld the idea (Doc. 16) that uniformity of faith among the student body must be enforced if the college was to be faithful to the intentions of its founders. The long arm of orthodoxy was thus to extend outside the walls of the college and to govern the beliefs and behavior of students even when they were in their homes.

The sympathizers of the Great Awakenings were by no means indifferent to the need for education; the religious movement led to the foundation of a series of institutions, of which the first was Princeton, chartered in 1746. A new note, imposed by the interdenominational politics of New Jersey, was struck in the Princeton charter (Doc. 17): students could not be excluded from or discriminated against in the college because of their religion. The college soon found, as others were to find, that this interdenominational liberality was an asset in appealing for funds (Doc. 18).

1. A College First Proposed for Massachusetts Bay, 1633

The author of this appeal for support for a college was "Apostle" John Eliot (1604–90), missionary to the Indians. Eliot was a graduate of Jesus College, Cambridge. He came to Boston in 1631, and at the time this letter was written he was a preacher in Roxbury. Later he became an Overseer of Harvard. See Samuel Eliot Morison, *Builders of the Bay Colony* (Boston, 1930), chap. x.

Now for your selfe to come, I doe earnestly desire it, if God so move your heart, & not only for the common wealth sake; but also for Larnings sake, which I know you love, & will be ready to furder, & indeede we want store of such men, as will furder that, for if we norish not Larning both church & common wealth will sinke: & because I am upon this poynt I beseech you let me be bould to make one motion, for the furtheranc of Larning among us: God hath bestowed upon you a bounty full blessing; now if you should please, to imploy but one mite, of that greate welth which God hath given, to erect a schoole of larning, a colledg among us; you should doe a most glorious work, acceptable to God & man; & the commemoration of the first founder of the means of Larning, would be a perpetuating of your name & honour among us:

... for a library, & a place for the exercize of Larning, its my earnest desire & prayre, that God would stir up the heart of some well wishers to Larning, to make an onsett in that kind, & indeed Sir I know none, every way more fitt then your selfe: I beseech you therfore consider of it, & doe that which may comfort us: & where as a library is your first project, & then a college; I conceive upon our experiens, that we shall most neede convenient chambers, to entertaine students at first, & a little room I feare, will hould all our first stock of bookes, & as they increase we may inlarge the roome: but with us in our young beginings, men want purses to make such buildings: & therfore publik exercizes of larning be not yet sett on foote, though we have many larned men, both gentlemen & ministers: but had we a place fitted, we should have

Franklin M. Wright, "A College First Proposed, 1633: Unpublished Letters of Apostle Eliot and William Hammond to Sir Simonds D'Ewes," *Harvard Library Bulletin*, VIII (Autumn, 1954), 273–74, 276.

our tearmes & seasons for disputations, & lectures, not only in divinity: but in other arts & sciences, & in law also: for that would be very material for the wellfaire of our common wealth: & now I will say no more, but pray that the Lord would move your heart (which yet I hope is allready moved) to be the first founder of so gloryous a worke, as this is: . . .

2. New England's First Fruits, 1643

The author of this pamphlet, a promotional tract designed to raise funds for the new college, has not been identified, though it is likely that President Henry Dunster (1609–58/59?) supplied some information to the writer. The document, reproduced only in part here, is one of the most important sources of information on early Harvard. See Worthington C. Ford on its authorship in *Proceedings of the Massachusetts Historical Society*, XLII (April, 1909), 259–66, and Morison, *Founding of Harvard College*, pp. 304–5.

IN RESPECT OF THE COLLEDGE, AND THE
PROCEEDINGS OF "LEARNING" THEREIN

I. After God had carried us safe to *New England,* and wee had builded our houses, provided necessaries for our liveli-hood, rear'd convenient places for Gods worship, and setled the Civill Government: One of the next things we longed for, and looked after was to advance *Learning* and perpetuate it to Posterity; dreading to leave an illiterate Ministery to the Churches, when our present Ministers shall lie in the Dust. And as wee were thinking and consulting how to effect this great Work; it pleased God to stir up the heart of one Mr. *Harvard* (a godly Gentleman, and a lover of Learning, there living amongst us) to give the one halfe of his Estate (it being in all about 1700.l.) towards the erecting of a Colledge: and all his Library: after him another gave 300.l. others after them cast in more, and the publique hand of the State added the rest: the Colledge was, by common consent, appointed to be at *Cambridge,* (a place very pleasant and accommodate) and is called (according to the name of the first founder) *Harvard Colledge.*

Reprinted in Samuel Eliot Morison, *The Founding of Harvard College* (Cambridge, Mass., 1935), pp. 432–33.

The Edifice is very faire and comely within and without, having in it a spacious Hall; (where they daily meet at Commons, Lectures and Exercises), and a large Library with some Bookes to it, the gifts of diverse of our friends, their Chambers and studies also fitted for, and possessed by the Students, and all other roomes of Office necessary and convenient, with all needfull Offices thereto belonging: And by the side of the Colledge a faire *Grammar* Schoole, for the training up of young Schollars, and fitting them for *Academicall Learning,* that still as they are judged ripe, they may be received into the Colledge of this Schoole: Master *Corlet* is the Mr., who hath very well approved himselfe for his abilities, dexterity and painfulnesse in teaching and education of the youth under him.

Over the Colledge is master *Dunster* placed, as President, a learned conscionable and industrious man, who hath so trained up, his Pupills in the tongues and Arts, and so seasoned them with the principles of Divinity and Christianity, that we have to our great comfort, (and in truth) beyond our hopes, beheld their progresse in Learning and godlinesse also; the former of these hath appeared in their publique declamations in *Latine* and *Greeke,* and Disputations Logicall and Philosophicall, which they have wonted (besides their ordinary Exercises in the Colledge-Hall) in the audience of the Magistrates, Ministers, and other Schollars, for the probation of their growth in Learning, upon set dayes, constantly once every moneth to make and uphold: The latter hath been manifested in sundry of them, by the savoury breathings of their Spirits in their godly conversation. Insomuch that we are confident, if these early blossomes may be cherished and warmed with the influence of the friends of Learning, and lovers of this pious worke, they will by the help of God, come to happy maturity in a short time.

Over the Colledge are twelve Overseers chosen by the generall Court, six of them are of the Magistrates, the other six of the Ministers, who are to promote the best good of it and (having a power of influence into all persons in it) are to see that every one be diligent and proficient in his proper place.

3. Statutes of Harvard, ca. 1646

This first code of Harvard laws was apparently patterned after the Elizabethan statutes of Cambridge. See Morison's annotations.

1. When any Scholar is able to Read Tully or such like classical Latin Author *ex tempore,* and make and speak true Latin in verse and prose *suo (ut aiunt) Marte,* and decline perfectly the paradigms of Nouns and verbs in the Greek tongue, then may he be admitted into the College, nor shall any claim admission before such qualifications.

2. Every one shall consider the main End of his life and studies, to know God and Jesus Christ which is Eternal life. John 17. 3.

3. Seeing the Lord giveth wisdom, every one shall seriously by prayer in secret, seek wisdom of Him. Prov. 2. 2, 3 etc.

4. Every one shall so exercise himself in reading the Scriptures twice a day that they be ready to give an account of their proficiency therein, both in theoretical observations of Language and Logic, and in practical and spiritual truths as their tutor shall require according to their several abilities respectively, seeing the Entrance of the word giveth light etc. Psalms 119, 130.

5. In the public Church assembly they shall carefully shun all gestures that show any contempt or neglect of God's ordinances and be ready to give an account to their tutors of their profiting and to use the helps of storing themselves with knowledge, as their tutors shall direct them. And all Sophisters and Bachelors (until themselves make common place) shall publicly repeat Sermons in the Hall whenever they are called forth.

6. They shall eschew all profanation of God's holy name, attributes, word, ordinances, and times of worship, and study with reverence and love carefully to retain God and his truth in their minds.

7. They shall honor as their parents, Magistrates, Elders, tutors and aged persons, by being silent in their presence (except they be called on to answer) not gainsaying showing all those laudable expressions of honor and reverence in their presence, that are in use as bowing before them standing uncovered or the like.

The Laws Liberties and orders of Harvard College Confirmed by the Overseers and President of the College in the Years 1642, 1643, 1644, 1645, and 1646. And Published to the Scholars for the Perpetual Preservation of their Welfare and Government, reprinted in Samuel Eliot Morison, *The Founding of Harvard College,* pp. 333–37.

8. They shall be slow to speak, and eschew not only oaths, lies, and uncertain rumors, but likewise all idle, foolish, bitter scoffing, frothy wanton words and offensive gestures.

9. None shall pragmatically intrude or intermeddle in other men's affairs.

10. During their residence, they shall studiously redeem their time, observe the general hours appointed for all the Scholars, and the special hour for their own Lecture, and then diligently attend the Lectures without any disturbance by word or gesture: And if of any thing they doubt they shall inquire as of their fellows so in case of non-resolution modestly of their tutors.

11. None shall under any pretence whatsoever frequent the company and society of such men as lead an ungirt and dissolute life.

Neither shall any without the license of the Overseers of the College be of the Artillery or traine-Band.

Nor shall any without the license of the Overseers of the College, his tutor's leave, or in his absence the call of parents or guardians go out to another town.

12. No Scholar shall buy sell or exchange any thing to the value of six-pence without the allowance of his parents, guardians, or tutors. And whosoever is found to have sold or bought any such thing without acquainting their tutor or parents, shall forfeit the value of the commodity, or the restoring of it, according to the discretion of the President.

13. The Scholars shall never use their Mother-tongue except that in public exercises of oratory or such like, they be called to make them in English.

14. If any Scholar being in health shall be absent from prayer or Lectures, except in case of urgent necessity or by the leave of his tutor, he shall be liable to admonition (or such punishment as the President shall think meet) if he offend above once a week.

15. Every Scholar shall be called by his surname only till he be invested with his first degree; except he be fellow-commoner or a Knight's eldest son or of superior nobility.

16. No Scholars shall under any pretense of recreation or other cause whatever (unless foreshowed and allowed by the President or his tutor) be absent from his studies or appointed exercises above an hour at morning-bever, half an hour at afternoon-bever; an hour and an half at dinner and so long at supper.

17. If any Scholar shall transgress any of the Laws of God or the House out of perverseness or apparent negligence, after twice admonition he shall be liable if not adultus to correction, if adultus his name shall be given up to the Overseers of the College that he may be publicly dealt with after the desert of his fault but in grosser offenses such gradual proceeding shall not be expected.

18. Every Scholar that on proof is found able to read the original of the Old and New Testament into the Latin tongue, and to resolve them logically withal being of honest life and conversation and at any public act hath the approbation of the Overseers, and Master of the College may be invested with his first degree.

19. Every Scholar that gives up in writing a Synopsis or summa of Logic, Natural and Moral Philosophy, Arithmetic, Geometry, and Astronomy, and is ready to defend his theses or positions, withal skilled in the originals as aforesaid and still continues honest and studious, at any public act after trial he shall be capable of the second degree of Master of Arts.

4. The Harvard Charter of 1650

The impetus behind the move for the charter came from President Dunster, who probably prepared the first draft.

WHEREAS THROUGH THE good hand of God many well devoted persons have been and daily are moved and stirred up to give and bestow sundry gifts, legacies, lands, and revenues for the advancement of all good literature, arts and sciences in Harvard College in Cambridge in the County of Middlesex and to the maintenance of the President and Fellows and for all accomodations of buildings and all other necessary provisions that may conduce to the education of the English & Indian youth of this Country in knowledge: and godliness. IT IS therefore ordered and enacted by this Court and the authority thereof that for the furthering of so good a work and for the purposes aforesaid from henceforth that the said College in Cambridge in Middlesex in New

Samuel Eliot Morison, *Harvard College in the Seventeenth Century*, I (Cambridge, Mass., 1936), 5–8.

England shall be a Corporation consisting of seven persons (to wit) a President, five Fellows, and a Treasurer or Bursar; and that Henry Dunster shall be the first President; Samuel Mather, Samuel Danford, Masters of Art; Jonathan Michell, Comfort Starre, and Samuel Eaton, Bachelors of Art; shall be the five Fellows and Thomas Danford to be present Treasurer, all of them being inhabitants in the Bay, and shall be the first seven persons of which the said Corporation shall consist. And that the said seven persons or the greater number of them procuring the presence of the Overseers of of [sic] the College and by their counsel and consent shall have power and are hereby authorized at any time or times to elect a new President, Fellows, or Treasurer so often and from time to time as any of the said person or persons shall die or be removed, which said President and Fellows for the time being shall for ever hereafter in name and fact be one body politic and corporate in Law to all intents and purposes, and shall have perpetual succession, and shall be called by the name of President and Fellows of Harvard College; and shall from time to time be eligible as aforesaid; and by that name they and their successors shall and may purchase and acquire to themselves or take and receive upon free gift and donation any lands, tenements or hereditaments within this jurisdiction of the Massachusetts not exceeding the value of five hundred pounds per annum and any goods and sums of money whatsoever to the use and behoof of the said President, Fellows, and Scholars of the said College and also may sue and plead or be sued and impleaded by the name aforesaid in all courts and places of judicature within the jurisdiction aforesaid; and that the said President with any three of the Fellows shall have power and are hereby authorized when they shall think fit to make and appoint a Common Seal for the use of the said Corporation. And the President & Fellows or the major part of them from time to time may meet and choose such Officers & Servants for the College and make such allowance to them and them also to remove and after death or removal to choose such others and to make from time to time such orders & bylaws for the better ordering & carrying on the work of the College as they shall think fit. Provided the said orders be allowed by the Overseers. And also that the President and Fellows or major part of them with the Treasurer shall have power to make conclusive bargains for lands & tenements to be purchased by the said Corporation for valuable consideration. AND for the better ordering of the government of the said College and Corporation be it enacted by the authority aforesaid that the President and three more of the Fellows shall and may from time to time upon due warning or notice given by the President to the rest hold a meeting for the debating and concluding of affairs concerning the profits and revenues of any lands and disposing of their goods. Provided that all the said disposings be according to the will of the donors. And for direction in all emergent occasions execution of all orders and bylaws and for the procuring of a general meeting of all the Overseers & society in great & difficult cases, and in cases of nonagreement, in all which cases aforesaid the conclusion shall be made by the major part, the said President having a casting voice, the Overseers consenting thereunto. And that all the aforesaid transactions shall tend to & for the use and behoof of the President, Fellows, Scholars & Officers of the said College, and for all accommodations of buildings, books and all other necessary provisions & furnitures as may be for the advancement & education of youth in all manner of good literature, arts and sciences. AND further be it ordered by this Court and the authority thereof that all the lands, tenements or hereditaments, houses or revenues within this jurisdiction to the aforesaid President or College appertaining, not exceeding the value of five hundred pounds per annum shall from henceforth be freed from all civil impositions, taxes & rates; all goods to the said corporation or to any Scholars thereof appertaining shall be exempt from all manner of toll, customs & excise whatsoever. And that the said President, Fellows & Scholars, together with the servants & other necessary Officers to the said President or College appertaining not exceeding ten, viz. three to the President and seven to the College belonging, shall be exempted from all personal, civil offices, military exercises or services, watchings and wardings, and such of their estates not exceeding one hundred pounds a man shall be free from all Country taxes or rates whatsoever and none others. IN WITNESS whereof the Court has caused the Seal of the Colony to be hereunto affixed. Dated the one & thirtieth day of the third month called May, Anno 1650.

THO: DUDLEY
Governor

5. *Cotton Mather's History of Harvard, 1702*

Mather (1663–1728), the great Puritan clergyman and scholar, was a graduate
of the Harvard class of 1678. His father, Increase, was president of Harvard from
1685 to 1701, and Cotton would have liked to succeed him. When it was first
published in London in 1702, Mather's *Magnalia Christi Americana; or, the Ecclesiastical History of New-England, from its First Planting in the Year 1620 unto
the Year of Our Lord, 1698,* was the most imposing literary work produced in
New England.

    1. THE nations of mankind, that have shaken off *barbarity,* have not
more *differed* in the *languages,* than they have *agreed* in this one principle, that *schools,* for the institution of young men, in all other liberal
sciences, as well as that of *languages,* are necessary to procure, and preserve, that *learning* amongst them, . . .

    The primitive *Christians* were not more prudently careful, to settle
schools for the education of persons, to succeed the more immediately
inspired ministry of the apostles, and such as had been ordained by the
apostles; (and the apostate *Julian,* truly imagined, that he could not
sooner undo *christianity,* than by putting of them down!) than the
Christians in the most early times of *New-England* were to form a
COLLEDGE, wherein a succession of a learned and able *ministry* might
be educated. And, indeed, they foresaw, that without such a provision
for a *sufficient ministry,* the churches of *New-England* must have been
less than a *business of one age,* and soon have come to nothing: the
other *hemisphere* of the world, would never have sent us over MEN
enough to have answered our necessities; but without a nursery for
such MEN among ourselves *darkness must have soon covered the land,
and gross darkness the people.* For some little while, indeed, there were
very hopeful effects of the pains taken by certain particular men of
great worth and skill, to bring up some in their own *private families,*
for *public services;* but much of *uncertainty* and of *inconveniency* in
this way, was in that little while discovered; and when wise men considered the question handled by *Quintilian, Utilius ne sit domi, atq;
intra privatos Parietes studentem continere, an frequentiæ scholarum,
et velut publicis præceptoribus tradero?* (Whether it is more expedient
to shut up the student at home and in his own closet, or to send him

---

Cotton Mather, *Magnalia Christi Americana* (Hartford, Conn., 1820), II, 6–10.

to the crowded school and to public teachers?) they soon determined it as *he* did, that *set-schools* are so necessary, there is no doing without them. Wherefore a COLLEDGE must now be thought upon: a *Colledge,* the best thing that ever *New-England* thought upon! As the admirable *Voctius* could happily boast of it, that whereas there are no less than *ten* provinces in the *Popish Belgium,* and there are no more than two Universities in them, there are but *seven* provinces in the *reformed Belgium,* and there are *five Universities* therein, besides other academical societies; thus the first Possessors of this *protestant* and *puritan* country, were zealous for an *University,* that should be more significant than the Seminaries of *Canada* and *Mexico; New-England* compared with other places, might lay claim to the character that *Strabo* gives of *Tarsus,* the city of our apostle *Paul's* first education; *they had so great a love to philosophy, . . . and all the liberal sciences, that they excelled* Athens, Alexandria, *and if there were any other place worth naming where the schools, and disputes of philosophy, and all humane arts maintained.* And although this country did chiefly consist of such as by the difficulties of subduing a wretched wilderness, were brought into such a condition of *poverty,* that they might have gone by the title, by which the modestly-clad *noblemen* and *gentlemen,* that first petitioned against the *Inquisition* in the *low countries,* were distinguished, namely, *a troop of beggars,* yet these *Gueux* were willing to let the richer colonies, which retained the ways of the Church of *England,* see *how much true religion was a friend unto good literature.* The reader knows that in every town among the *Jews,* there was a *school,* whereat children were taught the reading of the *law;* and if there were any town destitute of a *school,* the men of the place did stand excommunicate, until one were erected: besides and beyond which they had *midrashoth,* or divinity-*schools,* in which they expounded the law to their disciples. Whether the churches of *New-England* have been duely careful or no, about their other *schools,* they have not been altogether careless about their *midrashoth;* and it is well for them that they have not.

2. A general Court held at *Boston,* Sept. 8, 1630, advanced a *small sum* (and it was then a day of *small things,*) namely, four hundred pounds, by way of *essay* towards the building of something to begin a *Colledge;* and *New-Town* being the *Kiriath Sepher* (City of Books) appointed for the seat of it, the name of the town, was for the sake of somewhat now founding here, which might hereafter grow into an

University, changed into *Cambridge*. 'Tis true, the University of *Upsal* in *Sueden*, hath ordinarily about seven or eight hundred students belonging to it, which do none of them live *collegiately*, but board all of them here and there at private houses; nevertheless, the government of *New-England*, was for having their students brought up in a more *collegiate* way of living. But that which laid the most significant *stone* in the foundation, was the last will of MR. JOHN HARVARD, a reverend, and excellent minister of the gospel, who dying at *Charlstown*, of a consumption, quickly after his arrival here, bequeathed the sum of *seven hundred, seventy nine pounds, seventeen shillings and two pence*, towards the pious work of building a *Colledge*, which was now set a foot. A committee then being chosen, to prosecute an affair, so happily commenced, it soon found encouragement from several other *benefactors*: the other *colonies* sent some small help to the undertaking, and several particular gentlemen did more, than whole *colonies* to support and forward it: but because the memorable MR. JOHN HARVARD, led the way by a generosity exceeding the most of them, that followed *his* name was justly æternized, by its having the name of HARVARD COLLEDGE imposed upon it. While these things were a doing, a society of *scholars*, to lodge in the *new nests*, were forming under the conduct of one Mr. *Nathaniel Eaton* (or, if thou wilt, reader, *Orbilius Eaton*) a blade, who marvellously deceived the expectations of good men concerning him; for he was one fitter to be master of a *Bridewel* than a *Colledge*: and though his *avarice* was notorious enough to get the name of a *Philargyrius* (Money-lover) fixed upon him, yet his *cruelty* was more scandalous than his *avarice*. He was a *rare scholar* himself, and he made many more such; but their education truly was *in the school of Tyrannus*. Among many other instances of his *cruelty*, he gave one in causing two men to hold a young gentleman, while he so unmercifully beat him with a *cudgel*, that upon complaint of it, unto the court in *September*, 1639, he was fined an hundred *marks*, besides a convenient sum to be paid unto the young gentleman, that had suffered by his unmercifulness; and for his inhumane severities towards the *scholars*, he was removed from his trust. After this, being first excommunicated by the church of *Cambridge*, he did himself excommunicate all our churches, going first into *Virginia*, then into *England*, where he lived privately until the restauration of King *Charles* II. Then conforming to the *ceremonies* of the church of *England*, he was fixed at *Biddiford*, where he became (as

Apostata est Osor sui Ordinis,) a bitter *persecutor* of the christians, that kept faithful to the *way of worship,* from which he was himself an *apostate;* until he who had cast so many into *prison* for *conscience,* was himself cast into *prison* for *debt;* where he did, at length, pay one *debt,* namely, that unto *nature,* by *death.*

3. On *August* 27, 1640, the *magistrates,* with the *ministers,* of the colony, chose Mr. *Henry Dunster,* to be the President of their new *Harvard-Colledge.* And in time convenient, the General Court endued the Colledge with a *charter,* which made it a *corporation,* consisting of a *President,* two *Fellows,* and a *Treasurer* to all proper intents and purposes: only with powers reserved unto the *Governour, Deputy-Governour,* and all the *magistrates* of the colony, and the *ministers* of the six next towns for the time being, to act as *overseers,* or *visitors* of the society. The *tongues* and *arts* were now taught in the *Colledge,* and *piety* was maintained with so laudable a *discipline,* that many eminent persons went forth from hence, adorned with accomplishments, that rendered them formidable to *other parts* of the world, as well as to this country, and persons of good quality sent their sons from *other parts* of the world, for such an education, as this country could give unto them. The number of *benefactors* to the *Colledge,* did herewithal increase to such a degree of *benefits,* that although the President were supported still by a *salary* from the *Treasury* of the *colony,* yet the Treasury of the *Colledge* itself was able to pay many of its expences; especially after the incomes of *Charlestown ferry,* were by an act of the *General Court* settled thereupon. To enumerate these *benefactors* would be a piece of *justice* to their memory, and the catalogue of their *names,* and *works* preserved in the *Colledge,* has done them that *justice.* But as I find one article in that catalogue to run thus, *a gentleman not willing his name should be put upon record, gave fifty pounds;* thus I am so willing to believe, that most of those *good men* that are mentioned were content with a *record* of their *good deeds* in the *book of God's remembrance,* that I shall excuse this *book of our church history* from swelling with a particular mention of them: albeit for us to leave unmentioned in this place MOULSON, a SALTONSTAL, an ASHURST, a PENNOYER, a DODDRIDGE, an HOPKINS, a WEB, an USHER, an HULL, a RICHARDS, an HULTON, a GUNSTON, would hardly be excusable. And while these made their liberal contributions, either to the *edifice* or to the *revenue* of the *Colledge,* there were other that enriched its *library* by presenting of choice *books* with mathematical instruments, there-

unto, among whom Sir *Kenelm Digby,* Sir *John Maynard,* Mr. *Rich-ard Baxter* and Mr. *Joseph Hill,* ought always to be remembered. But the most considerable accession to this *library* was, when the Reverend Mr. *Theophilus Gale,* a well known *writer* of many *books,* and *owner* of more, bequeathed what he had, unto this *New-English* treasury of learning; . . .

4. When scholars had so far profited at the *grammar schools,* that they could read any *classical author* into English, and readily make and speak true *Latin,* and write it in *verse* as well as *prose;* and perfectly decline the *paradigms* of *nouns* and *verbs* in the Greek tongue, they were judged capable of admission in *Harvard-Colledge;* and upon the examination, were accordingly admitted by the President and Fellows; who, in testimony thereof signed a copy of the *Colledge laws,* which the scholars were each of them to transcribe and preserve, as the continual remembrancers of the duties, whereto their priviledges obliged them. While the *President* inspected the *manners* of the students thus entertained in the *Colledge,* and unto his morning and evening *prayers* in the hall, joined an *exposition* upon the chapters; which they read out of *Hebrew* into *Greek,* from the *Old Testament* in the morning, and out of *English* into *Greek,* from the *New* Testament in the evening; besides what *Sermons* he saw cause to preach in publick assemblies on the *Lord's day* at *Cambridge* where the students have a particular *gallery* allotted unto them; the *Fellows* resident on the place, became *Tutors,* to the several *classes,* and after they had instructed them in the *Hebrew language,* led them through all the *liberal arts,* e're their first *four years* expired. And in this time, they had their weekly *declamations,* on *Fridays* in the Colledge-hall, besides publick *disputations,* which either the *President* or the *Fellows* moderated. Those who then stood *candidates* to be *graduates,* were to attend in the *hall* for certain hours, on *Mondays,* and on *Tuesdays,* three weeks together towards the middle of *June,* which were called *weeks of visitation;* so that all comers that pleased, might examine their skill in the *languages* and *sciences,* which they now pretended unto; and usually, some or other of the *overseers* of the *Colledge,* would on purpose *visit* them, whilst they were thus doing what they called, *sitting of solstices:* when the *commencement* arrived, which was formerly the second *Tuesday* in *August,* but since, the first *Wednesday* in *July;* they that were to proceed *Bachelors,* held their *act* publickly in *Cambridge;* whither the *magistrates* and *ministers,* and other *gentlemen* then came, to put

respect upon their exercises: and these exercises were besides an *oration* usually made by the *President,* orations both *salutatory* and *valedictory,* made by some or other of the commencers, wherein all *persons* and *orders* of any fashion then present, were addressed with proper complements, and reflections were made on the most remarkable occurrents of the præceding year; and these orations were made not only in *Latin,* but sometimes in *Greek* and in *Hebrew* also; and some of them were in *verse,* and even in *Greek* verse, as well as others in *prose.* But the main exercises were *disputations* upon *questions,* wherein the *respondents* first made their *theses:* for according to *Vossius,* the very essence of the *Baccalaureat* seems to lye in the thing: BACCALAUREUS being but a name corrupted of *Batualius,* which *Batualius* (as well as the French *Bataile*) comes *à Batuendo,* a business that carries *beating* in it: . . . In the close of the day, the President, with the formality of delivering a *book* into their hands, gave them their *first degree;* but such of them as had studied *three years* after their *first degree,* to answer the *Horation* character of an artist, *Qui Studiis Annos Septem dedit insenuitque Libris et curis.* (Who seven long years has spent in student-toil.)

And besides their exhibiting *synopses* of the *liberal arts,* by themselves composed, now again publickly disputed on some *questions,* of perhaps a little higher elevation; *these* now, with a like formality, received their *second degree,* proceeding *Masters of Art.—Quis enim doctrinam amplectitur ipsam, præmia si tollas?* (For who would seek even learning itself, if you should strip it of its rewards?) The words used by the Præsident, in this action, were:

FOR THE BATCHELOURS

Admitto te ad Primum Gradum in Artibus, *scilicet, ad respondendum questioni, pro more Academiarum in* Angliâ.

Tibiq; Trado hunc Librum, *unà cum protestate publicè prælegendi, in aliquâ artium (quam profiteris) quotiescunq; ad hoc munus evocatus fueris.*

(I admit you to the first degree in Arts, that is to say, to the privilege of responding in debate, according to the custom of the English Universities; and I deliver to you this book, with the privilege of reading in public, in such profession as you shall select, as often as you are summoned to that duty.)

FOR THE MASTERS

Admitto te ad Secundum Gradum in Artibus, *pro more Academiurum in* Angliâ.

Tradoque tibi hunc Librum, *unà cum potestate profitendi, ubicunque ad hoc munus publicè evocatus fueris.*

(I admit you to the second degree in Arts, according to the custom of the English Universities; and I deliver to you this book, with the privilege of practising a profession, whenever you shall be called upon to do so.)

5. Mr. *Henry Dunster,* continued the President of *Harvard-Colledge,* until his unhappy entanglement in the snares of *Anabaptism,* fill'd the *overseers* with uneasie fears, lest the students by his means, should come to be ensnared: Which uneasiness was at length so signified unto him, that on *October* 24, 1654, he presented unto the overseers, an instrument under his hands; wherein he resigned his Presidentship, and they accepted his resignation. That brave old man *Johannes Amos Commenius,* the *fame* of whose worth hath been *trumpetted* as far as more than *three* languages (whereof every one is endebted unto his *Janua*) could carry it was indeed agreed withall, by our Mr. *Winthrop* in his travels through the *low countries,* to come over into *New-England,* and illuminate this *Colledge* and *country,* in the quality of a *President:* But the solicitations of the *Swedish* Ambassador, diverting him another way, that incomparable *Moravian* became not an *American.* On *November* 2, 1654, Mr. *Richard Mather* and Mr. *Norton,* were employed by the overseers, to tender unto Mr. *Charles Chauncey* the place of *President,* which was now become vacant; who on the twenty-seventh day of that month, had a solemn Inauguration thereunto. . . .

6. Cotton Mather on Harvard's First President, Henry Dunster

See Doc. 5. On the Dunster controversy, see Samuel Eliot Morison, *Harvard College in the Seventeenth Century,* I, chap. xv.

NOTWITHSTANDING the veneration which we pay to the *names* and *works* of those reverend men, whom we call *the fathers,* yet even the *Roman Catholicks* themselves confess, that those *fathers* were not *infallible. Andradius,* among others, in his defence of the council of *Trent,* has this passage, *There can be nothing devised more superstitious, than to count all things delivered by the fathers,* divine oracles. And, indeed, it is plain enough, that those excellent men, were not without *errors* and *frailties,* of which, I hope, it will not be the part of a *cham* to take some little notice. . . .

Wherefore it may not be wondred at, if among the first *fathers* of *New-England,* there were some things, not altogether so agreeable to the *principles,* whereupon the country was in the main established. But among those of our *fathers,* who differed somewhat from his *brethren,* was that learned and worthy man Mr. *Henry Dunster.*

He was the president of our *Harvard College* in *Cambridge,* and an able man: [as we may give some account, when the history of that *college* comes to be offered.]

But wonderfully falling into the errors of *Antipædobaptism,* the *overseers* of the college became solicitous, that the students there might not be unawares ensnared in the errors of their *president.* Wherefore they laboured with an extreme agony, either to rescue the good man from his *own mistake;* or to restrain him from imposing them upon *the hope of the flock,* of both which, finding themselves to despair, they did as quietly as they could, procure his *removal,* and provide him a successor, in Mr. *Charles Chauncey.*

He was a very good *Hebrician,* and for that cause, he bore a great part in the metrical version of the *Psalms,* now used in our churches. But after some short retirement and secession from all publick business, at *Scituate* in the year 1659, he went thither, where he bears his part in everlasting and cælestial *hallelujahs.* It was justly counted an instance

---

Magnalia Christi Americana, I, 366–67.

of an *excellent spirit,* in *Margaret Meering;* that though she had been excommunicated by the congregation of protestants, whereof Mr. *Rough* was pastor, and she seemed to have hard measure also in her excommunication; yet when Mr. *Rough* was imprisoned for the truth, she was very serviceable to him, and at length suffered martyrdom for the truth with him. Something that was not altogether unlike this *excellent spirit* was instanced by our *Dunster.* For, he died in such *harmony* of affection with the good men, who had been the authors of his removal from *Cambridge,* that he, by his *will,* ordered his body to be carried unto *Cambridge* for its burial, and bequeathed *legacies* to those very persons.

7. *Tutor Sever's Argument on the Constitution of Harvard College, 1723*

Nicholas Sever (1680–1764) was a member of the Harvard class of 1701 and became a tutor in 1716 after some years as a preacher in Dover, New Hampshire. During his tutorship he had a distinguished record as a troublemaker. In 1721, when the religious conservatives who controlled the General Court sought to break the power of the liberal President Leverett by removing three liberal ministers and replacing them with tutors, Sever joined the attack, out of which this appeal resulted. In 1723 the Overseers elected Sever to the Corporation, but he did not win his argument that the Corporation should be composed only of resident teachers. On Sever see Clifford K. Shipton's essay in *Sibley's Harvard Graduates,* V (Boston, 1937), 90–95; see also *ibid.,* VI (Boston, 1942), 153–58, on William Welsteed, another tutor involved in the controversy, and Part IV, Doc. 9.

To bring the matter to a point, the question is, who are by this charter to execute the laws and govern the College? And (with submission) there are a few lines in the charter which must be thought to determine that matter beyond all doubt, and they are these, viz.: "And for the better ordering of the government of the said College and Corporation, be it enacted, by the authority aforesaid, that the President and three more of the Fellows shall and may from time to time, upon due

Proceedings of the Massachusetts Historical Society, 1st series, XVI (February, 1878), 50–67.

warning or notice given by the President to the rest, hold a meeting for the debating and concluding of affairs touching the profits and revenues of any lands, and disposing of their goods; provided, that all the said disposing be according to the will of the donors, and for direction in all emergent occasions, *execution of all orders and by-laws*." Now, I think (with great submission) no words can express a thing more plainly and fully than this matter is here expressed, nor can any terms be used that are stronger than these. It is expressly said that the President and Fellows, or Corporation, shall meet upon all emergent occasions and for the execution of all orders and by-laws. The note of universality is here expressed, which makes the sense very strong. And, if the execution of all orders and by-laws belongs to the Corporation, what can be the business of the Fellows of the House and Tutors?

There is, indeed, another clause of the charter which has been improved against us, and that is it which empowers the Corporation to choose other officers and servants; and it has been said that these Fellows of the House and Tutors, which are now made use of to govern the College, come in properly under this head of officers and among the servants. But by officers and servants, then, for the College, we must understand such as steward, butler, handicraftsmen, and menial servants, which the college has continual occasion to make use of. And it is impossible that under this head of officers and servants any should be brought in to execute the laws and govern the College until that other part of the charter which was but now mentioned be razed out of it, which says that the Corporation shall execute all orders and by-laws. These two parts of the charter are distinct, and stand at some distance. I will set them together, and see how they will stand by one another. The one, and that which is expressed, is this, that the President and Fellows or Corporation shall execute all orders and by-laws; the other is that which empowers the Corporation to choose other officers and servants, which they suppose (it is not expressed, but the gentlemen of the Corporation suppose) may be vested with powers to execute the orders and by-laws of the College. Now, if the art of man can reconcile these two propositions to any tolerable sense,—viz., first, that the Corporation shall execute all orders and by-laws; and, secondly, that other officers and servants may execute the orders and by-laws of the College—we may then possibly be in an error. But to say that other officers and servants may be empowered to execute the orders and by-laws of the College, when the charter says expressly that this business shall be done by the Corporation and none else, is to attempt to reconcile a contradiction and make both the parts of it true.

Moreover, the business of the College is a great trust which the government has reposed in a corporation and their successors. Now, if they may empower other officers and servants to execute the laws of the College, by the same rule they may empower them also to make laws, and to dispose of the revenues and do all the business of the College; and by this means the design of the Government in committing so great a charge to a Corporation and their successors might be entirely defeated.

And thus the charter empowers the Corporation to govern the College without allowing them to substitute others in their room and stead, and without making any provision for anybody else to do that business. And no words can be found in the charter upon which an inferior judicature in the College to that of the President and Fellows, viz., consisting of President and Tutors, can be founded. . . .

Now since the charter, laws, form of instalment of Fellows, all agree in this point, that the President and Fellows or Corporation shall govern the College, and for that end suppose their residence in it, it must needs be so, and cannot possibly be otherwise.

And nothing (with submission) can be more clear and evident than that this was the constitution of the college government by the charter and laws, and that it was a fundamental principle in the charter, if any thing was so, that the College should be governed nextly and immediately by the Corporation, and under the countenance and with the approbation of the Honorable and Reverend Overseers in all great and difficult cases. So that what we aim at is not to break up and overthrow an ancient constitution, as has been suggested, but to recover a broken constitution, which the College has for some years been groaning and bleeding under, to its ancient, primitive, most perfect, and healthful state. . . .

And we do allow that by those ["Latin"] laws* several parts of the business of the College are put into the hands of the President or a Tutor; and, if it be desired, we will allow further that the whole

---

* These "Latin laws" are probably those printed by Cotton Mather in the *Magnalia* (Book IV, pp. 132–34) and thence transferred by Mr. Benjamin Peirce to the Appendix of his *History of Harvard University*.

immediate government of the College was committed to the President and Tutors, for so it was.

But then, for answer, Who were those Tutors, and what were their characters in the College? Were they only titular and upon no foundation, as we are? No, by no means. Mr. Leverett, the present President, and Mr. Brattle, were the men, and they were Fellows, too, upon the foundation; and their names are now to be seen as such in the charter of 1692, which the College was then upon; and nothing more can therefore be argued from thence but that the immediate government of the College was by those laws committed to the President and resident Fellows. And I suppose the only reason of so many non-resident Fellows as there were under that charter was that that charter had no reference to the Honorable and Reverend Overseers, as this has, or to any power of visitation abroad whatsoever, for which reason (by the way) I suppose the charter was disallowed of by the King. . . .

And now I think the College is at present very happy, in that it has so sufficient a guard and so strong a power of visitation abroad as this, consisting of your Honor and the Honorable Board and the Reverend the rest of the Overseers of the College; and I believe no man can question the strength and sufficiency of this great and learned body for a guard upon the College abroad; and, if the charter had had the same reference to this your learned and honorable body which this has, I believe nobody had thought of one non-resident Fellow, and there was then no such character known in the College as that of a Tutor distinct from a Fellow.

Now, to argue that because then the government of the College was put into the hands of a President and Tutors who were also Fellows upon a foundation, that therefore now it may be put into the hands of a President and Tutors who are not Fellows, and who are upon no foundation, is (with great submission) a strain in arguing which is beyond all reason in the world, and which can be admitted of by no man. . . .

I remember very well that some years since the non-residence of the President was complained of as greatly detrimental to the College, although he usually visited the College once a fortnight or oftener, and performed suitable exercises, both scholastical and theological. And surely the non-residence of the Fellows cannot be hurtful to the College also, who do not usually meet here more than twice or thrice a year, and when they do come (it being so seldom) cannot but come very much unacquainted with the affairs and business of the College. When they have been here, I suppose they have at all times truly aimed at the good of the College; but their unacquaintedness with the affairs of it has, I believe, been very hurtful.

I have the greatest esteem and veneration for the non-resident Fellows of the College, for their superior learning and piety; and I think myself unhappy in that it falls to my lot to express these sentiments upon this occasion, which I find are different from theirs, and nothing would have induced me to it but an apprehension of the necessity of it for the service of the College. But so long as the College has every way so sufficient a guard abroad to prevent any mal-administration in the business of it (and I believe scarce any College has a more effectual one), and so long as by non-residence the resident Fellows are crowded off from the foundation and divested of the powers of the charter, which is the case here, so long I say it is impossible (I speak it with the lowest submission) that the non-residence of Fellows should answer any other end in the College but to cramp and depress the characters of the resident ones, and render them insignificant and useless in the business of the College, unless it be to weaken the authority of the Overseers too, the non-residents always having been chosen out of their number. By this means, indeed, the government of the College is become strong abroad, but it is left feeble and defenceless at home. . . .

And I cannot but mention one circumstance in this state of things, which I look upon (with submission) as very inconsistent, and that is that the Fellows are not only non-resident, but that they are chosen out of the body of the Overseers, and thus matters are brought by the Fellows from themselves in Corporation to themselves as Overseers for confirmation. They must seem (with great submission) to be incompetent judges, among the Overseers, of matters that have passed through their own hands in Corporation. And if any thing should be amiss in the College at any time, and want a regulation by the Honorable and Reverend Overseers, by this means the proceeding must needs be greatly clogged and made very difficult. . . .

I have thought several times within these two or three years past that the College has been upon the very brink of great disorders; and, when we in our places have done the best we could to prevent them, we have seen and felt the feebleness of the college state. And, when we are made to signify just nothing in the College, our pupils observe it, and the natural tendency of it is to lessen that regard to us which they ought to have, and which they must have, and which if they have not, they had better be at home than at College under our care. And our part as Fellows of the House in this new model of the College affairs is but a mock business: it appears to be so, and has been greatly detrimental to the College.

By indulgence, and upon sufferance, and not upon charter, we have indeed, on our parts, been assisting in the business of the College, in this method, for some years past, but I believe everybody acquainted with the affairs of the College knows the difficulties the resident Fellows have met with in this method, and how hurtful this state of things has been in the College; and truly I believe everybody else that considers the bottom we are upon may be very likely to guess as much. . . .

Elections of officers, and exhibitions of the college money, are, I think, the two principal things now managed by the Corporation; and now, when Mr. Hollis's pious and generous donations come to be wholly applied, there will be at least forty persons benefited this way, either by small offices in the College, or else by the college money. Now I believe the non-resident gentlemen have not the least personal knowledge of half so many of the students belonging to the College, or, to be sure, of those that are any way suitable to receive these favors. Now the donors of money to the College have very strictly obliged the disposers of it to have a particular regard to the character and merit of persons, and the College charter no less strictly obliges them to observe the directions of the donors of money to the College in all those dispositions, which it is impossible for them to do while they are so unacquainted with persons in the College. They cannot act in this business upon any knowledge of their own. They must needs act very much in the dark in the bestowment of these favors. And, since there are such favors to be disposed of in the College and among our pupils nothing (with submission) can be more reasonable than that we should have an hand in the disposition; and this power, prudently managed by the residents, may be improved very much for the service of the College by encouraging the ingenious and industrious, and by discountenancing the slothful and vicious, if any such there shall be, as by the non-residents it cannot. . . .

We are regularly elected Fellows, and do not therefore ask for any new election. And, as for the distinction between Fellows of the

Corporation and Fellows of the House, it was never heard of in the College until very lately; and sometimes the gentlemen of the Corporation are upon our books styled Fellows of the House. There is no color of any foundation in the charter for such a distinction, and we therefore look upon it as a distinction without a difference; so that instead of five Fellows, which the charter allows of, there are now seven regularly elected and confirmed. And that such who have the business of a college should be divested of the powers of its charter, which were granted for their support and direction in that business, and for no other end, and especially when it has (upon every account) so sufficient a guard abroad as this has, is to us an inexplicable paradox in college affairs.

And now the design of this memorial is no other but that we who are regularly elected Fellows, and confirmed by the Honorable and Reverend Overseers, according to the directions of the charter, and as such have the care and business of the College committed to us,—that we may be enabled to proceed in that business regularly upon the charter, and according to the known laws of the College made or to be made; and that we may have such a subsistence as our predecessors in this business have formerly had, which has of late years been very much shortened, for what reasons we cannot tell. And we therefore assure ourselves (with humble submission) that your Honor, and the Honorable Board and the Reverend the rest of the Overseers of the College, will think it reasonable and necessary for the good of the College that the prayer of it should be granted.

N. SEVER

8. *Leverett's Answer to Sever, 1723*

John Leverett (1662–1724) was a member of the Harvard class of 1680. He became a tutor in 1685 and, during the long absence of Increase Mather, shared with William Brattle in the management of the college, until he was made president in 1707. A liberal in his religious views, he survived the persistent

"Memorial of the Corporation to the Lieutenant-Governor and Council," *Harvard College Records,* Part II ("Publications of the Colonial Society of Massachusetts, Collections," Vol. XVI [Boston, 1925]), pp. 489–500; also printed in Josiah Quincy, *The History of Harvard University,* I (Cambridge, Mass., 1840), 547–56.

hostility of the conservative faction in the legislature. See John L. Sibley's sketch
in *Sibley's Harvard Graduates,* III (Cambridge, Mass., 1885), 180–98, and Quincy,
History of Harvard, I, chaps. xiii–xiv.

The representation of the President and Fellows is as follows,

To the Honorable William Dummer, Esquire, Lieutenant-Governor
and Commander-in-chief in and over his Majesty's Province of the
Massachusetts Bay, in New England; and to the Honorable his Majesty's Council, the humble representation of the President and Fellows
of Harvard College upon the affairs of said College, now depending
in the General Court, occasioned by a late petition of Mr. Nicholas
Sever and Mr. William Welsteed. . . .

The first article in the report of the honorable Committee is, *"that
it was the intent of the College charter, that the Tutors of the said
College, or such as have the instruction and government of the students
there, should be Fellows and members of the Corporation of said College,* provided they exceed not five in number."

To this we reply, that, having had occasion often to peruse and consider the charter of the College, it still appears to us not to be the intent of said charter, that the Tutors of the College, or such as have the
instruction and government of the students there, should be Fellows
and members of the Corporation of said College, provided that they
exceed not five in number. And our reasons are these that follow.
First. If this had been the real intention of the General Court, who
made and gave the charter, it seems unaccountable to us, that it was
not plainly expressed, which might easily have been done, and we
humbly think ought to have been. But, instead of that, when the first
seven persons are named in the charter, it immediately adds, *all of
them being inhabitants in the Bay.* It could as easily have said, *all
of them being resident in the College, or within the town of Cambridge,* if that had really been the intention of the charter, and there
is no doubt with us but it would have said so. But it being given as a
reason or qualification, that they were *inhabitants of the Bay,* it seems
plainly to follow, that the charter never intended any such thing, as
that the members of the Corporation must be resident Fellows (or
Tutors) in the House. . . .

If, may it please your Honors, there be any thing else in the charter
that seems to require the residence of the Fellows of the Corporation
within the House, it seems to be that clause in it, *and, for direction in*

all emergent occasions, execution of all orders and by-laws, the con-
clusion shall be made by the major part, &c. &c. Now from hence some
may plead, that the Corporation's residing at the College is necessary
for the well-governing the students there, and for the executing the
good laws provided for that end.

To this we answer, that by the charter it is the province of the Corporation, *from time to time, to make such orders and by-laws for the
ordering and carrying on the work of the College as they shall think
fit, provided these orders be allowed by the Overseers.*

Now, may it please your Honors, when such laws are made, the
ordinary execution of them belongs to the President and Tutors residing in the House, who are in the immediate daily government of
it, and for this service, among others, they receive their salary. But
upon *emergent occasions, and in great and difficult cases,* the direction
of the charter is, that the President call the Corporation together to
advise and resolve, and, if need be, to *execute,* for the greater honor
and service to the College, which accordingly has been the practice, on
occasions that have called for severe censures or expulsions.

May it please your Honors, we humbly conceive, that the College
charter, empowering the Corporation to make orders and by-laws,
does also authorize and empower them to appoint and require all
officers, in their respective places within the College, to execute from
day to day the laws made and confirmed for the good order and government of the House. And in a particular manner we judge the
Tutors to be such officers, chosen and authorized for this very end, as
well as to instruct; and unto the President and them does the execution
of the by-laws and orders belong, in the daily ordering of matters
within the House. It is not therefore at all necessary (we humbly conceive), that the Tutors be of the Corporation in order to the execution
of the laws in the daily government of the House. Nay, what pretence
can there be, that persons must needs be lawgivers in order to their
having the executive trust and power committed to them?

We pray your Honors, therefore, to observe, that the execution of
all orders and by-laws, wherein the charter directs and expects the
convening and acting of the Corporation is only upon *emergent occasions, and in great and difficult cases,* in which cases a non-resident
Corporation are easily called together, and have usually been so.

But, if any should say that this clause, *the execution of all orders and
by-laws,* must be taken absolutely and unlimitedly, they must then

extend it to all and every particular in the daily administration and ordering the affairs of the House; and then 't would follow, that a student must not have leave to go out of Commons, or out of town, unless there be a major part of the Corporation actually consenting in such a permission to him given. As also that at least four of the Corporation must consent to the punishing a student for being absent from, or tardy at prayers, recitation, or for the least misdemeanor that is punishable by the laws and usage of the House.

Now this, in our apprehension, is so impracticable, not to say ridiculous. . . .

We ask, therefore, this favor of your Honors, to leave at least this our testimony and witness—that we apprehend and fear prejudice and detriment to the College in times to come, both as to its estate and also as to the government of it, if this *new and untried* method be gone into. And, if any great inconveniences or damage to the College do ensue thereupon, we are clear of them; nor will they be so easily retrieved, when they may be too late felt and bewailed.

But there is another thing which we also crave leave to recommend unto your Honors' wise and serious consideration, which is, *that the College Corporation is to have perpetual succession by election as vacancies happen.* So that if those three of the Corporation, whose ejection is thought and endeavoured by some, should be once *quit* of their station in it, or be made to *cease* together from it, the Corporation itself would then cease, and the charter become null and void, inasmuch as there will then remain but one Fellow, with the President and Treasurer, who cannot, by the charter, make an election to fill up the vacancy. For the charter plainly says, that the Corporation is to be continued by elections, and that there must be the *major part of seven* acting in those elections.

And thus, may it please your Honors, we have made answer to the first article, which is the main and great one, in the report of the honorable Committee; and we submit our reasons, weighty as they seem to us, to your Honors' most impartial and deliberate consideration.

We come now to the second article in the report of the honorable Committee, which is, *"that none of the said Fellows be Overseers."*

To this we briefly answer, that, should the Corporation consist of resident Tutors, it is not probable, if possible, that any of them should be of the Board of Overseers, the said Tutors, while such, not being like to be teaching elders in any of the neighbouring churches, nor of his Majesty's Council.

But then we still add, that some of the Fellows of the Corporation *have been* of the number of Overseers from time to time; and, as we think, to the *great benefit* of the College, so that till *now* it never was judged improper or unfit, or contrary to the intent of the charter, that some of the *Fellows of the Corporation* should be also of the Board of Overseers.

The last thing in the report of the honorable Committee is, *"that the President and Fellows of the said College, or the major part of them, are not warranted to fix or establish any salary or allowance for their service, without the approbation and consent of the Overseers."*

To this we humbly reply; we think, that prior acts of legislature are to be explained, restrained, or enlarged, according to the plain sense of subsequent acts of the same legislature. We readily own, that, from the first constitution of the Overseers, in 1642, the whole management of the affairs of the College was entirely in the hands of the Overseers. But when the same legislature, that had constituted and empowered them, did, in the the year 1650, make a charter for the College, and invested a Corporation with the powers therein granted, we humbly conceive, that *thenceforth* there remained no more power to the Overseers than what that charter leaves them.

We are humbly of opinion, that if the present powers of the Overseers are sought for, they are not so much to be looked for in the act for their original constitution as in the subsequent acts of the General Court, and particularly the charter of 1650. . . .

And thus we have made some reply to the report of the honorable Committee, in the several articles thereof; only, whereas in the preamble to their report, they are pleased to say, that these *their resolutions, if put in practice, would be more beneficial to the College than the enlarging the number of the Corporation;*

We must still crave leave humbly to insist on the contrary opinion, and say, that we should be heartily glad, and think it much for the safety of the College, if the honorable Court could in their wisdom think it proper to enlarge the Corporation to twice its present number or more, because of the large powers with which we think it is intrusted; always provided, that the resident Tutors should never be able to make a major part, *because we think it contrary to the light of nature, that any should have an overruling voice in making those laws by which themselves must be governed in their office work, and for which they receive salaries.*

Having thus answered to the report of the honorable Committee, we come now to offer a few words upon a clause or two in the petition of Mr. Sever and Mr. Welsteed, which they have lately presented to the General Court.

They recite a proviso, which his Excellency, the Governor, was pleased to make some time the last year, that three of us, ministers, should not be removed from the Corporation.

On this head we can assure your Honors, that none of us ever sought after such a proviso in our favor, directly nor indirectly, unless our open arguing and reasoning from time to time before the Board of Overseers may be so interpreted, which we humbly conceive it cannot justly be.

It has been openly declared before your Honors, again and again, as we do now declare, that we have never meant to argue for our own personal continuance in the Corporation, but only against a majority of the resident Tutors being of it.

We have no reason at all, for our own parts, to be *unwilling to part with our character* as Fellows of the Corporation, how meanly soever those gentlemen may think and are pleased to say reflectingly of us; and so far are we from desiring to continue in the Corporation, if it has not been, or may not be, for the service of the College, that it would be an ease and a pleasure to us to quit our station in it and see it better served by others, and more secured by their services. . . .

We truly and seriously declare, that we make not this representation for any by-ends or self-interest. Those of us, whose ejectment is so earnestly sought for, neither seek nor find any reward for all that time we spend, or pains we take, as members of the Corporation. If we have served the College in any kind or degree, we desire to thank God for the time and assistance. We heartily wish and pray for its welfare, and for the flourishing of religion and good literature in it, to the glory of God and the good of all his people, even to the latest posterity, if it may be the divine pleasure so to order it. . . .

> JOHN LEVERETT,
> *President of Harvard College,*
> in the name and at the
> desire of the Corporation

9. *Charter of William and Mary, 1693*

In Virginia, as in Massachusetts, talk of a college began in the early years of settlement; but it was not until 1693 that the Reverend James Blair (1655–1743), commissary for the Bishop of London and head of Virginia's Anglican church, went to London to secure the royal charter, here much abbreviated, that authorized the creation of the College of William and Mary. Blair was made president for life. While the lower schools called for in the charter began operation earlier, instruction at the college level probably began only around 1729, when the full body of teachers provided in the charter was at last engaged. On Blair see D. E. Motley, *Life of Commissary Jas. Blair* (Baltimore, 1901); on the college, Herbert Baxter Adams, *The College of William and Mary* (Washington, D.C., 1887).

WILLIAM and MARY, by the Grace of God, of England, Scotland, France and Ireland, King and Queen, Defenders of the Faith, &c. To all to whom these our present Letters shall come, Greeting.

Forasmuch as our well-beloved and faithful Subjects, constituting the General-Assembly of our Colony of Virginia, have had it in their Minds, and have proposed to themselves, to the End that the Church of Virginia may be furnished with a Seminary of Ministers of the Gospel, and that the Youth may be piously educated in good Letters and Manners, and that the Christian Faith may be propagated amongst the Western Indians, to the Glory of Almighty God; to make, found, and establish a certain Place of universal Study, or perpetual College of Divinity, Philosophy, languages, and other good Arts and Sciences, consisting of one President, six Masters or Professors, and an Hundred Scholars, more or less, according to the Ability of the said College, and the Statutes of the same; to be made, encreased, diminished, or changed there, by certain Trustees, nominated and elected by the General-Assembly aforesaid; to wit, our faithful and well-beloved Francis Nicholson, our Lieutenant-Governor in our Colonies of Virginia and Maryland, William Cole, Ralph Wormley, William Byrd, and John Lear, Esquires; James Blair, John Farnifold, Stephen Fouace, and Samuel Gray, Clerks; Thomas Milner, Christopher Robinson, Charles Scarborough, John Smith, Benjamin Harrison, Miles Cary, Henry Hartwell, William Randolph, and Matthew Page, Gentlemen, or the

Edgar W. Knight (ed.), *A Documentary History of Education in the South before 1860* (Chapel Hill, N.C., 1949), I, 401–39.

major Part of them, or of the longer Livers of them, on the South Side
of a certain River, commonly called York River, or elsewhere, where
the General-Assembly itself shall think more convenient, within our
Colony of Virginia, to be supported and maintained, in all Time
coming.

I. And forasmuch as our well-beloved and trusty the General-Assembly of our Colony of Virginia aforesaid, has humbly supplicated
us, by our well-beloved in Christ, James Blair, Clerk, their Agent duly
constituted, That we would be pleased, not only to grant our Royal
Licence to the said . . . Gentlemen, or the major Part of them, or of the
longer Livers of them, to make, found, erect, and establish the said
College, but also to extend our Royal Bounty and Munificence, towards
the Erection and Foundation of the said College, in such Way and
Manner, as to us shall seem most expedient: We taking the Premisses
seriously into our Consideration, and earnestly desiring, that as far in
us lies, true Philosophy, and other good and liberal Arts and Sciences
may be promoted, and that the Orthodox Christian Faith may be
propagated: And being desirous, that for ever hereafter, there should
be one such College, or Place of universal Study, and some certain and
undoubted Way within the said College, for the Rule and Government
of the same, and of the Masters or Professors, and Scholars, and all
others inhabiting and residing therein, and that the said College should
subsist and remain in all Time coming; of our special Grace, certain
Knowledge, and mere Motion, HAVE GRANTED and given Leave, and by
these Presents do grant and give Leave, for us, our Heirs and Successors, as much as in us lies, to the said . . . Gentlemen, That they or the
major Part of them, or of the longer Livers of them, for promoting the
Studies of true Philosophy, Languages, and other good Arts and Sciences, and for Propagating the pure Gospel of Christ, our only Media-
tor, to the Praise and Honor of Almighty God, may have Power to
erect, found, and establish a certain Place of universal Study, or perpetual College, for Divinity, Philosophy, Languages, and other good
Arts and Sciences, consisting of One President, Six Masters or Professors, and an Hundred Scholars, more or less, Graduates and Non-
Graduates, . . . [there follows the designation of a place].

II. And further, of our special Grace, certain Knowledge, and mere
Motion, we HAVE GRANTED, and given Leave, and by these Presents do
grant, and give Leave, for us, our Heirs and Successors, to the said
Francis Nicholson, William Cole, &c. that they, or the major Part of

them, or of the longer Livers of them, may be enabled to take, hold, and enjoy, and that they may be Persons apt and capable in Law, for taking, holding and enjoying all Manors, Lands, Tenements, Rents, Services, Rectories, Portions, Annuities, Pensions, and Advowsons of Churches, with all other Inheritances, Franchises, and Possessions whatever, as well Spiritual as Temporal, to the Value of Two Thousand Pounds a Year; and all other Goods, Chattels, Monies, and Personal Estate whatsoever, of the Gift of any Person whatsoever, that is willing to bestow them for this Use; or any other Gifts Grants, Assignments, Legacies, or Appointments, of the same, or of any of them, or of any other Goods whatsoever,: But with this express Intention, and upon the special Trust we put in them, that they the said Francis Nicholson, William Cole, &c. or the major Part of them, or of the longer Livers of them, shall take and hold the Premisses, and shall dispose of the same, and of the Rents, Revenues, or Profits thereof, or of any of them only for defraying the Charges that shall be laid out in Erecting and Fitting the Edifices of the said intended College, and furnishing them with Books, and other Utensils, and all other Charges pertaining to the said College, as they, or the major Part of them, shall think most expedient, until the said College shall be actually erected, founded, and established, and upon this Trust and Intention, that so soon as the said College shall, according to our Royal Intent, be erected and founded, the said Francis Nicholson, William Cole, &c. or the longer Livers or Liver of them, and their or his Heirs, Executors, Administrators, or Assigns, shall, by good and sufficient Deeds and Assurances in Law, Give, Grant, and Transfer to the said President and Masters, or Professors, or their Successors, the said Lands, Manors, Tenements, Rents, Services, Rectories, Portions, Annuities, Pensions, and Advowsons of Churches, with all other Inheritances, Franchises, Possessions, Goods, Chattels, and personal Estate aforesaid, or as much thereof as has not been laid out and bestowed upon the Building the said College, or to the other Uses abovementioned.

III. [Appoints James Blair first president "during his natural life."]

IV. [Gives trustees power to choose successive masters and professors.]

V. And further, we Will, and for us, our Heirs, and Successors, by these Presents, do GRANT, That when the said College shall be so erected, made, founded, and established, it shall be called and denominated, for ever, the College of William and Mary, in Virginia, and that the President and Masters, or Professors, of the said College, shall be a Body politic and incorporate, in Deed and Name; and that by the Name of the President, and Masters, or Professors, of the College of William and Mary, in Virginia, they shall have perpetual Succession; and that the said President, and Masters, or Professors, shall for ever be called and denominated the President, and Masters, or Professors, of the College of William and Mary, in Virginia: And that the said President, and Masters, or Professors, and their Successors, by the Name of the President, and Masters, or Professors, of the College of William and Mary, in Virginia, shall be Persons able, capable, apt, and perpetual in Law, to take and hold Lordships, Manors, Lands, Tenements, Rents, Reversions, Rectories, Portions, Pensions, Annuities, Inheritances, Possessions, and Services, as well Spiritual as Temporal, whatsoever, and all Manner of Goods and Chattels, both of our Gift, and our Heirs and Successors, and of the Gift of the said, Francis Nicholson, William Cole, [and, as above, names of other trustees], or of the Gift of any other Person whatsoever, to the Value of Two Thousand Pounds of lawful Money of England, Yearly, and no more, to be had and held by them and their Successors for ever.

VI. And also, that the said President and Masters or Professors, by and under the Name of the President and Masters or Professors of the College of William and Mary, in Virginia, shall have Power to plead, and be impleaded, to sue, and be sued, to defend, and be defended, to answer, and be answered, in all and every Cause, Complaint, and Action real, personal, and mixed, of what Kind and Nature soever they be, in whatsoever Courts and Places of Judicature belonging to us, our Heirs and Successors or to any other Person whatsoever, before all Sorts of Justices and Judges, Ecclesiastical and Temporal, in whatsoever Kingdoms, Countries, Colonies, Dominions, or Plantations, belonging to us, or our Heirs; and to do, act, and receive, these and all other Things, in the same manner, as our other liege People, Persons able and capable in Law, within our said Colony of Virginia, or our Kingdom of England, do, or may act, in the said Courts and Places of Judicature, and before the said Justices and Judges. . . .

VII. [Gives president and masters the use of the common seal of the college.]

VIII. And further, of our more especial Grace, we have Given and Granted, and for us, our Heirs, and Successors, we Give and Grant our special Licence, as far as in us lies, to the said . . . Gentlemen, that they, or any other Person or Persons, whatsoever, after the said College is so founded, erected, made, created, and established, may have Power to Give, and Grant, Assign, and Bequeath, all Manors, Lands, Tenements, Rents, Services, Rectories, Portions, Annuities, Pensions, and Advowsons of Churches, and all Manner of Inheritances, Franchises, and Possessions whatsoever, as well Spiritual as Temporal, to the Value of Two Thousand Pounds a Year, over and above all Burthens, and Reprisals, to the President, and Masters, or Professors, of the said College, for the Time being, and their Successors, to be had, held, and enjoyed, by the said President, and Masters, or Professors, and their Successors, for ever: And that they the said President, and Masters, or Professors aforesaid, may take and hold, to themselves, and their Successors, for ever, as is aforesaid, Manors, Lands, Tenements, Rents, Reversions, Services, Rectories, Portions, Pensions, Annuities, and all, and all Manner of Inheritances, and Possessions whatsoever, as well Spiritual as Temporal, to the aforesaid Value of Two Thousand Pounds a Year, over and above all Burthens, Reprisals, and Reparations: It not being our Will, that the said President, and Masters, or Professors, . . . for the Time being, or their Successors, shall be troubled, disquieted, molested, or aggrieved, by Reason, or Occasion, of the Premises, or any of them, by us, our Heirs, and Successors, or by any of our Justices, Escheators, Sheriffs, or other Bailiffs, or Ministers, whatsoever, belonging to us, our Heirs, and Successors.

IX. And further, we Will, and by these Presents, do declare, nominate, ordain, and appoint, the said . . . Gentlemen, and their Successors, to be the true, sole, and undoubted Visitors and Governors of the said College for ever: And we Give, and Grant to them, or the major Part of them, by these our Letters Patents, a continual Succession, to be continued in the Way and Manner hereafter specified; as also full and absolute Liberty, Power, and Authority, of making, enacting, framing, and establishing, such and so many Rules, Laws, Statutes, Orders, and Injunctions, for the good and wholesome Government of the said College, as to them the said Francis Nicholson, William Cole, &c. and their Successors, shall, from Time to Time, according to their various Occasions and Circumstances, seem most fit and expedient: All which Rules, Laws, Statutes, and Injunctions, so to be made, as aforesaid, we will have to be observed, under the Penalty, therein contained:

Provided notwithstanding, that the said Rules, Laws, Statutes, Orders, and Injunctions, be no way contrary to our Prerogative Royal, nor to the Laws and Statutes of our Kingdom of England, or our Colony of Virginia, aforesaid, or to the Canons and Constitutions of the Church of England, by Law established.

X. [Gives method of nominating and electing visitors and governors.]

XI. [Grants college officers power to elect a chancellor for a seven-year term.]

XII. [Empowers college officers to designate a meeting place for the visitors.]

XIII. [Empowers visitors to elect a rector annually.]

XIV. [Assigns funds to be used in construction of the college.]

XV. [Designates tobacco revenue to be applied to college construction.]

XVI. [Delegates interim powers to surveyor general.]

XVII. That the said Francis Nicholson, William Cole, and the rest of the said Trustees, or the major Part of them, or of the longest Livers of them, so soon as the said College shall be actually founded, and established, shall Give, Grant, Lett, and Alienate the said Twenty Thousand Acres of Land to the said President, and Masters, or Professors of the said College, to be had and held by them, and their Successors, for ever, by fealty, in free and common Soccage, paying to us, and our Successors, Two Copies of Latin Verses Yearly, . . . for ever, in full Discharge, Acquittance, and Satisfaction of all Quit-Rents, Services, Customs, Dues, and Burdens whatsoever, due, or to be due, to us, or our Successors, for the said Twenty Thousand Acres of Land, by the Laws or Customs of England, or Virginia.

XVIII. [Empowers college officers to elect a representative to House of Burgesses.]

XIX. And further, it is our Pleasure, that such further Confirmations and Ratifications of the Premisses shall be Granted, from Time to Time, by us, our Heirs, and Successors, to the said Francis Nicholson, and the rest of the Trustees above mentioned, and to their Successors, or to the President, and Masters, or Professors, of the said College, or to their Successors, for the Time being, upon their humble Petition under the Great Seal of England, or otherwise, as the Attorney General of us, our Heirs, or Successors, for the Time being, shall think fit and expedient.

In Testimony whereof, We have caused these our Letters to be made Patent: Witness our Selves, at Westminster, the Eighth Day of February, in the Fourth Year of our Reign.

By Writ of the Privy Seal.

PIGOTT

10. *Statutes of William and Mary, 1727*

THE PREFACE

Towards the cultivating the minds of men, and rectifying their manners, what a mighty influence the studies of good letters, and the liberal sciences have, appears from hence, that these studies not only flourished of old amongst those famous nations the Hebrews, Egyptians, Greeks, and Romans; but in the latter ages of the world likewise, after a great interruption and almost destruction of them, through the incursions of the barbarous nations, they are at last retrieved, and set up with honor in all considerable nations. Upon this there followed the reformation of many errors and abuses in the point of religion, and the institution of youth to the duties of Christian virtues and civility; and a due preparation of fit persons for all offices in church and state. But no where was there any greater danger on account of ignorance and want of instruction, than in the English colonies of America; in which the first planters had much to do, in a country over-run with woods and briers, and for many years infested with the incursions of the barbarous Indians, to earn a mean livelyhood with hard labor. There were no schools to be found in those days, nor any opportunity for good education. Some few, and very few indeed, of the richer sort, sent their children to England to be educated. And there, after many dangers from the seas and enemies, and unusual distempers, occasioned by the change of country and climate, they were often taken off by the small-pox, and other diseases. It was no wonder if this occasioned a great defect of understanding, and all sort of literature, and

Knight, *A Documentary History of Education in the South before 1860,* I, 501–27.

that it was followed with a new generation of men, far short of their fore-fathers, which, if they had the good fortune, tho' at a very indifferent rate, to read and write, had no further commerce with the muses, or learned sciences; but spent their life ignobly at the hoe and spade, and other employments of an uncultivated and unpolished country. There remained still notwithstanding, a small remnant of men of better spirit, who had either had the benefit of better education themselves in their mother-country, or at least had heard of it from others. These men's private conferences among themselves being communicated to greater numbers in the like circumstances, produced at last a scheme of a free-school and college, which was by them exhibited to the president and council, in the year 1690; a little before the arrival of Lieutenant-Governor Nicholson, which was afterwards recommended by them with applause to the next ensuing General Assembly. This work so luckily begun, made a very considerable progress under his government. For, altho' being tied up by injunctions from my Lord Effingham, Chief Governor, who was then in England, he was not allowed to call an assembly so soon as he would, yet that designed good work did not sleep in the mean time; for in that interval of assemblies be [*sic*] and the Council sent out briefs, by which, and their own good example, they invited and encouraged the subscriptions of the inhabitants. These briefs were recommended to the care and management of Mr. Commissary Blair, a minister, who had been one of the first projectors of this good work, and was a little before this made commissary to the Bishop of London; with the help of his surrogats some of the most creditable ministers of the country, and brought in subscriptions to the value of two thousand pounds sterling. Upon this followed that famous General Assembly of the year 1691. This assembly not only approved that scheme of a college, as well fitted to this country, but resolved upon an humble petition to King William and Queen Mary, for a charter to impower certain trustees that they named, to found such a college, and that their majesties would likewise assist in the funds necessary for building the edifices, and maintaining the president and masters. To deliver this petition, and to negotiate this whole affair, they made Mr. Blair their agent to sollicit it at the court of England. Tho' both the king and queen were exceeding well inclined, and the good bishops, especially Dr. Tillotson, Archbishop of Canterbury, and Dr. Compton, Bishop of London, gave all assistance; and Mr. Blair followed it with diligence and dexterity, it was a long time before all the difficulties, which were objected, were got over. But at last, after two years spent in that service, an ample charter was obtained, with several gifts, both for building, and endowment, for paying the president's and masters salaries; and Mr. Blair, by advice of the General Assembly in Virginia, and the bishops in England, being made president of the college, returned to see all put in execution. In which for many years afterwards he was involved in a great number of difficulties, some of which threatened the total subversion of the design. Especially when in the year 1705, the buildings and library were destroyed by fire; and there was no money to repair the loss. Yet at length, by patience and good husbandry of the revenues, and the bounty of Queen Anne, the work was finished a second time to every one's admiration. But to go on to another necessary branch of this design, which we are now about, other obstructions being in good measure removed, there seems to be nothing more necessary than that, according to the advice of our most Reverend Chancellor Dr. Wake, Archbishop of Canterbury, some rules and statutes should be made for the good government of the college, and of the president, and masters, and scholars, and all others, that either live in it, or are employed in the management of its affairs abroad, after mature deliberation with the said Lord Archbishop, our chancellor. But because in progress of time many things will be found to be more expedient, when from small beginnings the college shall have come to greater perfection; and some things too will want to be corrected and altered, as future cases and circumstances may require: All these things we are very willing to leave to the visitors and governors, for the time being, to be added, diminished and changed, according to the different circumstances of the college, for promoting the study of the learned languages, and liberal arts, according to the powers granted them by the college charter. Only that nothing may be enacted rashly, in the heat of disputation, no old statute suddenly changed, or new one made; we recommend it for a rule in these matters, that no new statute be enacted or prescribed, until it has been duly proposed, read and considered at two several meetings of the governors of the college.

CONCERNING THE COLLEGE SENATE

As to the number, authority, and power of the college senate, in chusing the chancellor, and the president, and masters, and in appointing and changing of statutes, all this is sufficiently set forth in the col-

lege charter. From whence it is evident, how much depends upon
them, and how far a good election of them conduces to the good government of the college.

Therefore in the election of all visitors and governors of the college,
let such be preferred as are persons of good morals, and found in the
doctrine of the reformed Church of England; and friends and patrons
of the college and polite learning; and gentlemen in good circumstances, such as by their interest, if there by occasion, can patronize
and serve the college.

Let the college senate beware, that no differences or parties be held
up and cherished, either amongst themselves, or the president and
masters; and let them take care that all things be transacted quietly
and moderately, without favor or hatred to any person whatsoever.

Let them maintain and support the ordinary authority of the president and masters in the administration of the daily government of the
college, and let them refer all common domestick complaints to them:
And not suffer themselves to be troubled, except in matters of great
moment, where there is some difficulty to be got over, or some corrup-
tion or ill practice to be reformed, or a new statute to be made, or some
other weighty business to be transacted.

In the election of a president or masters, let them have a principal
regard to their learning, piety, sobriety, prudence, good morals, order-
liness and observance of discipline, and that they be of a quiet and
peaceable spirit; and let them chuse such persons into the vacant places
without respect of persons.

OF THE CHANCELLOR

The chancellor is to be the the Mecoenas or patron of the college,
such a one as by his favor with the king, and by his interest with all
other persons in England, may be enabled to help on all the college
affairs. His advice is to be taken, especially in all such arduous and
momentous affairs, as the College shall have to do in England. If the
college has any petitions at any time to the king or queen, let them be
presented by their chancellor.

If the college wants a new president, or professor, or master, out of
Great-Britain, let the college senate rely chiefly on his assistance, advice,
and recommendation.

CONCERNING THE PRESIDENT, AND MASTERS, AND SCHOOLS

There are three things which the founders of this college proposed to themselves, to which all its statutes should be directed. The first is, that the youth of Virginia should be well educated to learning and good morals. The second is, that the churches of America, especially Virginia, should be supplied with good ministers after the doctrine and government of the Church of England; and that the college should be a constant seminary for this purpose. The third is, that the Indians of America should be instructed in the Christian religion, and that some of the Indian youth that are well-behaved and well-inclined, being first well prepared in the divinity school, may be sent out to preach the gospel to their countrymen in their own tongue, after they have duly been put in orders of deacons and priests.

For carrying on these noble designs, let there be four schools assigned within the college precincts; of which, together with the masters, or professors, belonging to them, some directions must be given.

THE GRAMMAR SCHOOL

. . . In this grammar school let the Latin and Greek tongues be well taught. As for rudiments and grammars, and classick authors of each tongue, let them teach the same books which by law or custom are used in the schools of England. Nevertheless, we allow the schoolmaster the liberty, if he has any observations on the Latin or Greek grammars, or any of the authors that are taught in his school, that with the approbation of the president, he may dictate them to the scholars. Let the master take special care, that if the author is never so well approved on other accounts, he teach no such part of him to his scholars, as insinuates any thing against religion and good morals.

Special care likewise must be taken of their morals, that none of the scholars presume to tell a lie, or curse or swear, or talk or do any thing obscene, or quarrel and fight, play at cards or dice, or set in to drinking, or do any thing else that is contrary to good manners. And that all such faults may be so much the more easily detected, the master shall chuse some of the most trusty scholars for public observators, to give him an account of all such transgressions, and according to the degrees of heinousness of the crime, let the discipline be used without respect of persons.

THE PHILOSOPHY SCHOOL

For as much as wee see now daily a further progress in philosophy, than could be made by Aristotle's *Logick* and *Physicks,* which reigned so long alone in the schools, and shut out all other; therefore we leave it to the president and masters, by the advice of the chancellor, to teach what systems of logick, physicks, ethicks, and mathematicks, they think fit in their schools. Further we judge it requisite, that besides disputations, the studious youth be exercised in declamations and themes on various subjects, but not any taken out of the Bible. Those we leave to the divinity school.

In the philosophy school we appoint two masters of professors, who for their yearly salary shall each of them receive eighty pounds sterling, and twenty shillings sterling a year from each scholar, except such poor ones as are entertained at the college charge, upon the foundations; for they are to be taught gratis.

One of these masters shall teach rhetorick, logick, and ethicks. The other physicks, metaphysicks, and mathematicks.

And that the youth of the college may the more chearfully apply themselves to these studies, and endeavour to rise to the academic degrees, we do, according to the form and institution of the two famous universities in England, allot four years before they attain to the degree of Bachelor, and seven years before they attain the degree Master of Arts.

THE DIVINITY SCHOOL

In this school let there be two professors, with a salary of one hundred and fifty pounds sterling to each; they are to have nothing from the students or candidates of theology.

Let one of these professors teach the Hebrew tongue, and critically expound the literal sense of the Holy Scripture both of the Old and New Testament.

Let the other explain the common places of divinity, and the controversies with hereticks; and let them have prelections and disputations on those subjects.

And let the students of divinity divide their time betwixt those two professors.

THE INDIAN SCHOOL

There is but one master in this school who is to teach the Indian boys to read, and write, and vulgar arithmetick. And especially he is to teach them thoroughly the catechism and the principles of the Christian religion. For a yearly salary, let him have forty or fifty pounds sterling, according to the ability of that school, appointed by the honorable Robert Boyle, or to be further appointed by other benefactors. And in the same school the master may be permitted to teach other scholars from the town, for which he is to take the usual wages of twenty shillings a year.

CONCERNING THE PRESIDENT

That every one may so much the more diligently wait upon his proper office, besides the six professors or masters, we have appointed a president to be supervisor of the rest. Let there be chosen for a president, a man of gravity, that is in holy orders, of an unblemished life, and good reputation, and not under thirty years of age. Of ecclesiastical benefices that have a cure of souls annexed, he shall not possess above one, and that of so near a distance from the college, that it may not hinder his ordinary care and attendance upon the college. Let the election of him be entrusted with the governors of the college. Besides learning, and an unblemished good life, care must be taken that he be a man of prudence, and skilful in business, and industrious and diligent in the management of all affairs; always preferring the honor and interest of the college, to his own or any other person's concerns. Let him have a watchful eye over the other masters and professors, that they be not absent from their employments. Let the masters often examine the scholars in his presence; and let him likewise often examine them a-part from their masters, that both masters and scholars may be excited to greater diligence in their studies. Let him likewise have a theological lecture four times a year in the explication of scripture, or some theological subject, or on some controversy against hereticks. And let him take care that the other two professors diligently attend their lectures and disputations. Let him diligently inspect into the revenues and expences of the college, and see that once a year at least a full account be perfected of all receipts and issues; and that if there be occasion for it, it be laid before the visitors and governors at their general meeting. Whatever business of the college requires epistolary commerce with any persons, he must take care to write about it, especially to the chancellor. He is to appoint the time for the ordinary meetings of himself and the masters, at which he is to preside. And to the end, that all things past at these meetings may be truly entered in books by the scribe of the meeting, the president shall first read over the minutes, and if there be occasion, correct the errors and omissions: He must provide in due time that the edifices be duly kept up and repaired. And that the visitors and governors of the college may be the better informed of every thing relating to it, let the president be always allowed to be, and accordingly let him be present at all their meetings and councils.

Let the president's yearly salary be two hundred pounds sterling, with an house and garden suitable to the place, so soon as the college revenues will bear all these expences.

OF THE ORDINARY GOVERNMENT OF THE COLLEGE

Let the ordinary government of the college be in the president and the six masters, viz. the two professors of divinity; and the two professors of philosophy, and the master of the grammar school, and the master of the Indian school. Let the power of calling, proroguing, and dismissing this sort of meetings be in the president. As to the business to be treated of in these meetings, in the first place it must be their care that all the statutes of the college be diligently put in execution. If any of the statutes are found to be inconvenient, so as to want to be amended or changed, let them modestly propose all such desired amendments to the general meeting of the visitors and governors, and submit them to their deliberation. Let all complaints and grievances, which the masters in their particular schools cannot redress, be brought first to the president, and by him to the meeting of the masters. To this meeting belongs the election and nomination of all officers that are necessary or requisite for the college business, such as the usher in the grammar school, the bursar, the library-keeper, the janitor, the cook, the butler, and gardener, the writing-master, the workmen for building or repairing; bailiffs and overseers. But in lesser matters the president's order by word of mouth may suffice. If any of the statutes are not backed and fortified with due penalties and mulcts, the setting of such mulcts and penalties is referred to this meeting of the president and masters. Let all things in this meeting, if possible, be transacted unanimously; if that cannot be, let the decision be by plurality of votes. If the votes are equal, the side on which the president is, shall be taken for the major part.

In all business of great weight and consequence especially if the president and masters cannot agree, let the college senate, consisting of the visitors and governors, be consulted; and by their determination let all the greater differences be decided.

For avoiding the danger of heresy, schism, and disloyalty, let the president and masters, before they enter upon these offices, give their assent to the articles of the Christian faith, in the same manner, and in the same words, as the ministers in England, by act of Parliament are obliged to sign the Articles of the Church of England. And in the same manner too they shall take the oaths of allegiance to the king or queen of England. And further, they shall take an oath that they will faithfully discharge their office, according to the college statutes, before the president and masters, upon the holy evangelists. All this under the penalty of being deprived of their office and salary.

OF THE SCHOLARS

There are two sorts of scholars; one is of them who are maintained at their own charge, and pay school wages in the schools where the masters are allowed to take wages as above; the other sort is of those who are maintained at the college's charge.

As to the first sort of scholars, we leave their parents and guardians at liberty whether they shall lodge and eat within the college or elsewhere in the town, or any country village near the town. For it being our intention that the youth, with as little charge as they can, should learn the learned languages and the other liberal arts and sciences: If any have their houses so near the college, that from thence the college bells can be heard, and the public hours of study be duly observed, we would not by these our statutes hinder them from boarding their own children, or their friends, or from lodging them at their own houses. Nevertheless we hope that all things relating to the table or lodging will be so well supplied within the college, that they can be no where cheaper or better accommodated.

Let the spare chambers of the college, over and above what are necessary for the president and masters, and other officers of the college, be let out at moderate rents to the better sort of the big boys; and let the money they yield be laid out in the reparation of the edifices of the college.

Out of the scholars let there be chosen to be put upon the foundation, as many as the college can maintain out of the funds allotted for that purpose. And let them be thereafter diligently instructed and maintained, till they are put in orders, and preferred to some place and office in the church. The election of this sort of scholars let it be in the visitors; and in that election let them chiefly regard besides their poverty, their ingeniousness, learning, piety, and good behaviour, as to their morals. And the more any one of the candidates excells in these things, he has so much the better title to be preferred; and let him be preferred accordingly.

OF THE COLLEGE BURSAR OR TREASURER

Because the circumstances of the college in this its infancy, will not as yet admit of many officers, who perhaps when it comes to be richer in revenues, and has a greater number of students, will become necessary: Therefore referring the rules concerning the butler, cook, janitor, library-keeper, gardener, and other officers, to the president and masters, who are to direct their offices and salaries, as the college shall find them useful and necessary; we shall only at present lay down some rules concerning the bursar or college treasurer.

It belongs to the bursar timely and diligently to gather in all the college revenues, or whatever else is due to it; and to keep the money in a strong chest. Likewise to pay to the president, masters, or professors, and the foundation scholars their several salaries, and to pay all other college debts and expences honestly, and in due time; and to take discharges and receipts for every thing. Let the accounts of all incomes and disbursements be exactly entered in account books; and after they are audited and examined once in half a year by the president and masters, that examination, and their discharge shall be entered in the same count-books, signed by the president's and masters names.

Let the president and masters from time to time chuse a man fit for this business, such a one as is responsible, and well able to pay, and who shall likewise give good security. For salary he shall have whatever the meeting of the visitors shall think reasonable, according to the trouble and desert of each bursar, besides his expences in suing at law for any debts due to the college, or any other charges he has been out in horses and messages, or in recovering the college dues, or carrying the money from Maryland, or any other very remote place....

We the subscribers James Blair, and Stephen Fouace, clerks, being the major part of the surviving trustees for the College of William and Mary, in Virginia, having considered the necessity there was to make statutes for the good government of the said college, do approve and confirm the aforesaid statutes contained in the twelve above written pages; and appoint them to be passed under the college seal. Reserving notwithstanding the power given by the charter to the visitors and governors of the same college, namely, that proceeding regularly they may add new statutes, or may even change these, as their affairs and circumstances from time to time shall require. As to which nevertheless, especially in the arduous affairs of great weight and moment, we are of opinion that the chancellor's advice should be first taken. Dated at London, the 24th day of June, in the year of our Lord one thousand seven hundred and twenty seven.

JAMES BLAIR
STEPHEN FOUACE

11. Yale Charter, 1745

Yale is still governed under this charter, which was secured in 1745 by the dynamic Rector Thomas Clap (1703–67), who hoped to give the president (now so named) a more central role in the affairs of the college. On Clap see Clifford K. Shipton's sketch in *Sibley's Harvard Graduates,* VII (Boston, 1945), 27–50, and Louis L. Tucker, "President Thomas Clap and the Rise of Yale College, 1740–1766," *The Historian,* XIX (1956–57), 66–81; see also Simeon E. Baldwin, "The Ecclesiastical Constitution of Yale College," *Papers of the New Haven Historical Society,* III (New Haven, Conn., 1882), 414–21.

Whereas, the said trustees, partners or undertakers, in pursuance of the aforesaid grant, liberty and lycence, founded a Collegiate School at New Haven, known by the name of Yale College, which has received the favourable benefactions of many liberal and piously disposed persons, and under the blessing of Almighty God has trained up many worthy persons for the service of God in the state as well as in church: And whereas the General Court of this Colony, assembled at New Haven the tenth day of October, in the year of our Lord one thousand seven hundred and twenty-three, did explain and enlarge the aforesaid powers and priviledges granted to the aforesaid partners, trustees or undertakers, and their successors, for the purpose aforesaid, as by

Charles J. Hoadly (ed.), *The Public Records of the Colony of Connecticut* (Hartford, Conn., 1876), IX, 113–18; reprinted in Edward C. Elliott and M. M. Chambers, *Charters and Basic Laws of Selected American Universities and Colleges* (New York, 1934), pp. 588–93.

the respective acts, reference thereto being had, more fully and at large may appear: And whereas . . . the present trustees, partners and undertakers of the said school, and successors of those before mentioned, have petitioned that the said school with all the rights, powers, priviledges and interests thereof, may be confirmed, and that such other additional powers and priviledges may be granted as shall be necessary for the ordering and managing the said school in the most advantageous and beneficial manner, for the promoting all good literature in the present and succeeding generations: Therefore,

The Governor and Company of his Majesty's said English Colony of Connecticut, in General Court assembled, this ninth day of May in the year of our Lord one thousand seven hundred and forty-five, enact, ordain and declare, and by these presents it is enacted, ordained and declared:

1. That the said Thomas Clap, Samuel Whitman, Jared Eliot, Ebenezer Williams, Jonathan Marsh, Samuel Cook, Samuel Whittelsey, Joseph Noyes, Anthony Stoddard, Benjamin Lord, and Daniel Wadsworth, shall be an incorporate society, or body corporate and politick, and shall hereafter be called and known by the name of The President and Fellows of Yale College in New Haven; and that by the same name they and their successors shall and may have perpetual succession, and shall and may be persons capable in the law to plead and be impleaded, defend and be defended, and answer and be answered unto, and also to have, take, possess, acquire, purchase or otherwise receive, lands, tenements, hereditaments, goods, chattels or other estates, and the same lands, tenements, hereditaments, goods, chattels or other estates to grant, demise, lease, use, manage or improve, for the good and benefit of the said college, according to the tenour of the donation and their discretion.

2. That all gifts, grants, bequests and donations of lands, tenements or hereditaments, of goods and chattels, heretofore made to or for the use, benefit and advantage of the Collegiate School aforesaid, whether the same be expressed to be made to the President or Rector and to the rest of the incorporate society of Yale College, or to the Trustees or Undertakers of the Collegiate School in New Haven, or to the trustees by any other name, stile or title whatsoever, whereby it may be clearly known and understood that the true intent and design of such gifts, grants, bequests and donations was to or for the use, benefit and advantage of the Collegiate School aforesaid and to be under the care and

disposal of the governors thereof, shall be confirmed, and the same hereby are confirmed and shall be and remain to, and be vested in the President and Fellows of the College aforesaid and their successors, as to the true and lawful successors of the original grantees.

3. That the said President and Fellows and their successors shall and may hereafter have a common seal, to serve and use for all causes, matters and affairs of them and their successors, and the same seal to alter, break and make new, as they shall think fit.

4. That the said Thomas Clap shall be, and he is hereby established, the present President, and the said Samuel Whitman, Jared Eliot, Ebenezer Williams, Jonathan Marsh, Samuel Cook, Samuel Whittelsey, Joseph Noyes, Anthony Stoddard, Benjamin Lord, and Daniel Wadsworth, shall be, and they are hereby established, the present Fellows of the said college; and that they and their successors shall continue in their respective places during life, or until they, or either of them, shall resign or be removed or displaced, as in this act is hereafter expressed.

5. That there shall be a general meeting of the President and Fellows of said College in the college library, on the second Wednesday of September annually, or at any other time and place which they shall see cause to appoint, to consult, advise and act in and about the affairs and business of the said College; and that on any special emergency the President and any two of the Fellows, or any four of the Fellows, may appoint a meeting at the said college: provided they give notice thereof to the rest by letters sent and left with them or at the places of their respective abode five days before such meeting; and that the President and six Fellows, or in case of death, absence or incapacity of the President, seven Fellows convened as aforesaid, (in which case the eldest Fellow shall preside,) shall be deemed a meeting of the President and Fellows of said College; and that in all the said meetings the major vote of the members present shall be deemed the act of the whole, and where an equi-vote happens, the President shall have a casting vote.

6. That the President and Fellows of the said College and their successors, in any of their meetings assembled as aforesaid, shall and may from time to time, as occasion shall require, elect and appoint a President or Fellow in the room and place of any President or Fellow who shall die, resign or be removed from his office, place or trust, whom the said Governor and Company hereby declare for any

disdemeanour, unfaithfulness, default or incapacity, shall be removable by the President and Fellows of the said college, six of them at least concurring in such act; and shall have power to appoint a scribe or register, a treasurer, tutors, professors, steward, and all such other officers and servants usually appointed in colleges or universities, as they shall find necessary and think fit to appoint, for the promoting good literature and the well ordering and managing the affairs of said college, and them or any of them at their discretion to remove, and to prescribe and administer such forms of oaths (not being contrary to the laws of England or of this Colony) as they shall think proper to be administered, to all the officers, instructors of the said college, or to such and so many of them as they shall think proper, for the faithful execution of their respective places, offices and trusts.

7. That the present President and Fellows of said college and their successors, and all such tutors, professors and other officers as shall be appointed for the publick instruction and government of said college, before they undertake the execution of their respective offices and trusts, or within three months after, shall publickly in the college hall take the oaths and subscribe the declaration appointed by an act of Parliament made in the first year of King George the first, entituled An Act for the further security of his Majesty's person and government and the succession of the crown in the heirs of the late Princess Sophia, being protestants, and for extinguishing the hopes of the pretended Prince of Wales and his open and secret abettors: that is to say, the President before the Governor, Deputy Governor, or any two of the Assistants of this Colony, for the time being, and the Fellows, tutors and other officers before the President for the time being, who is hereby impowered to administer the same; an entry of all which shall be made in the records of said college.

8. That the President and Fellows shall have the government, care and management of the said college, and all the matters and affairs thereunto belonging, and shall have power, from time to time as occasion shall require, to make, ordain and establish all such wholesome and reasonable laws, rules, and ordinances, not repugnant to the laws of England, nor the laws of this Colony, as they shall think fit and proper, for the instruction and education of the students, and ordering, governing, ruling, and managing the said college, and all matters, affairs and things thereunto belonging, and the same to repeal and alter, as they shall think fit; (which shall be laid before this Assembly

as often as required, and may also be repealed or disallowed by thi͙
Assembly when they shall think proper.)

9. That the President of said college, with the consent of the Fellows,
shall have power to give and confer all such honours, degrees or
lycences as are usually given in colleges or universities, upon such as
they shall think worthy thereof.

10. That all the lands and rateable estate belonging to the said college, not exceeding the yearly value of five hundred pounds sterling,
lying in this government, and the persons, families and estates of the
president and professors, lying and being in the town of New Haven,
and the persons of the tutors, students, and such and so many of the
servants of said college as give their constant attendance on the business of it, shall be freed and exempted from all rates, taxes, military
service working at highways, and other such like duties and services.

11. And, for the special encouragement and support of said college,
this Assembly do hereby grant unto the said President and Fellows
and their successors, for the use of the said college, in lieu of all former
grants, one hundred pounds silver money, at the rate of six shillings
and eight pence per ounce, to be paid in bills of publick credit, or
other currency equivalent to the said hundred pounds, (the rate or
value thereof to be stated from time to time by this Assembly,) in two
equal payments in October and May annually: this payment to continue during the pleasure of this Assembly.

In full testimony and confirmation of this grant and all the articles
and matters therein contained, the said Governor and Company do
hereby order that this act shall be signed by the Governor and Secretary, and sealed with the publick seal of the Colony, and that the same,
or a duplicate or exemplification thereof, shall be a sufficient warrant
to the said President and Fellows, to hold, use and exercise all the
powers and priviledges therein mentioned and contained.

12. Yale Laws of 1745

CHAPTER I

CONCERNING ADMISSION INTO COLLEGE

1. That none may Expect to be admitted into this College unless upon Examination of the Præsident and Tutors, They shall be found able Extempore to Read, Construe and Parce Tully, Virgil and the Greek Testament: and to write True Latin Prose and to understand the Rules of Prosodia, and Common Arithmetic, and shall bring Sufficient Testamony of his Blameless and inoffensive Life.

2. That no Person shall be admitted a Freshman into this College who is more than Twenty one Years old, unless by the special allowance of yᵉ President and Fellows or their Committee.

3. That no Person shall be admitted Undergraduate in this College until his Father, Guardian or some proper Person hath given a Sufficient Bond to the Steward of the College, to pay the Quarter Bills of the sᵈ Scholar allowed by the authority of College from Time to Time as long as He shall continue a Member of sᵈ College: which Bond The Steward Shall keep untill Such Scholar hath Taken his Second Degree, unless He Shall Receive Order from the President to Deliver it up before. . . .

CHAPTER II

OF A RELIGIOUS AND VIRTUOUS LIFE

1. All Scholars Shall Live Religious, Godly and Blameless Lives according to the Rules of Gods Word, diligently Reading the holy Scriptures the Fountain of Light and Truth; and constanly [sic] attend upon all the Duties of Religion both in Publick and Secret.

2. That the President, or in his absence One of the Tutors Shall constantly Pray in the College-Hall every morning and Evening: and Shall read a Chapter or Suitable Portion of the Holy Scriptures, unless there be Some other Theological Discourse or Religious Exercise: and Every Member of the College whether Graduates or Undergraduates,

---

Franklin B. Dexter, *Biographical Sketches of the Graduates of Yale College with Annals of the College History, 1745–1763*, II (New York, 1896), 2–18.

whether Residing in the College or in the Town of New-Haven Shall Seasonably Attend upon Penalty that every Undergraduate who Shall be absent (without Sufficient Excuse) Shall be Fined one Penny and for comeing Tardy after the Introductory Collect is made Shall be fin'd one half penny.

3. The President is hereby Desired as he hath Time & Opportunity to make and Exhibit in the Hall Such a publick Exposition, Sermon or Discourse as he shall think proper for the Instruction of ye Scholars, and when He Shall See cause So to do and Give public Notice thereof, Every Undergraduate Shall be Obliged to Attend upon the Same Penalty as aforesaid. . . .

5. No Student of this College Shall attend upon any Religious Meetings either Public or Private on the Sabbath or any other Day but Such as are appointed by Public Authority or Approved by the President upon Penalty of a Fine, Public Admonition, Confession or Otherwise according to the Nature or Demerit of the Offence.

6. That if any Student Shall Prophane the Sabbath by unnecessary Business, Diversion, Walking abroad, or makeing any Indecent Noise or Disorder on the Said Day, or on the Evening before or after, or Shall be Guilty of any Rude, Profane or indecent Behaviour in the Time of Publick Worship, or at Prayer at any Time in the College Hall, He Shall be punished, Admonished or otherwise according to the Nature and Demerit of his Crime. . . .

CHAPTER III

CONCERNING SCHOLASTICAL EXERCISES

1. Every Student Shall diligently apply himself to his Studies in his Chamber as well as attend upon all Public Exercises appointed by the President or Tutors, and no Student Shall walk abroad, or be absent from his Chamber, Except Half an hour after Breakfast, and an hour and an half after Dinner, and from prayers at Night to Nine o' the Clock, without Leave, upon Penalty of Two Pence or more to Six pence, at the Discretion of ye President and Tutors.

2. To this End the President or Tutors Shall, by Turns, or as They conveniently can visit Student's Chambers after Nine o'Clock, to See whether They are at their Chambers, and apply themselves to their Studies.

3. That the President and Each of the Tutors Shall according to the

best of their Discretion Instruct and bring forward their respective Classes in the Knowledge of the Three Learned Languages, and in the Liberal Arts and Sciences. In the first Year They Shall principally Study the Tongues & Logic, and Shall in Some measure pursue the Study of the Tongues the Two next Years. In the Second Year They Shall Recite Rhetoric, Geometry and Geography. In the Third Year Natural Philosophy, Astronomy and Other Parts of the Mathematicks. In the Fourth Year Metaphysics and Ethics. And the respective Classes Shall Recite Such Books, and in Such a manner as has been accustomed, or Such as the President upon the Consultation with the Tutors Shall think proper: but every Saturday Shall Especially be alloted to the Study of Divinity, and the Classes Shall dureing the whole Term recite the Westminster Confession of Faith received and approved by the Churches in this Colony, Wollebius, Ames Medulla, or any other System of Divinity by the Direction of the President and Fellows: and on Friday Each Undergraduate in his Order about Six at a Time Shall Declaim in the Hall in Latin, Greek, or Hebrew and in no other Language without Special Leave from the President; and Shall presently after Deliver up his Declamation to his Tutor, fairly written and Subscribed. And the two Senior Classes Shall Dispute in the Fall Twice a week; and if any Undergraduate Shall be Absent from Reciting or Disputeing without Sufficient Reason, He Shall be fined two Pence; and from Declaiming Six Pence.

CHAPTER IV

OF PENAL LAWS

1. If any Scholar Shall be Guilty of Blasphemy, Fornication, Robbery, Forgery, or any other such Great and Atrocious Crime he Shall be Expelled forthwith.

2. If any Scholar Shall deny the Holy Scriptures or any Part of Them to be the Word of God: or be guilty of Heresy or any Error directly Tending to Subvert the Fundamentals of Christianity, and continuing Obstinate therein after the first and Second Admonition, He shall be Expelled.

3. If any Scholar shall be Guilty of Profane Swearing, Cursing, Vowing, any Petty or Implicit Oath, Profane or Irreverent Use of the Names, Attributes, Ordinances or Word of God; Disobedient or Contumacious or Refractory Carriage towards his Superiours, Fighting,

Striking, Quarrelling, Challenging, Turbulent Words or Behaviour, Drunkenness, Uncleaness, Lacivious Words or Actions, wearing woman's Aparrel, Defrauding, Injustice, Idleness, Lying, Defamation, Tale bareing or any other Such like Immoralities, He Shall be Punished by Fine, Confession, Admonition or Expulsion, as the Nature and Circumstances of the Case may Require.

4. If any Person be Guilty of Stealing, He Shall besides the Fine Pay Trible [*sic*] Damage and in all other cases of Injustice Shall make full Restitution to the Party injured.

5. If any Scholar Shall break open any Other Scholars Door or Open it with a Pick-Lock or a False Key, He Shall be Fined One Shilling for the first Offence: and Two Shillings for the Second: and for the Third publickly admonished, Degraded or Expelled.

6. If any Scholar Shall Play at Cards or Dice at all: or at any Lawfull Game upon a Wager: or Shall bring any Quantity of Rum, Wine, Brandy or other Strong Liquor into College or into his Chamber where he Resides without Liberty from the President or Tutors, or Shall Go into any Tavern within Two miles of College and call for any Strong Liquor, or Spend his Time idly there unless with his Parent or Guardian, he shall for the first Offence be Fined Two Shillings and Sixpence, or be admonished: and for the Second Offence be Fined Five Shillings and be Degraded: and for the Third Offence be Expelled: and if any Scholar Shall Play at Swords, Files or Cudgels, He Shall be Fined not Exceeding One Shilling.

7. That if any Scholar Shall do any Damage to the College House, Glass, Fences, or any other Things belonging to College or Shall jump out of College Windows, or over the Board Fences, he Shall be Fined not exceeding One Shilling, and Pay all Damages to be charged in his Quarter Bill.

8. That Every Student Shall abstain from Singing, loud Talking and all other Noises in Studying Time, on Penalty of Four Pence: and if any Scholar Shall at any Time make any Rout, Disorder or Loud, Indecent Noises, Screamings or Hollowing or Shall call loud or Hollow to any other Scholar in the Presence of the President or Tutors, He Shall be fined not Exceeding Two Shillings.

9. That if any Scholar Shall associate himself with any Rude, Idle Disorderly Persons: or Shall Entertain Companions at his Chamber either in College or out after Nine o'Clock, or Shall Take any Person who is not a near Relation to Lodge with Him without Liberty from

the President or a Tutor he Shall be Fined not Exceeding Two Shillings.

10. That the President or Either of the Tutors may when he See Cause Break open any College Door to Suppress any Disorder; And if any Scholar Shall refuse to Give the President or Either of the Tutors admittance into his Chamber when Demanded, or to assist in Suppressing any Disorder when required; or to come when he is Sent for, or to Give in Evidence when he is called, he Shall be Fined Two Shillings; or be punished by Admonition, Confession, Degradation or Expulsion as the Nature of the Case may Require.

11. If any Scholar Shall behave himself obstinately, refractorily or Contemtionally [sic] toward the President or either of the Tutors, He Shall for the first Offence be punished by Fine, Admonition or Confession, or Being Deprived of the Liberty of Sending Freshman for a certain Time: For the Second Offence he Shall be Degraded or Expell'd.

12. That if any Scholar Shall write or Publish any Libel: or raise any false or Scandalous Report of the President or either of the Fellows or Tutors or the Minister of the first Church of New-Haven, or Shall directly or indirectly Say that either of Them is a Hypocrite, or Carnal or Unconverted, or use any Such reproachful or reviling Language concerning Them, He Shall for the first Offence make a Public Confession in the Hall; and for Second be Expelled.

13. If any Scholar Shall Go out of the College Yard without a Hat, Coat or Gown except at his Lawful Diversion, He Shall be Fined Three Pence: and if He Shall wear any indecent Apparrell He Shall be punished not exceeding Two Shillings.

14. If any Scholar Shall keep a Gun or Pistol, or Fire one in the College-Yard or College, or Shall Go a Gunning, Fishing or Sailing, or Shall Go more than Two Miles from College upon any Occasion whatsoever: or Shall be Present at any Court, Election, Town-Meeting, Wedding, or Meeting of young People for Diversion or any Such-like Meeting which may Occasion Mispence of precious Time without Liberty first obtain'd from the President or his Tutor, in any of the cases abovesaid he Shall be fined not exceeding Two Shillings.

15. That all the Scholars Shall behave Themselves inoffencively, blamelesly and justly toward the People in New-Haven: not unnecessarily Frequently their Houses, or Interesting Themselves into any Con-

troversey among Them. And upon Complaint of any Wrong done by any Scholar to any of Them, or any other Scholar, the President Shall Order Them to Do Justice and make Restitution. And if any Scholar Shall refuse So to do, He Shall be publickly Admonished, and if he continue Obstinate He Shall be Expelled and his Bond put in Sale if need be.

16. That Every Freshman Shall be Obliged to Go any reasonable and proper and reasonable Errand when he is Sent by any Student in any Superior Class; and if he Shall refuse So to Do he may be punished: provided that no Graduate Shall Send a Freshman out of the College Yard, and no Undergraduate Shall Send a Freshman anywhere in Studying Time, without Liberty first had from ye President or Oone [*sic*] of the Tutors. . . .

19. If any Scholar Shall make an assault upon the Person of yᵉ President or either of the Tutors or Shall wound, Bruise or Strike any of Them, He Shall forthwith be Expelled.

20. That no Scholar Shall undertake to Do or Transact any Matters or Affairs of Difficulty and Importance, or which are any ways new or beside the common & approved Customs & Practises of the College, without first Consulting with the President and Obtaining his Consent. . . .

CHAPTER V

OF CHAMBERS IN OR OUT OF COLLEGE

1. The President Shall from Time to Time Dispose of the Chambers and Studies in College and assign Them to particular Scholars to Live in according to his Discretion. And if any Scholar Shall not Dwell in or Shall Move out of any Chamber assigned to him, or into any other Chamber not assigned without Liberty, he Shall be Fined One Shilling, or otherwise Punished according to the Nature & Circumstances of the Offence. . . .

6. That Every Scholar who Shall Live out of College in the Town of New Haven Shall obtain Liberty of the President where to Live; and Shall not remove therefrom to any other House or Place without Liberty of the President, upon Penalty of Two Shillings.

7. That all Scholars who Live out of College in the Town of New Haven Shall be under the Same Regulations as those that live in. . . .

CHAPTER X

OF THE AUTHORITY OF COLLEGE

1. The Legislative Authority of college is in the President and Fellows; who have Power to make & establish all Such Laws, Rules or Orders and Directions (not repugnant to the Laws of the Civil Government) as They Shall think proper.

2. That the Executive Power of this College is principally in the President; who hath Power to Govern the College & every Student thereof whether Graduate or Undergraduate; and to Order and direct all the Affairs thereof according to Such Laws and Rules & Orders as are made by the President and Fellows & in Defect of them according to the Established Customs of the College, and where there are no Such then according to the best of his Judgment and Discretion, provided that in all Cases of Difficulty & Importance he Shall consult & advise with the Tutors: and when any extraordinary Emergency Shall happen which Shall be of great Importance & require a Speedy Determination, then the President with any Two of the Fellows Shall call a Meeting of the Corporation: or if that cannot conveniently be, then he Shall consult with as many as conveniently be got together.

3. That Each Tutor appointed by the President & Fellows Shall under the President have the Care, Inspection and Government of the College; and the Tuition of their respective Classes: and Shall have Power to punish any Undergraduate for any Breach of the College Laws not exceeding one Shilling, provided that when any matter of Difficulty fall out he shall not proceed without the Advice & Discretion of the President.

4. That no member of this College or any Person for him Shall make or Prosecute any Action, Suit or Complaint whatever against any other Member of Officer of this College for any Supposed Injury or Defect to or before Authority or Judges whatsoever besides the Authority of this College, upon Penalty, that any Scholar who Shall make Such Complaints or permit it to be made without Leave from the President or Fellows first obtain'd, Shall be forthwith Expell'd.

5. That every One who is chose President or Tutor of this College shall before he enter upon his Office, publickly, in the College-hall give his Consent to the Westminster Confession of Faith and Ecclesiastical Discipline recieved by the Churches of this Colony, & Established by the Laws of this Government.

ADDITION TO CHAPTER 4th, SECT. 9th

And if any Person or Persons whatsoever Shall Shew any ill treatment, Disrespect or Contempt towards the Authority of this College or Shall Counsel, Encourage or Support any Students in any disobedient, refractory, or contemptuous Carriage or Conduct towards the Laws or Authority of it; or Shall Intice, Seduce or Mislead any Student into any Evil Ways, Principles or Practises, the President with the Advice of the Tutors, Shall Prohibit such Person or Persons from coming within the College Limits, & also prohibit all the Students from all familiar Conversation, Dealing & Commerce with Him or Them, upon Such Penalties as the Nature & Circumstances of the Case may Require.

CHAPTER XI

OF THE LIBRARY

1. That no Person shall have Liberty to Take or Borrow any Book out of the Library except the President, Fellows, Tutors, Steward, Masters & Bachellors Residing att College, & the two Senior Classes; provided that the President may Give Liberty that the Sophimores may have Some particular Books upon the Rudiments of Languages and Logic, which are rarely taken out by any Superior Class. . . .

6. That the Senior Tutor for the Time being shall be Library keeper and Shall Give his Attendance in the Library twice a week, immediately after Dinner on Such Days as the President shall Order; and no Student shall have Liberty to have out above three Books at a time.

13. The Testimony of the Harvard Faculty against George Whitefield, *1744*

On this incident, see Richard Hofstadter and Walter P. Metzger, *The Development of Academic Freedom in the United States* (New York, 1955), pp. 161–63.

First then, we charge him, with *Enthusiasm*. Now that we may speak clearly upon this Head, we mean by an *Enthusiast,* one that acts, either according to Dreams, or some sudden Impulses and Impressions upon his Mind, which he fondly imagines to be from the Spirit of God, perswading and inclining him thereby to such and such Actions, tho' he hath no Proof that such Perswasions or Impressions are from the holy Spirit: For the perceiving a strong Impression upon our Minds, or a violent Inclination to do any Action, is a very different Thing from perceiving such Impressions to be from the Spirit of God moving upon the Heart: For our strong Faith and Belief, that such a Motion on the Mind comes from God, can never be any proof of it; and if such Impulses and Impressions be not agreeable to our Reason, or to the Revelation of the Mind of God to us, in his Word, nothing can be more dangerous than conducting ourselves according to them; for otherwise, if we judge not of them by these Rules, they may as well be the Suggestions of the evil Spirit: And in what Condition must that People be, who stand ready to be led by a Man that conducts himself according to his Dreams, for some ridiculous and unaccountable Impulses and Impressions on his Mind? . . .

In the next Place, we look upon Mr. *W.* as an uncharitable, censorious and slanderous Man; which indeed is but a natural Consequence of the heat of Enthusiasm, by which he was so evidentally acted; for this Distemper of the Mind always puts a Man into a vain Conceit of his own Worth and Excellency, which all his Pretences to Humility will never hide, as long as he evidently shews, that he would

---

The Testimony of the President, Professors, Tutors and Hebrew Instructor of Harvard College in Cambridge against the Reverend Mr. George Whitefield, and His Conduct (Boston, 1744), pp. 4, 8–10, 15.

have the World think he hath a greater Familiarity with God than other Men, and more frequent Communications from his Holy Spirit. Hence such a Man naturally assumes an Authority to dictate to others, and a Right to direct their Conduct and Opinions; and hence if any act not according to his Directions, and the Model of Things he had form'd in his own heated Brain, he is presently apt to run into slander, and stigmatize them as *Men of no Religion, unconverted,* and *Opposers of the Spirit of God:* And that such hath been the Behaviour of Mr. *W.* is also sufficiently evident as was the former Head. Hence were his monstrous Reflections upon the great and good Archbishop Tillotson, (as Dr. *Increase Mather* Stiles him) comparing his Sermons to the conjuring Books which the Apostles perswaded the People to destroy. . . .

The next Instance we shall note, is the reproachful Reflections upon the Society which is immediately under our Care. . . . Where are observable his Rashness and his Arrogance. His Rashness, in publishing such a disadvantageous Character of *Us, viz.* Because some Body had so inform'd him. Surely he ought, if he had followed our Saviour's Rule, to have had a greater Certainty of the Truth of what he publish'd of us to the whole World. But his Arrogance is more flagrant still, that such a young Man as he should take upon him to tell what Books we shou'd allow our Pupils to read. But then he goes further still, when he says, p. 95. both of *Yale College* as well as ours, *As for the Universities, I believe it may be said, Their Light is now become Darkness, Darkness that may be felt.* What a deplorable State of Immorality and Irreligion has he hereby represented *Us* to be in! And as this is a most wicked and libellous Falshood (at least as to our College) as such we charge it upon him. But why doth he say thus? Why, *because this is complain'd of by the most godly Ministers.* Here we are at a Loss to think whom he means by *the most godly Ministers.* Certainly not the Rev. Gentlemen of the Town of *Boston* (with whom nevertheless he was most acquainted) for they are in the Government of the College, have assisted in making the Laws by which it is govern'd, and constantly visit us by a Committee, and themselves four Times in a Year, and make Examination how the Laws are executed. Besides, we don't know that he hath been pleas'd to allow to any one of them any such religious Character, in any one of his Journals, as

should make us think he means them, but rather the reverse. Vid. p. 76
of his Journal from *N.E.* . . .

Harvard College, Dec. 28. 1744

> EDWARD HOLYOKE, *President*
> HENRY FLYNT, *Tut.* & *Soc.*
> EDWARD WIGGLESWORTH, *Soc.* & *S.T.P.* Holliss.
> JUDAH MONIS, *Instr. Hebr.*
> BELCHER HANCOCK, *Tut.*
> JOSEPH MAYHEW, *Tut.* & *Soc.*
> THOMAS MARSH, *Tut.*
> JOHN WINTHROP, *Math.* & *Phil. Nat. Prof.* Holliss.

14. Whitefield's Reply to the Harvard Faculty, 1745

See Doc. 13.

But that which affords you the greatest Occasion to denominate me
a censorious, uncharitable and slanderous Man, and which I apprehend
chiefly stirs up your Resentment against me is; to make Use of your
own Expression, "My reproachful Reflections, p. 9. upon the Society
which is immediately under our Care."—I think the Reflections are
these,—"And as far as I could gather from some who well knew the
State of it (the *College*) not far superiour to our Universities in Piety
and true Godliness.—Tutors neglect to pray with and examine the
Hearts of the Pupils.—Discipline is at too low an Ebb: Bad Books are
become fashionable among them: *Tillotson* and *Clark* are read, instead
of *Shepard, Stoddard,* and such like evangelical Writers."—And *Gentlemen,* were not these Things so at the Time in which I wrote?
Wherein then in writing thus have I slandered *Harvard College?*—
But then you say, pa. 10th, he goes further still, when he says, pa. 96th,
both of *Yale-College* as well as ours; "As for the Universities, I believe
it may be said, Their Light is now become Darkness, Darkness that
may be felt."—And must it not be so when Tutors neglect to pray
with and examine the Hearts of the Pupils, &c. And this is all I meant.
—For I had no Idea or representing the Colleges in such a deplorable

---

George Whitefield, *A Letter to the Reverend the President, and Professors, Tutors, and
Hebrew Instructor of Harvard College* . . . (Boston, 1745), pp. 12–13, 20–22.

State of Immorality and Irreligion as you *Gentlemen,* in your Testimony p ibid. seem to object.—I meant no more, than what the Rev. President meant, when speaking of the Degeneracy of the Times, in his Sermon at the annual Convention of Ministers, *May* 28th, 1741, he adds, "But alas, *how is the Gold become dim, and the most fine Gold changed?* We have lost our first Love: And tho' Religion is still in Fashion with us, yet its evident, that the Power of it is greatly decayed."—However I am sorry, I publish'd my private Informations, tho' from credible Persons, concerning the Colleges to the World: and assure you, that I should be glad to find the Reverend President was not mistaken when he undertook from his own Examination of Things, seven Months after, to "assure that venerable Audience on the Day of the Convention, that their Society hath not deserv'd the Aspersions which have of late been made upon it, either as to the Principles there prevalent, or the Books there read:" . . . For I unfeignedly wish your Prosperity, and therefore was as willing to publish the Reformation in the College, as ever I was to speak of its Declension.—From thence may there always proceed those Streams which may make glad the City of our God!

To proceed,—again you say, p. 11. "We think it highly proper to bear out Testimony against Mr. *Whitefield,* as we look upon him a Deluder of the People.—And here we mean more especially as to the Collections of Money, which when here before, by an extraordinary mendicant Faculty, He almost *extorted* from the People."—Extorted from the People? How *Gentlemen,* could that be when it was a public Contribution? I never heard the People themselves make any such Objection.—Nor did I ever see People in all Appearance offer more willingly: they seem'd to be those chearful Givers whom God declares he approves of. . . .

Is it enough for me to answer for my self, without having the Faults of others that came after me laid to my Charge also? Did not the Papists as justly, who charged *Luther* with all the Imprudencies of his Adherents, and the Confusions that attended the Reformation? Besides, I do not understand, who you mean by those *hot Men.*—Surely you do not include the Reverend Mr. *Tennent.*—Him God did make me an Instrument of sending to *New-England.*—I thank Him for it, as I believe several of *Harvard Colleges,* many Ministers, and Thousands of the common People, in the several Parts of *New-England,* will be found to do thro' the endless Ages of Eternity. As for others, I knew nothing of their coming, neither do I well know who you mean, and consequently can be no more justly charged with their Misconduct, than the first Founder of *Harvard College* can be charged with all the bad Principles and Practices which any of the Members of that Society have been guilty of since his Decease.—That *our* Labours, *viz.* Mr. *Tennent* and mine were remarkable bless'd, the Rev. Mr. President himself testified in the foremention'd Sermon pa. 23d. . . .

Gentlemen, I profess my self a *Calvinist* as to Principles, and preach no other Doctrines than those which your pious Ancestors and the Founders of *Harvard College* preached long before I was born.—And I am come to *New England* with no Intention to meddle with, much less to destroy the Order of the *New-England* Churches, or turn out the Generality of their Ministers, or re-settle them with Ministers from *England, Scotland,* and *Ireland,* as hath been hinted in a late Letter written by the Reverend Mr. *Clap,* Rector of *Yale-College:*—Such a Thought never enter'd my Heart; neither as I know of, has my Preaching the least Tendency thereunto.—I am determined to know nothing among you but Jesus Christ and him crucified.—I have no Intention of setting up a Party for my self, or to stir up People against their Pastors. . . .

15. *Wigglesworth's Reply to Whitefield, 1745*

Edward Wigglesworth (*ca.* 1693–1765) was a member of the Harvard Class of 1710. He became the first Hollis Professor of Divinity in 1722 and in later years a leader of the anti-evangelical clergy. At the time of his death the great majority of the pulpits of Massachusetts and northern New England were occupied by ministers he had trained at Harvard. See Shipton's sketch in *Sibley's Harvard Graduates,* V (Boston, 1937), 546–55.

And this brings us to your "reproachful Reflections upon the Society which is immediately under our Care." The Reflections are these, as you rehearse them, P 12. "As far as I could gather from some who well knew the State of it [the *College*] not far superiour to *our Universities,*

A Letter to the Reverend Mr. George Whitefield by way of Reply to his Answer to the College Testimony Against him and his Conduct (Boston, 1745), pp. 26–33, 58–59.

in Piety and true Godliness.—Tutors neglect to pray with and examine the Hearts of their Pupils.—Discipline is at too low an Ebb:—Bad Books are become fashionable among them.—*Tillotson* and *Clark* are read, instead of *Shepherd, Stoddard,* and such like evangelical Writers." For publishing this disadvantageous Character of us, only upon Hear say, and that too probably from Persons whom you had not had six Days Acquaintance with, we have charged you with Rashness, and Contradiction to our Saviour's Rule; and you are sensible that the President undertook, from his own Examination of Things, a few Months after, to contradict some Part of your evil Report concerning us, in the Face of a venerable and great Assembly, many of them well acquainted with the State of the College.—These Things you make no Reply to; nor do you attempt to prove the Truth of the Reproaches you have taken up against us, and spread as far as your Journals find a Reading: But gravely ask us, "Were not these Things so at the Time in which I wrote them?" And taking it for granted that they were, you go on and say, "Wherein then in writing thus, have I slandered *Harvard College?*" And you assure us, that you would "be glad to find, that the Rev. President was not mistaken in what he declared before the Convention, from his own Examination." We will not say here, what perhaps some would, that this is a lively Specimen of the prevailing of too much of *that Temper* in you still, which you tell us in your Life, P. 2. that you *soon gave pregnant Proofs of.* Instead of this, we only ask, how you expect to find (what you say you should be glad of) "That the President was not mistaken?" It seems neither *his* Word, nor *ours,* is of any Weight with you; but you still believe, that "Things were at the Time in which you wrote," as you have represented them. And therefore, tho' you say, "you are sorry that you published your *private Informations* concerning the Colleges to the World;" yet you still declare the *Reasons to be credible* from whom you had them; and are yet of Opinion, that *in writing thus, you have not slandered Harvard College.* We little expect therefore to convince *you;* but we believe we shall do a Pleasure to many *others* (whose Opinion of us we ought to value) if we proceed to consider the several Articles of your Representation of us.

And here you say, first, that "as far as you could gather from some, who knew the State of the College well, it is not far superiour to *our Universities* in Piety and true Godliness."—To know what you mean by this, we must look to the Character you give of the *Universities* in *England*. Now this we have in your Journal at *Williamsburgh*, P. 109. where speaking of the College at that Place, you say, "It may be of excellent Use, if learning *Christ* be made the Foundation of their Study, and other Arts and Sciences only introduced and pursued as subservient to that. For want of this, most of our *English* Schools and *Universities* are sunk into *meer Seminaries of Paganism. Christ or Christianity* is scarce so much as named among them."—As for this your Character of the *Universities* in *England,* we only say, that you have taught us to *believe you with Discretion,* by telling the World, that *our State,* with Respect to "Piety and true Godliness, is not far superiour to this."—Concerning our own Academy, we say, we are far from boasting of its *Piety and true Godliness.* We are heartily sorry, that there is not much more of these to be found among the Youth under our Care, than there is. And yet we may with great Truth, and without any Immodesty, affirm, that the *Knowledge of the only true God, and of Jesus Christ whom He hath sent,* is earnestly recommended to the Students as that, in Comparison whereof they ought to account all other Things but *Loss and Dung.* And we must farther tell you, that we cannot easily perswade ourselves, that any *credible Person,* who *well knew the State* of our Society, ever told you any Thing, from which he will own you could fairly gather, that it was "not far superiour for Piety and true Godliness, to such Universities as are sunk into *meer Seminaries of Paganism; where Christ or Christianity is scarce so much as named.*" Produce the *credible Person* who gave you this Information, or take the vile Slander upon yourself, and let Confusion cover you, till you have given Satisfaction for it, which the Laws of Christ, our King and Judge, require.

You go on and say, "Tutors neglect to pray with their Pupils." To which we answer, that this is either not true, or not any just Matter of Reproach, as you would have it tho't to be. If you intended, by this Account of us, to make the World believe, that *social* Worship of God is not maintained in the College, that *Tutors* and *Pupils* don't attend upon the publick reading of the holy Scriptures, and join together in solemn Prayers, Morning and Evening, you have represented us as sunk into something as bad, or worse, than *meer Paganism.* But then this Representation is so vile a Slander, that we can hardly believe, that, in the *six* Days you gave yourself to be acquainted with *credible* Persons, and take their *Information,* you met with a single Man, who was false and bold enough to give you such an Account of us.

If you say, that this was not your Meaning, that you intended no more than to let the World know, that besides those Prayers which *Tutors* and *Pupils* conjunctly offer up to God Morning and Evening, each *Tutor* don't take *his own Pupils* into his Chamber and pray with them again; how does this prove what you seem to have designed it for, *viz.* that our Society is "not far superiour to such as are sunk into *meer Siminaries* [*sic*] *of Paganism,*" as you say the *Universities* in *England* are? What Law of Christ hath made this an *ordinary* Duty of *Tutors,* that you should think the neglect of it such a Reproach, that the World ought to hear it? If some *credible* Person should tell you concerning any professed Christian *Housholder,* that besides worshipping God Morning and Evening with his whole Family, he did not divide it into three or four Parts, and pray with each of them again by themselves, would you think this such an heinous Neglect, that all the *British Dominions* ought to ring of it? And would you think that you represented the Conduct of such an *Housholder* in a *Christian Manner,* if you should print it in your *Journal,* that he *neglected to pray with his Children,* only because he never shut out the rest of his Family, when he pray'd with them? If you say, the Case of the *Tutors* differs from that of an *Housholder,* because it is not a *Tutor,* but the *President,* who is ordinarily the Mouth of the *College* in their Address to God; we answer, that this makes the Difference not great; forasmuch as if the *Tutors* have any thing upon their Hearts, which they desire their *Pupils* should hear them offer up to God for them, they have frequent Opportunities to present these Desires of their Souls to God in the Hearing of their *Pupils,* by the necessary of Absence of the *President,* upon one Account or other, from Morning or Evening Prayers; upon which occasions the *Tutors* supply his Place by Turns.

Your next Reflection upon our *College,* is, that "*Tutors* don't examine the Hearts of their *Pupils.*" What you intend by this, we are much at a Loss to conceive. Indeed we are very sensible, that it is a great Duty, which nearly concerns us all, to *examine our own Hearts* with the utmost Diligence and Care. But that it is our Duty *ordinarily* to *examine the Hearts of others,* is not so clear. *The Son of God, who hath his Eyes like unto a Flame of Fire,* hath said, *Rev.* 2.23. *All the Churches shall know, that I am He who searches the Reins and Heart.* Would you have *Tutors* invade *his* Prerogative, and *make the Churches know* that *others* beside the *Son of God* may, and ought, to undertake this Scrutiny? Or, do you intend the Expression in a *Popish* sense, and mean, that our *Tutors* neglect to bring their *Pupils* before them to *secret Confession,* as the *Romish Priests* do by their *People?* If this be your Meaning, speak out, *Sir,* and tell us plainly, that you think the *Popish* Practice of *Auricular Confession* ought to be introduced in the *College,* that it may with more Speed and Ease be propagated thro' the Country. Whenever you tell us thus in plain Terms, we shall be at no loss for an Answer. If you reply, that you meant nothing of all this, but only intended that the Souls of the *Pupils* are not taken Care of, by those who have the Government and Instruction of them, that "Christ, or Christianity is scarce so much as named among them," which you say is the Case of the *Universities* in *England;* and that the Counsels and Warnings of God are not set before them; we answer, that if this, and not something much worse, be what you meant by saying, "Tutors neglect to examine the Hearts of their Pupils," it is a very injurious and false representation. And you might easily have known it to be so, upon much less than *six* Days Enquiry, if your Ears had not been more open to *evil* Reports, than to *good* ones.—Is not every *Exposition* of the *President,* and every *Lecture* of the *Divinity* Professor, and Address to the *Students* upon the important Points of our holy Religion? Are not these *all* in some Measure *Profitable for Doctrine, for Reproof, for Correction, or for Instruction in Righteousness?* And is it not a distinguishing Advantage to *the Youth of the College,* which both they and their Friends ought to be very thankful to God for, that they have the Benefit of these four Times a Week, beside what they enjoy *in common with other Christians,* viz. *The Exercises of the Lord's Day,* and *Lectures* on other Days *out of the College?*—And as for the Tutors, whom you particularly charge with *Neglect,* if you mean, that they are generally so grosly negligent of their Duty, with Regard to taking proper Opportunities to talk seriously and closely with the *Pupils* about their spiritual Concerns, as does in any Measure justify your Reflections, they deny the Charge, and insist upon it, that it is a Slander.—And others of us can with Truth assure you and the World, that besides discharging the more *publick* Duties of our Stations, we have not been wanting to reprove, rebuke, exhort or Encourage and direct more *privately,* whenever we have had Reason to think, that the Case of any particular Person has called for it.

You tell us next, "that Discipline is at too low an Ebb."—This is a Reproach which we had little Reason to expect at the Time when you published it. We had not long before dropped one of our *Tutors* out of his Place, for very corrupt and dangerous Principles, as soon as they came to be certainly known. And we had kept him out till he had given Grounds for Charity to hope, that he was come to a sounder Mind. We had also expelled a *Professor* for immoral and scandalous Practices. And can it be supposed, that a Government, which upon just Occasion, would not spare its *own Officers,* would at the same Time wink at the Faults of Children?—We have since, for Immorality, expelled another *Tutor,* who was also a *Fellow* of the House. And these Acts of Discipline, we believe, will convince others, whatever you may think of them, that Discipline neither was, nor is at so *low an Ebb,* as to deserve that we should be reproached publickly with the want of it.—But you say, "Bad Books are become fashionable among them; *Tillotson* and *Clark* are read, instead of *Shepherd, Stoddard,* and such like Evangelical Writers."—We make no doubt but that *bad Books* were, and are, and always will be, too often read in a Society of such Numbers, where many are supplied with Money enough by their Parents to purchase a *bad Book,* if their Inclinations lead them to it. But the Question is, whether *bad Books* were then read with the Approbation or Knowledge of the *Governours* of the House? Now the surest Way to find this, is to examine what Books were then borrowed by the Scholars out of the *publick Library:* For other Books they may easily conceal, if they please, from their *Tutors.* Now upon a particular Enquiry into the *Library Records* on this Occasion, as the World hath been informed, by our worthy Friend Col. *Brattle,* in the *Boston Gazette, June* 22. 1741. it was found, with respect to the Books which you call *Bad* ones, that "from the 28th *Nov.* 1732. to that very Day (for almost nine Years) *Tillotson* had not been so much as once taken out of the *Library* by any *Undergraduate;* nor any of Dr. *Clark's* Works for above two Years: Whereas *Owen, Baxter, Flavel, Bates, Howe, Doolittle, Willard, Watts,* and *Guyse* (who be sure most of them may be reckoned *Evangelical Writers,* as well as *Shepherd* and *Stoddard*) have some or other of them been borrowed by *Undergraduates* during this whole Time; and that they are scarcely ever in the Library; and that these Books have been more commonly borrowed by the *Graduates,* than *Tillotson* and *Clark.* This Account (says he) I have before me, attested by the *Library Keeper,* and desire the Facts may be examined into by any one that doubts them."—We think we may leave it now to every unbiassed Conscience to determine, whether the Account you have given of the *Books* read at *College,* was fair and just, "at the Time in which you wrote."

However, if at that Time you believed this, and all the other Reproaches, you had taken up against us, to be true; and that the State of our *College* was "not far superiour to that of Universities, where Christ or Christianity is scarce so much as named;" why did you not act so much like a Christian yourself, as to signify your Apprehensions, and make what Remonstrances you tho't proper *privately,* in a Letter to the *President,* or to some other of the *Officers* of the Society? This we should have taken kindly; and if your Apprehensions had been well grounded, such a Way of communicating them, might have been a Means of much Good, and no Harm to us. But what good End could you propose to yourself in calumniating us thus *publickly,* in your *Journal,* without ever hearing what we had to say for ourselves? We put this Question seriously to your Conscience; for it is easy to see many things very *hurtful* to us, which you might have in View; such as discouraging publick spirited Persons from becoming *Benefactors* to our Society, which was to injure us in our *Estate* as well as *Name;* and such as discouraging Pious Parents from sending their Children to us for *Education,* which must, in a little Time, bring destitute Churches under a Necessity of seeking to other Countries for a Supply of Ministers. These, and such other *bad* Designs, it is very easy to conceive, that you might have in your Heart; but what Good you could propose to do us, by this Conduct, either upom [*sic*] *Temporal* or *Spiritual* Accounts, we confess it is out of our Reach to Comprehend. You might probably conclude it would raise our Resentment; but you had no just Reason to think that it was the proper Way to compass a Reformation of what might be amiss; and be sure not the Way prescribed for this End by our blessed Saviour, thus to traduce us in the most *publick* Manner you could, instead of informing us, (when you might so easily have done it) *privately,* of what you had heard to our Disadvantage. And to this tender Treatment of us, we think, you was obliged *meerly as a Gentleman,* if you had laid *Christianity* quite aside; since, as you acknowledge, you was *very civily treated* and *kindly entertained;* and since we believe you must be sensible, from the Sum collected at *Cambridge,* that the *College* contributed liberally to the Relief of your *poor Orphans.* . . .

However you tell us, "you are sorry," and we easily believe you: But for what? Not that you have greatly wronged the Colleges, and heinously violated the eighth and ninth Commandments of the moral Law; but "that you *publish'd* your *private Informations* to the World, tho' from *credible* Persons:" By which, and your asking us "if these Things were not so at the Time in which I wrote? and wherein then in writing thus have I slandered *Harvard College?*" we understand you to insist upon it still, that the Facts are all true, and that you are only sorry that you was *somewhat rash* in proclaiming that to the World, which was only whispered to you in the Ear, by some credible Persons, who are loth to be exposed. But till you bring these credible Persons out, you must take all upon yourself. It hath been hinted by one of your late zealous Advocates, that some of your Informers were *Overseers* of the College. But we can hardly perswade ourselves, that any of those Honourable and Reverend Gentlemen could so far forget their Character, as to turn Informers, to a meer Stranger (as you then was) of Enormities in the College, which they never took any Care to reform, since their Visitations have been no less than four in a Year, two by their Committees, and two by themselves in a Body. And it may be a Satisfaction to some, into whose Hands this Paper may fall, to know, that these *Overseers* are his Excellency the *Governour,* the Honourable the *Lieutenant Governour,* and his *Majesty's Council,* with the Rev. *Ministers* of *Boston,* and the five neighbouring Towns; upon all of whom you have implicitly reflected, (as well as upon the Gentlemen in the more immediate Government and Instruction of the College) that they should suffer us to sink into little better than *a Seminary of meer Paganism,* and never tell us of it, (as be sure they never did) when they visit us so often to enquire into our State, and rectify what they think amiss. It deserves to be remarked also, that Governour *Belcher* of whom you speak so often in your Journals, and with so much Respect, was in the *Chair,* and so at the Head of the *Overseers,* when you wrote these injurious Reflections upon the College. . . .

You profess yourself, P. 21. "a *Calvinist* as to Principle, and that you preach no other Doctrines than those which our pious Ancestors, and the Founders of *Harvard College* preached long before you was born." —We assure you, *Sir,* that the same Doctrines are at this Day preached in *Harvard* College, which were preached by our pious Ancestors. We have no Controversy with you so far as you are a Calvinist in Principle. And if you had never preached any other Doctrines than those of *Calvinism,* or of the Doctrinal Articles of the *Church of England,* we should not have taken any Exceptions at the *Matter* of your preaching.

You had told us, P. 16. that you "utterly detest *Antinomianism,* both in Principle and Practice."—Upon this we must observe here, since we did not do it in the proper Place, that in your second Letter to the Bishop of *London,* lately printed and spread among us, you transcribe a long Passage (which you had printed once before) out of the *Honeycomb of free Justification,* written by one Mr. *Eaton.* You insinuate, P. 13. of your Letter, that he wrote with *Piety and Judgment on the Head of Justification.* And notwithstanding your Zeal and Uncharitableness towards Dr. *Tillotson,* and the Author of the *Whole Duty af* [*sic*] *Man,* you don't give the least Hint that there is any thing false or dangerous in this *Honeycomb of free Justification:* And therefore, lest your Followers, by your Extracts from the Book, and Commendation of the Author, should be led to read the Book, and swallow all the Poison in it, before they are aware, we think our selves in Duty bound to warn them against it, as containing the very Dregs of *Antinomianism.*

16. The Cleaveland Affair at Yale, 1745

The Rector, of course, was Thomas Clap, who would make no compromises from what he considered to be the true line. See Doc. 11 and Part II, Doc. 4.

It is well known that Messieurs *Elisha* and *Solomon Paine of Canterbury,* Lay Exhorters, have advanced sundry Corrupt Principles and Dangerous Errors; by means whereof they have led many People in the Country and especially in the County of *Windham,* into Schisms and Separations; which had such a threatning Aspect upon these Churches, as gave occasion to the Ministers of that County, unanimously to publish a Letter or Declaration to their People, setting forth the pernicious Nature and Danger of those Errors, and warning them against running after the Teachers of them. And since the Ministers of that County are the most proper Judges in this Case, we shall choose to Represent it in their words.

"You well know there are divers Persons in several of our Societies, who have of late Separated themselves from the Congregations to the

The Judgment of the Rector and Tutors of Yale College, Concerning Two of the Students Who Were Expelled; Together with the Reasons of it (New London, Conn., 1745).

which they did belong, and have vented diverse Erroneous and dangerous Principles, calculated to Overthow the Institution of the Gospel Ministry, to render Vain the Ordinances of Christ's Appointment, to the Perverting of the Holy Scriptures, and making some of the great and most important Doctrines of them appear in a ridiculous Light; —And have followed several Persons who have set up for publick Teachers and Exhorters (as far as we can find) on the same Principles, and draw away the People after them, to the Neglect and Contempt of the Instituted Worship of God. Some of the most Considerable of these Errors are those that follow.

"1. That it is the Will of God to have a pure Church on Earth in this sense, That all the Converted should be Separated from the Unconverted.

"2. That the Saints certainly Know one another, and Know who are Christ's true Ministers, by their own inward Feeling, or a Communion between them in the inward Actings of their own Soul.

"3. That no other Call is necessary to a Person's undertaking to preach the Gospel, but his being a true Christian, and having an inward Motion of the Spirit, or perswasion in his own Mind that it is the Will of God he should preach and perform ministerial Acts: The Consequence of which is, That there is no standing instituted Ministry in the Christian Church which may be known by the visible Laws of Christ's Kingdom.

"4. That God disowns the Ministry and Churches in this Land, and the Ordinances as Administered in them.

"5. That at such Meetings of Lay-preaching, they have more of the Presence of God than in his Ordinances and under the Ministration of the present Ministry and Administration of the Ordinances in these Churches. And hereupon many have Chosen to follow after such as have set up themselves to be Preachers, Exhorters and Expounders of the Doctrines of the Scriptures; several of which there have sprung up of late in this County, the most famous of which is Mr. *Elisha Paine,* of whose Mistakes and Errors in these points we have diverse Intimations."

Then they proceed to recite sundry Evidences, by which it appears that the said *Paine* has declared,

"That it was made manifest to him, that Christ was about to have a pure Church; and that he had not done his duty in time past in promoting Separations and Divisions among the people, and that for the time to come he should endeavour to promote and encourage Separations, *pag.* 9. And asserted, That the Saints, by virtue of Grace in themselves, know the certainty of Grace in another: And charged Mr. Everet with Blasphemy for denying of it, *pag.* 11. And that the Union of a Christian to God or Christ, was the same in kind with the Union between the Humane Nature of Christ and the Divine; the only difference was, the Spirit was given to Christ without measure, but to Believers in measure: And when it was replied, That the Union between the Humane and Divine Nature of Christ, was a Union of the Second Person; but the spirit which dwelt in Believers was the Third Person. Mr. *Paine* replied, *That they were no otherwise Three Persons, than as they were Three distinct Officers."*

This he insisted upon with many other things of the like nature: Whereupon the said Ministers say;

"We thought ourselves bound, for the Honour of Christ & the Welfare of your Souls, to give an account of these things, that so you may see to what danger persons are Exposed in running after such Teachers, and how false are their pretences to the especial Impulses of the Holy Ghost, in calling them to preach,—That God has in his Providence Testified against their Practice; diverse of those who have undertaken this work have fallen into scandalous Sins and Miscarriages, and others into foul and dreadful Errors, miserable Weakness and strange perverting the Word of God."

Then the said Ministers proceed clearly to Confute those Errors from the Word of God and the Nature of the Things, shewing them to be Subversive of the very being of the Christian Church in any visible Form of it. And we cannot but signifie our Approbation of their just and seasonable Testimony against them.

In the next place, it appears to us, That *John Cleaveland* and *Ebenezer Cleaveland,* Students of this College, had imbibed and practiced sundry of those Principles and Errors, by their withdrawing from the publick Worship of God in the Congregation in *Canterbury* and attending upon the Meeting of those *Paines,* and by justifying these Errors before us. Particularly,

1. It appears to us that they had imbibed the Third Error there mentioned, (viz.) *That no other Call is necessary to a person's undertaking to preach the Gospel, but his being a true Christian and having an inward Motion of the Spirit; or a perswasion in his own Mind that it is the Will of God that he should Preach.* Tho' they sometimes added

this Proviso, *That such persons had a sufficient Ability to preach or teach to Edification:* And they particularly justified the preaching of the *Paines;* And *John Cleaveland* said, that *Solomon Paine* could preach better than he could, if he should study Divinity this Seven Years.

2. That they had imbibed the Fifth Error there mentioned (viz.) *That at such Meetings of Lay-preaching and Exhorting, they have more of the Presence of God than under the present Ministry: And that the extraordinary influences of the Spirit accompanied the preaching of these* Paines; and said, that thereby they were filled with such a strong and lively Impression of divine Things, as made them *come home Singing along the Streets.*

3. They asserted, *That every true Christian was as much United to God as Christ was;* and brought those words of Christ to prove it. *That they all may be one, even as we are one,* Joh 17.21, &c. But they being Examined about Mr. *Paine's* denying the Doctrine of the Trinity, said, *They did not know, or had not heard that he did deny it.*

We being apprehensive of the fatal Tendency of these and such like Errors, which the said *Cleavelands* had imbibed, and were likely more and more to imbibe, if they were permitted to attend upon the preaching of the *Paines;* and the danger that they might Infect and Corrupt the College (which would be very definitive to Religion) after discoursing with them several Times, proceeded to give the following Judgment;

Yale College, November 19th, 1744

THE RECTOR AND TUTORS

PRESENT,

UPON *Information that* John Cleaveland *and* Ebenezer Cleaveland, *Members of this College, withdrew from the publick Worship of God in the Meeting-house in* Canterbury, *carried on by* Mr. Cogswell, *a Licensed and Approved Candidate for the Ministry, preaching there at the desire of the first Parish or Society in* Canterbury, *with the special direction of the Association of the County of* Windham; *and that they the said* Cleavelands, *with sundry others belonging to* Canterbury *and* Plainfield, *did go to & attend upon a private separate Meeting in a private House, for divine Worship, carried on principally by one* Solomon Paine, *a Lay-Exhorter, on several Sabbaths in* September *or* October *last.*

The said *Cleavelands* being several times sent for, Acknowledged the Facts, as above related, and Justified what they had done, and gave in, the Reasons given in Writing by the said Separatists for their Separation, aforesaid; the most material of which are these, Viz. That the first Society in *Canterbury* keep up only the Form of Godliness and deny the Life, Power and Spirituality of it, and had given Mr. *Cogswell* a Call in order for Settlement, whom they the said Separatists had declared to be destitute of those essential Qualifications that ought to be in a Minister of Jesus Christ; and therefore cannot join with the Society in their Choice, but look upon it to be their indispensible Duty to Choose one after God's own heart, one that will be able to comfort the wounded with the same comfort wherewith he himself is comforted of God, and not a blind Guide; for then the Blind will lead the Blind into the ditch of God's eternal Wrath. And many of the said Society speak evil of those things, which they the said Separatists receive and hold to be the Effect of the Holy Ghost: Whereupon they look upon it a loud Call to them to come out from among them, &c. And do appoint the House of *Samuel Wadsworth* to be a place to Meet in by themselves to serve the Lord in spirit and in truth.

And the said *Cleavelands* say, That this being the Act of the major part of the Members in full Communion within the said Society, is a sufficient Warrant for them to join with them.

They also say, That the said *Solomon Paine* has sufficient Knowledge and Ability to Expound the Scripture and to Preach the Gospel, and therefore has a right to do it: And therefore they say, That in withdrawing from the publick Worship and attending upon the Preaching of the said *Solomon Paine,* they have not acted contrary to any divine or humane Law.

Whereupon it is Considered by the Rector and Tutors,

1. That we (depending in this matter upon the unanimous Judgment of the Association in the County of *Windham*) do Judge that the said Mr. *Cogswell* is sufficiently Qualified to be a Preacher of the Gospel; and therefore that the Reflections cast upon him, as aforesaid, are groundless.

2. That if there were any Reasons why the said Separatists should not choose to receive Mr. *Cogswell* as their Minister; or if it should be

doubtful whether it is convenient that Mr. *Cogswell* should be Ordained where so great a Number are against him, (which things properly belong to the hearing and judgment of a Council) yet we can't see that this could be any Justification of their setting up a Separation in the mean time.

3. That neither the major part of the Members in full Communion, nor any other persons in any Parish or Society, have any right or warrant, to appoint any House or Place for Worship on the Sabbath, distinct and separate from and in opposition to the Meeting-house, the publick Place appointed by the General Assembly and the Parish; but on the contrary, all such Places & separate Meetings are prohibited by the ancient Laws of this Government.

4. The principal Reasons assigned for this Separation manifestly import that spirit of uncharitable Censuring and rash Judging of mens Hearts and spiritual State, which has of late so much prevailed in the Country, and which is plainly prohibited in the Word of God.

5. There's scarce any thing more fully and strictly Enjoin'd in the Gospel than Charity, Peace and Unity among Christians; and scarce any thing more plainly and frequently forbidden than Divisions, Schisms and Separations: And therefore nothing can justifie a Division or Separation, but only some plain and express Direction in the Word of God; which must be understood as a particular Exception from the general Rule. And it appears to us that there is no Direction or Warrant in the Word of God to set up a Separation upon the Reasons there assigned.

6. That if it could be supposed that they had a Warrant to Separate from the Meeting-house, Preacher and Congregation where they belong'd, and attend upon some lawful Minister in another Place; yet this could not justifie them in attending upon the Ministry or Preaching of a Lay-Exhorter, who has no Right, License or Authority to Preach; and especially of one who is a common promoter of Separations and Disturber of the Christian Peace, not only in *Canterbury,* but also in *Windham, Mansfield* and other places.

7. That this practice of setting up Lay-Exhorters (which has of late prevailed in the Country) is without any Scripture Warrant, and is Subversive of the standing Order of a Learned Gospel Ministry, and naturally tends to introduce spiritual Pride, Enthusiasm and all manner of Disorders into the Christian Church.

Whereupon it is Considered and Adjudged by the *Rector* and *Tutors,*

That the said *John* and *Ebenezer Cleaveland,* in Withdrawing and Separating from the publick Worship of God, and Attending upon the Preaching of a Lay-Exhorter, as aforesaid, have acted contrary to the Rules of the Gospel, the Laws of this Colony and of the College; and that the said *Cleavelands* shall be publickly Admonished for their Faults, aforesaid: And if they shall continue to Justifie themselves and refuse to make an Acknowledgement they shall be Expelled.

THOMAS CLAP, *Rector*

About a Week after this *John Cleaveland* gave in a Paper, wherein he says, *"I did not know that it was a Transgression, either of the Laws of God or of this Colony, or of this College, for me, as a Member of and in Covenant with a particular Church, as is generally owned to be a Church of Jesus Christ, to meet together with the major part of said Church, for Social Worship, and therefore Beg and Intreat that my Ignorance may be suffered to Apologize for me in that respect."*

Upon which it was Considered:

First, That we have no Evidence, and never so much as heard, that that Company of men who Separated from the Congregation at *Canterbury* and Met at the House of *Samuel Wadsworth,* were owned to be a Church of Christ, by any Churches or Ministers (unless by Mr. *Crosswell*) but have always been Informed that they have been look'd upon by the Ministers and Churches in the County of *Windham,* as a company of persons Disorderly, Separated from their own Congregation, by the Influence of the *Paines,* upon the Principles mentioned in their Letter aforesaid; and that they were not the major part of the proper ancient Church in *Canterbury:* Tho we understand that Circumstance is disputed.

Secondly, The Plea, that the persons who met at the House of *Samuel Wadsworth,* were the major part of the Church, appears to be a meer pretence, and not the true and real principle of the Conduct of those persons: For these *Paines* have made and preach'd at Separations in *Windham, Mansfield,* and many other places; and we have been since Informed, That the said *Cleaveland* met with the Separations at *New-Haven* and *Milford,* in which places there was no pretence that the Separatists were the major part of the Church. So that it is very plain they acted upon the other principles before mentioned, which justifie the Separation of a Minor part as much as a Major.

Thirdly, He had no colour to plead Ignorance; for he had often heard the Rector declare in the College-Hall, *That these Separations and Lay-Exhorters, were contrary to the Word of God,* (tho' perhaps he might not believe it.) And the Book of the Laws and Customs of the College had some time before been read in the *College-Hall;* in which among other things there was this Clause, *That no Student shall attend upon any Religious Meetings but such as are appointed or approved by publick Authority, or by the Rector.* The Laws of the Government which he had broke, were also read to him—And here we think it proper to take Notice of one very false Representation in the Memorial; it is said, *That they Informed the Rector, &c. that they were entirely Ignorant what the Laws of the College were; for that they never had opportunity to see them, &c. and begg'd to see them, but were denied.* We have no remembrance, and do not believe, that they begg'd to see the Laws of the College, and know that they never were refused or denied: For we well remember that we had the Laws by us, and read that Paragraph which they had transgressed; and if we did not read it in their hearing it was because they did not desire it, and we supposed that they could not be ignorant of it; at least that the said *John* could not be ignorant, who had been at College Three Years: And some of the Scholars had Transcribed the Laws.

Fourthly, What ever might be his former Ignorance and Mistake, yet after all means of Light and Conviction, he still persisted in Justifying what he had done, and *would acknowledge no Error in it;* tho' somtimes he seem'd to be brought to such a doubt and stand in his own Mind, as that it seemed probable that he would have made some Acknowledgement, if he had not been prevented by ill Advice.—And since the principal End and Design of Erecting this College (as declared in Charter) was, *To Train up a Succession of Learned and Orthodox Ministers,* by whose Instruction and Example people might be directed in the ways of Religion and good Order; therefore to Educate persons whose principles and practices are directly Subversive of the Visible Church of Christ, would be contrary to the Original Design of Erecting this Society. And we conceive that it would be a Contradiction in the Civil Government, to Support a College to Educate Students to trample upon their own Laws, and brake up the Churches which they Establish and Protect, Especially since the General Assembly in *May* 1742, tho't proper to give the Governours of the College some special Advice & Direction upon that account; which was to this Effect, *That all proper Care should be taken to prevent the Scholars from imbibing those or such like Errors; and that those who would not be Orderly and Submissive, should not be allowed the Privileges of the College.* Neither can we conceive that it makes any odds, whether such pernicious Errors are imbibed and practised, and the Laws of GOD and the Civil Government are broken, in or out of the Vacancy or the Town of *New-Haven,* or with or without the Concurrence of their Parents, since the pernicious Consequences thereof to the *College* & *Religion* will be just the same.

THOMAS CLAP, *Rector*

CHAUNCEY WHITTELSEY ⎤
JOHN WHITING   ⎬ *Tutors*
THOMAS DARLING   ⎦

New-Haven, May 1st, 1745

17. Charters of the College of New Jersey (Princeton), 1746, 1748

George the Second, by the Grace of God, of Great Britain, France and Ireland, King, Defender of the Faith &c. To all to whom these presents shall come, Greeting.*

Whereas sundry *of our loving subjects,* well disposed & publick spirited Persons, have lately by their humble Petition presented to our Trusty and well beloved [John Hamilton Esqr. the President of our Council], *Jonathan Belcher, Esq., governor* and Commander in Chief of our Province of New Jersey in America, represented the great Necessity of coming into some Method for encouraging and promoting a learned Education of Our Youth in New Jersey, and have expres'd their earnest Desire that a College may be erected in our Said Province of New Jersey *in America* for the Benefit of the *inhabitants of the*

T. J. Wertenbaker, *Princeton, 1746–1896* (Princeton, N.J., 1946), pp. 396–404.

* The parts of the Charter of 1746 which were omitted in the Charter of 1748 have been placed in brackets; the parts of the Charter of 1748 not included in the Charter of 1746 appear in italics. The capitalization of the first charter has been followed, but not the punctuation. It is obvious that a few of the omissions in the first charter were made by the transcriber and did not occur in the original.—T. J. W.

Said Province *and other,* wherein Youth may be instructed in the learned Languages, and in the Liberal Arts and Sciences. . . . And whereas by the fundamental Concessions made at the first Settlement of New Jersey by the Lord Berkley and Sir George Carteret, then Proprietors thereof, and granted under their Hands, and the Seal of the said Province, and bearing Date the Tenth Day of February [1664], *in the year of our Lord one thousand six hundred and sixty-four,* it was, among[st] other Things, conceded and [granted] *agreed,* "that no Freeman within the said Provence of New Jersey, should at any Time be molested, punished, disquieted, or Called in Question for any difference in opinion or practice in matters of Religious Concernment, who do not actually disturb the civil Peace of the Said Province, but that all and every such Person [and] *or* Persons might from Time to Time & at all Times *thereafter* freely & truly have and enjoy his and their Judgments and Consciences in Matters of Religion throughout the said Province, they behaving themselves Peaceably and quietly and not using this Liberty to Licentiousness nor to the Civil Injury or outward Disturbance of others." As by the Said Concessions on Record in the Secretary's Office of New Jersey, at Perth Amboy, in Lib. 3 fol*io* 66 &c may appear. Wherefore *and for that* the said Petitioners have also expressed their earnest Desire that those of every Religious Denomination may have free and Equal Liberty and Advantage of Education in the Said College [notwithstanding] any different Sentiments in Religion *notwithstanding.* We being willing to grant the reasonable Request*s* & Prayer*s* of all our loving Subjects, and to promote a liberal and Learned Education among them—Know Ye, therefore that we considering the Premises, and being willing for the future that the best Means of Education be established in our Province of New Jersey, for the Benefit and Advantage *of the inhabitants* of that our said Province *and others,* Do of Our special Grace, certain Knowledge and mere Motion, by these Presents, will, ordain, grant, and constitute that there be a College erected in Our Said Province of New Jersey for the Education of Youth in the Learned Languages and in the Liberal Arts and Sciences. And that the Trustees of the said College and their Successors *for* ever May, and shall be one Body Corporate & Politick, in Deed, action & Name, and shall be called, *and* named and distinguis*h*ed, by the Name of the Trustees of the College of New Jersey.—And further we have willed, given, granted, Constituted and [Ordained] *appointed,* and by this our present Charter of Our especial

Grace, certain Knowledge & meer Motion. We do for Us, our Heirs and Successors [For ever] will, give, grant, constitute & ordain that there shall in the Said College from henceforth, and for ever be a Body politick Consisting of Trustees of the said College of New Jersey, and for the more full & perfect Erection of the said Corporation and Body Politick consisting of Trustees of the College of New Jersey, we of our Especial Grace, Certain Knowledge and meer Motion, do by these Presents for Us, our Heirs & Successors, create, make, ordain, constitute, Nominate and appoint [our Trusty & well beloved William Smith, Peter Van Brugh Livingston & William Peartree Smith, of the City of New York, Gentlemen, and our trusty & well beloved Jonathan Dickinson, John Pierson, Ebenezer Pemberton & Aaron Burr, Ministers of the Gospel with such others as they shall think proper to Associate until them not Exceeding the Number of twelve to be the Trustees of the Said College of New Jersey with full power and Authority to them, or any four, or greater Number of them, to nominate & appoint & associate unto them any Number of Persons, as Trustees, so that the whole Number of Trustees exceed not Twelve.] *the Governor and Commander in Chief of our said province of New Jersey, for the time being, and also our trusty and well beloved John Reading, James Hude, Andrew Johnston, Thomas Leonard, John Kinsey, Edward Shippen and William Smith, Esquires, Peter Van-Brugh Livingston, William Peartree Smith and Samuel Hazard, gentlemen, John Pierson, Ebenezer Pemberton, Joseph Lamb, Gilbert Tennent, William Tennent, Richard Treat, Samuel Blair, David Cowell, Aaron Burr, Timothy Jones, Thomas Arthur and Jacob Green, ministers of the gospel, to be Trustees of the said College of New Jersey.*

That the said Trustees do, at their first meeting, after the receipt of these presents, and before they proceed to any business take the oath appointed to be taken by an act, passed in the first year of the reign of the late King George the First, entitled, "An act for the further security of his Majesty's person and government, and the succession of the crown in the heirs of the late princess Sophia, being protestants, and for extinguishing the hopes of the pretended prince of Wales, and his open and secret abettors"; as also that they make and subscribe the declarations mentioned in an act of parliament made in the twenty-fifth year of the reign of King Charles the Second, entitled, "An act for preventing dangers which may happen from popish recusants";

and likewise take an oath for faithfully executing the office or trust reposed in them, the said oaths to be administered to them by three of his Majesty's justices of the peace, quorum unus; and when any new member or officer of this corporation is chosen, they are to take and subscribe the aforementioned oaths and declarations before their admission into their trusts or offices, the same to be administered to them in the presence of the Trustees, by such persons as they shall appoint for that service.

That no meeting of the Trustees shall be valid or legal for doing any business whatsoever, unless the clerk has duly and legally notified each and every member of the corporation of such meeting; and that before the entering on any business, the clerk shall certify such notification under his hand to the Board of Trustees.

That the said Trustees have full power and authority or any thirteen or greater number of them, to elect, nominate and appoint and associate unto them, any number of persons as Trustees upon any vacancy, so the whole number of Trustees exceed not twenty-three whereof the President of the said college for the time being, to be chosen as hereafter mentioned, to be one, and twelve of the said Trustees to be always such persons as are inhabitants of our said province of New Jersey.

And We do further of our special Grace, certain Knowledge & meer Motion, for us, Our Heirs & Successors, will, give, grant and appoint That the said Trustees and their Successors shall forever hereafter be in Deed, Fact & Name a Body corporate, & politick, and that they the Said Body Corporate & Politick shall be known & distinguished in all Deeds, Grants, Bargains, Sales, Writings, Evidences, [Monuments] *muniments* or otherwise howsoever, and in all Courts for ever hereafter Plead and be impleaded by the Name of the Trustees of the College of New Jersey. And that *they* the Said Corporation, by the Name aforesaid shall be able, and in Law capable for the use of the said College to have, get, acquire, purchase, receive and possess Lands, Tenements, Hereditaments, Jurisdictions & Franchises for themselves and their Successors, in Fee Simple or otherwise howsoever, and to purchase, receive, or build any House or Houses, or any other Buildings, as they shall think needful [and] *or* Convenient for the Use of the said College of New Jersey, and in such Place or Places in New Jersey as they the said Trustees shall agree upon. And also to receive, and dispose of any Goods, Chattels and other things of what Nature soever for the Use aforesaid. And also to have, accept & receive any

Rents, profits, Annuities, Gifts, Legacies, Donations and Bequests of
any kind whatsoever for the Use aforesaid, so nevertheless that the
Yearly *clear* Value of the premi[s]ses do not exceed the Sum of two
thousand Pounds Sterling. And therewith or otherwise to support and
pay as the Said Trustees & their Successors, or the Major Part of such
of them as according to the Provision herein after*wards* [made] are
regularly convened for that Purpose shall agree and see Cause, the
President, [&] Tutors and [their] *other* Officers [and] *or* Ministers
of the Said College, their respective annual Salaries, or Allowances,
and all such other necessary & contingent Charges as from time to
time shall arise and accrue relating to the said College.—And also to
grant, Bargain, sell, let, set or Assign Lands, Tenements or Hereditaments, Goods or Chattels, contract or do all other things whatsoever,
by the Name Aforesaid, and for the Use aforesaid, in as full and ample
Manner, to all intents & Purposes, as any Natural Person or other Body
politick or corporate is able to do by the Laws of our Realm of Great
Britain, or of our said province of New Jersey. And of our further
Grace, certain Knowledge, meer Motion, to the Intent that our said
Corporation & Body politick may answer the End of their Erection &
Constitution, and may have perpetual Succession, and continue for
ever, We do for Us, our Heirs and Successors, Hereby will, give and
grant unto the said Trustees of the College of New Jersey, and to
their Successors for ever, that when any [seven] *thirteen* of the *said*
Trustees, or of their Successors, are convened & met together *as aforesaid* for the Service of the said College *The Governor and Commander
in Chief of our said province of New Jersey, and in his absence, the
President of the said college, and in the absence of the said Governor
and President, the elde 1 Trustee present at such meeting, from time
to time, shall be President of the said Trustees in all their meetings, and*
at any Time or Times such [seven] *thirteen* Trustees *convened and
met as aforesaid,* shall be capable to act as fully and amply to all Intents and Purposes as if all the Trustees of the said College were personally present, *provided always, that a majority of the said Thirteen
Trustees be of the said province of New Jersey, except after regular
notice they fail of coming in which case those that are present are hereby empowered to act, the different place of their abode notwithstanding.* And all Affairs and Actions whatsoever under the Care of the

said Trustees shall be Determined by the Majority or greater Number of Those [seven] *thirteen* [Trustees] so convened & met together, *the President whereof shall have no more than a single vote.* And we do for us, our Heirs and Successors hereby will, give & grant full Power & Authority to any [Three] *six* or more of the said Trustees, to [appoint] *call* Meetings *of the said Trustees* from time to time [of the said seven Trustees] and to order Notice to the said [seven] Trustees [or any greater Number of them] of the Times & Places of Meeting for the Service aforesaid. . . . And also we do hereby for us, Our Heirs and Successors will, give & grant to the Said Trustees of the College of New Jersey, and to their Successors for ever, that the Said Trustees do elect, nominate and appoint such qualified persons as they or the Major Part of any [Seven] *thirteen* of them convened for that purpose, as above directed, shall think fitt to be the President of the Said College and to have the immediate Care of the Education & Government of such Students as shall be sent to & admitted in to the Said College for instruction and Education. . . . And also that the said Trustees do Elect, nominate and appoint so many Tutors and Professors to assist the President of the Said College in the Education & Government of the Students belonging to it, as they the said Trustees or their Successors, or the Major Part of any [Seven] *thirteen* of them, which shall convene for that Purpose as above directed, shall from time to time, and at any time hereafter think needful and serviceable to the Interests of the Said College. . . . And also that the Said Trustees and their Successors, or the Major Part of any [Seven] *thirteen* of them which shall convene for that Purpose as above directed, shall at any time Displace and discharge from the Service of the said College such President, Tutors or Professors and to elect others in their Room and Stead. . . . And also that the said Trustees or their Successors or the Major Part of any [seven] *thirteen* of them, which shall convene for that purpose, as above directed, do from time to time, as Occasion shall require elect, constitute and appoint a Treasurer, a Clerk, an Usher and a Steward for the Said College, and appoint to them, and each of them, their respective Business & Trust, & Displace & Discharge from the Service of the said College such Treasurer, Clerk, Usher or Steward, and to elect others in their Room & Stead, which President, Tutors, Professors, Treasurer*s*, Clerks, Ushers & Steward, so elected and appointed, We do for us, our Heirs & Successors by their Presents Constitute and Establish in their several Offices, and do give them, and Every of them, full Power and Authority to Exercise the same in the said College of New Jersey according to the Direction[s] and during the pleasure of the Said Trustees, as fully and freely as any other the like officers in our Universities or any of our Colleges in our Realm of great Britain Lawfully may or ought to do. . . . And also that the said Trustees and their Successors or the Major Part of any [seven] *thirteen* of them, which shall convene for that Purpose as above directed, as often as one, or more of the said Trustees shall happen to die, or by Removal or Otherwise shall [according to their Judgment] become unfitt, or uncapable *according to their judgment* to serve the Interest[s] of the said College, do as soon as conveniently may be after the Death, Removal or such Unfittness and Incapacity of such Trustee or Trustees *to serve the interest of the said college elect and appoint such other Trustee or Trustees,* as shall supply the place of him or them so dying or otherwise becoming unfitt or Uncapable to serve the Interest[s] of the said College, and every Trustee so Elected or appointed shall by virtue of these Presents and *of* such Election and Appointment be vested with all the powers and Privile[d]ges which any of the Other Trustees of the said College are hereby vested with. . . . And we do further of our especial Grace, certain Knowledge and meer Motion will, give, and grant and by these Presents do for us, our Heirs and Successors will, give, and grant unto the said Trustees of the College of New Jersey, that they and their Successors or the major part of any [seven] *thirteen* of them which shall convene for that Purpose, as is above directed, may make, and they are hereby fully [i]empowered, from Time to Time freely and lawfully to make & Establish such Ordinances, Orders and Laws as may tend to the good and wholesome Government of the said College, & all the students & the several[l] Officers & Ministers thereof, and to the publick Benefit of the same not repugnant to the Laws and Statutes of our Realm of great Britain, or of this our Province of New Jersey, and not excluding any Person of any religious Denomination whatsoever from free and Equal Liberty and Advantage of Education, or from any of the Liberties, Privile[d]ges or immunities of the Said College on account of his or their [speculative Sentiments in Religion and of his, or their] being of a Religious profession Different from the said Trustees of the College[.] and such ordinances, Orders & Laws which shall [as aforesaid be made] *be so as aforesaid made,* . . . We do by these Presents for us, our Heirs and Successors, ratify, allow of and Confirm, as good and Effectual to oblige and bind all the *said* students, and the several Officers & Ministers of the said College, and we do hereby authorize & [impower] *empower* the said Trustees of the College, and the President, Tutors and Professors by them elected and appointed to put such Ordinances, [Orders] and Laws in Execution, to all proper Intents and purposes. And we do further of our especial Grace, certain Knowledge and meer Motion, will, give and grant unto the said Trustees of the College of New Jersey, that for the Encouragement of Learning and Animating of the Students of *the* Said College to Diligence, Industry and a Laudable Progress in Literature that they and their Successors, [and] *or* the Major Part of any [seven] *thirteen* of them convened for that Purpose, as above directed, Do by the President of the said College for the time being, or by any other Deputed by them Give and Grant any such Degree or Degrees to any of the Students of the said College, or to any others by them thought worthy thereof as are usually granted in either of our Universities, or any other College in our Realm of great Britain, and that they do sign & seal Di[a]plomas or Certificates of such Graduations to be kept by the Graduates as perpetual Memorials and Testimonials thereof. . . .

And further of our especial Grace, certain Knowledge & meer Motion we do by these Presents for us, our Heirs and Successors, give and grant unto the said Trustees of the College of New Jersey and to their Successors that they and their Successors shall have a Common Seal under which they may pass all Di[a]plomas, or Certificates of Degrees, and all Other the Affairs & Business of and Concerning the said Corporation, or of and Concerning the Said College of New Jersey which shall be [i]engraven in such form, and with such Inscription*s* as shall be devised by the said Trustees of the said College [for the Time being,] or [by] the Major Part of any [seven] *thirteen* of them convened for the Service of the Said College as above directed. . . .

And we do further for us, Our Heirs and Successors, give & Grant unto the said Trustees of the [Said] College of New Jersey and their Successors, or the Major Part *of any thirteen* of them convened for the

Service of the said College, as [is] above directed, full Power and Authority from time to time to Nominate and Appoint all other Inferio[u]r Officers & Ministers which they shall think to be convenient & necessary for the Use of the [said] College, not herein particularly named or mentioned, and which are accustomary in our Universities or any of our Colleges in our Realm of great Britain, which Officers or Ministers we do hereby [i]empower to execute their Offices or Trusts as fully & freely as any other the like Officers [&] or Ministers in *and of* our Universities or any *other* College[s] in our Realm of great Britain, Lawfully may or ought to do.—

And Lastly our express Will and Pleasure is, and we do by these presents for us, our Heirs and Successors, give and grant *un*to the said Trustees of the College of New Jersey and to their Successors forever, that these our Letters patent, or the Enrol[l]ment thereof [in our Secretarys Office of our Province aforesaid] shall be good & effectual in the Law, to all intents & Purposes against us, our Heirs & Successors without any Other Licence, Grant or Confirmation from us, our Heirs & Successors hereafter by the said Trustees, to be had & attained, notwithstanding the not [writing] *reciting* or Misrecital, [of] *or* not naming or misnaming of The Aforesaid Offices, Franchises, Privileges, Immunities or Other the Premis[s]es, or any of them, and notwithstanding a Writ of ad quod Damnum hath not issued forth to [e]*i*nquire of the Premis[s]es or any of them before the ensealing hereof, any Statute, Act, Ordinance or Provision, or any other Matter or thing to the Contrary notwithstanding.

To have [&] to hold *and enjoy* all & Singular the Privileges, Advantages, Liberties, Immunities and all other the Premis[s]es herein & hereby granted & given, or which are meant, mentioned or intended to be herein and hereby given and granted Unto them the Said Trustees of the Said College of New Jersey and to their Successors forever.

In Testimony whereof we have caused these our Letters to be made patent, and the great seal of our Said Province of New Jersey to be hereunto Affixed. Witness our Trusty and well Beloved [John Hamilton Esqr. the President of our Council] *Jonathan Belcher, Esquire, Governor* and Commander in Chief of our said Province [&c] *of New Jersey.* This [Twenty second] *fourteenth* Day of [October] *September, and* in the [twentieth] *twenty second* Year of our Reign [Annoq:

Domini 1746] *year of our Lord,* one thousand seven hundred and forty eight.

L.S.
I have perused and considered the written Charter of incorpora-tion, and find nothing contained therein inconsistent with his Majesty's interest or the honor of the Crown.

(*Signed*)   J. WARRELL, *Att. Gen'l*

September the 13th, 1748.—This Charter, having been read in Coun-cil was consented to and approved of.

CHA. READ, *Cl. Con.*

Let the Great Seal of the Province of New Jersey be affixed to this Charter.

(*Signed*) J. BELCHER

To the Secretary of the Province of New Jersey

18. An Account of the College of New Jersey in 1754

This was a second, enlarged version of a pamphlet first published in 1752 by the trustees of the college. Gilbert Tennent (1703–64), was one of the leading evangelizers of the Middle Colonies. When the College of New Jersey was estab-lished, he became one of its trustees, and in 1753 he and the Reverend Samuel Davies (1723–61) went to England to solicit funds for it. Davies had been an active evangelist since 1747, and later became president of the college, 1757–61. The fund-raising trip of 1753, of which this document is a result, was a success: the two men raised more than £3,000. See T. J. Wertenbaker, *Princeton, 1746–1896,* pp. 32–35.

Nothing has a more direct Tendency to advance the Happiness and Glory of a Community, than the founding of *public Schools* and *Sem-inaries of Learning,* for the *Education of Youth,* and adorning their Minds with useful Knowledge and Virtue. Hereby the *Rude* and *Ig-norant* are civiliz'd and render'd humane; Persons, who would other-wise be useless Members of Society, are qualified to sustain with

---

Gilbert Tennent and Samuel Davies, *A General Account of the Rise and State of the College, Lately Established in the Province of New-Jersey in America* ... (London, 1754), pp. 3–7.

Honour, the Offices they may be invested with, for the public Service; Reverence of the *Deity, Filial-Piety,* and *Obedience* to the Laws, are inculcated and promoted.

The Sciences have no where flourish'd with more Success, than in our *Mother Country.* The Universities and Seminaries of Learning in *England* and *Scotland,* are annually sending abroad into the Kingdom, Proficients in all Kinds of Literature; Men of refin'd Sentiments, solid Judgments, and noble Principles; who spread (if the Expression may be allowed) a Kind of literary Glory over the *British* Nation.

AMERICA remain'd, during a long Period, in the thickest Darkness of *Ignorance* and *Barbarism,* till Christianity, at the Introduction of the *Europeans,* enlightened her *Hemisphere* with the salutary Beams of *Life* and *Immortality. Science,* her constant Attendant, soon rais'd her depress'd Head, and the *Arts* began to flourish. . . . At length, several Gentlemen residing in and near the Province of *New-Jersey,* who were Well-Wishers to the Felicity of their Country, and real Friends of *Religion* and *Learning,* having observ'd the vast Increase of those Colonies, with the Rudeness, and Ignorance of their Inhabitants, for want of the necessary Means of Improvement, first projected the Scheme of a Collegiate *Education* in that Province.

The immediate Motives to this generous Design, were,—the great Number of Christian Societies then lately form'd in various Parts of the Country, where many Thousands of the Inhabitants, ardently desirous of the Administration of religious *Ordinances,* were entirely destitute of the necessary Means of Instruction, and incapable of being relieved; —the urgent Applications that were annually made by those vacant Congregations to the *Clergy* in their collective Bodies; complaining in the most moving Manner, of their unhappy Circumstances, in being depriv'd of the ordinary Means of *Salvation,* and left to grope after Happiness, almost in the Obscurity of *Paganism,* tho' the Light of *Revelation* shone on their surrounding Neighbours;—the great Scarcity of Candidates for the *Ministerial Function,* to comply with these pious and christian Demands; the Colleges of *New-England,* educating hardly a competent Number for the Service of its own Churches. These Considerations were the most urgent Arguments for the immediate Prosecution of the abovementioned Scheme of Education.

Accordingly, in the Year 1747, a Petition was presented to his Excellency Jonathan Belcher, Esq; Governor of that Province (a Gentleman, who has long signaliz'd himself, as a Patron of *Religion* and

Learning,) praying his Majesty's Grant of a Charter, for the Establishment of a publick *Seminary of Literature* in *New-Jersey.* His Excellency, with the Approbation of the Council and Attorney General of the said Province, was pleased to comply with their Request; and order'd a Charter to pass the Seals, incorporating sundry Gentlemen, to the Number of Twenty-three; by the Name of *The Trustees of the College of* New-Jersey; and appointing the Governor of *New-Jersey,* for the Time being, who is his Majesty's Representative, to act as their President, when convened. This Charter places the Society upon the most *catholic* Foundation: All Protestants of every Denomination, who are loyal Subjects to our most Gracious Sovereign (the happy Effects of whose mild and equal Administration, the remotest Colonies of the *British* Empire sensibly experience, and gratefully acknowledge;) are admitted to the Enjoyment of all its Priviledges, and allowed the unlimited Exercise of their Religion.

The Trustees, thus authorized with ample Powers, for the Execution of this Laudable Design; in Conformity to the Plan of their Charter, applied themselves with the utmost Deliberation, to form and enact such Rules and Orders for the Regulation of the Methods of Instruction, and Conduct of the Students, as might tend to prevent the Entrance of Vice into the Society, and the Introduction of Idleness, Vanity, and extravagant Expences amongst its Members. It would be repugnant to the Design of a general Narrative, as well as impertinent to the Reader, to enter into a minute Detail of these several private Regulations. It will suffice to say, that the two principal Objects the Trustees had in View, were Science and Religion. Their first Concern was, to cultivate the Minds of the Pupils, in all those Branches of Erudition, which are generally taught in the Universities abroad: And to perfect their Design, their next Care was to rectify the Heart, by inculcating the great Precepts of *Christianity,* in order to make them good. . . .

As no human Institutions in a World of Imperfection and Error, are so completely model'd, as to exclude the Possibility of farther Emendation; it may be said, without any Intention of Disparagement to other learned Seminaries, that the Governors of this College have endeavour'd to improve, upon the commonly received Plans of Education. They proceed not so much in the Method of a dogmatic Institution, by prolix Discourses, on the different Branches of the *Sciences,* by burdening the Memory, and imposing heavy and disagreeable Tasks;

as in the *Socratic* Way of free Dialogue, between Teacher and Pupil, or between the Students themselves, under the Inspection of their Tutors. In this Manner, the Attention is engaged, the Mind entertain'd, and the Scholar animated in the Pursuit of Knowledge. In fine, the Arts and Sciences are convey'd into the Minds of Youth, in a Method, the most easy, natural, and familiar. But as Religion ought to be the End of all Instruction, and gives it the last Degree of Perfection: As one of the primary Views of this Foundation, was to educate young Gentlemen for the sacred Office of the *Ministry,* and fit them for the Discharge of so noble and Employment; *Divinity,* the Mistress of the *Sciences,* engages the peculiar Attention of the Governors of this Society. Stated Times are set apart for the Study of the *Holy Scriptures,* in the original Languages, and stated Hours daily consecrated to the Service of Religion. The utmost Care is taken to discountenance Vice, and to encourage the Practice of Virtue; and a manly, rational, and christian Behaviour in the Students. *Enthusiasm* on the one Hand, and *Prophaneness* on the other, are equally guarded against, and meet with the severest Checks.

Under such Management, this Seminary, from the smallest Beginnings, quickly drew the public Attention, enlarged the Number of her Pupils, raised her Reputation; and now, tho' in her Infancy, almost rivals her ancient *Sisters* upon the Continent.

Daily Observation evinces, that in Proportion as Learning makes its Progress in a Country, it softens the natural Roughness, eradicates the Prejudices, and transforms the Genius and Disposition of its Inhabitants. *New-Jersey,* and the adjacent Provinces, already feel the happy Effects of this useful Institution. A general Desire of Knowledge, seems to be spreading among the People: Parents are inspired with an Emulation of cultivating the Minds of their Offspring: Public Stations are honourable fill'd by Gentlemen, who have received their Education here: And from hence, many Christian Assemblies are furnish'd with Men of distinguished Talents for the Discharge of the *Pastoral Office.* . . .

It is hoped, that the Pious and Benevolent in *Great-Britain,* into whose Hands these Papers may fall, will extend their generous *Aids,* in the Prosecution and Completion of so excellent and useful a Design. A Design! upon the Success of which, the Happiness of Multitudes in sundry Colonies, and their numerous Posterity, in the present and future Ages far distant, in a great Measure depends. A Design! which not only tends to promote the Weal of the *British* Inhabitants, but also of the *German Emigrants;* and to spread the Gospel of Salvation among the benighted *Indian* Tribes, and attach them to his Majesty's Government. A Design! which is not calculated to promote the low Purposes of a Party,* but in its Views and Consequences affects the *Protestant* Interest in general, and *Great-Britain* in particular, both in *Religious* and *Civil* Respects; since by this, the *filial* Duty of her Descendants will be inculcated, their Manners reformed, and her Trade increased; which is the Basis of her Empire, Glory and Felicity.

---

* The Trustees of the said College have not made such Regulations as may burden the Consciences of any, or confine the Advantages of the Institution to a *Party;* nor did they desire such a Power; as is evident from . . . Words of the Charter—.

Part II

THE COLLEGIATE SYSTEM

IN THE

EIGHTEENTH CENTURY

Perhaps the most significant development in the colleges during the last half of the eighteenth century was the emergence of a measure of interdenominational sponsorship. Princeton, as we have seen, opened the door to an interdenominational student body (Part I, Docs. 17 and 18) but its control was solidly in the hands of the New-Side faction of the Presbyterian church. In those colonies that had a mixture of denominations, it became difficult to maintain complete sectarian control. When King's College (Columbia) was projected in New York as an Anglican institution, the strong Presbyterian faction rose up in protest and presented eloquent arguments against the sectarian domination of education (Docs. 1 and 2). In good measure the Presbyterian faction won its point; for although the president of King's was required by charter to be an Anglican, its first board of trustees included the pastors of the four non-Anglican denominations in New York City. When its president, Samuel Johnson, first advertised the opening of the college and set forth its plan of studies (Doc. 3), it was with the assurance that "there is no intention to impose on the scholars, the peculiar tenets of any particular sect of Christians." The early laws of

97

the college (Doc. 5), as well as the original advertisement, show a tendency to play up secular studies in addition to the inherited curriculum, including "the mathematical and experimental philosophy in all the several branches of it, with agriculture and merchandise." John Witherspoon, promoting the College of New Jersey (Princeton) in 1772 (Doc. 10), dwelled with some pride upon its scientific offerings.

The ideal of the sectarian college died hard, however, and even as the opening of King's College was being planned, the redoubtable Thomas Clap was writing a systematic defense (Doc. 4) of the notion of "The Religious Constitution of Colleges"—i.e., of the idea that a college should be organized and rigorously controlled by a single sect. The remaining colonial colleges followed the example set in the College of Philadelphia (later the University of Pennsylvania) and at King's College. In Philadelphia even the Roman Catholic priest was incorporated into the original interdenominational board of trustees. The College of Rhode Island (Brown), true to the province's heritage of tolerance was generously interdenominational (Doc. 9), while such later colonial colleges as Queen's College (Rutgers) and Dartmouth followed the same general principle. The principles of the Enlightenment and the idea of toleration were gaining ground in America and were having their effects upon the management of colleges. In 1757, after Thomas Clap had tried to have expelled from the Yale Corporation a pastor of the opposing faction of Congregationalists, a broadminded spokesman of the opposition, Shubael Conant, wrote a powerful little tract (Doc. 6) arguing for religious liberalism in the control of colleges.

By and large, however, it was Clap's ideal, rather than that of his opponents, that was to prevail in the near future for the great majority of small American colleges, for most of them were fated to be established by denominations and to live—as well as prosper, as some have maintained—under a sectarian yoke. In the closing decades of the eighteenth and the opening decades of the nineteenth centuries, as the college system proliferated rapidly throughout the country, the interdenominational example of the better-established, older colleges was lost to view. The older colleges were themselves weakened by the diffusion of the country's educational energies—a circumstance foreseen by the Overseers of Harvard as early as 1762 when they protested (Doc. 8) against the premature proposal of a new college in Hampshire County.

1. William Livingston Opposes a Sectarian College for New York, 1753

William Livingston (1723–90) was one of the most vigorous and prominent among a faction of Presbyterians who were opposed to the Anglican gentry in New York provincial politics. When a college was first proposed, he concluded that it was a step toward the establishment of Anglicanism in New York and set himself to block it. His friends established a weekly in 1752, the *Independent Reflector,* in which he published a series of spirited essays from which these excerpts are taken. Later, after retiring to New Jersey, he became governor of that state and a leader of the Revolution. On the King's College controversy see Dorothy R. Dillon, *The New York Triumvirate* (New York, 1949), and Milton M. Klein, "The American Whig: William Livingston of New York" (Ph.D. diss., Columbia University, 1954).

[MARCH 22, 1753]

There is no place where we receive a greater variety of impressions, than at colleges. Nor do any instructions sink so deep in the mind as those that are there received. . . . The students not only receive the dogmata of their teachers with an implicit faith, but are also constantly studying how to support them against every objection. The system of the college is generally taken for true, and the sole business is to defend it. Freedom of thought rarely penetrates those contracted mansions of systematical learning. But to teach the established notions, and main-tain certain hypotheses, *hic Labor hoc opus est.* Every deviation from the beaten tract, is a kind of literary heresy; and if the professor be given to excommunication, can scarce escape an anathema. Hence that dogmatical turn and impatience of contradiction, so observable in the generality of academics. To this also is to be referred, those voluminous compositions, and that learned lumber of gloomy pedants, which hath so long infested and corrupted the world. In a word, all those visionary whims, idle speculations, fairy dreams, and party distinctions, which contract and imbitter the mind, and have so often turned the world topsy-turvy.

[William Livingston and others (eds.)], *Weekly Essays on Sundry Important Subject, more particularly adapted to the Province of New York. Printed (until tyrannically suppressed) in 1753,* in Herbert and Carol Schneider (eds.), *Samuel Johnson, His Career and Writings* (New York, 1929), IV, 122–43.

I mention not this to disparage an academical education, from which I hope I have myself received some benefit, especially after having worn off some of its rough corners, by a freer conversation with mankind. The purpose for which I urge it, is to show the narrow turn usually prevailing at colleges, and the absolute necessity of teaching nothing that will afterwards require the melancholy retrogradation of being unlearned. . . .

At Harvard College in the Massachusetts-Bay, and at Yale College in Connecticut, the Presbyterian profession is in some sort established. It is in these colonies the commendable practice of all who can afford it, to give their sons an education at their respective seminaries of learning. While they are in the course of their education, they are sure to be instructed in the arts of maintaining the religion of the college, which is always that of their immediate instructors; and of combating the principles of all other Christians whatever. When the young gentlemen have run thro' the course of their education, they enter into the ministry, or some offices of the government, and acting in them under the influence of the doctrines espoused in the morning of life, the spirit of the college is transfused thro' the colony, and tinctures the genius and policy of the public administration, from the Governor down to the Constable. Hence the Episcopalians cannot acquire an equal strength among them, till some new regulations, in matters of religion, prevail in their colleges, which perpetually produce adversaries to the hierarchical system. Nor is it to be questioned, that the universities in North and South Britain, greatly support the different professions that are established in their respective divisions. . . .

MARCH 29, 1753

Should our college, therefore, unhappily thro' our own bad policy, fall into the hands of any one religious sect in the province: should that sect, which is more than probable, establish its religion in the college, show favor to its votaries, and cast contempt upon others; 'tis easy to foresee, that Christians of all other denominations amongst us, instead of encouraging its prosperity, will, from the same principles, rather conspire to oppose and oppress it. Besides English and Dutch Presbyterians, which perhaps exceed all our other religious professions put together, we have Episcopalians, Anabaptists, Lutherans, Quakers, and a growing Church of Moravians, all equally zealous for their discriminating tenets. Whichsoever of these has the sole government of the college, will kindle the jealousy of the rest, not only against the persuasion so preferred, but the college itself. Nor can any thing less be expected, than a general discontent and tumult; which, affecting all ranks of people, will naturally tend to disturb the tranquility and peace of the province.

In such a state of things, we must not expect the children of any, but of that sect which prevails in the academy will ever be sent to it: for should they, the established tenets must either be implicitly received, or a perpetual religious war necessarily maintained. Instead of the liberal arts and sciences, and such attainments as would best qualify the students to be useful and ornamental to their country, party cavils and disputes about trifles, will afford topics of argumentation to their incredible disadvantage, by a fruitless consumption of time. Such gentlemen, therefore, who can afford it, will give their sons an education abroad, or at some of the neighboring academies, where equally imbibing a zeal for their own principles, and furnished with the arts of defending them, an incessant opposition to all others, on their return, will be the unavoidable consequence. . . .

It is farther to be remarked, that a public academy is, or ought to be a mere civil institution, and cannot with any tolerable propriety be monopolized by any religious sect. The design of such seminaries, hath been sufficiently shown in my last paper, to be entirely political, and calculated for the benefit of society, as a society, without any intention to teach religion, which is the province of the pulpit: tho' it must, at the same time, be confessed, that a judicious choice of our principles, chiefly depends on a free education. . . .

APRIL 5, 1753

It has in my two last papers been shown, what an extensive and commanding influence the seat of learning will have over the whole province, by diffusing its dogmata and principles thro' every office of church and state. What use will be made of such unlimited advantages, may be easily guessed. The civil and religious principles of the trustees, will become universally established, liberty and happiness be driven without our borders, and in their room erected the banners of spiritual and temporal bondage. My readers may, perhaps, regard such reflections as the mere sallies of a roving fancy; tho', at the same time, nothing in nature can be more real. For should the trustees be prompted by ambition, to stretch their authority to unreasonable lengths, as undoubtedly they would, were they under no kind of restraint, the consequence is very evident. Their principal care would be to choose such persons to instruct our youth, as would be the fittest instruments to extend their power by positive and dogmatical precepts. Besides which, it would be their mutual interest to pursue one scheme. Their power would become formidable by being united: as on the contrary, a dissention would impede its progress. Blind obedience and servility in church and state, are the only natural means to establish unlimited sway. Doctrines of this cast would be publicly taught and inculcated. Our youth, inured to oppression from their infancy, would afterwards vigorously exert themselves in their several offices, to poison the whole community with slavish opinions, and one universal establishment become the fatal portion of this now happy and opulent province.

APRIL 12, 1753

Instead of a charter, I would propose, that the college be founded and incorporated by Act of Assembly, and that not only because it ought to be under the inspection of the civil authority; but also, because such a constitution will be more permanent, better endowed, less liable to abuse, and more capable of answering its true end. . . .

Another reason that strongly evinces the necessity of an Act of Assembly, for the incorporation of our intended academy, is, that by this means that spirit of freedom, which I have in my former papers, shown to be necessary to the increase of learning, and its consequential advantages, may be rendered impregnable to all attacks. While the government of the college is in the hands of the people, or their guardians, its design cannot be perverted. As we all value our liberty and happiness, we shall all naturally encourage those means by which our liberty and happiness will necessarily be improved: and as we never can be supposed wilfully to barter our freedom and felicity, for slavery and misery, we shall certainly crush the growth of those principles, upon which the latter are built, by cultivating and encouraging their opposites. Our college therefore, if it be incorporated by Act of Assembly, instead of opening a door to universal bigotry and establishment in church, and tyranny and oppression in the state, will secure us in the enjoyment of our respective privileges both civil and religious. For as we are split into so great a variety of opinions and professions; had each individual his share in the government of the academy, the jealousy of all parties combating each other, would inevitably produce a perfect freedom for each particular party.

Should the college be founded upon an Act of Assembly, the Legislature would have it in their power, to inspect the conduct of its governors, to divest those of authority who abused it, and appoint in their stead, friends to the cause of learning, and the general welfare of the province. Against this, no bribes, no solicitations would be effectual: no sect or denomination plead an exemption: but as all parties are subject to their authority; so would they all feel its equal influence in this particular. Hence should the trustees pursue any steps but those that lead to public emolument, their fate would be certain, their doom inevitable. Every officer in the college being under the narrow aspect and scrutiny of the civil authority, would be continually subject to the wholesome alternative, either of performing his duty, with the utmost exactness, or giving up his post to a person of superior integrity. By this means, the prevalence of doctrines destructive of the privileges of human nature, would effectually be discouraged, principles of public virtue inculcated, and every thing promoted that bears the stamp of general utility. . . .

APRIL 19, 1753

The Fifth Article I propose is, that no religious profession in particular be established in the college; but that both officers and scholars be at perfect liberty to attend any Protestant Church at their pleasure respectively: and that the Corporation be absolutely inhibited the making of any by-laws relating to religion, except such as compel them to attend Divine Service at some church or other, every Sabbath, as they shall be able, lest so invaluable a liberty be abused and made a cloak for licentiousness.

To this most important head, I should think proper to subjoin,

Sixthly: That the whole college be every morning and evening convened to attend public prayers, to be performed by the President, or in his absence, by either of the Fellows; and that such forms be prescribed and adhered to as all Protestants can freely join in. . . .

2. *The Issue of a Denominational College, 1754*

The first portion of this document is "A Brief Vindication of the Proceedings of the Trustees Relating to the College." It was published anonymously by the "impartial hand" of Benjamin Nicoll, one of the original Anglican trustees of King's College. The second portion is a protest by two leading men of the colony of New York, addressed to a member of the general assembly on May 30, 1754. James Alexander (1691–1756), one of the authors of this protest, was born in Scotland and came to America in 1715. He became an important figure in the law and politics of both New Jersey and New York and was associated with the other author, William Smith (1697–1769), in the famous case of Peter Zenger, involving freedom of the press. Smith and Alexander were both patrons and supporters of William Livingston (see Doc. 1). For an Anglican answer to the appeal of Smith and Alexander, see Herbert and Carol Schneider, *Johnson,* pp. 39–41.

This offer [of lands] of the rector, church wardens and vestry, was made in general terms; and neither the governor, council, or general assembly, calling upon the trustees for any report, occasioned the matter to stand in this state for a considerable time. The *Independent Reflector,* it seems, collecting from this proposal of the rector, church wardens and vestry, that it was very probable, as they were Churchmen, and believed something of the Christian religion, they would endeavor that something of that should be taught youth, in the course of their education at college; at length, grew so outragious as to reprint all the *Independent Whig's* trite reflections, only in other words, against priests and priestcraft, and the power of the clergy; and loudly sounded in our ears, the terrible dangers, the subjects of this province were in, from the growing power of the Church; though he all along insisted, there were ten to one against it in the government; so inconsistent was that author. What was the use of so much clamor in the government against priests and priestcraft, I could not then clearly see; being fully convinced, from what I daily saw, that the clergy had no power in the province, but such as their good conduct and behavior gave them a right to claim, and which I hope they will never want.

But, Mr. Reflector, not content with this, with the air of a dictator, proceeded to lay down rules and instructions for the establishing the college in this province; and among others, insisted, that as there were

Herbert and Carol Schneider (eds.), *Samuel Johnson,* IV, 191–203, 208–11.

different sects of Christians among us, therefore, in order to give every sect an equal interest in the college, no religion should be taught in it; and no form of prayer used, but such as was appointed by the legislature. I suppose he was in hopes that it would fall to him to compose the form for the legislature. Therefore, he chose to give us a specimen of his gifts in that way, by exhibiting a form of prayer made up of detached pieces of verses of Scripture, spliced together in such a manner, that it was almost any thing else, as much as a prayer. The drift and end of those prayers, I clearly perceived by this time, was to set the different sects of Christians at variance with the Church of England, and to embarrass and obstruct the affair of the college as much as was possible; that in the interim the favorite College of New Jersey, founded on a scheme agreeable to his own sentiments, and vigorously prosecuted at home and abroad, might take such root, as not easily to be hurt by any thing that could afterwards be done in this government, even though we all should join in erecting a college here. . . .

I therefore pass on to the eighth reason, "that the president by the charter, is to be a member of the Church of England"; and this I shall answer by inserting a paragraph of a letter from a friend of mine who appears to me to write judiciously on the subject.

"I am no Churchman, but I seriously believe the Christian religion, and think that the interest of that ought to be considered, in the forming every seminary of learning; and must frankly own, that had the people of my persuasion been able to make so valuable a donation, as that church has done, I should (from the writings of the Reflector) have annexed the like condition; and therefore do not wonder they have done it; and the more so, because 'tis pretty certain, without an annual tax upon the government, a proper person for a president cannot be maintained, but by choosing one of the ministers of that church, to that office, as no other congregation can spare any one of theirs, from parish duties enough, to attend to the office of president. I am pleased, that the little precedence that in all probability in such an undertaking would fall somewhere, is given to the Church; for besides the cognizance taken of it by law here, 'tis certain it is the church of the nation to which we belong; and talk what we will against it, has been the bulwark of the Protestant cause to this day. Besides, I am fully convinced, that every sect among us (after themselves) would choose the precedence should be in the national church. That church has used the power it enjoys by law for many years, and with moderation enough; and as I have no hope of having the precedence of my own way of thinking, I hope 'twill be fixed where it is, by the charter. For I would sooner trust the church which is bound by law than a new sect with whom, should they get into power, we must contend for those laws and privileges we enjoy under the present establishment. . . ."

ALEXANDER AND SMITH PROTEST

We whose names are under written, being two of five of his Majesty's council, for this province, who in the said committee dissented from the opinion then given by the Honorable Joseph Murray, Edward Holland and John Chambers, Esqrs. We also having proposed that the said petition should remain for further consideration of the said committee before report should be made thereon, and the said committee having determined against our opinions in that point also, and carried the proposal in the negative, have therefore thought fit, for the justification of our loyal intention towards his Majesty's service, and our hearty concern for the best good of his majesty's subjects in this province, and our true respect and deference to his honor the lieutenant governor, and the honorable board of his Majesty's council, with all humility herein to set forth the grounds and reasons why we are of opinion that the said petition, with the exclusive clauses therein contained, ought not to have been granted. Previous whereto we beg leave to declare that in the political light in which we consider the intended college, it appears to us that any constitutional preferment by act of the government within this province, of one denomination of Protestants exclusive of others, to any office that concerns the education of youth (a matter extremely interesting and important) will be injurious to the common rights of this people, naturally endanger the producing of factions and parties, tend to destroy that harmony which at present subsists among them, raise and maintain perpetual jealousies, feuds, animosities, divisions and hatred among his Majesty's subjects within this province; put it in the power of the party preferred to oppress the rest and tend to the advancement of particular interests and designs rather than the public good. And although we are of opinion that the state of this province ought to have been fully considered in a time of more leisure than our preparation for his Majesty's service on the public affairs at Albany and our business on the circuit would admit of, yet we thought it our duty at this time notwithstanding these disadvantages with regard to the present petition, to observe more particularly that it appears to us,

First, That the far greatest part (we suppose seven eighths) of the freeholders and inhabitants of this province are Protestants of religious denominations different from those of the Church of England established by law in South Britain, who are all zealously attached to the distinguishing characteristics of their own respective parties, and notwithstanding their different opinions in religion are all well affected to his Majesty's person and government and the Protestant succession of his royal house and are good and profitable members of this community; and (at least) as to the far greatest part of them, have not hitherto been disqualified by any act of legislature for public service in any office, either civil, military or literary within the government.

Secondly, That the free indulgence of liberty of conscience and an equal enjoyment of civil rights allowed to Protestants of all denominations, and the impartial distributing of offices of trust to Protestants of sufficient qualifications to discharge such offices within this province, has greatly tended to its present growth and prosperity; and that its future strength as a frontier province against the common enemy, very much depends upon the preservation of those liberties and rights without the least violation or infringement.

Thirdly, That the college established by the charter proposed, being evidently intended to draw to it the application of the public funds raised for the erecting a college or seminary of learning within this province, will contract the scheme of public education within narrower limits than appear to have been designed by the present public acts of legislation and will prove a manifest infringement upon the rights of the people who are all equally interested in the money raised for that purpose.

Fourthly, We conceive that a charter granted with such exclusive clauses, will prove a public grievance, and tend to disoblige the far greatest part of the people of this province, who will be disposed to think that this government treats them unkindly in judging them unfit to be trusted in the education of their own youth, in abridging their natural and civil rights and liberties, in an article of the highest importance; that it will tend to drive away the far greatest part of the youth of this province, into the neighboring colonies for an education, and transfer a considerable part of our wealth to the support of foreign colleges; will tend to prevent strangers from settling among us; obstruct the increase of the value of our lands, and his Majesty's revenues by quit-rents and in the event, have an unhappy tendency to continue this province as a frontier against the French in a weak and defenseless state.

Wherefore, We are humbly of opinion against the grant of the present petition (among other reasons that may be collected from the premisses) more particularly for that it appears to us,

First, As being unjust by any charter to exclude any Protestant denomination in this province from any offices in our college.

Secondly, As being inconsistent with religious liberty to impose any method of divine service unless it be formed for that purpose in such way as the legislature shall agree to.

Thirdly, As tending to monopolize learning to a small party, and to drive the greatest part of the youth intended for an education to seek it out of this province.

Fourthly, As subversive of the generous design of a public college, intended by the acts of legislature referred to in the petition, which do not exclude any denomination of Protestants from any office therein.

Fifthly, As dangerous to the peace and prosperity of this province, by establishing in a minor party a constitutional right with an exclusive dominion over the far greatest part of the inhabitants thereof.

Sixthly, As detrimental to his Majesty's interest, the honor of his government within this province, and the general good and welfare of the people that inhabit the same.

For these reasons we do enter our protestation against, and dissent from the grant of the prayer of the said petition with such exclusive clauses as are contained in it; protesting farther and declaring it to be our undoubted right and bounden duty for his Majesty's service and with regard to the civil and religious interests of the good people of this province, as occasion may require to publish this our protestation for the common good.

JAMES ALEXANDER
WILLIAM SMITH

3. Samuel Johnson Advertises the Opening of King's College (Columbia), 1754

Johnson (1696–1772) was a graduate and later a tutor at Yale. During his tutorship he became converted to episcopacy and decided to join the Church of England. For some years he had a small Anglican congregation in Stratford, Connecticut, but in 1754 the learned theologian and philosopher accepted an invitation to become the first president of King's College, an office he held until 1763.

To such parents as have now (or expect to have) children prepared to be educated in the College of New York:

I. As the gentlemen who are appointed by the assembly, to be trustees of the intended Seminary or College of New York, have thought fit to appoint me to take charge of it, and have concluded to set up a course of tuition in the learned languages, and in the liberal arts and sciences; they have judged it advisable, that I should publish this advertisement, to inform such as have children ready for a college education, that it is proposed to begin tuition upon the first day of July next, at the vestry room in the new school house, adjoining to Trinity Church in New York, which the gentlemen of the vestry are so good as to favor them with the use of in the interim, till a convenient place may be built.

II. The lowest qualifications they have judged requisite, in order to admission into the said college, are as follows, *viz.*, that they be able to read well, and write a good legible hand; and that they be well versed in the five first rules in arithmetic; *i.e.*, as far as division and reduction; and as to Latin and Greek, that they have a good knowledge in the grammars, and be able to make grammatical Latin, and both in construing and parsing, to give a good account of two or three of the first select Orations of Tully, and of the first books of Virgil's Aeneid, and some of the first chapters of the Gospel of St. John, in Greek. In these books therefore they may expect to be examined, but higher qualifications must hereafter be expected; and if there be any of the higher classes in any college, or under private instruction, that incline to come hither, they may expect admission to proportionably higher classes here.

From the *New York Gazette, or Weekly Post-Boy*, No. 592, June 3, 1754, in Herbert and Carol Schneider (eds.), *Samuel Johnson*, IV, 222–24.

III. And that people may be the better satisfied in sending their children for education to this college, it is to be understood, that as to religion, there is no intention to impose on the scholars, the peculiar tenets of any particular sect of Christians; but to inculcate upon their tender minds, the great principles of Christianity and morality in which true Christians of each denomination are generally agreed. And as to the daily worship in the college morning and evening, it is proposed that it should ordinarily consist of such a collection of lessons, prayers, and praises of the liturgy of the Church, as are, for the most part, taken out of the Holy Scriptures, and such as are agreed on by the trustees, to be in the best manner expressive of our common Christianity; and, as to any peculiar tenets, every one is left to judge fully for himself, and to be required only to attend constantly at such places of worship, on the Lord's Day, as their parents or guardians shall think fit to order or permit.

IV. The chief thing that is aimed at in this college is to teach and engage the children to know God in Jesus Christ, and to love and serve Him in all sobriety, godliness, and righteousness of life, with a perfect heart, and a willing mind; and to train them up in all virtuous habits and all such useful knowledge as may render them creditable to their families and friends, ornaments to their country, and useful to the public weal in their generations. To which good purposes it is earnestly desired, that their parents, guardians, and masters, would train them up from their cradles, under strict government, and in all seriousness, virtue and industry, that they may be qualified to make orderly and tractable members of this society;—and, above all that in order hereunto, they be very careful themselves, to set them good examples of true piety and virtue in their own conduct. For as examples have a very powerful influence over young minds, and especially those of their parents, in vain are they solicitous for a good education for their children if they themselves set before them examples of impiety, and profaneness, or of any sort of vice whatsoever.

V. And, lastly, a serious, virtuous, and industrious course of life being first provided for, it is further the design of this college to instruct and perfect youth in the learned languages, and in the arts of reasoning exactly, of writing correctly, and speaking eloquently; and in the arts of numbering and measuring, of surveying and navigation, of geography and history, of husbandry, commerce and government, and in the knowledge of all nature in the heavens above us, and in the air, water and earth around us, and the various kinds of meteors, stones, mines, and minerals, plants and animals, and of everything useful for the comfort, the convenience and elegance of life, in the chief manufactures relating to any of these things; and finally, to lead them from the study of nature to the knowledge of themselves, and of the God of nature, and their duty to Him, themselves, and one another, and everything that can contribute to their true happiness, both here and hereafter.

Thus much, Gentlemen, it was thought proper to advertise you of, concerning the nature and design of this college. And I pray God, it may be attended with all the success you can wish, for the best good of the rising generations; to which (while I continue here) I shall willingly contribute my endeavors to the utmost of my power. . . .

N.B. The charge of the tuition is established by the trustees to be only 25 s. for each quarter.

4. Thomas Clap Defends the Ideal of the Sectarian College, 1754

See Doc. 6 and Part I, Docs. 11, 16; and Richard Hofstadter and Walter P. Metzger, *The Development of Academic Freedom in the United States* (New York, 1955), pp. 163–77. The controversy is reassessed in Louis L. Tucker, "The Church of England and Religious Liberty at Pre-Revolutionary Yale," *William and Mary Quarterly*, 3d series, XVII (July, 1960), 314–28.

The Universities, in Scotland, have as great, or greater Privileges, than those in England. . . . Their Worship, is wholly under their own Regulation, and they are not subject, to any particular Parish, or Presbytery; but only to the general Assembly, of the Church of *Scotland;* to which, they send a President, or Professor, in the Quality of a Minister, as Presbyteries do. p. 32.

Religious Worship, Preaching, and Instruction on the Sabbath, being one of the most important Parts, of the Education of Ministers; it is more necessary, that it should be under the Conduct, of the Authority,

Thomas Clap, *The Religious Constitution of Colleges* (New London, Conn., 1754), pp. 5–8, 10–20.

of the College, than any other Part of Education. The Preaching, ought to be adapted, to the superior Capacity, of those, who are to be qualified, to be *Instructors of others;* and upon all Accounts *Superior,* to that, which is ordinarily to be expected, or indeed requisite, in a common Parish.

There are many different Principles, in Religion, and Kinds of Preaching, which, when they are in any Degree faulty, cannot always be easily remedied, by Complaint, to any other Authority. And therefore, every *religious Society,* naturally chooses, as far as may be, to have, the Nomination of their own Minister. And this is much more necessary in a *College,* where the Preaching, is of such general Importance, to a whole Country; and such special Care, should be taken, that it be, upon all Accounts, of the *best Kind.* And it cannot be reasonable, nor safe, that any particular Parish, especially, that which happens to be the nearest to a College, should appoint the Minister for it. . . .

And where, as it generally happens, there are sundry Places of Worship, in the City, where a College is; if the Students should disperse to all, and every one of them, this would break up all order in the Society, and defeat the Religious Design, and Instructions of it. . . .

Yale-College in *New-Haven;* does not come up, to the Perfection, of the Ancient Established Universities, in *Great Britain;* yet, would endeavour, to Imitate them, in most things, as far, as its present State, will admit of.

It was *Founded,* A. D. 1701. By *Ten Principal Ministers,* in the Colony of *Connecticut;* upon the Desire, of many other Ministers, and People in it; with the *License, and Approbation, of the General Assembly.* Their main Design, in that *Foundation,* was to *Educate Persons, for the Ministry of these* Churches, commonly called *Presbyterian,* or *Congregational,* according to their own *Doctrine, Discipline,* and *Mode of Worship.* . . .

The present Governors, of the College; esteem themselves, bound by *Law,* and the more *sacred Ties of Conscience, and Fidelity to their Trust, committed to them, by their Predecessors;* to pursue, and carry on, the pious Intention, and Design, of the *Founders;* and to improve, all the *College Estate,* descended to them, for that purpose. And therefore, about seven Years ago; began, to lay a Fund for the Support of a *Professor, of Divinity,* in the College; and being, of late Years, more sensible, of the *Necessity* of it; from, the unhappy, divided Circumstances, of *New-Haven;* and having receiv'd, some large Donations . . .

have determined, to settle, such a Professor; as soon, as, by Leasing more of the said Land, or other ways, a competent Support, can be obtained.

In the mean Time, they have desired, the *President;* with some Assistance, from themselves, and others; to carry on the Work, of a Professor, of Divinity; by Preaching, in the College Hall, every Lord's Day. Being hereunto, sufficiently warranted, from, the original Nature, Design, and Practice of Colleges, and Universities; (which are, superior Societies, for Religious Purposes;) and, the several special Clauses, in the Acts, of the General Assembly; That so, the Students, may have the Advantage, of such Preaching, and Instruction, as is *best adapted, to their Capacity, State, and Design.*

The Governors, of the College, cannot, consistent, with the Trust committed, to them; give up, the ordinary, public Instruction, of the Students; especially, in Matters of Divinity; to any, but their *own Officers* and *Substitutes.* For, they can have, no sufficient Security, as such Governors, that others, who are not, of their Nomination, and under their Authority, will Teach, or Instruct, according, to the Design, of the *Founders:* and, if they should deviate from it; the Governors, could have, no Authority, to prevent it. And, upon that account, it is more necessary, that the Governors of the College, should nominate the Preacher to it, than any *other Officer,* or Instructor.

Particularly, it cannot be reasonable; that, either of the three, religious Assemblies, in *New-Haven,* should choose, a Minister, for the College; or that, the College, should be *obliged, to attend* upon such Preaching, as they, or either of them, should *choose.* They would not allow, that the College, should choose a Minister for *them;* much less, is it reasonable, that they, should choose a Minister, for the *College;* which is a religious Society, of a superior, more general, and more important Nature.

This would be, to subject the College, to a Jurisdiction out of itself; in the most important Point, of it's Institution, and Design. And no Society, or Body Politick, can be *safe,* but only, in it's having, a Principle of self-Preservation; and a Power, of Providing, every thing necessary, for it's own Subsistance, and Defence.

Indeed, as the College, receives it's Charter, and Part, of it's Support, from the *Government;* it is necessarily, *dependent* upon them; and under their Direction; and must choose, such a Minister as is agreeable to them; or otherwise, they may, withdraw their special Protection, and Support. And it cannot, reasonably, be suppos'd; that, the General Assembly, would neglect, this part, of their Superintendency; and suffer it, to be exercised, by any, particular Parish. For, by this means, it might easily happen, that the College, might be subjected, to such Preaching, as would be contrary, to the Minds, of the Generality, of the Colony; as well, as, the Design, of the *Founders.*

Some indeed, have supposed, that, the only Design of Colleges, was to teach the Arts, and Sciences; and that Religion, is no part, of a College Education: And therefore, there ought to be, no religious Worship upheld, or enjoined, by the Laws of the College; but every Student, may Worship, where, and how, he pleaseth; or, as his Parents, or Guardian, shall direct.

But, it is probable, that there is not a College, to be found upon Earth, upon such a Constitution; without any Regard, to Religion. And we know, that Religion, and the Religion of these Churches, in particular; both, as to *Doctrine,* and *Discipline,* was the main Design, of the *Founders,* of this College; (agreeable, to the minds, of the *Body, of the People;*) and, this Design, their Successors, are bound in Duty, to pursue. And indeed, Religion, is a matter, of so great Consequence, and Importance; that, the Knowledge, of the Arts, and Sciences, how excellent soever, in themselves, are comparatively, worth but little, without it. . . .

And, if Parents, have a *Right,* to order, what Worship, their Children shall attend, at College; it would take, the Power, wholly out, of the Hands, of the Authority, of College, as to matters of Religion; and there may be, as many Kinds, of Religious Worship, at College; as there are, different Opinions, of Parents.

And, if Parents, give the *Law;* they must also, affix the *Penalty;* and indeed, *inflict it themselves.* But Parents, at a Distance, cannot, Govern, their Children, at College; neither, is it practicable, that, they should give, such, a just *System of Rules,* as the Authority, of College *can,* or *ought,* to put in Execution.

For, we may suppose, for Instance; that, there may be, an Assembly, of *Jews,* or *Arrians,* in *New Haven;* and then, the Authority, of College, may be obliged, to punish, the Students, for not attending, such a Worship, as they esteem, to be *worse than none;* and such, as they are obliged, by the Statutes, of the *Founders,* not to permit, the Students, to attend upon.

It has been said; that, *Liberty of Conscience,* ought, to be allowed to all; to Worship, as they please.

Upon which, it has been considered; that, the College acts, upon the Principles, of Liberty, of Conscience, in the *fullest Sense;* and suppose, that any Man, under the Limitations of the Law; may Found a College, or School, for such Ends, and Purposes; and upon such Conditions, and Limitations, with Respect to those, who are allow'd, the Benefit of it, *as he in his Conscience,* shall think best. And that *his* Conscience, who has the Property, of a Thing; or gives, it, upon Conditions; ought to Govern, in all Matters, relating to the Use, of that thing; and not, his Conscience, who is allowed, to take the Benefit; who, has *no Right* to it, but according to the *Will,* and Conditions of the Proprietor, or Donor. And Liberty of Conscience in, him, who is allow'd, to take the Benefit, extends no further, than to determine, whether he will accept it upon those Conditions. And to challenge the Benefit, without complying with the Conditions, would be, to rob the Proprietor, (or Feoffee in Trust,) of his Property; and Right of Disposal.

The great Design, of Founding this School, was to Educate Ministers in our *own Way;* and in order to attain this End; the *Founders,* and *their Successors,* apprehend it to be necessary, that the Students, should ordinarily attend, upon the *same Way of Worship:* and should they give up, that Law, and Order; the College would serve Designs, and Purposes, *contrary* to that, for which it was *originally Founded:* which, in *Point of Conscience,* and Fidelity, to their Trust; *they cannot permit.* And in this Point, the College, Exercises, no kind of *Power,* or *Authority;* but only that, which Results, from the *natural Liberties,* and Privileges of all free, and *Voluntary Societies* of Men; which is to determine, *their own Design,* amongst themselves; and the Conditions, of their own Favors, and Benefits to *others.*

Yet the Governors of the College, have always freely admitted, Protestants, of all Denominations, to enjoy the Benefit, of an Education in it; they attending upon, (as they always have done,) our Way of Worship; while they are there.

It has also been said; that, all the Students, ought to attend, the Worship, of the Church of *England;* or so many of them, as shall see Cause; or, as their Parents shall order, or permit.

That, the Church of England, is the *Established Religion,* of this Colony; and that those, who do not conform to it, are *Schismaticks.*

Upon which, it has been consider'd, that the Act of Parliament, in the Common Prayer Book, for the Establishment, of the Church of

England, is expressly limitted, to *England, and Wales, and the Town of Berwick, upon Tweed.* And it is, a well known Maxim in the Law; *that the Statutes of England, do not extend to the Plantations; unless, they are Expressly mentioned.* . . .

It has also been said; that, Governor *Yale,* and Bishop *Berkley,* who were Church Men, made large *Donations,* to this College.

Upon which, it has been consider'd that; when any Donation is given, after the Foundation is laid, the Law presumes, that it was the Intention, of the *Donors,* that their Donations, should be improved, according, to the Design, of the *Founders.* The Law presumes, that every Man, knows the Law, in that thing, wherein he Acts: And since, by Law, the Statutes of the Founders, cannot be altered, it presumes, that the Donor, had not any Design to do it. And there is not, the least Reason to suppose, that the Governor, or Bishop, intended, or Expected, that, upon their Donations, any alteration should be made, in the Laws of the College; or any Deviation, from the Design, of the Founders, towards *the Church of England or* any other way.

If it was so; it seems, as if they intended, to *Buy* the College, rather than make a *Donation,* to it. And if there was Evidence, that they made their Donations, upon that *Condition;* the College would *Resign* them back again.

And since, there is not, the least Reason to suppose that, they, expected, or desired, that, upon their Donations, any Alteration should be made, in the Laws of College; we see no Obligation to do it, in Point of *Gratitude.* . . .

Yet, we have a just Sense, of the Generosity, of those Gentlemen; and for that, and many other Reasons, are Willing to do, all that we can, to gratify, the Gentlemen, of the Church of England; consistant with the Design and Statutes, of the Founders; and particularly, have given Liberty, to those Students, who have been educated, in the Worship, of the Church of England; and are, of that Communion; to be absent, at those Times, when the Sacrament is Administered, in that Church; and upon Christmas; and, at some such other Times, as will not be, an Infraction upon, the general, and *standing Rules,* of College.

It has been further said, that there are, a Number of Church Men, in this Colony; who, in the annual public Taxes, contribute something, towards the Support, of the College.

Upon which, it has been consider'd; that, when a Community, are jointly, at some public Charge; it is equitable, that the Benefit, of each

Individual, should be consulted, so far, as it is consistant, with the general Design, and Good of the whole, or the Majority. And tho' it is impossible, that such a Benefit, should be Mathematically proportioned, to each Individual; yet this College, has educated, as many Episcopal Ministers, and others, as they desired, or stood in need of; which has been a sufficient Compensation, for their Paying, about, a Half Peny Sterling, per Man; in the annual Support, of the College.

And it may still continue to be, as serviceable, to the Church of England, as it has been, if they please; for the Orders of it, remain in Substance, just the same.

It may further be consider'd, that this College, was Founded, and in a good measure, Indowed, many Years, before there were any Donations made, by Church-Men; or so much, as one Episcopal Minister, in the Colony. And if Mens contributing, something, towards the Support of the College; gives, them a Right, to order, what Worship, their Children shall attend upon, while at College; it gives the same Right, to Parents, of all other Denominations; which to admit, as was before Observ'd, would defeat the Design of the *Founders;* and destroy, the religious Order, of the College; which ought, *sacredly,* to be observed.

5. *Laws and Orders of King's College, 1755*

See Doc. 3.

I. OF ADMISSION

First. None shall be admitted (unless by a particular act of the governors) but such as can read the first three of Tully's Select Orations and the three first books of Virgil's Aeneid into English, and the ten first chapters of St. John's Gospel in Greek, into Latin and such as are well versed in all the rules of Clark's Introduction so as to make true grammatical Latin and are expert in arithmetic so far as the rule of reduction to be examined by the president or fellows:

2ndly. Every scholar shall have a copy of these laws and his admittatur shall be signed at the end of them by the president upon his

---

Herbert and Carol Schneider (eds.), *Samuel Johnson,* IV, 225–29.

promising all due obedience to them which promise shall be expressed in writing under his hand.

First. The examination of candidates for the degree of Bachelor of Arts shall be held in the college hall about six weeks before commencement by the president or fellows when any of the governors or any who have been Master of Arts in this college may be present and ask any question they think proper and such candidates as have resided four years and are then found competently versed in the sciences wherein they have been instructed shall then be admitted to expect their degree at commencement which shall be on the second Wednesday in May.

2ndly. Such as have diligently pursued their studies for three years after being admitted to their Bachelor's degree; and have been guilty of no gross immorality shall be admitted to the degree of Master of Arts.

3rdly. No candidate shall be admitted to either of these degrees without fulfilling the terms above appointed unless in case of extraordinary capacity and diligence and by a particular act of the governors of the college.

4thly. Every one that is admitted to either degree shall pay a pistole to the president.

First. The president or one of the professors or fellows in his absence shall every morning and evening read the form of prayers established by the governors of the college and according to the rules and method therein prescribed.

2ndly. Every student shall constantly attend the said public service at such stated hours as the president shall appoint and those that absent themselves shall for every offense be fined twopence, and one penny for not coming in due season, unless they can allege such reasons for their absence or tardiness as shall appear sufficient to the president.

3dly. Every pupil shall constantly attend on the public worship every Lord's Day at such church or meeting as his parents or guardians order him to frequent and for every neglect shall be obliged to perform such extraordinary exercise as the president and professors or fellows shall appoint unless he hath some reasonable excuse admitted to be sufficient by the president.

4thly. Every pupil shall behave with the utmost decency at public worship, or in the hall and whoever is proved guilty of any profane or indecent behavior as talking, laughing, justling, winking, etc., he shall submit to an admonition for the first offense and to an extraordinary exercise for the second, and if obstinate, expelled.

IV. OF MORAL BEHAVIOR

First. If any pupil shall be convicted of drunkenness, fornication, lying, theft, swearing, cursing, or any other scandalous immorality he shall submit to open admonition and confession of his fault or be expelled if his crime is judged to heinous for any lesser punishment and especially if he be contumacious.

2ndly. None of the pupils shall frequent houses of ill fame, or keep company with any persons of known scandalous behavior and such as may endanger either their principles or morals; and those that do so shall first be openly rebuked and if they obstinately persist in it they shall be expelled.

3rdly. None of the pupils shall fight cocks, play at cards, dice or any unlawful game upon penalty of being fined not exceeding five shillings for the first offense, and being openly admonished and confessing their fault for the second, and expulsion, if contumacious.

4thly. If any pupil shall be convicted of fighting, maiming, slandering, or grievously abusing any person he shall be fined three shillings for the first offense and if he repeats his offense he shall be further punished by fine, admonition, suspension, or expulsion according to the aggravation of his fault, especially if contumacious.

5thly. If any pupil be convicted of any dilapidations of the college or any injury done to the estates, goods or persons of any others he shall be obliged to make good all damages.

V. OF BEHAVIOR TOWARDS AUTHORITY AND SUPERIORS

First. If any pupils be disobedient to the president, professors or fellows of the college or treat them or any others in authority with any insulting, disrespectful or contemptuous language or deportment, he shall be fined not exceeding five shillings for the first offense or submit to open admonition and confession of his fault, according to the nature of it and be expelled if he persists contumacious.

2ndly. Every pupil shall treat all his superiors and especially the authority of the college with all duty and respect by all such good manners and behavior as common decency, and good breeding require, such as rising, standing, uncovering the head, preserving a proper distance and using the most respectful language, etc., and he that behaves otherwise shall be punished at the discretion of the president and fellows or governors according to the nature and degree of his ill behavior.

VI. OF COLLEGE EXERCISES AND DUE ATTENDANCE

First. The business of the first year shall be to go on and perfect their studies in the Latin and Greek classics and go over a system of rhetoric, geography and chronology and such as are designed for the pulpit shall also study the Hebrew.

2ndly. The business of the second and third years shall be after a small system of logic to study the mathematics and the mathematical and experimental philosophy in all the several branches of it, with agriculture and merchandise, together with something of the classics and criticism all the while.

3rdly. The fourth year is to be devoted to the studies of metaphysics, logic and moral philosophy, with something of criticism and the chief principles of law and government, together with history, sacred and profane.

4thly. The pupils in each of their terms shall be obliged, at such times as the president shall appoint, to make exercises in the several branches of learning suitable to their standing both in Latin and English, such as declamations and dissertations on various questions pro and con, and frequently these and syllogistical reasonings.

5thly. Whoever shall misbehave in time of exercise by talking, laughing, or justling one another, etc., shall be fined one shilling for each offense.

6thly. All the pupils shall be obliged to apply themselves with the utmost diligence to their studies and constantly attend upon all the exercises appointed by the president or their tutors or professors for their instruction.

7thly. None of the pupils shall be absent from their chambers or neglect their studies without leave obtained of the president or their respective tutors, except for morning and evening prayers and recitation and half an hour for breakfast and an hour and half after dinner and from evening prayer till nine of the clock at night. The penalty, four pence or some exercise for each offense.

8thly. If any student shall persist in the neglect of his studies either through obstinacy or negligence and so frequently fails of making due preparation for recitation and other appointed exercises and if he refuse to submit and reform after due admonition he shall be rusticated, *i. e.,* suspended for a time, and if he does not bring sufficient evidence of his reformation he shall be expelled.

9thly. No student shall go out of town without the president's or his tutor's leave, unless at the stated vacation upon penalty of five shillings and for repeating his fault he shall be rusticated, and if contumacious, expelled.

N.B. The stated vacations are a month after commencement, one week at Michaelmas and a fortnight at Christmas, and Easter Week, *i.e.,* from Good Friday till the Friday following, which last being so near commencement is to be considered as only a vacation from exercises but not from the college or daily morning and evening prayers, and so does not come within the last prohibition.

All the fines shall be paid to the treasurer of the college to be laid out in books and disposed of as a reward to such of the scholars as shall excell in the course of their studies in their several classes as the president, professors and tutors or the major part of them shall direct.

6. *Shubael Conant Attacks Heresy-hunting at Yale, 1757*

See Doc. 4 and Part I, Docs. 11, 16; Louis L. Tucker, "President Thomas Clap and the Rise of Yale College, 1740–1766," *The Historian,* XIX (1956–57), 66–81; and Hofstadter and Metzger, *The Development of Academic Freedom in the United States,* pp. 163–74.

The Foundation on which the Corporation take upon themselves an Authority, to bring him under Examination, is the Law or Ordinance, made by the Corporation, at their Meeting, *November* 21, 1751, and published by the President, in his *Defence &c.* By which 'tis decreed, that when it is suspected by any of the Corporation, that either the

Shubael Conant, *Letter to a Friend . . . on the Subject of the Reverend Mr. Noyes's . . . Examination by the Corporation of Yale–College, and their erecting a Church Within the Same . . .* (New Haven, 1757), pp. 3–5, 7–8, 10–11, 13–20, 23–31.

President, or any Fellow, or Professor of Divinity, or any Tutor, of the College, has fallen from the Profession of his Faith, (required to be made at the Time of his Admission into his Office) and is gone into any contrary Scheme of Principles, he *shall* be examined by the Corporation. . . .

'Tis in it self unjust, and injurious thus to subject the Members, and Officers of that Body to Examination, on Suspicion of Heresy or Defection from their professed Faith. They are all obliged to give very full Proof of their Soundness in Faith, before they are admitted to their respective Offices. And when they have been once tried, and approved by the Corporation, they have certainly a *just Right* to a good Character, 'till they themselves have forfeited it; and ought to be esteemed and treated as found in the Faith, 'till the Contrary appears. To bring their Character into Question, upon the *bare Suspicion* of any of their Fellow-Members, is very unfare. If any One will bring any Accusation against them, let them be tried, and have Liberty to defend themselves. But if the Accusation can't be proved; how scandalous is it, to have recourse to Suspicions, and evil Surmisings, and make the poor suspected Man his own Accuser; and seek to draw out of his own Mouth, the Matter of his Condemnation; by subjecting him to answer all the ensnaring Questions, that the evil Surmiser sees fit to ask him. And in such a Case you may be sure, that he will do his utmost this Way, in Order to justify his Suspicion.

A Man's being bro't under Examination in such a Case, will infallibly hurt his Character, even tho' he should be acquitted: And he is left without Remedy, against him who has done him Wrong.

In all Cases, which in their Nature admit of Proof; the only just Way of proceeding against Men, is by express Charges, and supporting them by Evidence. . . . Such a Way of proceeding against Men as this Ordinance warrants, is inconsistent with the legal Rights of *English-men,* and the divine Rights of Christians. . . .

It may be said here, that 'tis uncharitable and injurious to suppose the Corporation will ever be so unjust as to go into the Examination of any of their Officers, unless there is *just* Ground to suspect them. But it ought to be observed that I am not speaking of what the Equity of the Judges will dispose them to do; but what the Law warrants, and allows to be done. The Law, it is plain, makes no Difference between a *just,* and an *unjust* Suspicion. According to that, 'tis enough, that the Man is suspected by a *proper Officer.* The Law regards not at all, whether the Suspicion be well grounded, or not. All that the Law regards in the Case, is that the Suspicion proceed from a right Person. If all the World should suspect any of the Members of the Corporation, or other Officers of the College, to be Hereticks, and that on most just Grounds, this Law takes no Notice of it: But if any Member of the Corporation, suspects any of them, this, of it self, is sufficient to subject them to Examination, and makes it the Duty of the Court to examine them. Whereas the old Law of the Trustees, did *not at all* regard the *Persons* of the Suspectors, but *only* the *Grounds* of the Suspicion.—I believe the Judges are better than the Law: And that they will be found wise, and more equitable *Judges,* than Law-Givers. But tho' we have good and upright Judges, yet we are not quite secure, 'till we have good Laws too. For my Part, I choose to live under a Government, whose Laws won't suffer the Judges to be arbitrary, and oppressive, tho' they were disposed to be so; rather than under One whose Judges, won't practise that Oppression and Tyranny, which the Laws allow. . . .

If a Set of Narrow-Spirited Bigots, who strain up the *Calvinistick* Doctrines to the highest Pitch, and interpret *moderate, catholick Calvinism,* to be a Defection from the Standard-Faith; whose Narrowness, and Haughtiness is such, that they can't bear that Others should depart a Hair's-Breadth from their Sentiments, in the Doctrines, wherein they esteem Orthodoxy chiefly to consist; but they are ready to cry out against them, and run them down as Corrupters of the Faith: If such Men should ever become Members of the Corporation; 'tis easy to see, what a Use they may make of this Ordinance, in intimidating, vexing, and injuring such of their Members, and Officers as are moderate, catholick, charitable *Calvinists;* by their suspicious Examinations, and Censures of them.—Or if a Set of ambitious, designing Men, who are carrying on Party-Designs, and Schemes of Self-Exaltation, should ever become Judges in this Court of Inquisition; what Advantages does this Law of Examination put into their Hands, against such of their Fellow-Members, as cross their Schemes, and stand in their Way? 'Tis but to suggest to the Board, a Suspicion of their being Hereticks, and bring them under Examination; and by asking them a multitude of Questions, upon a great Variety of Subjects, they may easily catch something, from some of their Answers, which, such a Sort of Men will know how to turn against them, as the Matter of their Condemnation. And the College Standard of right Belief, would, in such a Case, afford to such a Set of Men, a vast Advantage against Those they want to humble, and subdue. For it contains a *vast Number* of Articles; and some of them are carried to such an *excessive Height,* and others of them are so *extremely disputable,* that the soundest Believers, and greatest and best Divines, supposing they are honest Men, may find it impossible to give a satisfactory Answer to *all* the Questions, which their Judges may ask them, out of their two Standard-Books. . . .

When the New-Light Errors, and Disorders, first broke in upon us, Mr. *Noyes* was an open Opposer, as was the *President* and Corporation.—He was presently stigmatized by the Party, as an unconverted Teacher, and as an *Arminian;* as were most of the Ministers, who stood firm in those Times.—A Party of his People were soon ripe for a Separation: And being once separated; were greatly encouraged and strengthened, from abroad, and grew and multiplied apace.—The Scholars were, many of them, much infected with the Disease of the Day; were very ungovernable, despised Mr. *Noyes,* and lusted after the separate meetings, and were hardly restrained from them. 'Twas thought, in those Times, that they were counseled, and countenanced in that Matter, by some Persons abroad, out of Favour to the Separation.—The Corporation was represented in a bad Light, by the Friends to New-Light; and 'twas rumoured that they were leaning towards *Arminianism;* the *President* in particular was suspected; and all this, it was thought, was done with Design to work themselves, by Degrees, into the Corporation, and make the College the Property of the *New-Light* Party in the Government: Who were, at that Time, manifestly labouring to bring the Authority of the Government into their Hands. During these Transactions, the *President* and Mr. *Noyes,* to all Appearance, were very good Friends; and the Former, supported the Interest of the Latter, with Strength and Honour; against the Power of *New-Light.*—But the Disturbances, and Disaffection to Mr. *Noyes,* both in Town and Colege, raised from that Quarter, grew higher and higher; insomuch that the Corporation, and Town both, thought it needful, for the Cure of the growing Evil, that Mr. *Noyes* should have a Colleague.—Sundry Attempts were made for that Purpose, without Success. 'Twas suspected, Mr. *Noyes* was not so hearty in that Affair, as he ought to have been.—The *President,* and most (I don't know but all) of the Corporation, were disgusted with him, on that Account. Many think he was to blame, in not forwarding that Design, so cordially as he should have done. How that is I don't know. But here, I suppose the Breach of Friendship between the *President* and Mr. *Noyes* begun.—By this Time there was a considerable Change in the Members of the Corporation. . . . It happened that this Assembly, a little after rejecting the Motion in Favour of a Professor; at the Request of President *Burr,* granted a Lottery, for the Use of his College. This was laid hold on. And 'twas urged by the College Politicans, that the Reason why the Assembly was so ready to assist the *Jersey* College, and so backward in the Affair of the Professor, was that they were well satisfied of *their* Orthodoxy, but were jealous of *Our's:* 'Twas therefore thought necessary, to give some further Proof of the Corporation's Soundness, and Zeal for Orthodoxy, and against *Arminianism.* By this Engine the Corporation was drawn in, to pass their Resolves, and Laws of *November* 1751, published in the *President's* Defence; but not without Opposition, and sundry negative Voices.—This gained the Corporation the Confidence of one Sort of Men in the Government; and increased the Jealousy of Others, that Orthodoxy was going to be made the Stirrup, for some Men to mount the Saddle by.—After this, the Affair of the Professor's Support was again urged in the Assembly, but without Success. The final Issue was, that instead of adding any Thing for that Service, they kept back the annual Supply of £. 100 which they used to give the College; finding the College could support their present Charge without it; and judging it needless and inexpedient, for them to set up a Professor at present. This Opposition, has all along been represented, by the *President,* and many Others, as proceeded from the great Power of the *Arminian* Party in the Government: Who are represented as opposing these Measures of the Corporation, out of Aversion to *Calvinism,* and a secret Design of spreading their own Principles, and engrossing the College, and Government to themselves. —There are doubtless some *Arminians* among the Opposers of these College Measures, as there are some *Antimonians,* and *New-Lights* among the Favourers of them. And I know too, there are many sincere *Calvinists* who Oppose those Measures, and many more at present, than there were at first.

The President, has been observed, from the first Opening of this new Opposition, and Distinction of Parties, which took its Rise from the Methods that were used to bring the Assembly to support the Professor, gradually to grow cold to such of his former *Old-Light* Friends, as any Ways Oppose the new Measures, both in the Corporation, and out of it. And latterly he has made the new Members of the Corporation his Confidents, and Cabinet; while the old Members, who stood firm in shaking Times of *New-Light,* and now Oppose the present Measures, and New Schemes of the Corporation, are little Regarded.

Mr. *Noyes* in particular, has been a constant Opposer of the New Schemes, and Politicks of the College, from their first Beginning. . . .

But supposing it *True* that Mr. *Noyes* borders a little upon *Arminianism;* how is the College affected, or indangered thereby? He has no Concern with the Instruction of the College. They don't attend on his Ministry, but are a Church by themselves, as Independent on him, as any other Minister of the Government. He has no Influence in the Corporation, that can possibly suggest the least fear for the College's Purity, from him. If he preaches corrupt Doctrines to his own People. They may have their Remedy according to our Constitution. He is accountable to his associated Brethren in the Ministry. And 'tis their proper Business, if he is accused of Heresy to them, diligently to enquire into the Matter. . . .

I beg your Pardon Sir, for being so Lengthly upon this Part of my Letter: And now proceed to give you some of my Thoughts upon the Affair of the Corporation's erecting a Church in the College; which was done at their last Meeting.

It appears to me an entirely *needless* Thing. If it was not safe to trust the College under Mr. *Noyes's* Ministry, lest the Scholars should learn of him to be poor Preachers, and *Arminians;* that Danger was sufficiently guarded against before, by withdrawing the College from his Meetings, and turning the Professor, into a Chaplain. The President, and other Communicants at College, might, I believe, have continued still to communicate with the Parish-Church, without Danger of being Infected by the Errors of the Administrator; which are so secret, it seems as to be rather suspected, than publickly divulged by him. . . .

But to all this, it may perhaps be replied, "That Colleges" (*as such*) "are religious Societies of a *Superior Nature* to all Others; as being Societies of *Ministers,* for the training up Persons for the Work of the Ministry. . . ." That *Yale-College* in particular is such.—Consequently, the Governors of it, have an absolute Right, and Authority, to separate the College from the Parish Church, and form it into a distinct Church, and separate worshiping Assembly: And therefore, that there is no cause of Complaint, that they have erected a Church at College.

If you please, Sir, we will a little examine these *high* Pretensions, and Claims, of *Yale-College.* It Claims by its President, to be a religious Society of a *superiour Nature* to all Parish-Churches. . . . The Reason assign'd, of this superior Nature of Colleges to all Other, &c. is this, "For whereas Parishes, are Societies, for training up the *common People,* Colleges are Societies of Ministers, for training up Persons, for the *Work of the Ministry."—Societies of Ministers.*—Some may be so, perhaps: But 'tis most certain that *all* are not so. *Yale-College* in particular, is not. The President is a Minister, but he does not preside there, in the Character of a Minister, but in that of the *legal* Head, and Governor of that School. There is not one act of his Office *as President,* but what a *Layman* might as lawfully perform as he, supposing he was invested with the Presidentship.—The Fellows and Overseers of the College are Ministers of the Church. But they don't take the Oversight and Direction of the College upon themselves, by virtue of their being *Ministers;* but by virtue of a *civil* Appointment and Authority, derived to them by the *Charter of the Government.* They don't act in that Office, in their *ministerial,* but in a political Capacity, as Persons put in Trust, with the ordering and government of that collegiate School; by an Authority, derived from the King. There is no one proper Act of the ministerial Office; which they may do, to the College, or any Members of it; but that any other Ministers may do the same, as well as they, upon a proper Call thereto: And there is no one Act, *peculiar* to their Office, *as* Trustees or *Fellows,* but what a *Layman* might perform with as much Propriety as they, if he was invested with the same Office or Trust. There is nothing in the Nature of that Office, which confines it to *Clergymen;* nor in the Charter of the Assembly; by which the College is incorporated, and invested with all its Powers: And almost all the Colleges in *America,* have *Laymen* joined with *Clergymen* in the Oversight and Government of them. And I believe most People begin to think, it would be best for our College; and the whole Community if it was so, at *Yale-College* too.

The Tutors, and other subordinate Officers, are not Ministers in the Church of *Christ.*

The Under-graduates, are not Ministers: And there is not one in four of them, that will ever be such. But supposing they were all to be made Ministers, in due Time; 'tis Time enough to honour them as Ministers, when they are *so.*

Our Divinity Professor, is a Minister, and now acts in his Station, as College Pastor, in the Character and Capacity of a Minister of *Jesus Christ.* And he is the only Officer of the College, that does so. All the Rest act in a political Capacity, and by an Authority derived to them from the *civil* Magistrate. How then is *Yale-College* a Society of Ministers? There are but twelve Ministers that have any special Relation to the College; and but one that acts in that Relation, in his Ministerial Character and Office. There seems to me, to be *no Sense,* in calling the College a Society of Ministers. The House of Lords may as well be called, the House of Bishops, because some Men who are Bishops in the Church, sit there, as Barons, of the Realm, by a civil Right, and Authority. . . .

But it will still be said, if our College is not a Society of Ministers; yet it must be acknowledged that the Corporation, in whose Hands the Authority and Government of the College, is lodged, are *Ministers,* and some of the *principal* Ministers in the Government: And on this Account, the College may claim a superior Nature, to all the Parish Churches in the Government. *Very well.* Some of our Churches are dignified, by having *Magistrates,* and *Governors* among their Members. They are therefore, superior in their Nature, to the other Churches; who can pretend to nothing higher, than a *Captain* or *Justice.* . . .

"The other Branch of the Argument is this, That Parishes are Societies, for training up the *common People,* whereas the College is for training up Persons for the *Work of the Ministry.*" 'Tis acknowledged that one principal Reason of erecting our College, was to give Youth such an Education, as might lay a proper Foundation for their being furnished, *by further Studies,* for that important and honourable Work. But the View was not confined to this one Object, nor are the Instructions, and Education, which are given at College. The Scholars spend four Years at College. About three fourths of this Time, is spent in the Study of the Languages, and Arts, the rest in Divinity. By this Education, a Foundation is laid, for after Improvements, in Divinity, or any other Kinds of Study, as they are inclined. . . . But in Comparing herself with the Parish Churches, which are Corporations of a quite different Nature, and Design, and exalting herself above them all, *She is not Wise.* By thus boasting, and glorying over *all* ecclesiastical Societies, because she teaches her Sons, Latin and Greek, Logick, Philosophy, Mathematicks, Ethicks, and a *little Smattering* of Divinity; as tho' she was blessed with a superior Nature to all Others, and by, thereupon, assuming to herself, Powers, and Prerogative, which don't belong to her; she renders herself as contemptible, as a young assuming Coxcomb. . . .

But however *Colleges are,* at least, *religious Societies;* if they are not superior to all Others.

This I shall now examine a little. A *religious* Society, according to my Notion of it, is a Society founded for religious Purposes, and Services, whose proper and special Business, is to teach and practise Religion, and the Worship of God; and which is invested with spiritual Rights, and Powers, or Authority. Such are the Churches of *Christ.* . . . 'Tis not a Church, by its Charter, or any Act of the first Trustees, or Founders; as the President calls them. Nor has it any Power, inherent in itself, to form itself into a Church, or to invest itself, with the religious Rights and Powers, proper and peculiar to such Societies.—The Founders gave the College no such Power. On the contrary, subjected it to the Attendance on the publick Worship of the Parish Church, where it is situated.—The Charters of the Assembly, whether the Old or New, neither made the College a Church, nor gave it Power, to form itself into a Church.—There is a Clause in the new Charter, granting generally, Power to appoint a Scribe or Register, a Treasurer, Tutors, Professors, Steward, and all such other Officers and Servants, usually appointed in Colleges, or Universities; from which some Plead the Right of our College to form itself into a Church, because the Universities of *Oxford* and *Cambridge,* whose Constitution are agreeable to the Hierarchy of the Church of *England,* have Churches within them; but the Universities and Colleges in *Scotland,* which are more proper for us *Dissenters* to copy after, I have been well assured from divers Gentlemen, who have had their Education there, and now reside among us, have no Churches within themselves. But this Clause of the College Charter, can reasonably be understood only of civil Powers and Privileges. For civil Societies and Communities, can't form a religious Society, and communicate religious Rights and Powers, to another Community, which they have not in themselves; any more than Churches, or religious Societies, can form civil Societies, and invest them with civil Rights and Powers. . . .

The Governors of our College, by Virtue of their Office, as such, can admit Members into that Society, and cast them out of it, Order their Education and Discipline: But they can't, as such Officers, admit Men, as Members of the Church, and Kingdom of *Christ,* nor cast them out of it, nor govern their Instruction and Discipline, as Members of that Community, nor administer the Sacraments of the Church. . . .

The President and Fellows, considered as acting in their political

Capacity, as Governors of the College, have no more Authority to set up a Church in the College, that [*sic*] a Minister, who is also a Justice of the Peace, has, in his political Capacity and acting as a civil Officer, to admit Men into the Church, or cast them out of it.

7. Commencement Exercises at King's College, 1758

This item appeared in the *New York Mercury* for June 26, 1758. Its author is unknown.

Mr. Printer, please to insert the following in your next paper. Wednesday last being the day appointed by the Governors of King's College, in this city, for the commencement, I had the pleasure of being present at the first solemnity of the kind ever celebrated here; which was, thro' the whole, conducted with much elegance and propriety. The order of the procession from the vestry room, where the college is now held, to St. George's Chapel, was as follows: The President, with his Honor the Lieutenant Governor, who, by his presence graced the solemnity, were preceded by the candidates for Bachelor's and Master's Degrees, with their heads uncovered, and were followed by the Governors of the college, the clergy of all denominations in this city, and other gentlemen of distinction of this and the neighboring provinces. After short prayers suitable to the ocassion, the Reverend Dr. Johnson, the President, from the pulpit, opened the solemnity, with a learned and elegant *Oratio Inauguralis*. The exercises of the Bachelors were introduced by a polite salutory oration, delivered by Provost, with such propriety of pronunciation, and so engaging an air, as justly gained him the admiration and applause of all present. This was followed by a metaphysical thesis, learnedly defended by Ritzema against Ver Planck and Cortlandt, with another held by Reed, and opposed by two Ogdens. The Bachelor's exercises were closed by a well composed, genteel English oration, on the advantages of a liberal education, delivered by Cortlandt, whose fine address added a beauty to the sentiment, which give universal satisfaction to that numerous assembly. After this Mr. Treadwell, in a clear and concise manner, demonstrated the revolution

Herbert and Carol Schneider, *Samuel Johnson*, IV, 280–81.

of the earth around the sun, both from astronomical observations, and the theory of gravity, and defended the thesis against Mr. Cutting and Mr. Wetmore, a candidate for the Degree of Master of Arts. This dispute being ended, the President descended from the pulpit, and being seated in a chair, in a solemn manner, conferred the honors of the college upon those pupils who were candidates for a Bachelor's Degree, and on several gentlemen who had received degrees in other colleges. The exercises were concluded with a Valedictory oration (in Latin) by Mr. Cutting, universally esteemed a masterly performance. The President then addressed himself in a solemn pathetic exhortation, to the Bachelors, which could not fail of answering the most valuable purposes, and leaving a lasting impression on the minds of all the pupils. The whole solemnity being finished by a short prayer, the procession returned back to the City-Arms, where an elegant entertainment was provided by the governors of the college. This important occasion drew together a numerous assembly of people of all orders, and it gave me a sincere pleasure to see the exercises performed in a manner which must reflect honor upon the college and incite every friend of his country, to promote so useful, so well regulated an institution.

8. Harvard Opposes a New College in the West, 1762

12. Particularly as our college, yet in its infant state, is hitherto but meanly endowed, and very poor, the unhappy consequences of which are too obvious; and we think that the founding another college would be the most probable and effectual way to prevent its being hereafter endowed in such a manner as all who desire its prosperity doubtless wish to see it. For, if such a college as is proposed were founded in Hampshire, it cannot be thought that persons living in that part of the country, who might be favorers of it, in respect of its vicinity, or

1762. 18 March. Reasons against founding a College, or Collegiate School in the County of Hampshire, humbly offered to the consideration of his Excellency Francis Bernard, Esquire, Governor of the Province of Massachusetts Bay &c., by the Overseers of Harvard College, in New England, in Josiah Quincy, *The History of Harvard University* (Cambridge, Mass., 1840), II, 469–70, 472–73.

on any other account, would be willing to bear a part in endowing that at Cambridge, whether in a legislative or private capacity. It may naturally be concluded that they would rather endeavour to obstruct all schemes and proposals to this end; judging very justly, that the growth and flourishing of their own college depended in some measure upon the languishing and depression of the other. At least it may be concluded, that they would represent it as a heavy, intolerable grievance to be obliged by law to do any thing towards the encouragement and support of a college, from which they expected no immediate benefit, while they had one of their own to support, on which they had their dependence, and which stood in at least equal need. And besides, if such a college were founded, it might probably receive some legacies, or private donations, which would otherwise come to the College in Cambridge. So that we conceive the latter would at least lose some friends and benefactors, if not find some positive enemies, by the establishing another college in the manner intended. And the certain consequence of such a division and opposition of interests, as we think must needs be occasioned by this means, will be the keeping low, and greatly cramping, that college, whose prosperity we so justly and sincerely desire.

13. Moreover, if another college were founded, as has been proposed, yet it cannot be reasonably thought that in many years to come, the means of education therein, would be near so good as they are even already in Harvard College: they will doubtless be far inferior. And yet, from the motives of nearness or novelty, of convenience, of supposed cheapness, or some other, we think it not unlikely that after a few years, a great proportion of the youth of the Province might actually be sent thither, instead of being sent to Cambridge to be educated, which would not only be a direct, great, and manifest prejudice to Harvard College, but consequently a real hurt to the general interest of literature and religion in the country. For although more of our youth might by this means receive what is usually called a liberal education, and which might pass for a very good one with many, yet we apprehend this would be rather a disadvantage than the contrary, as it would prevent a sufficient, though smaller number of our youth, being sent to Cambridge, where they would unquestionably be much more thoroughly instructed and far better qualified for doing service to their country. And the natural consequence hereof would be, not only the filling too many important civil offices, but a great part of

our pulpits, with comparatively unlettered persons, at once to the detriment both of the Commonwealth, and of the churches here established. . . .

17. . . . You have too much candor and goodness, Sir, to impute it to us, as a criminal partiality, if we highly honor the memory of our forefathers; the first European settlers of this country. And on no one account, their unfeigned piety excepted, is their memory more respectable, more venerable to us, than on account of their known great regard for learning; their love and strong attachment to which prompted them so early, and while they were struggling with unnumbered difficulties, to make an establishment for it, even in a wilderness. This they did at a great expense for them, considering their circumstances and abilities, however small it may seem in any other view; herein, probably, consulting the welfare of posterity and future ages, rather than their own immediate benefit. They did it with the pleasing hopes, that the seminary of learning, of which they then laid the foundation, would at length, by the prudent care and the ingenuous liberality of successive generations, one day arrive to the dignity and extensive usefulness of an University, and become a distinguished ornament of the New World, in some measure as the Universities of Oxford and Cambridge were of the Old. And we cannot but think, that they were very happy in the choice of a situation for this seminary, at once so healthy and agreeable, and as near as could well be in the centre, or at an equal distance from the eastern and western limits of the government; in which the common convenience was provided for. Nor was the prudence of the government less conspicuous in the provision made for the well ordering, for the instruction and government of this Society; particularly, if we may be allowed to say it, in respect of the persons to whom the inspection and oversight of it were committed; and who have all along given a vigilant and constant attention thereto. Which, by the way, they could not have done to so good effect, had it been situated at a much greater distance from this capital.

18. We devoutly adore the good Providence of God, which hath from the beginning presided over this seminary, and raised up worthy benefactors to it from time to time, as well in Europe as America. So that it hath, from its first institution, furnished these churches with faithful and able ministers, and the Commonwealth with worthy members, by whom the important offices in the government have been sustained with ability, fidelity, and reputation. . . .

9. *Charter of Rhode Island College (Brown University)*, *1764*

The first draft of this charter was written by Ezra Stiles (see Part III, Doc. 4), but the Providence Baptists in the Rhode Island Assembly objected that the Congregationalists would be given too much power; the revisions emerged from this dispute.

DRAFT AND REVISION OF CHARTER

. . . the Trustees shall and may be [thirty-five] *thirty-six;** of which [nineteen] *twenty-two* shall forever be elected of the denomination called Baptists [,] or *Anti-Pedobaptists,* [seven] *five* shall forever be elected of the denomination called [Congregationalists or Presbyterians] *Friends or Quakers,* [five] *four* shall forever be elected of the denomination called [Friends or Quakers] *Congregationalists,* and [four] *five* shall forever be elected of the denomination called Episcopalians [:]; and that the succession in this branch shall be forever chosen and filled up from the respective denominations in this proportion, and according to these numbers, which are hereby fixed. . . .
And that the number of the Fellows, [(] inclusive of the President [,] (who shall always be a Fellow) [,] shall and [may be] *maybe* twelve; of which eight shall *be* forever elected of the denomination called [Congregationalists] *Baptists, or Anti-Pedobaptists,* and the rest indifferently of any and all denominations. . . .
. . . and they are hereby declared [and established] the first and present Fellows and Fellowship, to whom the President, when hereafter elected (*who shall forever be of the denomination called Baptists or Anti-Pedobaptists*), shall be joined to complete the number.
And furthermore, it is declared and ordained, that the succession in both branches shall at all times hereafter be filled up and supplied according to these numbers, and this established and invariable pro-

---

Reuben A. Guild, *Life, Times and Correspondence of James Manning and the Early History of Brown University* (Providence, 1864), pp. 470–78.

* The parts of Stiles's draft which were omitted from the charter of 1764 have been placed in brackets; the parts of the charter of 1764 not included in Stiles's draft appear in italics.

portion, from the respective denominations, by the *separate* election [and concurrence] of both branches of this Corporation. . . .

. . . And in case any President, Trustee, or Fellow shall see cause to change his religious denomination, [or remove out of this Colony,] this Corporation are hereby empowered to declare his or their place or places vacant, and may proceed to fill it up accordingly[;], *as before directed;* [which upon the request of either branch being omitted by the body, either branch may proceed to declare and fill up their vacancy separately as aforesaid; otherwise] each Trustee and Fellow, not an officer of instruction, shall continue in his office during life, or until resignation. And further, in case either of the religious denominations should decline taking a part in this catholic, comprehensive, and liberal institution, the Trustees and Fellows shall and may complete their number, by electing from their respective denominations [indifferently,] always preserving their respective proportions herein before prescribed and determined: And all elections shall be by ballot, or written suffrage. . . .

And furthermore, it is hereby enacted and declared, that into this liberal and catholic institution shall never be admitted any religious tests; but, on the contrary, all the members hereof shall forever enjoy full, free, [unmolested, and absolute] *absolute, and uninterrupted* liberty of conscience: And that the places of [Presidents,] Professors, Tutors, and all other officers, *the President alone excepted,* shall be free and open for all denominations of Protestants: And that youth of all religious denominations shall and may be freely admitted to the equal advantages, emoluments, and honors of [this] *the* College or University; and shall receive a like fair, generous, and equal treatment during their residence therein, they conducting themselves peaceably, and conforming to the laws and statutes thereof: [And that to all the purposes of this Corporation persons of different sects shall be sufficiently distinguished and known by their free profession or declaration, and by their general attendance on the public worship of their respective denominations: And it is hereby ordained and declared, that in this College shall no undue methods or arts be practised to allure and proselyte one another, or to insinuate the peculiar principles of any one or other of the denominations into the youth in general; which, as well as the monopoly of offices, might discourage the sending of students to this College, involve unhappy controversies among the instructors, and defeat this good design: And it is thereupon agreed, declared, constituted and established, that everything of this nature shall be accounted a misdemeanor, mutually avoided as much as possible, and by all the denominations, generously disdained and discountenanced as beneath the dignity, and foreign from the true intention, of this Confederacy: That accordingly the public teaching shall in general respect the sciences, and that the sectarian differences of opinion, and controversies on the peculiarities of principle, shall not make any part of the public and classical instruction: Although all religious controversies may be studied freely, examined, and explained by the President, Professors, and Tutors, in a personal, separate, and distinct manner to the youth of any and each denomination, *they or their parents requesting the same.* [Italics in original Stiles.—eds.] And that in this the President, Professors, and Tutors shall treat the religion of each denomination with peculiar tenderness, charity, and respect; so that neither denomination shall be alarmed with jealousies or apprehensions of any illiberal and disingenuous attempts upon one another, but on the contrary an open, free, undesigning, and generous harmony; and a mutual honorable respect shall be recommended and endeavored, in order to exhibit an example in which literature may be advanced, on Protestant harmony, and the most perfect religious liberty: Yet, nevertheless, shall be publicly taught and explained to all the youth, the existence, character, and dominion of the Supreme Being, the general evidences of natural and revealed religion, and the principles of moral philosophy, and a constant regard be paid to, and effectual care taken of the morals of the College.] *And that the public teaching shall, in general, respect the sciences; and that the sectarian differences of opinion shall not make any part of the public and classical instruction: Although all religious controversies may be studied freely, examined, and explained by the President, Professors, and Tutors, in a personal, separate, and distinct manner, to the youth of any and each denomination: And above all, a constant regard be paid to, and effectual care taken of, the morals of the college.*

10. John Witherspoon's Account of the College of New Jersey, 1772

John Witherspoon (1723–94) was an active clergyman in the Scottish Presbyterian church when he was called in 1768 to assume the presidency of the College of New Jersey. A commanding figure, he was most successful in promoting the little college, adding much to its endowment, its student body, and its faculty. It occurred to Witherspoon that some of the well-to-do Englishmen in the West Indies might be induced to send their sons and their money to the college if they could be persuaded that it was healthier and more conducive to the protection of their morals than education in England. His appeal to them, given in greater part here, also serves the purpose of giving a brief rounded account of one of the most flourishing colonial colleges on the eve of the Revolution. Witherspoon was later active in political affairs and was one of the signers of the Declaration of Independence. See Varnum L. Collins, *President Witherspoon: A Biography* (2 vols.; Princeton, 1925).

It is unnecessary to begin this Address by a laboured encomium on Learning in general, or the importance of public Seminaries for the Instruction of Youth. Their use in every country; their necessity in a new or rising country; and, particularly the influence of Science, in giving a proper direction and full force to industry or enterprize, are indeed so manifest, that they are either admitted by all, or the exceptions are so few as to be wholly unworthy of regard.

In a more private view, the importance of Education is little less evident. It promotes virtue and happiness, as well as arts and industry. On this, as on the former, it is unnecessary to enlarge; only suffer me to make a remark, not quite so common, that, if there is any just comparison on this subject, the children of persons in the higher ranks of life, and, especially, of those who by their own activity and diligence, rise to opulence, have of all others the greatest need of an early, prudent and well conducted education. The wealth to which they are born becomes often a dangerous temptation, and the station in which they enter upon life, requires such duties, as those of the finest talents can scarcely be supposed capable of, unless they have been improved and cultivated with the utmost care. Experience shews the use of a liberal Education in both these views. It is generally a preservative from vices

Address to the Inhabitants of Jamaica, and Other West-India Islands in Behalf of the College of New-Jersey (Philadelphia, 1772).

of a certain class, by giving easy access to more refined pleasures, and inspiring the mind with an abhorrence of low riot and contempt for brutal conversation. It is also of acknowledged necessity to those who do not wish to live for themselves alone, but would apply their talents to the service of the public and the good of mankind. Education is therefore of equal importance in order either to enjoy life with dignity and elegance, or imploy it to the benefit of society, in offices of power or trust.

But leaving these general topics, or rather, taking it for granted that every thing of this kind is by intelligent persons, especially parents, both believed and felt; I proceed to inform the public that it is intended to sollicit Benefactions from the wealthy and generous, in behalf of a College of considerable standing, founded at Nassau-Hall in Princeton, New-Jersey. In order to this it is necessary for me—1. To shew the great advantage it will be to the inhabitants of the West-Indies, to have it in their power to send their children to approved places of education on the continent of America, instead of being obliged to send them over, for the very elements of Science, to South or North-Britain. 2. To point out the situation and advantages of the College of New-Jersey in particular. And as I was never a lover either of florid discourse, or ostentatious promises, I shall endeavour to handle these two points with all possible simplicity, and with that reserve and decency which are so necessary, where comparison in some respects cannot be avoided.

On the first of these points, let it be observed,

That places of education on the continent of America are much nearer to the West-Indies than those in Great-Britain; and yet sufficiently distant to remove the temptation of running home and lurking in idleness. This is a circumstance, which, other things being supposed equal, is by no means inconsiderable. Parents may hear much oftener from and of their children, and may even visit them, as is known to have been the case here, with no great loss of time for business, and to the advantage of their own health. They may also much more speedily and certainly be informed, whether they are profiting and have justice done them, or not, and remove or continue them at pleasure. . . .

Let it be further observed, that the climate of the continent of North-America is certainly much more healthy in itself, and, probably also, more suited to the constitutions of those who have been born in the West-Indies, than that of Great-Britain. Health is the foundation of every earthly blessing, and absolutely necessary, both to the receiving instruction in youth, and being able in riper years to apply it to its proper use. Parental tenderness will make every one feel the importance of this to his own children. . . .

It is hoped it will appear, that it would be much more to the advantage of the Gentlemen of the West-Indies to give their Children their Grammar-School and College Education, at least to their first degree in the Arts, in an American Seminary, if conducted by persons of ability and integrity, than to send them to Great-Britain; and that for two important reasons, first the better to secure their instruction, and secondly for the preservation of their morals.

1. For the greater security of their instruction. The Colleges in Britain have by no means that forcible motive that we have, not only to teach those who are willing to learn, but to see that every one be obliged to study, and actually learn, in proportion to his capacity. These old foundations have stood so many ages, have had their character so long established, and are, indeed, so well known to be filled with men of the greatest ability, that they do not so much as feel any injury, in point of reputation, from one or more coming out of College almost as ignorant as they went in. The truth is, I do not think they ought to lose any character by it. Every one knows, that it is owing to the idleness or profligacy of the boy, and not the insufficiency of the master. When the numbers of one class are from a hundred to a hundred and thirty, or perhaps more, and when they do not live in College, how is it possible the master can keep them to their private studies, or even with any certainty discern whether they study diligently or not. A good Professor is easily and speedily distinguished by his own performances, by the esteem, attachment, and progress of the diligent, but very little, if at all, hurt by the ignorance of the negligent. . . .

On the other hand, the young Seminaries in America have their character constantly at stake for their diligence, as one or two untaught coming out from us affects us in the most sensible manner. As to the College of New-Jersey in particular, we have seen the importance of this in so strong a light, that whereas before we had half-yearly, we now have quarterly examinations carried on with the utmost strictness, when all who are found deficient are degraded to the inferior class. So impartially have these trials been conducted, that nothing is more usual than for those who suspect themselves, especially, if their relations are near, to pretend sickness and avoid the examination, that they may afterwards fall back without the dishonour of a sentence. Further, all the scholars with us, as soon as they put on the gown, are obliged to lodge in College, and must of necessity be in their chambers in study-hours: nor is it in the least difficult to discover whether they apply carefully or not. The teachers also live in College, so that they have every possible advantage; not only for assisting the diligent but stimulating the slothful.

2. The second reason for prefering an American education is, that their morals may be more effectually preserved. This, by all virtuous and judicious parents, will be held a point of the last consequence. The danger they run of contracting vicious habits by being sent to Britain, has been often complained of, and therefore, I suppose, is matter of experience. If so, it will not be difficult to assign the causes of it, which may be safely mentioned, because they carry on imputation upon the Schools or Colleges to which they are sent. They generally are, and are always supposed to be, of great wealth. The very name of a West-Indian has come to imply in it great opulence. . . . There are also in every considerable place in Great-Britain, but especially the principal cities where the Colleges are fixed, a constant succession and variety of intoxicating diversions, such as Balls, Concerts, Plays, Races, and others. These, whatever may be pleaded for some of them in a certain measure for those further advanced, every body must acknowledge, are highly pernicious to youth in the first stages of their education. . . .

These Colleges must necessarily, in time, produce a number of young men proper to undertake the office of private tutors in gentlemen's families. There are some who prefer a private to a public education at any rate, especially in the very first stages, and some find it necessary as not being able to support their expence of sending their children so early, and keeping them so long from home. Now all who know the situation of things in Britain must be sensible, how difficult it is to get young men of capacity or expectation to leave their native country in order to undertake the instruction of Gentlemen's Children. In this office there is little prospect of increase of fortune, to balance the risk of going to a new and dangerous, or supposed dangerous climate. But those who are born and educated in American will not only increase the number of such Teachers, but they will have no such hideous apprehensions of going to any part of the continent or islands. Whatever is done, therefore, to raise and support proper Seminaries in America will, in time, be followed by this great and general benefit, which I have been assured is very much needed in many or most of the West-India Islands.

I will now proceed to speak a little of the Constitution and Advantages of the College of New-Jersey in particular. . . .

The regular course of instruction is in four classes, exactly after the manner and bearing the names of the classes in the English Universities; Freshman, Sophomore, Junior and Senior. In the first year they read Latin and Greek, with the Roman and Grecian antiquities, and Rhetoric. In the second, continuing the study of the languages, they learn a compleat system of Geography, with the use of the globes, the first principles of Philosophy, and the elements of mathematical knowledge. The third, though the languages are not wholly omitted, is chiefly employed in Mathematics and Natural Philosophy. And the senior year is employed in reading the higher classics, proceeding in the Mathematics and Natural Philosophy, and going through a course of Moral Philosophy. In addition to these, the President gives lectures to the juniors and seniors, which consequently every Student hears twice over in his course, first, upon Chronology and History, and afterwards upon Composition and Criticism. He has also taught the French language last winter, and it will continue to be taught to all who desire to learn it.

During the whole course of their studies the three younger classes, two every evening formerly, and now three, because of the increased number, pronounce an oration on a stage erected for that purpose in the hall, immediately after prayers, that they may learn by early habit presence of mind and proper pronunciation and gesture in public speaking. This excellent practice, which has been kept up almost from the first foundation of the College, has had the most admirable effects. The senior scholars every five or six weeks pronounce orations of their own composition, to which all persons of any note in the neighbourhood are invited or admitted.

The College is now furnished with all the most important helps to instruction. The Library contains a very large collection of valuable books. The lessons of Astronomy are given upon the Orrery, lately invented and constructed by David Rittenhouse, Esq; which is reckoned by the best judges the most excellent in its kind of any ever yet produced; and when what is commissioned and now upon its way is added to what the College already possesses, the appartus for Mathematics and Natural Philosophy will be equal, if not superior, to any on the continent.

As we have never yet been obliged to omit or alter it for want of scholars, there is a fixed annual Commencement on the last Wednesday of September, when, after a variety of public exercises, always attended by a vast concourse of the politest company, from the different parts of this province and the cities of New-York and Philadelphia, the students whose senior year is expiring are admitted to the degree of Batchelors of Arts; the Batchelors of three years standing, to the degree of Masters; and such other higher degrees granted as are either regularly claimed, or the Trustees think fit to bestow upon those who have distinguished themselves by their literary productions, or their appearances in public life.

On the day preceeding the Commencement last year there was (and it will be continued yearly hereafter) a public exhibition and voluntary contention for prizes, open for every member of College. These were first, second, and third prizes, on each of the following subjects. 1. Reading the English language with propriety and grace, and being able to answer all questions on its Orthography and Grammar. 2. Reading with Latin and Greek languages in the same manner with particular attention to true quantity. 3. Speaking Latin. 4. Latin versions. 5. Pronouncing English orations. The preference was determined by ballot, and all present permitted to vote, who were graduates of this or any other College.

As to the government of the College, no correction by stripes is permitted. Such as cannot be governed by reason and the principles of honour and shame are reckoned unfit for residence in a College. The collegiate censures are, 1. Private admonition by President, Professor, or Tutor. 2. Before the Faculty. 3. Before the whole class to which the offender belongs. 4. And the last and highest, before all the Members of College assembled in the hall. And, to preserve the weight and dignity of these censures, it has been an established practice that the last or highest censure, viz. public admonition, shall never be repeated upon the same person. If it has been thought necessary to inflict it upon any one, and if this does not preserve him from falling into such gross irregularities a second time, it is understood that expulsion is immediately to follow.

Through the narrowness of the funds the government and instruction has hitherto been carried on by a President and three Tutors. At last Commencement the Trustees chose a Professor of Mathematics, and intend, as their funds are raised to have a greater number of Professorships, and carry their plan to as great perfection as possible. . . .

The circumstances to which I would entreat the attention of impartial persons are the following.

1. The College of New-Jersey is altogether independent. It hath received no favour from Government but the charter, by the particular friendship of a person now deceased. It owes nothing but to the benefactions of a public so diffusive that it cannot produce particular dependance, or operate by partial influence. From this circumstance it must be free from *two* great evils, and derive the like number of solid advantages. There is no fear of being obliged to choose Teachers upon Ministerial recommendation, or in compliance with the over-bearing weight of family interest. On the contrary the Trustees are naturally led, and in a manner forced to found their choice upon the characters of the persons and the hope of public approbation. At the same time those concerned in the instruction and government of the College are as far removed, as the state of human nature will admit, from any temptation to a fawning cringing spirit and mean servility in the hope of Court favour or promotion.

In consequence of this it may naturally be expected, and we find by experience that hitherto in fact the spirit of liberty has breathed high and strong in all the Members. I would not be understood to say that a Seminary of Learning ought to enter deeply into political contention; far less would I meanly court favour by professing myself a violent partisan in any present disputes. But surely a constitution which naturally tends to produce a spirit of liberty and independance, even though this should sometimes need to be reined in by prudence and moderation, is infinitely preferable to the dead and vapid state of one whose very existence depends upon the nod of those in power. Another great advantage arising from this is the obligation we are under to recommend ourselves, by diligence and fidelity, to the public. Having no particular prop to lean to on one side, we are obliged to stand upright and firm by leaning equally on all. We are so far from having our fund so complete as of itself to support the necessary expence, that the greater part of our annual income arises from the payments of the Scholars, which we acknowledge with gratitude have been for these several years continually increasing.

2. This leads me to observe, that it ought to be no inconsiderable

recommendation of this College to those at a distance, that it has the esteem and approbation of those who are nearest it and know it best. The number of Under graduates or proper Members of College, is near four times that of any College on the continent to the southward of New-England, and probably greater than that of all the rest put together. This we are at liberty to affirm has in no degree arisen from pompous descriptions, or repeated recommendations in the public papers. We do not mean to blame the laudable attempts of others to do themselves justice. We have been often found fault with, and perhaps are to blame for neglect on this particular. It is only mentioned to give full force to the argument just now used; and the fact is certainly true. I do not remember that the name of the College of New-Jersey has been above once or twice mentioned in the news papers for three years, except in a bare recital of the acts of the annual Commencements. The present Address arises from necessity, not choice; for had not a more private application been found impracticable, the press had probably never been employed.

3. It may not be amiss to observe on this subject, that the great utility of this Seminary has been felt over an extensive country. Many of the Clergy, Episcopal and Presbyterian, in the different colonies, received their education here, whose exemplary behaviour and other merit we suffer to speak for themselves. We are also willing that the public should attend to the characters and appearance of those Gentlemen in the Law and Medical departments, who were brought up at Nassau-Hall, and are now in the cities of New-York and Philadelphia, and in different parts of the continent or islands. Two at least of the Professors of the justly celebrated Medical School lately founded in Philadelphia, and perhaps the greatest number of their pupils received their instruction here. We are not afraid, but even wish that our claim should be decided by the conduct of those in general who have come out from us, which is one of the most conclusive arguments, for *a tree is known by its fruits.* . . .

4. The place where the College is built is most happily chosen for the health, the studies and the morals of the scholars. . . . It is upon the great post-road almost equally distant from New-York and Philadelphia, so as to be a center of intelligence, and have an easy conveyance of every thing necessary, and yet to be wholly free from the many temptations in every great city, both to the neglect of study and the practice of vice. . . . It is not in the power of those who are in great

cities to keep the discipline with equal strictness, where boys have so many temptations to do evil, and can so easily and effectually conceal it after it is done. With us they live all in College under the inspection of their Masters, and the village is so small that any irregularity is immediately and certainly discovered, and therefore easily corrected.

It has sometimes happened, through rivalship or malice, that our discipline has been censured as too severe and rigorous. This reproach I always hear not with patience only but with pleasure. . . .

5. This College was founded, and hath been conducted upon the most Catholick Principles. The Charter recites as one of its grounds, "That every religious denomination may have free and equal liberty and advantage of education in the said College, any different sentiments in religion notwithstanding." Accordingly there are now, and have been from the beginning, scholars of various denominations from the most distant colonies, as well as West-India Islands; and they must necessarily confess that they never met with the least uneasiness or disrespect on this account. Our great advantage on this subject is the harmony of the Board of Trustees, and the perfect union in sentiment among all the Teachers both with the Trustees and with one another. On this account there is neither inclination or occasion to meddle with any controversy whatever. The author of this Address confesses that he was long accustomed to the order and dignity of an established church, but a church which hath no contempt or detestation of those who are differently organized. And, as he hath ever been in that church an opposer of lordly domination and sacerdotal tyranny, so he is a passionate admirer of the equal and impartial support of every religious denomination which prevails in the northern colonies, and is perfect in Pennsylvania and the Jerseys, to the unspeakable advantage of those happy and well constituted governments.

With respect to the College of New-Jersey, every question about forms of church government is so entirely excluded, that, though I have seen one set of scholars begin and finish their course, if they know nothing more of religious controversy than what they learned here, they have that Science wholly to begin. This is altogether owing to the union of sentiment mentioned above: for, if you place as Teachers in a College persons of repugnant religious principles, they must have more wisdom and self-denial than usually fall to the lot of humanity, if the whole Society is not divided into parties and marshalled under names, if the changes are not frequent, and, when they take place, as well known as any event that can happen in such a society. On the contrary there is so little occasion with us to canvass this matter at all, that, though no doubt accident must discover it as to the greatest number, yet some have left the College as to whom I am wholly uncertain at this hour to what denomination they belong. It has been and shall be our care to use every mean in our power to make them good men and good scholars; and, if this is the case, I shall hear of their future character and usefulness with unfeigned satisfaction, under every name by which a real Protestant can be distinguished.

Having already experienced the generosity of the public in many parts of the continent of America, I cannot but hope that the Gentlemen of the Islands will not refuse their assistance, according to their abilities, in order to carry this Seminary to a far greater degree of perfection than any to which it has yet arrived. The express purpose to which the benefactions now requested will be applied, is the establishment of new professorships, which will render the Institution not only more complete in itself, but less burthensome to those who have undertaken the important trust. The whole branches of Mathematics and Natural Philosophy are now taught by one Professor; and the President is obliged to teach Divinity and Moral Philosophy as well as Chronology, History, and Rhetoric, besides the superintendance and government of the whole. The short lives of the former Presidents have been by many attributed to their excessive labours, which, it is hoped, will be an argument with the humane and generous to lend their help in promoting so noble a design.

Part III

THE NATION, THE STATES,
AND THE SECTS

THE AMERICAN REVOLUTION transformed thinking on education, as on many other matters, and the legal independence of the states, followed by the creation of the new federal government, raised new questions about what the institutional setting of American higher education should be. Should education be left in the hands of the sects? Should the states, which had already begun to enlarge their roles as sponsors of education in an age of revolt against established churches, make themselves the primary or sole agents promoting colleges? Should the new federal union create its own university as a standard-setter and cultural center? If many competing agencies were at work in the educational field, would they not hamstring each other and create a collegiate chaos? How were the small and rather limited colleges of the colonial period to be enlarged into true universities, centers of general advanced study?

No one doubted the importance of education to the new society emerging in America, and good nationalists agreed with the framers of the first charter for a state university, that of Georgia (Doc. 1), that to send American youth abroad for their education would be a "humiliating acknowledgment" of "ignorance or inferiority." In the South and Southwest, liberal educational theorists, influenced by the

Enlightenment, hoped to rescue the collegiate system from sectarianism; and, taking advantage of the fact that a system of private sectarian colleges had not yet been established, they founded state institutions. The University of Georgia was chartered in 1785; it was soon followed by the University of North Carolina in 1789 (Doc. 5), the University of Tennessee in 1794, and the South Carolina College (later the University of South Carolina) in 1801. Still later, Jefferson, disappointed at the development of his alma mater, William and Mary, planned what was expected to be the most ambitious of the state institutions, the University of Virginia. The state university idea spread rapidly westward. In Michigan, for example, the legal foundations of a university were laid in territorial days (Doc. 11) in 1817, twenty years before Michigan became a state. The pompous terminology in which this "Catholepistemiad" was laid out did not augur well, but Michigan became one of the most distinguished of the state universities.

The period from the close of the Revolution through the first two decades of the nineteenth century was one of searching and reconsideration in educational theory. The liberals, as exemplified by Benjamin Rush (Docs. 2 and 5), hoped to make American education more secular and scientific, more general and practical, and to overleap the bounds and limits of the traditional classical college with its sectarian sponsorship. Even the older private schools, like King's, now renamed Columbia, and Yale yielded (Doc. 4) to greater state interference without actually becoming state institutions. Washington more than once proposed a national university to Congress (Doc. 3) as an aid to national unity, on the ground that "the more homogeneous our citizens can be made in [principles, opinions, and manners], the greater will be our prospect of permanent union." He was emulated in this respect by James Madison (Doc. 8), and the idea once received the indorsement of a committee of Congress (Doc. 9) in the nationalistic high tide following the War of 1812. Robert Finley, the president of the University of Georgia, once went so far as to propose national uniformity in textbooks (Doc. 16) as part of a scheme to make the nation's higher education genuinely systematic.

But the national university never came to be, and Thomas Jefferson was probably closer to the characteristic American preference for decentralization when he pitted his hopes upon the states as the sponsors of higher education. As early as 1800 he was planning a university

(Doc. 7) "on a plan so broad & liberal & *modern,* as to be worth patronizing with the public support, and be a temptation to the youth of other states to come and drink the cup of knowledge & fraternize with us." In 1818 the Rockfish Gap Commission (Docs. 12 and 13), appointed to pick a site for the University of Virginia, presented a full-fledged statement of the state university ideal that embodied many of Jefferson's ideas. The legislature responded less promptly than Jefferson had hoped (Doc. 17) and gave him to feel that Virginia might never be able to compete with Massachusetts in education (for the germs of sectional hostility had already begun to eat away at the "fraternization" that Jefferson had envisaged in 1800). But the project went onward, and in 1824 Jefferson's friend Francis Walker Gilmer went abroad on a quest for some of the best professorial talents in Europe (Doc. 18)—over the solemn warning of John Adams (Doc. 20), who predicted that European professors would merely bring with them the dogmatic controversies of the European past. By 1824 a somewhat modernized plan of studies had been drawn up by Rector Jefferson and the Board of Visitors (Doc. 19).

State universities, notably in the South and West, were to remain an important part of American education, though their full flowering did not come until after the Civil War. The immediate future of higher education lay with the small private college. A turning point in this respect was the Dartmouth College case of 1819. Dartmouth had become involved in state politics in 1816 when the Jeffersonian Republicans reorganized the college, under a revised charter, as Dartmouth University. The college trustees refused to abide by the law and kept a college operating in Hanover side by side with the newly created institution. The Republican court of New Hampshire decided that the newly created Dartmouth was the valid one, but the college trustees appealed to the Supreme Court. There Daniel Webster (Doc. 14) eloquently argued that the Dartmouth charter was a contract and that the attempt to change it was an impairment of the obligation of contract in violation of the federal Constitution. He further argued that the college would constantly skirt destruction if it could be made the frequent object of changes in public opinion or the vicissitudes of party politics. In a momentous decision (Doc. 15) John Marshall expressed his agreement with Webster both on the question of contract and on the argument that the college was a private rather than a public corporation. This decision had profound consequences for all corporations, including business enterprises. In the educational field it meant that private colleges, once chartered, would now be secure from state interference; and it helped to create a firm legal foundation for the little colleges that soon began to mushroom wildly throughout the country.

The gravest problem confronting the collegiate system, as it proliferated throughout the rapidly developing country, was the failure of the sects to co-operate. A few years before the Dartmouth College case, a review of theological and collegiate education (Doc. 10) found the country's colleges largely under sectarian control. Distinguished educators like Philip Lindsley in the South (Doc. 21), Julian M. Sturtevant in the West (Doc. 22), and Francis Wayland in New England (Doc. 23) all saw the colleges as resting mainly in the hands of the sects; and they found in sectarianism the besetting problem of educational organization. Lindsley, surveying the condition of the colleges in 1837 (Doc. 24) from the vantage point of his own University of Nashville, set the goal of nonpartisanship in religion and politics—freedom from the "political or sectarian college."

1. Charter of the University of Georgia, 1785

Although the University of Georgia was the earliest "state" institution by reason of the charter of 1785, here reprinted in part, it was not until 1881 that the state appropriated funds directly for its support. On the "profitless dispute" over which was the "first" state university, see John S. Brubacher and Willis Rudy, *Higher Education in Transition* (New York, 1958), pp. 141–42, 423 n.

As it is the distinguishing happiness of free governments, that civil order should be the result of choice, and not necessity, and the common wishes of the people become the laws of the land, their public prosperity, and even existence, very much depends upon suitably forming the minds and morals of their citizens. Where the minds of the people in general are viciously disposed and unprincipled, and their

"By the representatives of the freemen of the State of Georgia in general assembly, and by the authority of the same. An Act for the more full and complete establishment of a public seat of learning in this State," in Robert and George Watkins (eds.), *A Digest of the Laws of the State of Georgia . . . to 1798 . . .* (Philadelphia, 1800), pp. 299–302.

conduct disorderly, a free government will be attended with greater confusions, and with evils more horrid than the wild uncultivated state of nature: It can only be happy where the public principles and opinions are properly directed, and their manners regulated. This is an influence beyond the sketch of laws and punishments, and can be claimed only by religion and education. It should therefore be among the first objects of those who wish well to the national prosperity, to encourage and support the principles of religion and morality, and early to place the youth under the forming hand of society, that by instruction they may be moulded to the love of virtue and good order. Sending them abroad to other countries for their education will not answer these purposes, is too humiliating an acknowledgment of the ignorance or inferiority of our own, and will always be the cause of so great foreign attachments, that upon principles of policy it is not admissible.

This country, in the times of our common danger and distress, found such security in the principles and abilities which wise regulations had before established in the minds of our countrymen, that our present happiness, joined to pleasing prospects, should conspire to make us feel ourselves under the strongest obligation to form the youth, the rising hope of our land, to render the like glorious and essential services to our country. . . .

4th. As the appointment of a person to be the president and head of the university is one of the first and most important concerns, on which its respect and usefulness greatly depend, the board of trustees shall first examine and nominate, but the appointment of the president shall be by the two boards jointly, who shall also have the power of removing him from office for misdemeanor, unfaithfulness, or incapacity. . . .

7th. The trustees shall have the power of filling up all vacancies of their own board, and appointing professors, tutors, secretary, treasurers, steward, or any other officers which they may think necessary, and the same to discontinue or remove, as they may think fit; but not without seven of their number, at least, concurring in such act.

8th. The trustees shall prescribe the course of public studies, appoint the salaries of the different officers, form and use a public seal, adjust and determine the expences, and adopt such regulations, not otherwise provided for, which the good of the university may render necessary.

9th. All officers appointed to the instruction and government of the university, shall be of the christian religion; and within three months after they enter upon the execution of their trust, shall publicly take the oath of allegiance and fidelity, and the oaths of office prescribed in the statutes of the university; the president before the governor or president of council, and all other officers before the president of the university.

10th. The president, professors, tutors, students, and all officers and servants of the university whose office require their constant attendance, shall be, and they are hereby excused from military duty, and from all other such like duties and services; and all lands and other property of the university is hereby exempted from taxation.

11th. The trustees shall not exclude any person of any religious denomination whatsoever, from free and equal liberty and advantages of education, or from any of the liberties, privileges, and immunities of the university in his education, on account of his or their speculative sentiments in religion, or being of a different religious profession.

12th. The president of the university, with consent of the trustees, shall have power to give and confer all such honors, degrees and licenses as are usually conferred in colleges or universities, and shall always preside at the meeting of the trustees, and at all the public exercises of the university. . . .

JOSEPH HABERSHAM
Speaker

Savannah, January 27, 1785

2. *Benjamin Rush on a Federal University, 1788*

Benjamin Rush (1745–1813) was born on a plantation near Philadelphia and was a graduate of Princeton (1760), later a student of medicine at the College of Philadelphia and at Edinburgh. He began medical practice in Philadelphia in 1769, published the first American chemistry textbook in 1770, became a member of the American Philosophical Society and a leading exponent of the abolition of slavery. A member of the Continental Congress, he was a signer of the Declaration of Independence and subsequently served during the Revolutionary War as surgeon-general of the armies of the Middle Department. Although his fame was due mainly to his work in medicine, he remained active in public affairs and in education as well

"To Friends of the Federal Government: A Plan for a Federal University," in L. H. Butterfield (ed.), *Letters of Benjamin Rush* (Princeton, N.J., 1951), I, 491–95.

and was one of the first planners of Dickinson College and a member of its Board of Trustees (see Part IV, Doc. 1). Rush was among the earliest advocates of a federal university. This paper originally appeared under a pseudonym in the Philadelphia *Federal Gazette,* October 29, 1788. The proposal that only graduates of the federal university be eligible to federal service would surely have been unpopular, and it has been suggested that this accounts for the omission of this piece from Rush's *Essays* (1798). See Doc. 6 and N. G. Goodman, *Benjamin Rush, Physician and Citizen* (Philadelphia, 1934), and H. G. Good, *Benjamin Rush and His Services to American Education* (Berne, Ind., 1918).

"Your government cannot be executed. It is too extensive for a republic. It is contrary to the habits of the people," say the enemies of the Constitution of the United States.—However opposite to the opinions and wishes of a majority of the citizens of the United States, these declarations and predictions may be, they will certainly come to pass, unless the people are prepared for our new form of government by an education adapted to the new and peculiar situation of our country. To effect this great and necessary work, let one of the first acts of the new Congress be, to establish within the district to be allotted for them, federal university, into which the youth of the United States shall be received after they have finished their studies, and taken their degrees in the colleges of their respective states. In this University, let those branches of literature only be taught, which are calculated to prepare our youth for civil and public life. These branches should be taught by means of lectures, and the following arts and sciences should be the subjects of them.

1. The principles and forms of government, applied in a particular manner to the explanation of every part of the Constitution and laws of the United States, together with the laws of nature and nations, which last should include every thing that relates to peace, war, treaties, ambassadors, and the like.

2. History both ancient and modern, and chronology.

3. Agriculture in all its numerous and extensive branches.

4. The principles and practice of manufactures.

5. The history, principles, objects and channels of commerce.

6. Those parts of mathematics which are necessary to the division of property, to finance, and to the principles and practice of war, for there is too much reason to fear that war will continue, for some time to come, to be the unChristian mode of deciding disputes between Christian nations.

7. Those parts of natural philosophy and chemistry, which admit of an application to agriculture, manufactures, commerce and war.

8. Natural history, which includes the history of animals, vegetables and fossils. To render instruction in these branches of science easy, it will be necessary to establish a museum, as also a garden, in which not only all the shrubs, &c. but all the forest trees of the United States should be cultivated. The great Linnaeus of Upsal enlarged the commerce of Sweden, by his discoveries in natural history. He once saved the Swedish navy by finding out the time in which a worm laid its eggs, and recommending the immersion of the timber, of which the ships were built, at that season wholly under water. So great were the services this illustrious naturalist rendered his country by the application of his knowledge to agriculture, manufactures and commerce, that the present king of Sweden pronounced an eulogium upon him from his throne, soon after his death.

9. Philology which should include, besides rhetoric and criticism, lectures upon the construction and pronunciation of the English language. Instruction in this branch of literature will become the more necessary in America, as our intercourse must soon cease with the bar, the stage and the pulpits of Great Britain, from whence we received our knowledge of the pronounciation of the English language. Even modern English books should cease to be the models of style in the United States. The present is the age of simplicity in writing in America. The turgid style of Johnson—the purple glare of Gibbon, and even the studied and thick set metaphors of Junius, are all equally unnatural, and should not be admitted into our country. . . . The cultivation and perfection of our language becomes a matter of consequence when viewed in another light. It will probably be spoken by more people in the course of two or three centuries, than ever spoke any one language at one time since the creation of the world. When we consider the influence which the prevalence of only *two* languages, viz. the English and the Spanish, in the extensive regions of North and South America, will have upon manners, commerce, knowledge and civilization, scenes of human happiness and glory open before us, which elude from their magnitude the utmost grasp of the human understanding.

10. The German and French languages should be taught in this University. The many excellent books which are written in both these languages upon all subjects, more especially upon those which relate

to the advancement of national improvements of all kinds, will render a knowledge of them an essential part of the education of a legislator of the United States.

11. All those athletic and manly exercises should likewise be taught in the University, which are calculated to impart health, strength, and elegance to the human body.

To render the instruction of our youth as easy and extensive as possible in several of the above mentioned branches of literature, let four young men of good education and active minds be sent abroad at the public expense, to collect and transmit to the professors of the said branches all the improvements that are daily made in Europe, in agriculture, manufactures and commerce, and in the art of war and practical government. This measure is rendered the more necessary from the distance of the United States from Europe, by which means the rays of knowledge strike the United States so partially, that they can be brought to a useful focus, only by employing suitable persons to collect and transmit them to our country. It is in this manner that the northern nations of Europe have imported so much knowledge from their southern neighbours, that the history of agriculture, manufactures, commerce, revenues and military arts of *one* of these nations will soon be alike applicable to all of them.

Besides sending four young men abroad to collect and transmit knowledge for the benefit of our country, *two* young men of suitable capacities should be employed at the public expense in exploring the vegetable, mineral and animal productions of our country, in procuring histories and samples of each of them, and in transmitting them to the professor of natural history. It is in consequence of the discoveries made by young gentlemen employed for these purposes, that Sweden, Denmark and Russia have extended their manufactures and commerce, so as to rival in both the oldest nations in Europe.

Let the Congress allow a liberal salary to the Principal of the university. Let it be his business to govern the students, and to inspire them by his conversation, and by occasional public discourses, with federal and patriotic sentiments. Let this Principal be a man of extensive education, liberal manners and dignified deportment.

Let the Professors of each of the branches that have been mentioned, have a moderate salary of 150*l.* or 200*l.* a year, and let them depend upon the number of their pupils to supply the deficiency of their maintenance from their salaries. Let each pupil pay for each course of lectures two or three guineas.

Let the degrees conferred in this university receive a new name, that shall designate the design of an education for civil and public life.

In thirty years after this university is established, let an act of Congress be passed to prevent any person being chosen or appointed into power or office, who has not taken a degree in the federal university. We require certain qualifications in lawyers, physicians and clergymen, before we commit our property, our lives or our souls to their care. We even refuse to commit the charge of a ship to a pilot, who cannot produce a certificate of his education and knowledge in his business. Why then should we commit our country, which includes liberty, property, life, wives and children, to men who cannot produce vouchers of their qualifications for the important trust? We are restrained from injuring ourselves by employing quacks in law; why should we not be restrained in like manner, by law, from employing quacks in government?

Should this plan of a federal university or one like it be adopted, then will begin the golden age of the United States. While the business of education in Europe consists in lectures upon the ruins of Palmyra and the antiquities of Herculaneum, or in disputes about Hebrew points, Greek particles, or the accent and quantity of the Roman language, the youth of America will be employed in acquiring those branches of knowledge which increase the conveniences of life, lessen human misery, improve our country, promote population, exalt the human understanding, and establish domestic, social and political happiness.

Let it not be said, "that this is not the *time* for such a literary and political establishment. Let us first restore public credit, by funding or paying our debts, let us regulate our militia, let us build a navy, and let us protect and extend our commerce. After this, we shall have leisure and money to establish a University for the purposes that have been mentioned." This is false reasoning. We shall never restore public credit, regulate our militia, build a navy, or revive our commerce, until we remove the ignorance and prejudices, and change the habits of our citizens, and this can never be done 'till we inspire them with federal principles, which can only be effected by our young men meeting and spending two or three years together in a national University, and afterwards disseminating their knowledge and principles through every county, township and village of the United States. 'Till this be done

—Senators and Representatives of the United States, you will undertake to make bricks without straw. Your supposed union in Congress will be a rope of sand. The inhabitants of Massachusetts began the business of government by establishing the University of Cambridge, and the wisest Kings in Europe have always found their literary institutions the surest means of establishing their power as well as of promoting the prosperity of their people.

These hints for establishing the Constitution and happiness of the United States upon a permanent foundation, are submitted to the friends of the federal government in each of the states, by a private

CITIZEN OF PENNSYLVANIA

3. Washington to Congress on a National University, 1790, 1796

All of the first six presidents of the United States agreed on the desirability of a national university, and Washington, Jefferson, Madison, and John Quincy Adams sent requests to Congress asking for the establishment of such an institution. Washington left a bequest to Congress for this purpose, but it was never used. For the idea of a national university, see Edgar B. Wesley, *Proposed: The University of the United States* (Minneapolis, Minn., 1936), and J. S. Brubacher and Willis Rudy, *Higher Education in Transition,* chap. xi.

JANUARY 8, 1790

Nor am I less persuaded that you will agree with me in opinion, that there is nothing which can better deserve your patronage than the promotion of Science and Literature. Knowledge is in every country the surest basis of public happiness. In one in which the measures of Government receive their impression so immediately from the sense of the Community as in ours, it is proportionably essential. To the security of a free Constitution it contributes in various ways: By convincing those who are intrusted with the public administration, that every valuable end of Government is best answered by the enlightened confidence of the people: and by teaching the people themselves to know and to

John C. Fitzpatrick (ed.), *Writings of George Washington, 1745–1799,* XXX (Washington, D.C., 1939), 493–94; XXXV (Washington, D.C., 1940), 316–17.

value their own rights; to discern and provide against invasions of them; to distinguish between oppression and the necessary exercise of lawful authority; between burthens proceeding from a disregard to their convenience and those resulting from the inevitable exigencies of society; to discriminate the spirit of Liberty from that of licentiousness, cherishing the first, avoiding the last, and uniting a speedy, but temperate vigilance against encroachments, with an inviolable respect to the Laws.

Whether this desirable object will be best promoted by affording aids to seminaries of learning already established, by the institution of a national University, or by any other expedients, will be well worthy of a place in the deliberations of the Legislature. . . .

DECEMBER 7, 1796

The Assembly to which I address myself, is too enlightened not to be fully sensible how much a flourishing state of the Arts and Sciences contributes to National prosperity and reputation. True it is, that our Country, much to its honor, contains many Seminaries of learning highly respectable and useful; but the funds upon which they rest, are too narrow, to command the ablest Professors, in the different departments of liberal knowledge, for the Institution contemplated, though they would be excellent auxiliaries.

Amongst the motives to such an Institution, the assimilation of the principles, opinions, and manners of our Country men, but the common education of a portion of our Youth from every quarter, well deserves attention. The more homogeneous our citizens can be made in these particulars, the greater will be our prospect of permanent Union; and a primary object of such a National Institution should be, the education of our Youth in the science of *Government*. In a Republic, what species of knowledge can be equally important? and what duty, more pressing on its Legislature, than to patronize a plan for communicating it to those, who are to be the future guardians of the liberties of the Country?

The Institution of a Military Academy is also recommended by cogent reasons. However pacific the general policy of a Nation may be, it ought never to be without an adequate stock of Military knowledge for emergencies. The first would impair the energy of its character, and both would hazard its safety, or expose it to greater evils when War could not be avoided. Besides that War might often not depend upon its own choice. In proportion as the observance of pacific maxims might exempt a Nation from the necessity of practising the rules of the military Art, ought to be its care in preserving and transmitting, by proper establishments, the knowledge of that Art. Whatever argument may be drawn from particular examples, superficially viewed, a thorough examination of the subject will evince, that the Art of War is at once comprehensive and complicated; that it demands much previous study; and that the possession of it, in its most improved and perfect state, is always of great moment to the security of a nation. This, therefore, ought to be a serious care of every Government; and for this purpose, an Academy, where a regular course of instruction is given, is an obvious expedient, which different Nations have successfully employed.

4. Ezra Stiles on Changes in the Yale Corporation, 1792

Ezra Stiles (1727–95) is the commanding figure in the history of Yale College during the latter part of the eighteenth century. There he was student (1742–46), tutor (1749–55), and president (1778–95). While serving as pastor of the Second Congregational Church of Newport, Rhode Island (1755–77), Stiles also played an important role in the chartering of Rhode Island College (Brown University)—see Part II, Doc. 9. During his Yale presidency Stiles demonstrated immense learning in languages and history, profound intellectual curiosity in scientific matters, devotion to the American Revolution, and skill in administration. No man then in academic life displayed more admirably the viewpoint of the American Enlightenment.

A major development during his regime was a change in the college charter, whereby several state officials were made ex officio members of the Yale Corporation with all the rights of the original Fellows and Yale received some financial aid from the state. The following excerpts from his *Diary* in the early summer of 1792 record his views on the matter.

The best brief survey to date of Stiles's life, apart from his massive *Literary Diary* (3 vols.) cited below, is Harris Elwood Starr's account in Dumas Malone (ed.), *Dictionary of American Biography*, XVIII (New York, 1936), 18–21. On

F. B. Dexter (ed.), *The Literary Diary of Ezra Stiles* (New York, 1901), III, 460–63, 452–56. Reprinted with the permission of Yale University Library.

his undergraduate years at Timothy Clap's Yale (see Part I, Doc. 11), see Edmund
S. Morgan, "Ezra Stiles: The Education of a Yale Man, 1742–46," *Huntington
Library Quarterly,* XVII (May, 1954), 251–68.

[May 31, 1792] While at Hartford at Election, I had much Conversation of the proposal for joyning Civilians to the Corporation, which
many are much engaged for. They said if the Corporation would only
consent to joyn Civilians, *any number,* it would give Satisfaction. In
1777 I was convinced that they replied nothing short of a Majority. But
they would never bring it out. They dwelt only on generals; sometimes
saying if two or 3, *any number* were joyned, all would go well. But
whenever I askd whether any Thing short of an Equality or Majority
would give Satisfaction, they either replied nothing or evaded; saying
if we would only agree to associate any Civilians, they doubted not all
would be settled. I knew otherwise from the first—& knew that this
Surrendery could never be carried in the then Corporation—& besides
tho' I did not see but that admission of a few Civilians might be done
with safety, yet I never could see that this would give radical Satisfaction; & I never could see that it would be wise to give it up to a Majority of Civilians & out of the hands of Ecclesiastics. At this time I
determined to investigate the matter thoroughly. All pretended to an
open free Conference, & unreserved Communication on both sides, the
Committee of Assembly & Corporation who were all present at this
Interview at Hartford. And yet I plainly perceived that both were on
the Reserve & cautious.

In a distinct Interview at this Election with 3 Gent. separately who
have always been deep in the Scheme for bringing in Civilians I
pressed them with several investigating Questions.

Mr. M— had proposed joyning the Gov., Lieutenant G. & Council,
the Speaker of the House, & Chief Just. of the Superior Court to be in
all Successions. I started 2 Difficulties. 1. That the Corporation might
have Causes come before the Sup. Court, in which Case, the Judge
must be taken off the Bench. 2. As the Gov. & Council were a Court of
Errors, if a Cause in which Y[ale] C[ollege] was a party shd. come up
to that Court, the whole must be taken off if of the Corporation & so
there be no Court to sit on such a Cause. He did not reply to this so as
to remove the Difficulty: but said if the Gov. & Council shd. not do, a
Board of Civilians (not official Characters) might be appointed. Upon
which among other Queries, as who shd. fill up the Succession, them-

selves or Assembly, I asked what Number? He said any Number. I asked if an equal Number of Civ. & Eccl. would satisfy? He said yes. If a less number? He did not know; but however if once consented to an Alteration Things could be easily settled to mutual Satisfaction. I then stated, supposing it shd. be agreed that the Corporation shd. consist of two Thirds Ecclesiastics & one Third Civilians, & this be a permanent & fundamental Constitution? I saw in an Instant he hesitated, & said he doubted whether it would give Satisfaction; and that he was sorry the Corporation did not shew a Disposition to negotiate upon the matter, as this was a very opportune Time for it.

After this on the same day I spent 2 hours with Mr. S—. We conversed on three modes. 1. Gov. & Council. 2. A distinct Board with a negative on the Corporation. 3. Enlargment of the number of the Fellows by associating Civilians, & leaving both open to future Elections, so that they might possibly hereafter be all Ecclesiastics, or all Civilians, or always mixt. We canvassed each. Among other Things I again stated that the Corporation be permanently fixt one Third Civilians, & 2/3 Ecclesiastics: & asked if this would satisfy the Assembly & public? And he fully answered, it would not.

The next day Mr. C— attackt me upon the subject of an Alteration. I went over much the same as with Mr. M. He said he was not sollicitous as to the Mode, if Civilians were conjoyned in any form, it would satisfy. I then observed that after hearing much said on the subject, I was at a loss for Gentlemen's real minds; but that I thot that 2 Modes might give radical Satisfaction, tho' I doubted whether either could be carried thro' the Assembly. 1. The Gov. & Council. He said it would. 2. A Board of Civilians superior in Number or perhaps equal to Ecclesiastics, & this either conjoyned with or distinct from & with a negative on the Eccl. or present Board. He said it would. I then told him I wished to submit to his Judgment, whether a Constitution in which it shd be fundamental that the Civilians be one Third, the Eccl. Two Thirds, would be acceptable? I instantly perceived him hesitate—then said an Equality would do, but he believed the proposal of 2/3 & 1/3 would give Umbrage & excite Jealousies & Fears or apprehension least the Clergy were aiming at a Superiority over the Civilians. I plainly saw his Mind, & his Idea on the public Mind, that nothing short of Superiority or at least Equality would effect a radical Coalition. In conversing on filling or keeping up the succession in a supposed equal Board, He proposed it shd. be perpetuated in their own Election. I asked whether this could be carried thro' the Assembly, he hesitated a little & said he did not wish to have the Assembly fill up the Vacancies by their own Election as Vacancies fell; and especially as he knew, that the secret Society of nocturnal Stelligeri (now disgraced) intended to move in the Assembly, if ever Things were ripened so far, that the *whole Corporation* like the Judges of Courts, shd be *annually* appointed & chosen by the Assembly, & would be resolute to carry it, which he by no means approved. But he supposed a Constitution satisfactory to all parties might be carried thro' the Assembly in such form as shd. be agreed on, & greatly to the Honor & Emolument of the College. Thus I see, that after all the Talk & Negotiating nothing will give radical Satisfaction, but such a Mutilation as is a total Abolition & Surrendery of the College Constitution, & wresting it out the Hands of Ministers into the Hands of Civilians. The pursuing the matter any further will necessarily lead us to give Offence to Civilians & increase their Disgust, unless we shd make a Surrendery.

When I came into the Presidency 1777, all the Fellows were of one Mind on this same Question which was then very formally agitated & discussed between a Committee of Assembly & the Corporation. I have lived to see some alterations in old & new Members. I have lived to see a time when could the matter be ripened & prepared & fairly laid before the Fellows *without endangering the whole,* & their Opinion or Vote taken on the Reception or Rejection of a New Charter permanently establishing Two Thirds & One Third as before, it would be accepted by a Majority of the Body, perhaps 7 out of 11. But they all fear least we shd be carried too far. And as far as I know or can judge on their Sentiments, for all are cautious, on a Charter of Equality or Superiority of Civilians, I believe all would concurr in *not* receiving it, at most two would accept it perhaps, & yet I very much doubt whether more than one, & he reluctantly—& these two would not vote it if they found the rest of their Brethren against it. It would assuredly come to this, which would disgust the Assembly & public. This the Corporation have no Desire to do, tho' they have no pecuniary Expectations from the Assembly, which would never do much in money matters or giving Funds or endowing Professorships, even if the College was altered to their Minds. They would make the Scholars support the Instructors.

Civilians I doubt not would rule the College well, & so do Ecclesiastics. Three Quarters of the Clergy & more are fond of its present Constitution. And yet the 2/3 & 1/3 would in my Opin. have so effectively secured it, that would such an alteration have really sweetned & calmed the incessant Complaints of the public, I shd have concurred & believe it would have succeeded. But as fr. the beginning I foresaw that this could not be effected and that if effected, would yet give no Satisfaction; I was always therefore fr. the beginning averse & reluctant against taking up & agitating the Question, & wished it might never come up in my day. I promised Fidelity to the Constitution of the College at my first accession: and however light & easy it may be with unprincipled Politicians to sell, alter & destroy the fundamental Constitutions of well formed Societies for supposed better Forms, yet I never could bring my Mind to feel easy in enterprizing the Ruin & Eversion of so wise & excellent a Constit. as that of Yale Colege, for no other Reason than that it is in the Hands of sensible pious and learned Ecclesiastics, however disgustful to Civilians especially to those of a deistical Turn, or who however firm Revelationists have imbibed under the Idea of liberal Sentiments principles in Law, Polity & Government which endanger the Loss of all Religion, especially Congregationalism, from the civil State. As a Friend to the Ch[urc]hs & Pastors, to the Cause that brought our pious Ancestors to America, as a Friend to Virtue & Literature, I am decidedly now, as I have been from the Beginning, for Adherence to the present Charter. It is and doubtless always will be the only Amer. College in the Hands of Ecclesiastics. If well conducted, it may exhibit a noble Example & be a standing Monument & Proof, that Ecclesiastics can conduct an Institution for the highest Literature, with a Success & Glory equal to the other Sister Colleges, tho' all governed by a Mixture of Civilians & Ecclesiastics.

I am apprehensive that the Civilians or Committee will joyn with their Report to this Assembly, the Recommendation of a Junction of the Gov. & Council with the Corporation either with or without a Negative; and address this offer to the Corporation for their Concurrence or Rejection. I should be sorry to be embarrassed with such an Address. I foresee we shall be entangled & at great Difficulty. A Rejection would be converted into Obloquy against the College & increase the Offence & Disgust of the Civilians; & an Adoption will not only wrest the College out of the Hands of Ecclesiastics, but bring the deistical & mixt Characters hereafter ascending into the Council to such a Controll & Influence in this Institution as to neutralize & gradually to annihilate the Religion of the College, & so to lower down & mutilate the Course of Education, & model it to the Tast of the Age, as that in a few years we shall make no better Scholars than the other Colleges, or the Univ. of Oxford & Cambridge. May that superintending Provid. which has watched over the College hitherto continue its guardian & Protector. But I rather anticipate disageeable [*sic*] Consequences from these pressing & insidious Negotiations for an Alteration of the College Constitution.

If a Board of Civilians (not Gov. & Council) shd be proposed, I forsee 2 Things. 1. That there will be an uncomfortable Struggle for a Mixture constitutionally of Cong., Baptists, Episcopalians, Separatists, and those who under the Idea of Catholicism will be neutrals, Deists, Indifferentists. 2. That with respect to this Board, no religious Tests must be admitted, not so much as whether they are Revelationists, & the Door must be kept open for Deists & Enemies to all Sects of Xtians. 3. That this will produce an Effort for the Abolition to the present religious Test & Subscription as a qualification for the ecclesiastical Branch. The same for qualifying Tutors, Presidents & Professors as well as Fellows. In short the Religion & that good Order which arises from the Religion of the original Institution must be laid prostrate. This would be justly grievous to the 160 Ministers of the State; & excite them to set up a voluntary independent Institution for the Education of Ministers in the learned Languages, the Sciences & Theology. And their Assiduity would make such an Institution, tho' indigent, of higher Reputation for real Scholarship & Security of Morals than the proposed one by Civilians, unless there shd be Security that future Civilians would be like their Predecessors of the last Century in N. England, cordial Friends to *Religion* as well as *Learning,* which is no longer to be expected in these States, under the Example of Congress & all the present Assemblies of the States, in which there is such a mixture of, not only diff. Sects, but even Debauchees, Deists & Infidels. . . .

[June] 27. At [six hours] P. M. the Corporation voted an Acceptance of the Act of Assembly, nine yeas, Mr. Taylor hesitated wishing for longer Consideration, but against rejecting—doubtful.

This brings the Gov. D. Gov. [Governor, Deputy Governor] & 6 Senior Assistants into the Corporation, 4 Civilians & 6 Ecclesiastics to be a Quorum & the present Corporation to perpetuate their own Succession. And an addition of 30 Thousd Doll. to the Coll. Estate.

28. This Morning the Board compleated the Vote of yesterday *in form,* when it passed unanimously, Mr. Taylor acceding. He & Mr.

Ely were for postponing for further learning the Opinion of the
Clergy. . . . I am not certain that Mr. Hart wished for Alteration but
Mr. Williams, Ely & Taylor did—but they were all convinced that
there would be danger that the Alterations would be for the worse.
They wished the President & Professor of Divinity shd. be in the election of Ministers exclusively, but they foresaw if Amendments were
proposed on our part, they risqued urging Amendments on the part
of the Civilians & overthrowing the whole, or making it less acceptable
than at present: and the present plan was nearly to their mind if they
had any Civilians joyned. Mr. T. was agt. any Civilians being joyned
least we shd. not stop, till some future Corporation by Intrigue might
be induced to surrender all into the Hands of a Plurality of Civilians—
in which case it was agreed that the Constitution of College would be
fundamentally altered from its original Foundation, of which we were
all unanimously tenacious. It was put whether if it had been proposed
to add 8 Ministers, the Reception would have been giving up the
Charter or Constitution? it was on all hands agreed, not: even if ever
so many Ministers had been joyned. It was then put if a Majority or
say 12 or more Civilians were joyned, would this be giving up the
Charter & Constitution? it was agreed that it clearly would be:—if a
Minority of Civilians added would this &c—All were satisfied it would
not be, but Mr. Taylor—& he only because the same power of the Body
that could give up or receive a Minority might proceed to further
Reception, till all was lost from the Ecclesiastics. The Danger of this
was attended to. It was considered that the Civilians were convinced
of the good Economy & Government of the College & heartily tired
out of a 40 years storming against it & finding they could not kill it,
as it had got good Reputation & about £1200 per ann. Revenue &
could subsist, unless the Charter was forceably rent away, which however they mediated 15 years ago they now gave up: that while N. York,
Pensylvania & other surrounding States were patronizing Literature
& doing great Things making bounteous Donations to their Colleges,
they were ashamed Connecticutt shd do nothing for an Institution in
good Reputation thro' the U. S. and therefore wanted to do something
to purpose: they were convinced that to set up another College, which
the State could do, would injure both, & that one was sufficient for this
State, as they were building Colleges all around us. They were therefore disposed to be tired of an Effort against [Yale] C[ollege] & wished
to be concerned in building it up & to settle the long Noise about Ci-

vilians, with getting even only a Minority, or any Thing so as to so far carry their point as to have Civilians more or less in the Government of College. In short they were ripe to settle on any Terms & save Appearances, especially as the Committee of Assembly were so well satisfied with the good state of Coll. as to be ready to recommend an ample Endowment even without any addition of Civilians. But in this state of their feelings they were disposed to risque & propose one plan, & adventured the present Offer, hoping & wishing it might conciliate all parties. The Enemies of Coll. & to this plan, (not numerous), wished we might reject it; that this might excite a Resentment thro' the State & turn this very Donation of 9 or £10,000 to building another College under the Government of libertine, Deistical & duped Civilians. But the main Body of the Assembly were ready for Amnesty & an honourable & respectful Coalition & Harmony. The Corporation considering these public Ideas & the preparation of the pub[lic] mind, after an Irritation of 50 years or half a century, for Pacification & Harmony, judged that there was no prospect perhaps for another Century that the Civilians would feel disposed to try another Demand upon the Corporation for augmenting the Number of Civilians into a Majority—& that before that Time probably Moses & Aaron would be so cemented, harmonized & conected & consolidated in Union, that the very Civilians themselves would not be disposed to enterprize such a project: that on the whole the Prospect was that this Proportion of Civilians & Ministers would be lasting—and that as the latter have the Majority & power of self-perpetuation, it must be their own Unfaithfulness if Religion and every sacerdotal Interest shd not be permanently secured. Thereupon they felt satisfied that all the religious & important Ends of the primary Institution might be preserved & perhaps perpetuated on the present plan; & so became willing to adopt it. Upon the whole, it was the opinion of the Corporation not only that it was safe & best to adopt it, but that it was expedient to coalesce & adopt it now, without *Negotiation or Procrastination.* It was feared that Procrastination would give the Enemies opportunity to excite Ferments, Animosities & Jealousies, give occasion to Friends to become cool by Delay, & perhaps but lay a foundation for loosing all, or shd we finally accept it, yet an Acceptance might meet a dissatisfied & alienated public. Whereas, as this was their own offer, & a generous Offer, & the public in the moment of a sweetned state, after a long Disgust, & Conflict, it was of Importance by an immediate Reception to prevent on our part uncomfortable Consequences. Therefore they accepted it.

I am of Opin. that President Clap, & our Predecessors in the Corporation if now living, with all their Ideas & Attachment to the original Constitution, would have accepted it. I hope this Work is of God, & that it may be considered as the marvellous Disposal of his Providence who has the Command of all Hearts. It was most unexpected to me, that there could possibly have been effected such a Change on the Minds of the general Assembly & public, & such Condescentions & Liberality in their Offers. And I can ascribe it to none but him who turns the Hearts of men as the Rivers of Waters are turned & can make even Nations willing in a Day. How long this apparent good Humour in the public may last, we know not. I rejoyce in the present good Prospect, & desire to leave Futurity to the Supreme Disposer of Events: being satisfied with having acted rightly & wisely on the present Occasion.

I anticipate that this will bring forward Professors obnoxious to me, & who will at length enterprize Mischief to me personally. But I commend myself & the College to the Father of Wisdom, & desire to leave my all with him; satisfied that he will do right, whatever Mortifications & Disappointments in Providence may be in Reserve for me: and that the Affairs of College, as a religious & literary Institution, will be well superintended.

5. William R. Davie's Plan of Education for the University of North Carolina, 1795

William R. Davie (1756–1820) was born in England and taken in his childhood to the Waxhaw settlement in South Carolina. He took his B.A. at Princeton in 1776, began the practice of law in North Carolina, and then launched upon a career as a military officer in the Revolution. He was a member of the Federal Convention and a leading proponent of the ratification of the Constitution in his state. From 1786 to 1798 he served almost continuously in the North Carolina legislature, and it was during this period that he took the leadership in the movement to establish

A copy of this plan is included in Edgar W. Knight (ed.), *A Documentary History of Education in the South before 1860,* III (Chapel Hill, N.C., 1952), 23–26; another copy is given in R. D. W. Connor (ed.), *A Documentary History of the University of North Carolina, 1776–1799* (Chapel Hill, N.C., 1953), I, 451–55. Reprinted with the permission of the University of North Carolina Archives, University of North Carolina Library.

the University of North Carolina, chartered in 1789. In 1798 he was elected governor. See Kemp P. Battle, *History of the University of North Carolina,* Vol. I (Raleigh, N.C., 1907), and B. P. Robinson, *William R. Davie* (Chapel Hill, N.C., 1957).

THE PLAN OF EDUCATION UNDER THE PROFESSORSHIPS
OF THE UNIVERSITY

First—The President
　　Rhetoric & Belles lettres.
　　Rhetoric on the plan of Sheridan.
　　Belles Lettres, on the plan of Blair & Rollin.

PROFESSORSHIPS

First—Professor of Moral and political Philosophy and History.
　　Moral and political Philosophy by the Study of the following Authors.
　　Paley's Moral & Political Philosophy.
　　Montesquieu's Spirit of Laws.

Civil Government and Political Constitutions

Adams' Defence & De Lolme.
The Constitutions of the United States.
The Modern Constitution of Europe.

The Law of Nations

Vattell's Law of Nations.
Burlamaquis principles of Natural and political law.

History

Priestley's Lectures on History and General policy.
Millots Ancient and Modern History.
Hume's History of England with Smollets continuation.
Chronology on the most approved plan.

Second—Professor of Natural philosophy, Astronomy and Geography
　　Natural philosophy under the following heads—

General Properties of Matter

Laws of Motion
Mechanical powers
Hydrostatics

Hydraulics
Pneumatics
Optics
Electricity
Magnetism
Geography
The Use of the Globes
The Geometrical, political & Commercial relations of the different
  Nations of the Earth
Astronomy on the plan of Furgerson

Third—Professor of Mathematics.
  Arithmetic in a Scientific manner
  Algebra, and the application of Algebra to Geometry
  Euclid's Elements
  Trigonometry and the application of Trigonometry to the Mensura-
    tion of heights and distances, of Surfaces & Solids, and Surveying
    and Navigation
  Conic Section
  The Doctrine of the Sphere & Sylinder
  The projection of the Sphere
  Spherical Trigonometry
  The doctrine of fluxions
  The doctrine of chances & Annuities

Fourth—Professor of Chymistry & the Philosophy of Medicine, Agriculture and the Mechanic Arts.
  Chymistry upon the most approved plan.

Fifth—Professor of Languages.

The English Language

Elegant Extracts in prose and verse
Scott's Collection

Latin Language

Virgil—Cicero's Orations—Horaces Epistles including his Art of
  poetry.
Greek Language, Lucian. Xenophon.

6. *Benjamin Rush on Republican Education, 1798*

See Doc. 2.

The business of education has acquired a new complexion by the independence of our country. The form of government we have assumed, has created a new class of duties to every American. It becomes us, therefore, to examine our former habits upon this subject, and in laying the foundations for nurseries of wise and good men, to adapt our modes of teaching to the peculiar form of our government.

The first remark that I shall make upon this subject is, that an education in our own, is to be preferred to an education in a foreign country. The principle of patriotism stands in need of the reinforcement of prejudice, and it is well known that our strongest prejudices in favour of our country are formed in the first one and twenty years of our lives. . . .

I conceive the education of our youth in this country to be peculiarly necessary in Pennsylvania, while our citizens are composed of the natives of so many different kingdoms in Europe. Our schools of learning, by producing one general, and uniform system of education, will render the mass of the people more homogeneous, and thereby fit them more easily for uniform and peaceable government.

I proceed in the next place, to enquire, what mode of education we shall adopt so as to secure to the state all of the advantages that are to be derived from the proper instruction of youth; and here I beg leave to remark, that the only foundation for a useful education in a republic is to be laid in Religion. Without this there can be no virtue, and without virtue there can be no liberty, and liberty is the object and life of all republican governments.

Such is my veneration for every religion that reveals the attributes of the Deity, or a future state of rewards and punishments, that I had rather see the opinions of Confucius or Mahomed inculcated upon our youth, than see them grow up wholly devoid of a system of religious principles. But the religion I mean to recommend in this place, is that of the New Testament.

Benjamin Rush, *Essays, Literary, Moral and Philosophical* (2d ed.; Philadelphia, 1806), pp. 6–10, 12–13, 15–20.

It is foreign to my purpose to hint at the arguments which establish the truth of the Christian revelation. My only business is to declare, that all its doctrines and precepts are calculated to promote the happiness of society, and the safety and well being of civil government. A Christian cannot fail of being a republican. The history of the creation of man, and of the relation of our species to each other by birth, which is recorded in the Old Testament, is the best refutation that can be given to the divine right of kings, and the strongest argument that can be used in favor of the original and natural equality of all mankind. A Christian, I say again, cannot fail of being a republican, for every precept of the Gospel inculcates those degrees of humility, self-denial, and brotherly kindness, which are directly opposed to the pride of monarchy and the pageantry of a court. A Christian cannot fail of being useful to the republic, for his religion teacheth him, that no man "liveth to himself." And lastly, a Christian cannot fail of being wholly inoffensive, for his religion teacheth him, in all things to do to others what he would wish, in like circumstances, they should do to him.

I am aware that I dissent from one of those paradoxical opinions with which modern times abound; and that it is improper to fill the minds of youth with religious prejudices of any kind, and that they should be left to choose their own principles, after they have arrived at an age in which they are capable of judging for themselves. Could we preserve the mind in childhood and youth a perfect blank, this plan of education would have more to recommend it; but this we know to be impossible. The human mind runs as naturally into principles as it does after facts. It submits with difficulty to those restraints or partial discoveries which are imposed upon it in the infancy of reason. . . . Do we leave our youth to acquire systems of geography, philosophy, or politics, till they have arrived at an age in which they are capable of judging for themselves? We do not. I claim no more then for religion, than for the other sciences, and I add further, that if our youth are disposed after they are of age to think for themselves, a knowledge of one system, will be the best means of conducting them in a free enquiry into other systems of religion, just as an acquaintance with one system of philosophy is the best introduction to the study of all the other systems in the world. . . .

While we inculcate these republican duties upon our pupil, we must not neglect, at the same time, to inspire him with republican principles. He must be taught that there can be no durable liberty but in a republic, and that government, like all other sciences, is of a progressive nature. The chains which have bound this science in Europe are happily unloosed in America. Here it is open to investigation and improvement. While philosophy has protected us by its discoveries from a thousand natural evils, government has unhappily followed with an unequal pace. It would be to dishonor human genius, only to name the many defects which still exist in the best systems of legislation. We daily see matter of a perishable nature rendered durable by certain chemical operations. In like manner, I conceive, that it is possible to combine power in such a way as not only to encrease the happiness, but to promote the duration of republican forms of government far beyond the terms limited for them by history, or the common opinions of mankind. . . .

Having pointed out those general principles, which should be inculcated alike in all the schools of the state, I proceed now to make a few remarks upon the method of conducting, what is commonly called, a liberal or learned education in a republic.

I shall begin this part of my subject, by bearing a testimony against the common practice of attempting to teach boys the learned languages, and the arts and sciences too early in life. The first twelve years of life are barely sufficient to instruct a boy in reading, writing and arithmetic. With these, he may be taught those modern languages which are necessary for him to speak. The state of the memory, in early life, is favorable to the acquisition of languages, especially when they are conveyed to the mind, through the ear. It is, moreover, in early life only, that the organs of speech yield in such a manner as to favour the just pronunciation of foreign languages.

Too much pains cannot be taken to teach our youth to read and write our American language with propriety and elegance. The study of the Greek language constituted a material part of the literature of the Athenians, hence the sublimity, purity and immortality of so many of their writings. The advantages of a perfect knowledge of our language to young men intended for the professions of law, physic, or divinity are too obvious to be mentioned, but in a state which boasts of the first commercial city in America, I wish to see it cultivated by young men, who are intended for the compting house, for many such, I hope, will be educated in our colleges. The time is past when an academical education was thought to be unnecessary to qualify a young man for merchandize. I conceive no profession is capable of receiving more embellishments from it. The French and German languages should likewise be carefully taught in all our Colleges. They abound with useful books upon all subjects. So important and necessary are those languages, that a degree should never be conferred upon a young man who cannot speak or translate them.

Connected with the study of languages is the study of Eloquence. It is well known how great a part it constituted of the Roman education. It is the first accomplishment in a republic, and often sets the whole machine of government in motion. Let our youth, therefore, be instructed in this art. We do not extol it too highly when we attribute as much to the power of eloquence as to the sword, in bringing about the American Revolution.

With the usual arts and sciences that are taught in our American colleges, I wish to see a regular course of lectures given upon History and Chronology. The science of government, whether it relates to constitutions or laws, can only be advanced by a careful selection of facts, and these are to be found chiefly in history. Above all, let our youth be instructed in the history of the ancient republics, and the progress of liberty and tyranny in the different states of Europe. I wish likewise to see the numerous facts that relate to the origin and present state of commerce, together with the nature and principles of Money, reduced to such a system, as to be intelligible and agreeable to a young man. If we consider the commerce of our metropolis only as the avenue of the wealth of the state, the study of it merits a place in a young man's education; but, I consider commerce in a much higher light when I recommend the study of it in republican seminaries. I view it as the best security against the influence of hereditary monopolies of land, and, therefore, the surest protection against aristocracy. I consider its effects as next to those of religion in humanizing mankind, and lastly, I view it as the means of uniting the different nations of the world together by the ties of mutual wants and obligations.

Chemistry by unfolding to us the effects of heat and mixture, enlarges our acquaintance with the wonders of nature and the mysteries of art; hence it has become, in most of the universities of Europe, a necessary branch of a gentleman's education. In a young country, where improvements in agriculture and manufactures are so much to be desired, the cultivation of this science, which explains the principles of both of them should be considered as an object of the utmost importance.

Again, let your youth be instructed in all the means of promoting national prosperity and independence, whether they relate to improvements in agriculture, manufactures, or inland navigation. Let him be instructed further in the general principles of legislation, whether they relate to revenue, or to the preservation of life, liberty or property. Let him be directed frequently to attend the courts of justice, where he will have the best opportunities of acquiring habits of comparing, and arranging his ideas by observing the discovery of truth, in the examination of witnesses, and where he will hear the laws of the state explained, with all the advantages of that species of eloquence which belongs to the bar. Of so much importance do I conceive it to be, to a young man, to attend occasionally to the decisions of our courts of law, that I wish to see our colleges established, only in county towns.

But further, considering the nature of our connection with the United States, it will be necessary to make our pupil acquainted with all the prerogatives of the national government. He must be instructed in the nature and variety of treaties. He must know the difference in the powers and duties of the several species of ambassadors. He must be taught wherein the obligations of individuals and of states are the same, and wherein they differ. In short, he must acquire a general knowledge of all those laws and forms, which unite the sovereigns of the earth, or separate them from each other.

I beg pardon for having delayed so long to say any thing of the separate and peculiar mode of education proper for women in a republic. I am sensible that they must concur in all our plans of education for young men, or no laws will ever render them effectual. To qualify our women for this purpose, they should not only be instructed in the usual branches of female education, but they should be taught the principles of liberty and government; and the obligations of patriotism should be inculcated upon them. The opinions and conduct of men are often regulated by the women in the most arduous enterprizes of life; and their approbation is frequently the principal reward of the hero's dangers, and the patriot's toils. Besides, the first impressions upon the minds of children are generally derived from the women. Of how much consequence, therefore, is it in a republic, that they should think justly upon the great subject of liberty and government!

The complaints that have been made against religion, liberty and learning, have been, against each of them in a separate state. Perhaps like certain liquors, they should only be used in a state of mixture. They mutually assist in correcting the abuses, and in improving the good effects of each other. From the combined and reciprocal influence of religion, liberty and learning upon the morals, manners and knowledge of individuals, of these, upon government, and of government, upon individuals, it is impossible to measure the degrees of happiness and perfection to which mankind may be raised. For my part, I can form no ideas of the golden age, so much celebrated by the poets, more delightful, than the contemplation of that happiness which it is now in the power of the legislature of Pennsylvania to confer upon her citizens, by establishing proper modes and places of education in every part of the state.

7. *Jefferson Plans the University of Virginia, 1800*

The University of Virginia, finally opened for instruction in 1825, was the first full-fledged state university, both in the sense that it offered a program of advanced instruction and that it was a completely public enterprise, unlike its predecessors which were partly private. The university, the product of many years of devotion and work on Jefferson's part, was one of the three achievements for which he wished to be remembered. In the 1770's Jefferson had tried to reform his alma mater, the College of William and Mary. When his efforts failed to bring about the desired results, he turned to the idea of achieving them through a state university, modern, non-denominational, basically secular, republican, and capable of teaching advanced studies. This letter to Joseph Priestley represents one of the earlier statements of his ideal for the state university. See Roy J. Honeywell, *The Educational Work of Thomas Jefferson* (Cambridge, Mass., 1931); Philip A. Bruce, *History of the University of Virginia, 1819–1919,* Vol. I (New York, 1920). On the development of the state university idea, see Merle Curti and Vernon L. Carstensen, *The University of Wisconsin, 1848–1925* (Madison, Wis., 1949), Vol. I, chap. i.

We wish to establish in the upper & healthier country, & more centrally for the state an University on a plan so broad & liberal & *modern,* as to be worth patronizing with the public support, and be a temptation to the youth of other states to come, and drink of the cup of knowledge & fraternize with us. The first step is to obtain a good plan; that is a judicious selection of the sciences & a practicable regrouping of some of them together, & ramifying of others, so as to adapt the professor-

Thomas Jefferson to Joseph Priestley, Philadelphia, January 18, 1800, Jefferson MSS, Vol. CVI, Library of Congress.

ships to our uses, & our means. . . . There is no one in the world who equally with yourself unites this full possession of the subject with such a knowledge of the state of our existence, as enables you to fit the garment to him who is to *pay* for it & to *wear* it. To you therefore we address our solicitations, and to lessen to you as much as possible the ambiguities of our object, I will venture even to sketch the sciences which seem useful & practicable for us, as they occur to me while holding my pen. Botany, Chemistry, Zoology, Anatomy, Surgery, Medicine, Natl Philosophy, Agriculture, Mathematics, Astronomy, Geology, Geography, Politics, Commerce, History, Ethics, Law, Arts, Finearts. This list is imperfect because I make it hastily, and because I am unequal to the subject. It is evident that some of these articles are too much for one professor & must therefore be ramified; others may be ascribed in groups to a single professor. This is the difficult part of the work, & requires a head perfectly knowing the extent of each branch, & the limits within which it may be circumscribed, so as to bring the whole within the powers of the fewest professors possible, & consequently within the degree of expence practicable for us. We should propose that the professors follow no other calling, so that their whole time may be given to their academical functions; and we should propose to draw from Europe the first characters in science, by considerable temptations, which would not need to be repeated after the first set should have prepared fit successors & given reputation to the institution. From some splendid characters I have received offers most perfectly reasonable and practicable. . . .

8. James Madison on a National University, 1810

See Doc. 3.

Whilst it is universally admitted that a well instructed people alone can be permanently a free people, and while it is evident that the means of diffusing and improving useful knowledge from so small a proportion of the expenditures for national purposes, I cannot presume it to be unseasonable to invite your attention to the advantages of

James D. Richardson (ed.), *Messages and Papers of the Presidents,* I (Washington, D.C., 1896), 485.

superadding to the means of education, provided by the several States, a seminary of learning, instituted by the National Legislature, within the limits of their exclusive jurisdiction, the expense of which might be defrayed or reimbursed out of the vacant grounds which have accrued to the nation within those limits.

Such an institution, though local in its legal character, would be universal in its beneficial effects. By enlightening the opinions, by expanding the patriotism, and by assimilating the principles, the sentiments, and the manners, of those who might resort to this temple of science, to be redistributed, in due time, through every part of the community, sources of jealousy and prejudice would be diminished, the features of national character would be multiplied, and greater extent given to social harmony. But, above all, a well constituted seminary in the center of the nation, is recommended by the consideration that the additional instruction emanating from it would contribute not less to strengthen the foundations than to adorn the structure of our free and happy system of government.

9. A Congressional Committee Indorses a National University, 1816

After Madison had proposed a national university in four annual messages, the congressional committee to whom this matter was referred made the following favorable report on December 11, 1816. It was accompanied in 1817 by a bill for a national university, as also in 1816. But many, including President Monroe, believed that a constitutional amendment was necessary for such an establishment. The House of Representatives voted against a proposed amendment. Leading the committee that favored Madison's idea was Richard H. Wilde (1789–1847) of Augusta, Georgia. He was born in Dublin, engaged in mercantile pursuits in Augusta after 1802, practiced law there, was periodically elected to Congress, and moved to New Orleans in 1843, becoming professor of law at the University of Louisiana. See Doc. 3.

Your committee, therefore, have ventured to suggest some of the reasons which recommend the present as a favorable time for investigating, and perhaps, also, for adopting the plan they have proposed.

Annals of Congress, 9 Cong., 2 sess., pp. 257–60.

Among these, the prosperous state of our finances, leaving a large unappropriated surplus, the probability of a long continued peace, the flourishing condition of our capital, and the facility with which a portion of the public property within it might now be advantageously disposed of, so as at once to increase the convenience of the city, and support the proposed institution, may fairly be enumerated.

Besides, the information heretofore collected has enabled the committee to report at an early period, and it is believed that the present session, though inevitably a short one, will not present so many objects of great difficulty or deep interest, as entirely to exclude others of a more tranquil and less obtrusive character, to which it is possible a portion of time might be profitable devoted.

The acquisition of a scientific and literary reputation, not unworthy of their naval and military renown, can never be beneath the ambition of a people, since the most durable of all glory is that of exalted intellect.

The world is still a willing captive to the spells of ancient genius; and the rivalry of modern empires will be perpetuated by their arts and their learning, the preservers of that fame which arms alone may indeed win, but can never keep.

Any measure which contributes, however remotely, to give American literature a rank and name among mankind, cannot, therefore, be regarded with indifference by our citizens; and every effort towards that end must be witnessed at the present moment with unusual satisfaction, since it will present the interesting spectacle of a young nation, bending its whole strength to the pursuit of true greatness, and anxious to emulate all that is amiable in peace as well as all that is noble in war.

That the institution contemplated will have a happy influence on the harmony of our country and the unity of our national character, has been often supposed, and your committee feel inclined to anticipate effects no less happy from its operation on the genius of our people.

If American invention, unassisted as it has been, already excites the astonishment of Europe, what may not be expected from it when aided and encouraged? And why should not aid and encouragement be yielded by institutions like the present, founded and endowed by the munificence of the State? In our own day we have seen them work wonders in physical science, even when directed by a stern, jealous, and exacting Government, which, while training the mind to be quick, dexterous and daring, darkened its vision, and circumscribed its flight.

Is it here alone they would be impotent, where no depth could be hidden from its glance, no height forbidden to its wing?

But your committee, fearful of exhausting your patience, forbear to extend this report by arguments which it is easier to multiply than to withhold; for the same reason they refrain from answering objections which could not be stated without injury, since, in replying to them, force and perspicuity must be sacrificed to conciseness. Nor can such a course be required where it is intended merely to present a general result, not the particular process of reasoning by which that result has been obtained. Your committee, however, desire it to be understood, that they have not declined examining any objection which occurred to them, and though some have been found which it must be confessed are not without difficulty, all are thought capable of a satisfactory answer.

Under a conviction, therefore, that the means are ample, the end desirable, the object fairly within the legislative powers of Congress, and the time a favorable one, your committee recommend the establishment of a National University, and have directed their chairman to submit a bill and estimates for that purpose.

10. The Sectarian Status of American Colleges in 1813

This unsigned article provides a useful review of the relation between colleges and sects at the time of its writing. It expresses a minority viewpoint on the Protestant control of higher learning, that of liberal Boston Unitarianism, in contrast to the predominant point of view of the Presbyterians at Princeton and the Congregationalists under Timothy Dwight's leadership at Yale. The founder and editor of this short-lived journal (1812–13) was Andrews Norton (1786–1853), graduate of Harvard in 1804, Dexter Professor of Sacred Literature in the Harvard Divinity School (1819–30), a renowned biblical scholar, and the Unitarian "Pope." There is reason to believe that the author of this long review was Horace Holley (1781–1827), then minister of the Hollis Street Unitarian Church in Boston, who later was the liberal president of Transylvania University in Lexington, Kentucky, from 1818 to 1827.

"[Review of] A Contrast between Calvinism and Hopkinsianism. By the Rev. Ezra Stiles Ely . . . ," *General Repository and Review*, III (April, 1813), 355–65.

On Norton see A. P. Peabody, *Reminiscences of Harvard* (Boston, 1888), pp. 73–
78, and S. E. Morison, *Three Centuries of Harvard* (Cambridge, Mass., 1936), pp.
241–45.

It is but a few years since religious parties have been roused to vigorous exertions on the subject of Theological Seminaries distinct from
our colleges. The policy is now so well understood, and so many seminaries of this kind are, or are about to be established, that no sect can
consider its hopes as worth much without a school to educate and
raise up defenders. And this is equally true in respect to catholic
Christians as mere sectarians.

1. "The Theological Seminary of the Presbyterian church in the
United States of America."

We begin with this, although it is of later date than that at Andover
and some others. We wish to correct an impression too common on the
public mind, that Andover is about to go on without any effectual opposition. Andover has checks upon it in abundance from every quarter,
insomuch that its future rank among similar institutions in our country
will probably be very different from what its friends now suppose.

We have a pamphlet now before us, entitled, "The Plan of a Theo-
logical Seminary, adopted by the General Assembly of the Presbyterian
Church in the United States of America, in their Session of May last,
A.D. 1811; together with the measures taken by them to carry the
Plan into effect." This Seminary, we understand, was established at
Princeton, in connexion with that college, by a vote of the General
Assembly in May 1812, according to the general conditions hereafter
to be mentioned. As this institution is of great consequence in our inquiries after checks upon Andover, we shall now proceed to show that
the same opposition to New England Calvinism, which we have found
in the Letters, is jealously provided for and established in this Institution. We have thus a full knowledge of the future policy of the General Assembly.

The Plan says, of the objects of the Seminary, p. 4. "It is to form men
for the Gospel ministry, who shall truly believe, and cordially love,
and therefore endeavour to propagate and defend, in its *genuineness;*
simplicity, and *fulness,* that system of religious belief and practice,
which is set forth in the Confession of Faith, Catechisms, and Plan of
Government and Discipline of the Presbyterian Church; and thus to

perpetuate and extend the influence of true evangelical piety and gospel order."

In the pamphlet not a word is said about making the Bible the standard of faith, by which to try the Confession, should any teacher or student find it to need improvement. At page 10 it is asserted indeed, that the Bible is in harmony with the Confession, but the latter is the standard throughout. "Genuineness," "simplicity," and "fulness" are words of a very different meaning from that convenient phrase "for substance," which New England subscribers have adopted in assenting to a creed which they do not fairly and fully believe. Men must not only subscribe or assent to the Confession "for substance," at Princeton, but "truly," "cordially," in its "genuineness, simplicity, and fulness." The *middle-ground* men, and thorough Andoverians, would here be equally rejected. After the mangling of the Westminster Confession at Andover, and the light given us in the Letters, we can have no doubt at whom these jealous provisions are aimed. The plain English is, *Andoverians, we know you, stand off, or be converted from your errors.*

P. 5. "It is to preserve the unity of our church by educating her ministers in an enlightened attachment, not only to the same doctrines, but to the same plan of government."

The Andoverians are heretical by this standard, both in "doctrines" and "plan of government." Hence they must not be permitted any longer to destroy *"the unity of our Church."*

P. 10. "Every person, elected to a professorship in this Seminary, shall, on being inaugurated, solemnly subscribe to the Confession of Faith, Catechisms, and Form of Government of the Presbyterian Church, agreeably to the following formula, viz.—'In the presence of God, and of the directors of this Seminary, I do solemnly, and *ex animo,* adopt, receive, and subscribe the Confessions of Faith and Catechisms of the Presbyterian Church in the United States of America, *as the confession of my faith;* or, as a summary and just exhibition of that system of doctrine and religious belief, which is contained in Holy Scripture, and therein revealed by God to man for his salvation: and I do solemnly *ex animo* profess to receive the Form of Government of said Church, as agreeable to the inspired oracles. And I do solemnly promise and engage, not to inculcate, teach, or *insinuate* any thing which shall appear to me to contradict or contravene, *either directly or impliedly,* any thing taught in said Confession of Faith or Catechisms; nor to oppose any of the fundamental principles of Presbyterian Church government, while I shall continue a professor in this seminary.' "

Why all these guards? Why is all ambiguity, all chance for explanation, so jealously shut out? Why are the words "insinuate," "directly or impliedly," put into this oath of obedience to the decrees of the Westminster Divines?—For the same reason with the words in the former extract. The Andoverians begin to get into the Presbyterian Churches with their "new light," and their "improvements," and have alarmed the fears of the General Assembly. The reformed, amputated, and enlarged state of the Westminster creed, as received at Andover, is quite a different sort of Calvinism and orthodoxy from the standards at Princeton. The two can never meet, till one shall yield, or both exchange their human compositions for the Word of God.

P. 12. "The faculty shall be empowered *to dismiss* from the seminary any student who shall prove *unsound in his religious sentiments.*"

What an effect must this have upon a student's inquiries after truth? A formal decree, from the ecclesiastical authority in the church he has chosen, that he is *"unsound in his religious sentiments,"* if he depart from the Confession, certainly must close his eyes to all "new light," and be as effectual a bar to "improvements," as the Provost himself could wish. This is worse than Andover. There the charge, that freedom of inquiry was not indulged, has, if we mistake not, been anxiously repelled. Here the fact that it is prohibited appears in the very face of their laws. These Presbyterian gentlemen are driving back with full sail into the ignorance and bigotry of the dark ages.

P. 22. "The committee appointed to confer with the committee of the Trustees of New Jersey College, reported, among other things, that they deem it expedient, on the part of this Assembly, to appoint a committee, with ample powers to meet a committee on the part of the Trustees of the College of New Jersey, invested with similar powers, to frame the plan of a constitution for the Theological Seminary, containing the fundamental principles of a union with the Trustees of that College, and the Seminary already established by them, *which shall never be changed or altered without the mutual consent of both parties:* provided it should be deemed proper to locate the Assembly's Seminary at the same place with that of the College."

P. 23. The several articles already quoted, the joint committee, in their proposed conference for a union, are "in no case to be permitted to contravene."

This union with the college and location of the Theological Seminary at Princeton, we understand, as before mentioned, were agreed upon last May. Put this in connexion with Dr. Smith's resignation, who is considered too rational and catholic for the purposes of this Seminary, and with Dr. Green's election to the presidency, whose sentiments we have already seen, and we can have no doubt how both the college and the seminary are to be governed hereafter. Some of the Andoverians have, we understand, heretofore calculated upon Dr. Green as a middle man, between Presbyterian and New England Calvinism, and supposed if he would not directly aid the introduction of the latter into the jurisdiction of the General Assembly, that at least he would not oppose it. But he and the school of the Assembly must now be the defenders of rigid and exclusive Presbyterianism, both in doctrines and government. Here then is a rival interest and a check to Andover, which there can be no hope of subduing, but which must, on the contrary, be vigorously guarded in order that New England herself may be hereafter kept safe from the encroachments and conquests of the enemy. We wish neither of these Theological Schools success in their warfare. The public will be most benefited by the continuance of the contest without victory to either, till both come back from Calvin to Christ.

2. The Theological Seminary at Andover.

The Presbyterians are jealous of and opposed to this school for the following reasons:—

It is Congregational, or at most Consociational, and does not fit young men to be good Presbyterians.—It subscribes only the Shorter Catechism of their standards, leaving out the Confession of Faith, the Larger Catechism, and Form of Government.—It has so explained away even the Shorter Catechism, that subscription to the whole Andover creed does not amount to Presbyterian Calvinism. It has various passages in its creed, which add *positive* to the *negative* heresy already mentioned, and which allow the Hopkinsians to introduce all their peculiarities into the system of instructions.—Its students actually prove to be at variance with some of the favorite definitions of the Westminster Confession, and are found to be zealous, active Calvinists, according to the "new light" and the "improvements" of Edwards, West, Spring, and other such writers, who "in some very material

points," preach "another gospel indeed."—It is under the decided management of Hopkinsian policy. The *middle-ground* men have either
become cold toward it, or have floated with the popular tide.—It has
sent some pupils already among the Presbyterians, who have alarmed
and offended them: And it is preparing more.—It now forms the great
standard of New England Calvinism, and must continue under the
influence of those causes, which will forever prevent its becoming the
instrument of the General Assembly, or of any other body of Presbyterians.—It allows a greater latitude of inquiry than its new rival, and
will produce men better fitted for controversy.—It wants the control
of the New England Churches, and in order to get this, it cannot
flatter the ambition of the Presbyterians.—It denounces the Presbyterian
practice in baptism, as loose and unscriptural, and promotes disunion
on this subject, whenever its disciples are settled among the Presbyterians[.]—Both institutions wish for power in each other's bounds;
are rival candidates for the favor and patronage of the Calvinistic
public; and must feel, as the Presbyterians at least have abundantly
shown, the spirit of competition.

The Andoverians, we have no doubt, desire at present to have as
little said on the subject of this difference as possible. They are much
less afraid that Presbyterianism will get into New England, than the
Presbyterians are that they will bring their principles into the middle
and southern states, since to do this there is no necessity to change the
form of church government, and therefore success may be obtained
more secretly. The present policy however at Andover, not to give
publicity to the differences between themselves and the Presbyterians,
must be temporary. For this there are several reasons.

The Andoverians are now bent on getting a system of ecclesiastical
councils, or of church government, established in New England, which
shall produce uniformity of sentiment in their creed, and union of
operation against the catholic Christians. As there is a strong, hereditary jealousy of the horns of Presbyterianism in New England, it
would undoubtedly aid the plan of Consociations, if the Andoverians
should gradually allow the public to know the differences between
them and the Presbyterians. It is a clear case, that the Presbyterian
system cannot now be destroyed out of New England; and also that
it cannot extensively be established in it. The ambition of Andover
must be chiefly to govern within these limits; and the sooner she can

get the plan of consociations established, the better it will be for her power.

The Andoverians have really the best side of the controversy. They have been more hardly pushed by the Anti-Calvinists than the Presbyterians have been, and have digested their system into a form more susceptible of defence. This therefore is a reason for making the differences more public. By acknowledging, explaining, and defending these differences, the Andoverians will perfectly secure the affection and unite the forces of the New England Calvinists. It may reasonably be doubted, whether there be a Calvinist in New England, who would agree to the explanations of the New York Calvinists. There is indeed yet urged in New England a nominal distinction of Calvinist and Hopkinsian; but this distinction is fast merging in the general prevalence of a popular form of Hopkinsianism.

It is now the best time that Andover can ever expect to unite and bring New England under her power. The causes to promote free inquiry are every day multiplying, and delay at Andover can only increase the obstacles to her ambition.

We are satisfied therefore that the Andoverians, whatever caution and prudence they may use in the mode of operation, will steadily be preparing to defend and spread their sentiments in opposition to the Presbyterians wherever they find them, at home or abroad. They are not wanting in talent to discover their policy, nor are they tardy or timid in adopting the means of executing it. The two great schools, which we have just mentioned, must always hold each other in check. The causes must operate to produce this effect, whether they be laid before the public or not.

3. The Theological Seminary of the Reformed Dutch Church at New Brunswick.—This is under the care of Dr. Livingston, the writer of one of the Letters, and whose sentiments we have already seen. This School will indeed be in "doctrinal concord" with the Presbyterians, but will not aid the sectarian purposes of either party. It is jealous of, and a check upon both.

4. The Theological Seminary of the Associate Reformed Church, established at New York, under the care of Dr. Mason.

This will defend the doctrines of the Westminster Confession, but cannot act in concert with any other school or combination mentioned. It has no local interest to induce it to mediate between Andover and the General Assembly, and its Principal has already denounced the

Eastern Calvinism. As a specimen of the character and spirit of this institution, take the following. "With his third year, the student shall commence the study of systematic theology; and as a basis for it, *he shall commit to memory,* during the two previous years, the whole *text of the Confession of Faith and Larger Catechism.*" The Synod directs—"That every student, on his admission, bind himself in a *written obligation,* to strict obedience, to diligence, to peace, *and not to propagate, directly or indirectly, any opinion contrary to the known faith of the Associate Reformed Church.*" This known faith is the Confession, &c. It is also directed—"That students of *other denominations* be admitted into the Seminary *upon the same terms as are exacted from those of the Associate Reformed Church.*" The influence of Dr. Mason's school, under all the advantages from its position and from his extensive and various connexions, must be great.

5. The Romanists and Methodists have Theological Seminaries in Maryland, the former of which is flourishing, but the state of the latter is not known to us.

The Episcopalians have not, as far as we know, any Theological Seminary in form, and at this we confess ourselves surprised, especially when we consider their wealth and advantages in New York.

The German Lutherans in 1807 had collected some funds and made some arrangements toward establishing a Theological Seminary. Whether this has since been done, we do not know. They have educated young men for the ministry under individual clergymen, appointed by the Synod for the purpose.

The Baptists are in expectation of a Theological Seminary, as connected with a College in the District of Maine, a grant for which was obtained the last session of the General Court in Massachusetts. This will be a powerful source of sectarian influence, but will aid much to balance religious parties.

6. The Theological Instruction at Cambridge.

Of this we gave some account in our first number. We would add, that the advantages for students are much increased since that time. The Library is now kept open as a reading room every day in the week except Sunday. Beside his lectures delivered on Tuesday afternoon, Professor Ware, somewhat more than a year since, commenced a course of lectures delivered on Saturday forenoon. These are on subjects of biblical criticism and interpretation. They are very highly esteemed by those who have heard them, and who are best capable of judging of their merit. They have been distinguished for great perspicuity of explanation, for great correctness in the statement of facts and principles, and of the very happy and full selection of examples by which these are illustrated. They are the result of extensive reading, of much thought, and of much study of the scriptures. As far as they have been delivered, they would, in our opinion, if published, form a work as valuable, for its size, to a theological student, as any work on the same subjects with which we are acquainted. These lectures are, we believe, an advantage which the theological instruction at Cambridge possesses over any other in our country; and one of no small importance, both on account of the information which they directly communicate, and on account of the taste, which they are adapted to produce for the studies of which they treat.

On the subject of a Theological Seminary in form and well endowed at Cambridge, we cannot say much. But we will at least express our strong conviction of the policy, practicability, and unparalleled utility, of such a seminary in this place, connected with this university, with the advantage of the best theological library on this side of the Atlantic, and upon the spot where, of all others, rational and catholic Christianity has the most patronage and the best hopes. Good men ought promptly to unite in this enterprise, so honorable to the best feelings and principles of our nature; so necessary to the cause of truth; so dear to our hopes for the welfare of succeeding generations; and so interwoven with the progress of the human mind in all that is worth obtaining here or hereafter. Upon the rich men of our metropolis we would urge this subject. We would say that no time better than the present can be expected for this purpose. As you value truth, virtue, piety, and happiness, speedily endow a Theological Seminary at Cambridge, as the great defender of the true Protestant cause, as the source of rational, catholic, and evangelical Christianity, and as the glory of your age, and the hope of posterity.

IV. The religious influence exerted upon, or by, Literary Institutions.

Under this head, our limits will allow us to give little more than a catalogue, and we shall only mention those which we think important in this relation.

We shall use the word CATHOLIC, for those colleges which adopt the Bible as the rule of faith without any supplement, and whose system of instruction favors rational and simple Christianity. Any man is a sectarian, whether Papist or Protestant, who insists upon others subscribing a creed, or standard, of his own or his party, beside the Bible, in order to Christian communion. The two titles, *catholic* and *sectarian,* are not to be applied according to the respective number of either class, but according to the general, or party standard of faith, which may be adopted. The general standard of faith, i.e. the standard which all Christians profess to receive, is the Bible. The party standard is the given creed of the sect. Those who have separated from the standard left by Christ and his apostles are sectarians. Those who hold to it are the true catholics.

Harvard University. Catholic.

Yale College. Andoverian.

Dartmouth College. This is divided, but the Andoverian party expect to prevail.

Williams College. Andoverian.

Brown University. A majority of the governors are Baptists.

Burlington College. Catholic.

Middlebury College. Andoverian.

Bowdoin College. Catholic.

Schenectedy College. Liberally Presbyterian.

Columbia College. Of this College Dr. Mason is at present the Provost. Arminians and Calvinists are united in its government. But the Calvinists will probably prevail. Both however are opposed to Andover.

Hamilton College. Dr. Backus, the new President, will endeavour to make this Andoverian.

Princeton College. Presbyterian.

Queen's College. Dutch Presbyterian.

Dickinson College. Probably Presbyterian.

The University of Pennsylvania. What religious influence it has is probably in favor of rational and catholic Christianity, since this is the natural effect of scientific attainments.

St. Mary's College. Papal.

Cokesbury College. Methodist.

The Institution at Annapolis we suppose to be under Episcopal influence.

William and Mary College. Probably Catholic in what religious influence it has.

The University of North Carolina. This being a state institution, we suppose its influence not to be sectarian.

Washington and Greenville Colleges. Probably Presbyterian.

The University of South Carolina. From the manner in which this is governed, by members chosen from all parts of the state, we have a right to presume that it is catholic in its religious influence.

The University of Georgia. At present, as Dr. Kollock is at the head, it is probably Presbyterian in its religious influence.

One remark we would make about all or nearly all the literary institutions in our country. They are dependent very much upon public opinion for their success; they are, by this consideration, led to impress religious sentiments upon the minds of the young men under their care with caution, in regard to any sectarian peculiarities, that parents of the different denominations may not be offended. So far as this consideration has influence, it produces catholicism. Upon the whole, we think the religious influence of the Literary Institutions of the country is well balanced, as it respects those, whose influence is sectarian, and such as will promote catholicism and free inquiry.

11. Establishment of the Catholepistemiad, 1817

The author of this hopelessly polysyllabic plan for what became the University of Michigan was Judge Augustus B. Woodward (1774-1827), originally a New Yorker and a graduate of Columbia College (1793). After a brief career as a lawyer, real estate speculator, and amateur scientist, this versatile man was appointed in 1805 by Thomas Jefferson as one of the judges of the new Territory of Michigan. He was the first compiler of Michigan's code of laws. In 1816 he published his book, *A System of Universal Science,* which contains the germ of this ambitious plan for a state university. The University of Michigan began modestly under this plan, but by the 1850's it was second in size among the state institutions only to the University of Virginia.

On the early history of Michigan see William W. Bishop, "Judge Woodward and the Catholepistemiad," *Michigan Alumnus Quarterly Review,* LI (Summer, 1945), 323-36; Egbert R. Isbell, "The Universities of Virginia and Michigania," *Michigan Historical Magazine,* XXVI (1942), 39-53; Willis Dunbar, "Public Versus Private Control of Higher Education in Michigan," *Mississippi Valley Historical Review,* XXII (December, 1935), 385-406.

AN ACT TO ESTABLISH THE CATHOLEPISTEMIAD, OR
UNIVERSITY, OF MICHIGANIA

Be it enacted by the Governor and the Judges of the Territory of Michigan that there shall be in the said Territory a *catholepistemiad,*

Frank E. Robbins (ed.), *Records of the University of Michigan, 1817-1837* (Ann Arbor, Mich., 1935), pp. 3-6, 31-32.

or university, denominated the *catholepistemiad,* or university, of Michigania. The *catholepistemiad,* or university of Michigania shall be composed of thirteen *didaxiim* or professorships: first, a *didaxia* or professorship, of *catholepistemia,* or universal science, the *didactor* or professor, of which shall be president of the institution; second, a *didaxia,* or professorship, of *anthropoglossica,* or literature, embracing all the *epistemiim,* or sciences, relative to language; third, a *didaxia,* or professorship, of *mathematica,* or mathematics; fourth, a *didaxia,* or professorship, of *physiognostica,* or natural history; fifth, a *didaxia,* or professorship, of *physiosophica,* or natural philosophy; sixth, a *didaxia,* or professorship, of *astronomia,* or astronomy; seventh, a *didaxia,* or professorship, of *chymia,* or chemistry; eighth, a *didaxia,* or professorship, of *iatrica,* or medical sciences; ninth, a *didaxia,* or professorship, of *aeconomica,* or economical sciences; tenth, a *didaxia,* or professorship, of *ethica,* or ethica[1] sciences; eleventh, a *didaxia,* or professorship, of *polemitactica,* or military sciences; twelfth, a *didaxia,* or professorship, of *diegetica,* or historical sciences; and, thirteenth, a *didaxi[a]* or professorship of *ennaeica,* or intellectual sciences, embracing all the *epistemiim,* or sciences, relative to the minds of animals, to the human mind, to spiritual existences, to the deity, and to religion, the *didactor,* or professor, of which shall be vice-presiden[t] of the institution. The *didactors,* or professors, shall be appointed and commissioned by the Governor. There shall be paid, from the treasury of Michigan, in quarterly payments, to the president of the institution, to the vice-president, and to each *didactor,* or professor, an annual salary, to be, from time to time, ascertained by law. More than one *didaxia,* or professorship, may be conferred upon the same person. The president and *didactors,* or professors, or a majority of them, assembled, shall have power to regulate all the concer[ns] of the institution, to enact laws for that pu[r]pose, to sue, to be sued, to acquire, to hol[d] and to aliene, property, real, mixed, and personal, to make, to sue, and to alter, a seal, to establish colleges, academies, schools, libraries, musaeums, athenaeums, botanic gardens, laboratories, and other useful literary and scientific institutions, consonant to the laws of the United States of America and of Michigan, and to appoint officers, instructors and instructrixes, in, among, and throughout, the various counties, cities, towns, townships, and other geographical divisions, of Michigan. Their name and stile as a corporation shall be "The *catholepistemiad,* or university, of Michigania." To every subordinate instructor, and instructrix, appointed by the *catholepistemiad,* or university, there shall be paid, from the treasury of Michigan, in quarterly payments, an annual salary, to be, from time to time, ascertained by law. The existing public taxes are hereby increased fifteen per cent; and, from the proceeds of the present, and of all future public taxes, fifteen per cent are appropriated for the benefit of the *catholepistemiad,* or university. The treasurer of Michigan shall keep a separate account of the university fund. The *catholepistemiad,* or university, may propose and draw four successive lotteries, deducting from the prizes in the same fifteen per cent for the benefit of the institution. The proceeds of the preceding sources of revenue, and of all subsequent, shall be applied in the fir[st] instance, to the acquisition of suitable land[s] and buildings, and books, libraries, and apparatus, and afterwards to such purposes as shall be, from time to time, by law directed. The *honorarium* for a course of lectures sh[all] not exceed fifteen dollars, for classical instruction ten dollars a quarter, and for ordinary instruction six dollars a quarter. If the judges of the court of any county, or a majority of them, shall certify that the parent, or guardian, of any person has not adequate means to defray the expense of the suitable instruction, and that the sam[e] ought to be a public charge, the *honorarium* shall be paid from the Treasury of Michigan. An annual report of the state, concerns, and transactions, of the institution shall be laid before the legislative power for the time being. This law, or any part of it, may be repealed by the legislative power for the time being.

Made, adopted, and published, from the laws of seven of the original states, to wit the states of Connecticut, Massachusetts, New-Jersey, New-York, Ohio, Pennsylvania, and Virginia, as far as necessary and suitable to the circumstances of Michigan; at the City of Detroit, on Tuesday the twenty sixth day of August, in the year one thousand eight hundred seventeen.

WILLIAM WOODBRIDGE
Secy of Michigan, and at present Acting Governour thereof

A. B. WOODWARD
Presiding Judge of the Supreme Court of the Territory of Michigan

JOHN GRIFFIN
One of the Judges of the Territory of Michigan

AN ACT TO ASCERTAIN THE ANNUAL SALARIES OF THE PRESIDENT,
VICE-PRESIDENT, PROFESSORS, INSTRUCTORS, AND INSTRUC-
TRIXES, OF THE UNIVERSITY, FOR THE TIME BEING

*Be it enacted by the Governor and the Judges of the Territory of
Michigan,* That, for the time being, the annual salary of the president
of the University shall be twenty-five dollars, of the vice-president
eighteen dollars, and seventy-five cents, of each professor twelve dollars
and fifty cents, and of each instructor and instructrix twenty-five
dollars.

Made, adopted, and published, from the laws of one of the original
States, to wit: the State of New York, as far as necessary and suitable
to the circumstances of Michigan, at the city of Detroit, on Tuesday,
the twenty-sixth day of August, in the year one thousand eight hundred
seventeen.

WILLIAM WOODBRIDGE
*Secr'y of Michigan, and at present Acting Gov-
ernor thereof*

A. B. WOODWARD
*Presiding Judge of the Supreme Court of the
Territory of Michigan*

JOHN GRIFFIN
One of the Judges of the Territory of Michigan

AN ACT DEFINING THE POWERS OF THE TRUSTEES AND VISITORS
APPOINTED BY THE UNIVERSITY OF MICHIGANIA AND ALSO
THE QUALIFICATIONS OF INSTRUCTORS

Be it enacted by the University of Michigania that the Trustees and
Visitors of the several literary institutions established by the University, be and they are hereby invested with the following powers viz:
The Trustees and Visitors of each institution, whether it be Primary
School, Classical Academy or College, shall have power to call their
own meetings, appoint their own Officers, devise and carry into effect
measures which they may deem proper for the raising of funds, and
erect such buildings as may be convenient for the institution. And
these funds and buildings shall always be appropriated to the institution for which they were procured, and shall not be otherwise applied
but by the mutual approbation of the University and the said Trustees
and Visitors.

It shall also be the duty of the Trustees and Visitors to recommend suitable persons as instructors or Professors in that institution of which they are Trustees and Visitors; and the persons they recommended if approved by the University shall receive commissions accordingly, with the emoluments attached to them.

But if the Trustees and Visitors shall find upon trial that the persons they employed are not competent to the task assigned, or are guilty of misdemeanour, they shall report these facts to the University in order to have the said persons displaced.

It is likewise required of the Trustees that they watch over the interests generally, of the institution to which they shall have been appointed, and to see that the course of studies prescribed by the University is strictly pursued and that all other laws and regulations are duly observed.

Sect. 2. And be it further enacted that no person shall receive or hold a commission as instructor in any of the branches of Science prescribed by the University, unless he shall prove himself fully competent thereto, and unless he be strictly moral and discreet in his deportment and behaviour, and possess the capacity and maintain the habit of preserving good order and discipline amongst his pupils.

Passed at the City of Detroit on Tuesday the twenty-first day of October One thousand Eight hundred and Seventeen.

JOHN MONTEITH
President of the University of Michigania

12. Report of the Rockfish Gap Commission on the Proposed University of Virginia, 1818

See Introduction and Doc. 13.

3. 4. In proceeding to the third and fourth duties prescribed by the legislature of reporting "the branches of learning, which shall be taught in the University, and the number and description of the pro-

"Report of the Rockfish Gap Commission Appointed to Fix the Site of The University of Virginia," August 4, 1818, Virginia State Archives, Richmond, Virginia; first printed in *Journal of the House of Delegates, 1818–1819* (Richmond, 1818), pp. 9–16, and reprinted with permission of the Virginia State Archives.

fessorships they will require" the commissioners were first to consider at what point it was understood that university-education should commence? Certainly not with the Alphabet for reasons of expediency & unpracticability, as well as from the obvious sense of the Legislature, who, in the same act make other provision for the primary instruction of the poor children, expecting doubtless that, in other cases, it would be provided by the parent, or become perhaps a subject of future, and further attention for the legislature. The objects of this primary education determine its character & limits.—These objects would be,

To give to every citizen the information he needs for the transaction of his own business.

To enable him to calculate for himself, and to express & preserve his ideas, his contracts & accounts in writing.

To improve by reading, his morals and faculties.

To understand his duties to his neighbors, & country, and to discharge with competence the functions confided to him by either

To know his rights; to exercise with order and justice those he retains; to choose with discretion the fiduciary of those he delegates; and to notice their conduct with diligence with candor & judgment.

And, in general, to observe with intelligence and faithfulness all the social relations under which he shall be placed.

To instruct the mass of our citizens in these their rights, interests and duties, as men and citizens, being then the objects of education in the primary schools, whether private or public, in them should be taught reading, writing & numerical arithmetic, the elements of mensuration (useful in so many callings) and the outlines of geography and history, and this brings us to the point at which are to commence the higher branches of education, of which the legislature require the development: those for example which are to form the statesmen, legislators & judges, on whom public prosperity, & individual happiness are so much to depend:

To expound the principles and structure of government, the laws which regulate the intercourse of nations, those formed municipally for our own government, and a sound spirit of legislation, which banishing all arbitrary and unnecessary restraint on individual action shall leave us free to do whatever does not violate the equal rights of another.

To harmonize and promote the interests of agriculture, manufac-

tures & commerce and by well informed views of political economy to
give a free scope to the public industry.

To develop the reasoning faculties of our youth, enlarge their minds
cultivate their morals, and instil into them the precepts of virtue and
order:

To enlighten them with mathematical and physical sciences which
advance the arts and administer to the health, the subsistence and
comforts of human life:

And generally to form them to habits of reflection, and correct action, rendering them examples of virtue to others and of happiness
within themselves.

These are the objects of that higher grade of education, the benefits
and blessings of which the legislature now propose to provide for the
good & ornament of their country the gratification and happiness of
their fellow citizens, of the parent especially & his progeny on which
all his affections are concentrated.—

In entering on this field, the commissioners are aware that they have
to encounter much difference of opinion as to the extent which it is
expedient that this institution should occupy. Some good men, and
even of respectable information, consider the learned sciences as useless
acquirements; some think that they do not better the condition of
man; and others that education, like private & individual concerns,
should be left to private & individual effort; not reflecting that an establishment, embracing all the sciences which may be useful & even
necessary in the various vocations of life, with the buildings & apparatus belonging to each, are far beyond the reach of individual
means, & must either derive existence from public patronage or not
exist at all. This would leave us then without those callings which
depend on education, or send us to other countries, to seek the instruction they require. But the Commissioners are happy in considering
the statute under which they are assembled as proof that the legislature
is far from the abandonment of objects so interesting: they are sensible
that the advantages of well directed education, moral, political & economical are truly above all estimate. Education generates habits of
application, of order and the love of virtue; and controuls, by the force
of habit, any innate obliquities in our moral organization. We should
be far too from the discouraging persuasion, that man is fixed, by the
law of his nature, at a given point: that his improvement is a chimæra,
and the hope delusive of rendering ourselves wiser, happier or better

than our forefathers were. As well might it be urged that the wild &
uncultivated tree, hitherto yielding sour & bitter fruit only, can never
be made to yield better: yet we know that the grafting art implants a
new tree on the savage stock, producing what is most estimable both
in kind & degree. Education, in like manner engrafts a new man on
the native stock, & improves what in his nature was vicious & perverse, into qualities of virtue & social worth; and it cannot be but that
each generation succeeding to the knowledge acquired by all those
who preceded it, adding to it their own acquisitions & discoveries, and
handing the mass down for successive & constant accumulation, must
advance the knowledge & well-being of mankind; not *infinitely,* as
some have said, but *indefinitely,* and to a term which no one can fix
or foresee. Indeed we need look back half a century, to times which
many now living remember well, and see the wonderful advances in
the sciences and arts which have been made within that period. Some
of these have rendered the elements themselves subservient to the purposes of man, have harnessed them to the yoke of his labours, and effected the great blessings of moderating his own, of accomplishing
what was beyond his feeble force, & of extending the comforts of life
to a much enlarged circle, to those who had before known its necessaries only. That these are not the vain dreams of sanguine hope, we
have before our eyes real & living examples. What, but education, has
advanced us beyond the condition of our indigenous neighbors? and
what chains them to their present state of barbarism and wretchedness,
but a bigotted veneration for the supposed superlative wisdom of their
fathers and the preposterous idea that they are to look backward for
better things and not forward, longing, as it should seem, to return to
the days of eating acorns and roots rather than indulge in the degen-
eracies of civilization. And how much more encouraging to the
achievements of science and improvement, is this, than the despond-
ing view that the condition of man cannot be ameliorated, that what
has been, must ever be, and that to secure ourselves where we are, we
must tread with awful reverence in the footsteps of our fathers. This
doctrine is the genuine fruit of the alliance between Church and State,
the tenants of which, finding themselves but too well in their present
condition, oppose all advances which might unmask their usurpations,
and monopolies of honors, wealth and power, and fear every change,
as endangering the comforts they now hold. Nor must we omit to
mention, among the benefits of education, the incalculable advantage

of training up able counsellors to administer the affairs of our Country in all its departments, Legislative, Executive, and Judiciary, and to bear their proper share in the councils of our national Government; nothing, more than education, advancing the prosperity, the power and the happiness of a nation. . . .

The considerations which have governed the specification of languages to be taught by the professor of modern languages were that the French is the language of general intercourse among nations, and as a depository of human science is unsurpassed by any other language living or dead: that the Spanish is highly interesting to us, as the language spoken by so great a portion of the inhabitants of our continents, with whom we shall probably have great intercourse ere long; and is that also in which is written the greater part of the earlier history of America.

The Italian abounds with works of very superior order, valuable for their matter, and still more distinguished as models of the finest taste in style and composition: and the German now stands in a line with that of the most learned nations in richness of erudition and advance in the sciences. It is too of common descent with the language of our own country, a branch of the same original Gothic stock, and furnishes valuable illustrations for us. But in this point of view the Anglo-Saxon is of peculiar value. We have placed it among the modern languages because it is in fact that which we speak, in the earliest form in which we have knowledge of it. it has been undergoing, with time, those gradual changes which all languages, antient and modern, have experienced: and, even now, needs only to be printed in the modern character and orthography, to be intelligible, in a considerable degree to an English reader. . . .

Medicine, where fully taught, is usually subdivided into several professorships, but this cannot well be without the accessory of an hospital, where the student can have the benefit of attending clinical lectures & of assisting at operations of surgery. With this accessory, the seat of our University is not yet prepared, either by its population, or by the numbers of poor, who would leave their own houses, and accept of the charities of an hospital. For the present therefore we propose but a single professor for both medicine & anatomy. By him the elements of medical science may be taught, with a history & explanations of all its successive theories from Hippocrates to the present day: and anatomy may be fully treated. Vegetable pharmacy will make a

part of the botanical course, & mineral & chemical pharmacy, of those
of mineralogy & chemistry. This degree of medical information is such
as the mass of scientific students would wish to possess, as enabling
them, in their course thro life, to estimate with satisfaction the extent
& limits of the aid to human life & health, which they may understand-
ingly expect from that art: and it constitutes a foundation for those
intended for the profession, that the finishing course of practice at the
bedsides of the sick, and at the operations of surgery in a hospital, can
neither be long nor expensive. To seek this finishing elsewhere, must
therefore be submitted to for a while.

In conformity with the principles of our constitution, which places
all sects of religion on an equal footing, with the jealousies of the different sects in guarding that equality from encroachment & surprise,
and with the sentiments of the legislature in favor of freedom of religion manifested on former occasions, we have proposed no professor
of Divinity; and tho rather, as the proofs of the being of a god, the
creator, preserver, & supreme ruler of the universe, the author of all
the relations of morality, & of the laws & obligations these infer, will
be within the province of the professor of ethics; to which adding the
developments of these moral obligations, of those in which all sects
agree with a knowledge of the languages, Hebrew, Greek and Latin, a
basis will be formed common to all sects. Proceeding thus far without
offence to the constitution, we have thought it proper, at this point, to
leave every sect to provide as they think fittest, the means of further
instruction in their own peculiar tenets.

We are further of opinion that, after declaring by law that certain
sciences shall be taught in the university, fixing the number of professors they require, which we think should at present, be ten, limiting
(except as to the professors who shall be first engaged in each branch)
a maximum for their salaries, (which should be a certain but moderate
subsistence, to be made up by liberal tuition fees, as an excitement to
assiduity,) it will be best to leave to the discretion of the visitors, the
grouping of these sciences together, according to the accidental qualifications of the professors; and the introduction also of other branches
of science, when enabled by private donations, or by public provision,
and called for by the encrease of population, or other changes of circumstances; to establish beginnings, in short, to be developed by time,
as those who come after us shall find expedient. They will be more

advanced than we are, in science and in useful arts, and will know best what will suit the circumstances of their day. . . .

Signed and certified by the members present, each in his proper handwriting, this 4th day of August 1818.

TH: JEFFERSON	PHIL: C: PENDLETON
CREED TAYLOR	SPENCER ROANE
PETER RANDOLPH	JOHN M. C. TAYLOR
WM: BROCKENBROUGH	J. G. JACKSON
ARCHD. RUTHERFORD	THOS. WILSON
ARCH: STUART	PHIL SLAUGHTER
JAMES BRECKENRIDGE	WM. H. CABELL
HENRY E. WATKINS	NAT. H. CLAIBORNE
JAMES MADISON	WM. A. C. DADE
ARMISTEAD T. MASON	WILLIAM JONES
H. HOLMES	

13. Edward Everett on the Proposed University of Virginia, 1820

On Everett see Part IV, Doc. 23.

We beg leave to commend the whole Report to our readers, as an uncommonly interesting and skilful paper; well assured that they will overlook a little *neologism* in the language, and a few unauthorised words such as *location, centrality, grade,* and *sparse,* for the sake of the liberal zeal for science which it breathes and inculcates.

The general subject of academical education is so important that we venture to ask the attention of our readers a little longer to it. There are two questions to be asked on the subject of universities, first, what a university ought to be, second, how shall it be founded and supported.

Though used in the same general sense in Europe and America the word university is commonly applied by us to institutions considerably different from the European, at least, from the continental establishments: for the plans of the English universities coincide essentially with those of the best American ones. The universities on the continent

Edward Everett, "University of Virginia," *North American Review,* X (January, 1820), 124–27.

are properly speaking professional schools; places to which young men have carried their classical studies to a high degree of perfection, at gymnasia or high schools, resort for the study of their profession, of law, physic or divinity. It is here too, that they prepare themselves for another profession, scarcely known with us, viz. the Classical. All who look forward to places of instruction at the universities or the academies, who propose to get their living as professors or schoolmasters, together with the students of theology, to which class in fact the other for the most part belongs, these all make philology in its widest sense a great and constant study. Nor is it to be supposed that the other students who are preparing themselves in the faculties of law, physic, and divinity confine themselves illiberally to the routine of the professional lectures. There are some kindred branches of knowledge cultivated by the students of each profession, and a few of popular and universal interest attended to by all. Antiquities, the branches of natural science, history, geography, statistics, diplomacy, mechanical processes, agriculture, forestry, the fine arts, archaiology, or the remains of ancient art, hold out attractions for some in each of the professions; and especially occupy the attention of the young men of leisure and fortune, who without devoting themselves to any particular profession, wish to obtain a finished education.

Is nothing of all this wanted in our country? Is it not a defect of our university system, as well as of the English, that no reference is had to the destination of the student, but that he is required to dip into the whole circle of science? No more of the ancient languages is taught at the universities to those, who are hereafter to expound the Hebrew and Greek scriptures, than to those who mean to live in law and politics. Nor are the natural sciences farther explained to him, who is to be a surgeon or physician, than to the future lawyer or minister. How extremely loose men's notions on this subject are, may be seen from the practice of some of our universities, where anatomical demonstrations are made to all the members of the college class, of whom not a sixth part will treasure up the difference between a vein and an artery, a nerve and an absorbent vessel. The report before us, provides for a similar amount of medical instruction without considering that it is too superficial for the professional student, and will in two years, not to say months, be wholly forgotten by all the rest.

But some one may reply, that besides our universities we have professional schools. There are the medical schools at Baltimore, Philadelphia, New York, New Haven, Boston, and Hanover; there are the law schools at Litchfield and Cambridge; the divinity schools at Princeton, New York, Cambridge, and Andover. It is true there are these institutions, more or less resorted to, and more or less deserving to be. But there are two things to be answered to this. The one is that after all, for whatever cause it be, a small part of the professional education which the country requires is sought at these places. Take the country through, and we are nearly sure that not more than half the physicians, and quite sure that not near even that proportion of the lawyers and ministers are educated at these schools. So that if the want of places for professional education be a real defect, these schools do not remedy the want. But secondly, it cannot be expected that they should remedy it. If a part of the fault lies in the state of our society, where it is too easy for any body and every body, with or without merit or education, to get well on, another and perhaps the greater part of the fault lies in the institutions themselves. They are not attractive enough. With two or three exceptions, which it is not necessary to name, they do not hold out very high inducements, even in the single thing, in which they profess to deal. In most of our professional schools even the one little nostrum of which the name is painted up in gilded letters on the sign-board, is dealt out to moderate amount, and not always of the first quality. But more than this, these professional schools suffer from this very division and partition of branches. Learning is not such a wretched mechanical thing, that you can cut it in pieces and carry the parts hundreds of miles from each other, and they will still retain all their properties. It is a living body; its different members belong together, commune vinculum habent; they never possess their true nature and activity when they are sundered. There is a proper corporate spirit in a Universitas Artium, in a place where all the branches of useful knowledge, all the parts of a finished education are brought together to emulate each other, to illustrate, to adorn, to aid each other, and but a small part of this spirit goes with the separate portions of the dismembered whole when removed to a distance from each other. There are many great establishments wanting in an unisity, above all a grand library. The resources of a single professional school are inadequate to procure these. There are many subsidiary and illustrative branches of knowledge belonging to all professions, but not peculiarly so to any, and these can never be expected, can never be supported at a single professional school. At which school, for instance, the medical at Philadelphia, the legal at Litchfield, or the theological at Andover, would you fix a professor of statistics and geography?

Others will start from the beginning, and say that the whole thing is useless, that we do not want any professional institutions; that it is best to learn in the old way, in the office of the lawyer and the study of the doctor or the minister. This notion, it is true, is so fast disappearing that it may seem fighting with shadows to assail it....

14. Daniel Webster Argues the Dartmouth College Case, 1819

The famous last four paragraphs of this document were not a part of the official Court report of the case. They were later written from memory by an observer, Chauncey A. Goodrich, in a letter to Rufus Choate, November 25, 1852. See Rufus Choate, *A Discourse Delivered before the Faculty, Students, and Alumni of Dartmouth College . . . July 27, 1853, Commemorative of Daniel Webster* (Boston and Cambridge, 1853), pp. 34–40; on the authenticity of this account see Carroll A. Wilson, "Familiar 'Small College' Quotations, I: Daniel Webster and Dartmouth," *The Colophon*, N.S., III (Winter, 1938), 14–21.

The background of this case is too complex for a brief review, but in essence the issue was whether the state legislature of New Hampshire could retroactively alter the charter of Dartmouth College. Such a change, introduced in 1816, by which the college was changed to a "university" and otherwise altered, was contested by the trustees of the original college, who engaged Daniel Webster (1782–1852) of the class of 1801 to argue their case before the Supreme Court on appeal from the Supreme Court of New Hampshire. It was the first of his famous arguments before the Court. The decision, in which the Court upheld the case of the college (see Doc. 15), was momentous, both for American business and for American education. In defending the sanctity of charters, it gave sweeping protection to corporate business; in assuring the promoters of private colleges that once they had obtained a state charter they were secure in the future control of the institution, it underwrote the development of small colleges and weakened the position of state universities.

On the local background of the controversy, see William G. North, "The Political Background of the Dartmouth College Case," *New England Quarterly,*

"The Trustees of Dartmouth College *v.* Woodward," *Reports of Cases Argued and Decided in the Supreme Court of the United States,* IV (Newark, N.J., 1882), pp. 555–57, 560–64, 566–69, 574, 582–84, 587–89, 594–96, 598–600; first printed in 4 Wheaton 555–600 (1819).

XVIII (June, 1945), 181–203; on its consequences for subsequent legal cases involving colleges, see Gordon R. Clapp, "The College Charter," *Journal of Higher Education,* V (February, 1934), 79–87. For a full account of the case, with references to the outstanding literature on the subject, see Charles Grove Haines, *The Role of the Supreme Court in American Government and Politics, 1789–1835* (Berkeley, 1944), chap. xi.

The twelve trustees were the sole legal owners of all the property acquired under the charter. By the acts others are admitted, against their will, to be joint owners. The twelve individuals who are trustees, where [*sic*] possessed of all the franchises and immunities conferred by the charter. By the acts, nine other trustees, and twenty-five overseers, are admitted against their will, to divide these franchises and immunities with them. If, either as a corporation or as individuals, they have any legal rights, this forcible intrusion of others violates those rights, as manifestly as an entire and complete ouster and dispossession. These acts alter the whole constitution of the corporation. They affect the rights of the whole body, as a corporation, and the rights of the individuals who compose it. They revoke corporate powers and franchises. They alienate and transfer the property of the college to others. By the charter, the trustees had a right to fill vacancies in their own number. This is now taken away. They were to consist of twelve, and by express provision, of no more. This is altered. They and their successors, appointed by themselves, were forever to hold the property. The legislature has found successors for them, before their seats are vacant. The powers and privileges which the twelve were to exercise exclusively, are now to be exercised by others. By one of the acts, they are subjected to heavy penalties if they exercise their offices, or any of those powers and privileges granted them by charter, and which they had exercised for fifty years. They are to be punished for not accepting the new grant, and taking its benefits. This, it must be confessed, is rather a summary mode of settling a question of constitutional right. Not only are new trustees forced into the corporation, but new trusts and uses are created. The college is turned into a university. Power is given to create new colleges, and to authorize any diversion of the funds which may be agreeable to the new boards, sufficient latitude is given by the undefined power of establishing an institute. To these new colleges, and this institute, the funds contributed by the founder, Dr. Wheelock, and by the original donors, the Earl of Dartmouth and others, are to be applied, in plain and manifest disre-

gard of the uses to which they were given. The president, one of the
old trustees, had a right to his office, salary, and emoluments, subject
to the twelve trustees alone. His title to these is now changed, and he
is made accountable to new masters. So also all the professors and tutors. If the legislature can at pleasure make these alterations and
changes in the rights and privileges of the plaintiffs, it may, with
equal propriety, abolish these rights and privileges altogether. The
same power which can do any part of this work can accomplish the
whole. And, indeed, the argument on which these acts have been
hitherto defended goes altogether on the ground that this is such a
corporation as the legislature may abolish at pleasure, and that its
members have no rights, liberties, franchises, property or privileges,
which the legislature may not revoke, annul, alienate or transfer to
others whenever it sees fit.

It will be contended by the plaintiffs that these acts are not valid and
binding on them without their assent. 1. Because they are against
common right, and the constitution of New Hampshire. 2. Because
they are repugnant to the constitution of the United States. . . .

In the very nature of things, a charter cannot be forced upon anybody. No one can be compelled to accept a grant; and without acceptance the grant is necessarily void. It cannot be pretended that the legislature, as successor to the king in this part of his prerogative, has any
power to revoke, vacate, or alter this charter. If, therefore, the legislature has not this power by any specific grant contained in the constitution; nor as included in its ordinary legislative powers; nor by reason of its succession to the prerogatives of the crown in this particular;
on what ground would the authority to pass these acts rest, even if
there were no special prohibitory clauses in the constitution, and the
bill of rights?

But there are prohibitions in the constitution and bill of rights of
New Hampshire, introduced for the purpose of limiting the legislative power, and of protecting the rights and property of the citizens.
One prohibition is, "that no person shall be deprived of his property,
immunities, or privileges, put out of the protection of the law, or deprived of his life, liberty, or estate, but by judgment of his peers, or the
law of the land." In the opinion, however, which was given in the
court below, it is denied that the trustees, under the charter, had any
property, immunity, liberty or privilege, in this corporation, within the
meaning of this prohibition in the bill of rights. It is said, that it is a

public corporation, and public property. That the trustees have no greater interest in it than any other individuals. That it is not private property, which they can sell, or transmit to their heirs; and that, therefore, they have no interest in it. That their office is a public trust like that of the governor, or a judge: and that they have no more concern in the property of the college than the governor in the property of the state, or than the judges in the fines which they impose on the culprits at their bar. That it is nothing to them whether their powers shall be extended or lessened, any more than it is to the courts, whether their jurisdiction shall be enlarged or diminished. It is necessary, therefore, to inquire into the true nature and character of the corporation, which was created by the charter of 1769. . . .

The corporation in question is not a civil, although it is a lay corporation. It is an eleemosynary corporation. It is a private charity, originally founded and endowed by an individual, with a charter obtained for it at his request, for the better administration of his charity. "The eleemosynary sort of corporations are such as are constituted for the perpetual distributions of the free alms or bounty of the founder of them, to such persons as he has directed. Of this are all hospitals for the maintenance of the poor, sick, and impotent; and all colleges both in our universities and out of them." Eleemosynary corporations are for the management of private property, according to the will of the donors. They are private corporations. A college is as much a private corporation as a hospital; especially a college founded as this was, by private bounty. A college is a charity. "The establishment of learning," says Lord Hardwicke, "is a charity, and so considered in the statute of Elizabeth. A devise to a college, for their benefit, is a laudable charity, and deserves encouragement." The legal signification of a charity is derived chiefly from the statute 43 Eliz., c. 4. "Those purposes," said Sir W. Grant, "are considered charitable which that statute enumerates." Colleges are enumerated as charities in that statute. The government, in these cases, lends its aid to perpetuate the beneficent intention of the donor, by granting a charter, under which his private charity shall continue to be dispensed, after his death. This is done either by incorporating the objects of the charity, as, for instance, the scholars in a college, or the poor in a hospital; or by incorporating those who are to be governors, or trustees, of the charity. In cases of the first sort, the founder is, by the common law, visitor. In early times it became a maxim, that he who gave the property might regulate it in future. *Cujus est dare, ejus est disponere.* This right of visitation descended from the founder to his heir, as a right of property, and precisely as his other property went to his heir; and in default of heirs, it went to the king, as all other property goes to the king, for the want of heirs. The right of visitation arises from the property. It grows out of the endowment. The founder may, if he please, part with it at the time when he establishes the charity, and may vest it in others. Therefore, if he chooses that governors, trustees, or overseers, should be appointed in the charter, he may cause it to be done, and his power of visitation will be transferred to them, instead of descending to his heirs. The persons thus assigned or appointed by the founder will be visitors, with all the powers of the founder, in exclusion of his heir. The right of visitation, then, accrues to them as a matter of property, by the gift, transfer, or appointment of the founder. This is a private right which they can assert in all legal modes, and in which they have the same protection of the law as in all other rights. As visitors, they may make rules, ordinances, and statutes, and alter and repeal them, as far as permitted so to do by the charter. Although the charter proceeds from the crown, or the government, it is considered as the will of the donor. It is obtained at his request. He imposes it as the rule which is to prevail in the dispensation of his bounty in all future times. The king, or government, which grants the charter, is not thereby the founder, but he who furnishes the funds. The gift of the revenues is the foundation. . . . In New England, and perhaps throughout the United States, eleemosynary corporations have been generally established in the latter mode, that is, by incorporating governors or trustees, and vesting in them the right of visitation. Small variations may have been in some instances adopted; as in the case of Harvard College, where some power of inspection is given to the overseers, but not, strictly speaking, a visitatorial power, which still belongs, it is apprehended, to the fellows, or members of the corporation. In general, there are many donors. A charter is obtained, comprising them all, or some of them, and such others as they choose to include, with the right of appointing their successors. They are thus the visitors of their own charity, and appoint others, such as they may see fit, to exercise the same office in time to come. All such corporations are private. The case before the court is clearly that of an eleemosynary corporation. It is, in the strictest legal sense, a private charity. In *King* v. *St. Catharine's Hall,* that college is called a private eleemosynary lay corporation. It was endowed by a private founder, and incorporated by letters patent. And in the same manner was Dartmouth College founded and incorporated. Dr. Wheelock is declared by the charter to be its founder. It was established by him, on funds contributed and collected by himself. As such founder, he had a right of visitation, which he assigned to the trustees, and they received it by his consent and appointment, and held it under the charter. He appointed these trustees visitors, and in that respect to take place of his heir; as he might have appointed devisees to take his estate, instead of his heir. Little, probably, did he think, at that time, that the legislature would ever take away this property and these privileges, and give them to others. Little did he suppose that this charter secured to him and his successors no legal rights. Little did the other donors think so. If they had, the college would have been, what the university is now, a thing upon paper, existing only in name. The numerous academies in New England have been established substantially in the same manner. They hold their property by the same tenure, and no other. Nor has Harvard College any surer title than Dartmouth College. It may, to-day, have more friends; but to-morrow it may have more enemies. Its legal rights are the same. So also of Yale College; and indeed of all the others. When the legislature gives to these institutions, it may, and does, accompany its grants with such conditions as it pleases. The grant of lands by the legislature of New Hampshire to Dartmouth College, in 1789, was accompanied with various conditions. When donations are made, by the legislature, or others, to a charity already existing, without any condition, or the specification of any new use, the donation follows the nature of the charity. Hence the doctrine, that all eleemosynary corporations are private bodies. They are founded by private persons, and on private property. The public cannot be charitable in these institutions. It is not the money of the public, but of private persons, which is dispensed. It may be public, that is general, in its uses and advantages; and the state may very laudably add contributions of its own to the funds; but it is still private in the tenure of the property, and in the right of administering the funds. If the doctrine laid down by Lord Holt, and the House of Lords, in *Phillips* v. *Bury,* and recognized and established in all the other cases, be correct, the property of this college was private property; it was vested in the trustees by the charter, and to be administered by them, according to the will of the founder and donors, as expressed in the charter. They were also visitors of the charity, in the most ample sense. They had, therefore, as they contend, privileges, property, and immunities, within the true meaning of the bill of rights. They had rights, and still have them, which they can assert against the legislature, as well as against other wrong-doers. It makes no difference, that the estate is holden for certain trusts. The legal estate is still theirs. They have a right in the property, and they have a right of visiting and superintending the trust; and this is an object of legal protection, as much as any other right. The charter declares, that the powers conferred on the trustees, are "privileges, advantages, liberties, and immunities;" and that they shall be forever holden by them and their successors. The New Hampshire bill of rights declares, that no one shall be deprived of his "property, privileges, or immunities," but by judgment of his peers, or the law of the land. The argument on the other side is, that although these terms may mean something in the bill of rights, they mean nothing in this charter. But they are terms of legal signification, and very properly used in the charter. They are equivalent with franchises. Blackstone says that franchise and liberty are used as synonymous terms. . . . The granting of the corporation is but making the trust perpetual, and does not alter the nature of the charity. The very object sought in obtaining such charter, and in giving property to such a corporation, is to make and keep it private property, and to clothe it with all the security and inviolability of private property. The intent is, that there shall be a legal private ownership, and that the legal owners shall maintain and protect the property, for the benefit of those for whose use it was designed. Who ever endowed the public? Who ever appointed a legislature to administer his charity? Or who ever heard, before, that a gift to a college, or hospital, or an asylum, was, in reality, nothing but a gift to the state? . . .

That the power of electing and appointing the officers of this college is not only a right of the trustees as a corporation generally, and in the aggregate, but that each individual trustee has also his own individual franchise in such right of election and appointment, is according to the language of all the authorities. Lord Holt says, "it is agreeable to reason and the rules of law that a franchise should be vested in the corporation aggregate, and yet the benefit of it to redound to the particular members, and to be enjoyed by them in their private capacity. Where the privilege of election is used by particular persons, it is a particular right, vested in every particular man."

It is also to be considered that the president and professors of this college have rights to be affected by these acts. Their interest is similar to that of fellows in the English colleges; because they derive their living wholly, or in part, from the founder's bounty. The president is one of the trustees, or corporators. The professors are not necessarily members of the corporation; but they are appointed by the trustees, are removable only by them, and have fixed salaries, payable out of the general funds of the college. Both president and professors have free-holds in their offices; subject only to be removed by the trustees, as their legal visitors, for good cause. All the authorities speak of fellow-ships in colleges as freeholds, notwithstanding the fellows may be liable to be suspended or removed, for misbehavior, by their consti-tuted visitors. Nothing could have been less expected, in this age, than that there should have been an attempt, by acts of the legislature, to take away these college livings, the inadequate, but the only support of literary men, who have devoted their lives to the instruction of youth. The president and professors were appointed by the twelve trustees. They were accountable to nobody else, and could be removed by nobody else. They accepted their offices on this tenure. Yet the legis-lature has appointed other persons, with power to remove these offi-cers, and to deprive them of their livings; and those other persons have exercised that power. No description of private property has been regarded as more sacred than college livings. They are the estates and freeholds of a most deserving class of men; of scholars who have con-sented to forego the advantages of professional and public employ-ments, and to devote themselves to science and literature, and the in-struction of youth, in the quiet retreats of academic life. Whether, to dispossess and oust them; to deprive them of their office, and turn them out of their livings; to do this, not by the power of their legal visitors, or governors, but by acts of the legislature; and to do it without for-feiture, and without fault; whether all this be not in the highest de-gree an indefensible and arbitrary proceeding, is a question, of which there would seem to be but one side fit for a lawyer or a scholar to espouse. . . .

If it could be made to appear that the trustees and the president and professors held their offices and franchises during the pleasure of the legislature, and that the property holden belonged to the state, then, indeed, the legislature have done no more than they had a right to do. But this is not so. The charter is a charter of privileges and immunities; and these are holden by the trustees expressly against the state forever.

It is admitted that the state, by its courts of law, can enforce the will of the donor, and compel a faithful execution of the trust. The plaintiffs claim no exemption from legal responsibility. They hold themselves at all times answerable to the law of the land for their conduct in the trust committed to them. They ask only to hold the property of which they are owners, and the franchises which belong to them, until they shall be found, by due course and process of law, to have forfeited them. It can make no difference whether the legislature exercise the power it has assumed, by removing the trustees and the president and professors, directly, and by name, or by appointing others to expel them. The principal is the same, and in point of fact, the result has been the same. If the entire franchise cannot be taken away, neither can it be essentially impaired. If the trustees are legal owners of the property, they are sole owners. If they are visitors, they are sole visitors. No one will be found to say, that if the legislature may do what it has done, it may not do anything and every thing which it may choose to do, relative to the property of the corporation, and the privileges of its members and officers.

If the view which has been taken of this question be at all correct, this was an eleemosynary corporation; a private charity. The property was private property. The trustees were visitors, and their right to hold the charter, administer the funds, and visit and govern the college, was a franchise and privilege, solemnly granted to them. The use being public, in no way diminishes their legal estate in the property, or their title to the franchise. There is no principle, nor any case, which declares that a gift to such a corporation is a gift to the public. The acts in question violate property. They take away privileges, immunities, and franchises. They deny to the trustees the protection of the law; and they are retrospective in their operation. In all which respects, they are against the constitution of New Hampshire.

2. The plaintiffs contend, in the second place, that the acts in question are repugnant to the 10th section of the 1st article of the constitution of the United States. The material words of that section are: "No state shall pass any bill of attainder, *ex post facto* law, or law impairing the obligation of contracts." . . .

There are, in this case, all the essential constituent parts of a contract. There is something to be contracted about; there are parties, and there are plain terms in which the agreement of the parties, on the subject of the contract, is expressed. There are mutual considerations and inducements. The charter recites, that the founder, on his part, has agreed to establish his seminary in New Hampshire, and to enlarge it, beyond its original design, among other things, for the benefit of that province; and thereupon a charter is given to him and his associates, designated by himself, promising and assuring to them, under the plighted faith of the state, the right of governing the college, and administering its concerns, in the manner provided in the charter. There is a complete and perfect grant to them of all the power of superintendence, visitation, and government. Is not this a contract? If lands or money had been granted to him and his associates, for the same purposes, such grant could not be rescinded. And is there any difference, in legal contemplation, between a grant of corporate franchises and a grant of tangible property? No such difference is recognized in any decided case, nor does it exist in the common apprehension of mankind.

It is therefore contended, that this case falls within the true meaning of this provision of the constitution, as expounded in the decisions of this court; that the charter of 1769 is a contract, a stipulation, or agreement; mutual in its considerations, express and formal in its terms, and of a most binding and solemn nature. That the acts in question impair this contract, has already been sufficiently shown. They repeal and abrogate its most essential parts. . . .

The case before the court is not of ordinary importance, nor of every-day occurrence. It affects not this college only, but every college, and all the literary institutions of the country. They have flourished, hitherto, and have become in a high degree respectable and useful to the community. They have all a common principle of existence—the inviolability of their charters. It will be a dangerous, a most dangerous experiment, to hold these institutions subject to the rise and fall of popular parties, and the fluctuations of political opinions. If the franchise may be at any time taken away, or impaired, the property also may be taken away, or its use perverted. Benefactors will have no certainty of effecting the object of their bounty; and learned men will be deterred from devoting themselves to the service of such institutions, from the precarious title of their officers. Colleges and halls will be deserted by all better spirits, and become a theatre for the contention of politics. Party and faction will be cherished in the places consecrated to piety and learning. These consequences are neither remote nor possible only. They are certain and immediate.

When the court in North Carolina declared the law of the state, which repealed a grant to its university, unconstitutional and void, the legislature had the candor and the wisdom to repeal the law. This example, so honorable to the state which exhibited it, is most fit to be followed on this occasion. And there is good reason to hope that a state which has hitherto been so much distinguished for temperate councils, cautious legislation, and regard to law, will not fail to adopt a course which will accord with her highest and best interest, and, in no small degree, elevate her reputation. It was for many obvious reasons most anxiously desired that the question of the power of the legislature over this charter should have been finally decided in the state court. An earnest hope was entertained that the judges of that court might have viewed the case in a light favorable to the rights of the trustees. That hope has failed. It is here that those rights are now to be maintained, or they are prostrated forever. *Omnia alia perfugia bonorum, subsidia, consilia, auxilia, jura ceciderunt. Quem enim alium appellem? quem obtestor? quem implorem? Nisi hoc loco, nisi apud vos, nisi per vos, judices, salutem nostram, quae spe exigua extremaque pendet, temerimus; nihil est praeterea quo confugere possimus.*

This, Sir, is my case! It is the case, not merely of that humble institution, it is the case of every College in the land. It is more. It is the case of every Eleemosynary Institution throughout our country—of all those great charities founded by the piety of our ancestors to alleviate human misery, and scatter blessings along the pathway of life. It is more! It is, in some sense, the case of every man among us who has property of which he may be stripped, for the question is simply this: Shall our State Legislatures be allowed to take *that* which is not their own, to turn it from its original use, and apply it to such ends or purposes as they, in their discretion, shall see fit!

Sir, you may destroy this little Institution; it is weak; it is in your hands! I know it is one of the lesser lights in the literary horizon of our country. You may put it out. But, if you do so, you must carry through your work! You must extinguish, one after another, all those greater lights of science which, for more than a century, have thrown their radiance over our land!

It is, Sir, as I have said, a small College. And yet, *there are those who love it*—.

Sir, I know not how others may feel (glancing at the opponents of the College before him), but, for myself, when I see my alma mater surrounded, like Caesar in the senate house, by those who are reiterating stab after stab, I would not, for this right hand, have her turn to me, and say, *Et tu quoque mi fili! And thou too, my son!*

15. Chief Justice John Marshall's Opinion in the Dartmouth College Case, 1819

See Doc. 14.

This court can be insensible neither to the magnitude nor delicacy of this question. The validity of a legislative act is to be examined; and the opinion of the highest law tribunal of a state is to be revised: an opinion which carries with it intrinsic evidence of the diligence, of the ability, and the integrity with which it was formed. . . .

It can require no argument to prove that the circumstances of this case constitute a contract. An application is made to the crown for a charter to incorporate a religious and literary institution. In the application, it is stated that large contributions have been made for the object, which will be conferred on the corporation as soon as it shall be created. The charter is granted, and on its faith the property is conveyed. Surely in this transaction every ingredient of a complete and legitimate contract is to be found.

The points for consideration are:

1. Is this contract protected by the constitution of the United States?
2. Is it impaired by the acts under which the defendant holds?

1. On the first point it has been argued that the word "contract," in its broadest sense, would comprehend the political relations between the government and its citizens, would extend to offices held within a state for state purposes, and to many of those laws concerning civil institutions, which must change with circumstances, and be modified by ordinary legislation; which deeply concern the public, and which, to

"The Trustees of Dartmouth College *v.* Woodward," *Reports of Cases Argued and Decided in the Supreme Court of the United States,* IV (Newark, N.J., 1882), 625–54; first printed in 4 Wheaton 625–54 (1819).

preserve good government, the public judgment must control. That
even marriage is a contract, and its obligations are affected by the laws
respecting divorces. That the clause in the constitution, if construed in
its greatest latitude, would prohibit these laws. Taken in its broad unlimited sense, the clause would be an unprofitable and vexatious interference with the internal concerns of a state, would unnecessarily and
unwisely embarrass its legislation, and render immutable those civil
institutions which are established for purposes of internal government,
and which, to subserve those purposes, ought to vary with varying
circumstances. That as the framers of the constitution could never
have intended to insert in that instrument a provision so unnecessary,
so mischievous, and so repugnant to its general spirit, the term "contract" must be understood in a more limited sense. That it must be
understood as intended to guard against a power of at least doubtful
utility, the abuse of which had been extensively felt; and to restrain
the legislature in future from violating the right to property. That
anterior to the formation of the constitution, a course of legislation
had prevailed in many, if not in all, of the states, which weakened the
confidence of man in man, and embarrassed all transactions between
individuals, by dispensing with a faithful performance of engage-
ments. To correct this mischief, by restraining the power which produced it, the state legislatures were forbidden "to pass any law impairing the obligation of contracts," that is, of contracts respecting property, under which some individual could claim a right to something
beneficial to himself; and that since the clause in the constitution must
in construction receive some limitation, it may be confined, and ought
to be confined, to cases of this description; to cases within the mischief
it was intended to remedy.

The general correctness of these observations cannot be controverted. That the framers of the constitution did not intend to restrain
the states in the regulation of their civil institutions, adopted for internal government, and that the instrument they have given us is not to
be so construed, may be admitted. The provision of the constitution
never has been understood to embrace other contracts than those
which respect property, or some object of value, and confer rights
which may be asserted in a court of justice. It never has been understood to restrict the general right of the legislature to legislate on the
subject of divorces. . . .

The parties in this case differ less on general principles, less on the true construction of the constitution in the abstract, than on the application of those principles to this case, and on the true construction of the charter of 1769. This is the point on which the cause essentially depends. If the act of incorporation be a grant of political power, if it create a civil institution to be employed in the administration of the government, or if the funds of the college be public property, or if the state of New Hampshire, as a government, be alone interested in its transactions, the subject is one in which the legislature of the state may act according to its own judgment, unrestrained by any limitation of its power imposed by the constitution of the United States.

But if this be a private eleemosynary institution, endowed with a capacity to take property for objects unconnected with government, whose funds are bestowed by individuals on the faith of the charter; if the donors have stipulated for the future disposition and management of those funds in the manner prescribed by themselves, there may be more difficulty in the case, although neither the persons who have made these stipulations nor those for whose benefit they were made, should be parties to the cause. Those who are no longer interested in the property, may yet retain such an interest in the preservation of their own arrangements as to have a right to insist that those arrangements shall be held sacred. Or, if they have themselves disappeared, it becomes a subject of serious and anxious inquiry, whether those whom they have legally empowered to represent them forever may not assert all the rights which they possessed, while in being; whether, if they be without personal representatives who may feel injured by a violation of the compact, the trustees be not so completely their representatives, in the eye of the law, as to stand in their place, not only as respects the government of the college, but also as respects the maintenance of the college charter.

It becomes, then, the duty of the court most seriously to examine this charter, and to ascertain its true character. . . .

Are the trustees and professors public officers, invested with any portion of political power, partaking in any degree in the administration of civil government, and performing duties which flow from the sovereign authority?

That education is an object of national concern, and a proper subject of legislation, all admit. That there may be an institution founded by government, and placed entirely under its immediate control, the officers of which would be public officers, amenable exclusively to government, none will deny. But is Dartmouth College such an institution? Is education altogether in the hands of government? Does every teacher of youth become a public officer, and do donations for the purpose of education necessarily become public property, so far that the will of the legislature, not the will of the donor, becomes the law of the donation? These questions are of serious moment to society, and deserve to be well considered. . . .

Whence, then, can be derived the idea that Dartmouth College has become a public institution, and its trustees public officers, exercising powers conferred by the public for public objects? Not from the source whence its funds were drawn; for its foundation is purely private and eleemosynary. Not from the application of those funds; for money may be given for education, and the persons receiving it do not, by being employed in the education of youth, become members of the civil government. Is it from the act of incorporation? Let this subject be considered.

A corporation is an artificial being, invisible, intangible, and existing only in contemplation of law. Being the mere creature of law, it possesses only those properties which the charter of its creation confers upon it, either expressly or as incidental to its very existence. These are such as are supposed best calculated to effect the object for which it was created. Among the most important are immortality, and, if the expression may be allowed, individuality; properties by which a perpetual succession of many persons are considered as the same, and may act as a single individual. They enable a corporation to manage its own affairs, and to hold property without the perplexing intricacies, the hazardous and endless necessity, of perpetual conveyances for the purpose of transmitting it from hand to hand. It is chiefly for the purpose of clothing bodies of men, in succession, with these qualities and capacities, that corporations were invented, and are in use. By these means, a perpetual succession of individuals are capable of acting for the promotion of the particular object, like one immortal being. . . .

From this review of the charter, it appears that Dartmouth College is an eleemosynary institution, incorporated for the purpose of perpetuating the application of the bounty of the donors, to the specified objects of that bounty; that its trustees or governors were originally named by the founder, and invested with the power of perpetuating themselves; that they are not public officers, nor is it a civil institution, participating in the administration of government; but a charity school, or a seminary of education, incorporated for the preservation of its property, and the perpetual application of that property to the objects of its creation. . . .

According to the theory of the British constitution, their parliament is omnipotent. To annul corporate rights might give a shock to public opinion, which that government has chosen to avoid; but its power is not questioned. Had parliament, immediately after the emanation of this charter, and the execution of those conveyances which followed it, annuled the instrument, so that the living donors would have witnessed the disappointment of their hopes, the perfidy of the transaction would have been universally acknowledged. Yet then, as now, the donors would have had no interest in the property; then, as now, those who might be students would have had no rights to be violated; then, as now, it might be said, that the trustees, in whom the rights of all were combined, possessed no private, individual, beneficial interest in the property confided to their protection. Yet the contract would at that time have been deemed sacred by all. What has since occurred to strip it of its inviolability? Circumstances have not changed it. In reason, in justice, and in law, it is now what it was in 1769.

This is plainly a contract to which the donors, the trustees, and the crown (to whose rights and obligations New Hampshire succeeds), were the original parties. It is a contract made on a valuable consideration. It is a contract for the security and disposition of property. It is a contract, on the faith of which real and personal estate has been conveyed to the corporation. It is then a contract within the letter of the constitution, and within its spirit also, unless the fact that the property is invested by the donors in trustees for the promotion of religion and education, for the benefit of persons who are perpetually changing, though the objects remain the same, shall create a particular exception, taking this case out of the prohibition contained in the constitution.

It is more than possible that the preservation of rights of this description was not particularly in the view of the framers of the constitution when the clause under consideration was introduced into that instrument. It is probable that interferences of more frequent recurrence, to which the temptation was stronger, and of which the mischief was more extensive, constituted the great motive for imposing this restriction on the state legislatures. But although a particular and a rare case may not, in itself, be of sufficient magnitude to induce a rule, yet it must be governed by the rule, when established, unless some plain and strong reason for excluding it can be given. It is not enough to say that this particular case was not in the mind of the convention when the article was framed, nor of the American people when it was adopted. It is necessary to go farther, and to say that, had this particular case been suggested, the language would have been so varied, as to exclude it, or it would have been made a special exception. The case being within the words of the rule, must be within its operation likewise, unless there be something in the literal construction so obviously absurd, or mischievous, or repugnant to the general spirit of the instrument, as to justify those who expound the constitution in making it an exception.

On what safe and intelligible ground can this exception stand[?] There is no exception in the constitution, no sentiment delivered by its contemporaneous expounders, which would justify us in making it. . . .

Almost all eleemosynary corporations, those which are created for the promotion of religion, of charity, or of education, are of the same character. The law of this case is the law of all. . . .

The opinion of the court, after mature deliberation, is, that this is a contract, the obligation of which cannot be impaired without violating the constitution of the United States. This opinion appears to us to be equally supported by reason, and by the former decisions of this court.

2. We next proceed to the inquiry whether its obligation has been impaired by those acts of the legislature of New Hampshire to which the special verdict refers. . . .

The obligations, then, which were created by the charter to Dartmouth College, were the same in the new that they had been in the old government. The power of the government was also the same. A repeal of this charter at any time prior to the adoption of the present constitution of the United States, would have been an extraordinary and unprecedented act of power, but one which could have been contested only by the restrictions upon the legislature, to be found in the constitution of the state. But the constitution of the United States has imposed this additional limitation, that the legislature of a state shall pass no act "impairing the obligation of contracts."

It has been already stated that the act "to amend the charter, and enlarge and improve the corporation of Dartmouth College," increases the number of trustees to twenty-one, gives the appointment of the additional members to the executive of the state, and creates a board of overseers, to consist of twenty-five persons, of whom twenty-one are also appointed by the executive of New Hampshire, who have power to inspect and control the most important acts of the trustees.

On the effect of this law, two opinions cannot be entertained. Between acting directly, and acting through the agency of trustees and overseers, no essential difference is perceived. The whole power of governing the college is transferred from trustees appointed according to the will of the founder, expressed in the charter, to the executive of New Hampshire. The management and application of the funds of this eleemosynary institution, which are placed by the donors in the hands of trustees named in the charter, and empowered to perpetuate themselves, are placed by this act under the control of the government of the state. The will of the state is substituted for the will of the donors, in every essential operation of the college. This is not an immaterial change. . . . This system is totally changed. The charter of 1769 exists no longer. It is re-organized; and re-organized in such a manner as to convert a literary institution, moulded according to the will of its founders, and placed under the control of private literary men, into a machine entirely subservient to the will of government. This may be for the advantage of this college in particular, and may be for the advantage of literature in general, but it is not according to the will of the donors, and is subversive of that contract, on the faith of which their property was given. . . .

It results from this opinion, that the acts of the legislature of New Hampshire, which are stated in the special verdict found in this cause, are repugnant to the constitution of the United States; and that the judgment on this special verdict ought to have been for the plaintiffs. The judgment of the State Court must therefore be reversed.

[Mr. Justice Washington and Mr. Justice Story rendered separate concurring opinions. Mr. Justice Duvall dissented.]

16. Robert Finley on National Uniformity in Textbooks, ca. 1815

Robert Finley (1772–1817) was born in Princeton and graduated from the College of New Jersey at the age of fifteen. Later he studied theology with John Witherspoon (see Part II, Doc. 10) and was ordained in 1795 in the Presbyterian church. From 1807 to 1817 he was a trustee of his alma mater, and among his other interests was the organization of the American Colonization Society. He accepted the presidency of the University of Georgia in 1817 shortly before his premature death.

To introduce entire uniformity into the American system of education, would it not be advisable for those colleges which can be brought to adopt the same elementary books in the several departments, classical, mathematical and philosophical, to select, arrange and publish a complete set of studies, to be distinguished and known as the particular studies of these institutions? And, should this arrangement be found impracticable, would it not be highly advantageous for each college to make this selection for its own use, and as far as necessary, for the accommodation of its subordinate schools? By this measure

1. Money *might* be saved to the learner.

Most of the books now used in schools and colleges, are published in a style of execution more costly than necessary, and are bought at too dear a rate. In many instances the expense of procuring a whole work is incurred, while only a small portion of it is read or studied. The paper is often thin and perishable, and the binding very slight and inferior. In the proposed publication these disadvantages might easily be remedied. The materials and the workmanship should be of the most substantial and durable nature. All unnecessary matter it is proposed to leave out.

2. On the plan here contemplated, *accuracy,* in classical books, might be restored.

The Latin and Greek authors printed in this country abound so exceedingly with typographical errors that very great injury is sustained from the use of them in schools. When inaccuracies frequently occur, the teacher is incessantly harrassed and the business of school inter-

Isaac V. Brown, *Memoirs of the Rev. Robert Finley* (New Brunswick, N.J., 1819), pp. 350–53, 355, 356–59.

rupted, by applications to have the classical text examined, and existing errors exposed and corrected. In this manner much time is lost and the school is injured; and, besides, the student, always ready to impute difficulty to inaccuracy and to suspend his efforts till doubt is removed, finds his diligence in application and independent exercise of thought much impaired. These disadvantages have been experienced so seriously, that it has been judged expedient in some instances to keep a European edition, of the principal authors read, as a standard to refer to—a fact disgraceful and humiliating to American scholars!

3. The proposed publication *might* be made entirely free from those *impurities,* with which some of the best classical writers unhappily abound. Retaining passages, which convey insinuations against religion and morals and which are of an obscene and vitiating tendency in those books which are very early put into the hands of youth, to be carefully studied, is very manifestly dangerous and improper. It would be a favor, of no common magnitude, to the principles and morals of literary youth, to have every thing licentious, low, and polluting, removed from our classical authors. A remedy might thus be furnished for the evils and the dangers arising from making our young men whom we wish to lead to the knowledge of the one only living and true God, too early and too intimately acquainted with Grecian and Roman Polytheism—with the fictions and absurdities of their mythology—and with the vices and follies of their imaginary deities.

4. This measure would contribute very extensively to that *uniformity* which is so much desired. Wherever this work would circulate, the plan of education pursued in the institution, which had given it existence might be fully understood, and easily followed. The public in general, teachers, and schools especially, would know precisely in what manner, the preliminary studies of a candidate for that college must be conducted, to obtain for him an easy and honorable admission into it.

Might we not adopt with some prudent modifications in our literary institutions, that part of the ancient Jewish system of education, in which they trained their pupils to an acquaintance with mechanical pursuits, in connexion with letters and science, and while they strengthened and enriched the minds of their scholars with literary culture, established them in the practical knowledge of the useful arts and mechanical employments of life? If acquiring practical knowledge of mechanics, of gardening, of agriculture could be made to occupy a portion of that time which is commonly spent in idleness and amusement, and be brought to answer the purpose of necessary exercise, several additional objects of considerable importance would be in some degree gained, by the alteration. . . .

The last consideration is, that every man, whatever his grade of talent, his degree of education, and his sphere in life, ought to have a practical acquaintance with some mechanic art. Should he never pursue any branch of mechanical employ, his progess through life, his respectability, ease and comfort, will be greatly promoted by a general acquaintance with the common necessary and useful arts and occupations of men. . . .

Great exertions have recently been made to establish new colleges in several states in the union, and measures have been adopted in some of the best institutions in our country, to enlarge and ameliorate their capacity for the accommodation and instruction of youth. But, notwithstanding, a *University* located near the centre of the United States, amply endowed and extensively patronised by the national government, is a desideratum of great magnitude. The wise and patriotic Washington suggested an idea of this nature in his last will and testament, and the reasons on which he founded that intimation are still applicable in all their force. . . .

The colleges of the United States are so circumscribed in their resources and restricted in their views, as to embrace in their system of instruction only those subjects which are most common and essential in a literary course. Other objects, hitherto neglected, are becoming highly interesting. A *university,* established on a widely extended scale, so as to comprehend them all, would be truly worthy of national attention, and extensively conducive to national honour and interest.

This institution, besides the classical, mathematical and philosophical professorships, ought to possess,

1. A theological department, amply endowed for the purpose of teaching the elements of natural and revealed religion, biblical and ecclesiastical history, moral and theological science in general.

2. It ought to include a professorship for the languages of modern Europe.

This would be a great convenience to young men of talent and enterprise, seeking education principally as an auxiliary in the honourable pursuits of foreign commerce. It would afford to American genius a more direct and easy access to those stores of polite and accomplished literature, which have been accumulating for centuries in the South of

Europe, but from which our sons must be excluded while ignorant of the languages which are the only key to their depositories. And it would be an important accommodation to that part of our citizens who inhabit the regions in the South and West, where the French and Spanish especially, are becoming almost vernacular tongues.

3. A professorship for the purpose of extending the knowledge of the languages of the various nations of America, Asia and Africa.

This would facilitate the necessary intercourse with the American tribes both in treaty and in traffic; it would furnish a ready and happy assistant in carrying on the lucrative commerce with the Eastern World; it would extensively aid the glorious cause of foreign missions, in promoting which, every American statesman and philanthropist should feel a pride and an interest; it would enlarge the compass of human knowledge, by extending the sphere of education in this Western land; and in the course of time, by its indirect operation on the aborigines of India, Africa and America, it might have extensive influence in producing that community of sentiment and manners, that amelioration of aspect and condition, which will soon, we hope, be exhibited by the human race.

4. In this institution provision should be made, in the best manner practicable, for exciting, directing and aiding the efforts of American genius, in the cultivation of the *fine arts*.

With success in this department of science, the honour of the nation is closely connected. Europe claims pre-eminence in the arts, and looks down upon the United States with disdain. Let every encouragement and facility for the successful cultivation of American talent and taste, be afforded by a liberal and enlightened government, jealous of its own honour, and anxious for the best improvement of its own sons, in those arts and accomplishments which peculiarly liberalize, elevate and adorn the human character.

5. This establishment ought to afford to American youth, the means of obtaining accurate theoretic and practical knowledge of *agriculture*.

The course of improvement which this country seems destined to undergo, by means of canals, turnpikes, bridges, fortifications, &c. &c. will demand increasing skill in mechanic arts and operations. The American people have also manifested a strong predilection for manufacturing pursuits of various kinds. These objects respectively are highly deserving of national patronage. But, from the extent of our territory, the excellence of our climate, the fertility of our soil, the ideas, habits and necessities of the people, *agriculture* appears likely to be the general and predominant occupation of the American States. And as a warrant for making a system of instruction on this subject, an appendage of a great literary institution, it may be recollected that the example has been set in many of the most celebrated universities of Europe. . . .

17. Jefferson on the Virginia Legislature's Attitude toward a University, 1821

See Doc. 7. Jefferson's remarks here suggest how much educational plans were already affected by sectional hostility and rivalry in the years just after the Missouri controversy. Joseph Carrington Cabell (1778–1856) was Jefferson's chief co-worker in establishing the University of Virginia.

Even with the whole funds we shall be reduced to 6 professors. While Harvard will still prime it over us with her 20 professors. How many of our youths she now has, learning the lessons of anti-Missouri-anism, I know not; but a gentleman lately from Princeton, told me he saw there the list of the students at that place, and that more than half were Virginians. These will return home, no doubt, deeply impressed with the sacred principles of our Holy Alliance of Restrictionists.

18. Francis W. Gilmer's Mission for Jefferson, 1824

Francis Walker Gilmer (1790–1826) was born in Virginia and graduated (1810) from William and Mary. Having read law with the distinguished lawyer William Wirt, he settled down to an outstanding career at the bar, which left him time for the development of his many literary interests. He declined an appointment as

Thomas Jefferson to Joseph C. Cabell, Monticello, January 31, 1821, Jefferson MSS, Vol. CCXIX, Library of Congress.

R. B. Davis (ed.), *Correspondence of Thomas Jefferson and Francis Walker Gilmer, 1814–1826* (Columbia, S.C., 1946), pp. 92–94, 101–3, 106–9. The letters from Gilmer are reprinted with the permission of the Missouri Historical Society. Jefferson's letter is reprinted with the permission of the Alderman Library, University of Virginia.

professor of law in the University of Virginia but agreed to go to Great Britain at
Jefferson's request to get books and equipment and recruit professors for the new
institution. He succeeded in bringing five foreign scholars who helped to get
the university off to a reputable start, but the ardors of his trip contributed to his
premature death. See Doc. 7, and W. P. Trent, "English Culture in Virginia,"
Johns Hopkins University Studies in History and Political Science, VII (1889),
Nos. 5–6.

Hatton, July 20th. 1824

DEAR SIR:

Education at the universities has become so expensive, that it is almost exclusively confined to the nobility and the opulent gentry, no
one of whom, could we expect to engage. Of the few persons at oxford, or cambridge, who have any extraordinary talent, I believe 99
out of 100, are designed for the profession of law, the gown, or aspire
to political distinction; and it would be difficult to persuade one of
these, even if poor, to repress so far the impulse of youthful ambition
as to accept a professorship in a college, in an unknown country. They
who are less aspiring, who have learning, are caught up at an early
period in their several colleges; soon become fellows, & hope to be masters, which with the apartments, garden, and 4. 5 or 600 £ sterling a
year, comprises all they can imagine of comfort or happiness. Just at
this time too, there are building at Cambridge, two very large colleges
attached to Trinity, and King's which will be the most splendid of all.
This creates a new demand for professors, and raises new hopes in the
graduates.

all these difficulties, are multiplied by the system we have been compelled to adopt, in accumulation so many burthens on one professor.
To all the branches of Natural Philosophy, to add chemistry, & astronomy, each of very great compass, strikes them here with amazement.

The unprecedented length of the session you propose, is also a dis-
maying circumstance, as this will probably be altered in time, it is I
think to be regretted, that we had not begun with longer vacations. At
cambridge and oxford there are three vacations. The longest is from
about the 1st. July, to the 10th. october, altogether, there is a holiday
of near 5 months. I inquired at Cambridge if there was any good reason for this long recess. They answered "it is indispensable, no one
could study in such hot weather."—"It is necessary to refresh the constitution, oppressed by the continued application of many months."

&c. If the heat is insufferable in England, what must it be in our July, August &c. when there is to be no vacation?

I see distinctly, that it will be wholly impossible, to procure professors *from either university* by the time you wished. Whether I can find them elsewhere in England is most doubtful, in time I fear not. I shall not return without engaging them, if they are to be had, in G. B. or Germany. I have serious thoughts of trying Gottingen, where the late political persecutions of men of letters, will naturally incline them to us, and where classical literature at least, is highly cultivated. Dr. Parr seems to prefer this course, but I shall not be hasty in adopting it, as I fear the want of our language, will prove a great obstacle. . . .

F. W. GILMER

London, 15 September 1824

DEAR SIR:

I have given you so much bad news, that I determined to delay writing a few days, that I might communicate something more agreable.

When I returned from Edinburgh, where my ill success, is in part to be ascribed (I am well assured,) to the ill will of some of our Eastern Bretheren, who had just before me, been in Scotland, I determined to remain at London, as the most convenient point for correspondence; Here, assisted by Key our mathematician (with whom I am more pleased the more I see of him,) and several men of character & learning, I have been busily engaged since I last wrote. I have had the good fortune to enlist with us for the ancient languages, a learned and highly respectable Cantab. but there have been two obstacles, that have made me pause long, before I conclude with him. He has no knowledge of Hebrew, which is to be taught at the university. This I easily reconciled to my duty, from the absolute necessity of the case. oriental literature is very little esteemed in England, and we might seek a whole year, & perhaps not at last find a real scholar in Latin & Greek, who understands Hebrew. The other difficulty is more serious. Mr. Long the person I mean, is an alumnus of Trinity College, Cambridge. He is entitled to his fellowship, only on condition of his presenting himself at the meeting, in the first week of July next: failure to do this, no matter under what circumstances, will deprive him of about £300 *per annum.* That would be a great sacrifice. Still he seems to me so decidedly superior to his competitors, who do not lie under the incapacity of being of clerical character, that I believe I shall not be faithful to my trust, if I do not engage him, with a reservation of the privilege of being at Cambridge, for a week *only* in July. That is my present impression, and very strongly fixed. Tho', there was another most competent professor I could have, but for his being a clergyman.

The professor of anatomy &c. is a very intelligent & laborious gentleman, a Dr. Dunglison now of London, and a writer of considerable eminence on various medical & anatomical subjects.

The professors of natural philosophy & of natural history, still remain to be procured. I despair of finding Chemistry with natural history. It may go with natural philosophy, especially as the mathematician can take astronomy, or it may belong [to] Dr. Dunglison, who is very desirous of having it with his department.

Another week will inform me, what can be done about the two vacant chairs.

The library & apparatus, have given me great difficulty & trouble. I delayed as long as possible, speaking for them, to have the assistance of the professors. But the time for shipping them now presses so close, I have made out a catalogue of such as we must have, and have ordered the books & instruments, to be shipped as soon as possible. The present aspect of affairs assures me, we shall be able to open the university on the 1st of February as you desired.

The professors vary in age from about 26 to 43 or 4. Blaetterman is already married, and by a very singular coincidence, wholly unknown to me at the time, each of the others, tho' now unmarried will take out a young English wife. Tho' if they would take my advice, they would prefer Virginians: notwithstanding Dr. Parr has engaged to marry me in England, without his fee, which here is often considerable.

Having already declined the honor so flatteringly conferred upon me, I no longer feel at liberty to express any wish upon the subject. But really everything promises to make a professorship at the university one of the most pleasant things imaginable.

I have had no assistance (I wish I could say that were all) from a single American now in England. Leslie in Scotland, and Dr. Birkbeck (cousin to the Ilinois B——k) of London, have taken most interest in the matter. Mackintosh is too lazy for any thing, & Brougham's letters I found introduced me to eminent men, but they never took the right way, or to the right means for us—they talk of plate, furniture &c. for the pavilions, while we want men for work. I have had but a single letter from America, that gave me the very agreable news, that you were all well in albemarle

F. W. Gilmer

Monticello Oct. 12.24

Dear Sir:

. . . In that of July 20 you mentioned the possibility that you might be detained longer than we had expected, perhaps to Dec. or Jan. and wished a remittance of 6 or 700 D. [$700] for expences, if lengthened as possibly might be. This, with your other letters (at that time received) was communicated to the Visitors at their session of the 4th instant. in the present state of their funds they could do nothing more than express their willingness that you should take this from the monies placed in your hands for books, apparatus &. they would deeply regret that any difficulty of this kind should withdraw you from your post, re infectâ and have more at heart your ultimate success than the time of your stay or mode of employing this pecuniary deposit, necessary to ensure it.—your idea of going to Germany for Professors is not approved. the science of a Professor would be of little importance if he has not the easy and copious use of language to communicate it. we think Ireland a better recourse, were England and Scotland to fail. the greatest of all misfortunes would be your return without any. it would produce in the mind of the legislature a belief that the enterprise had proved abortive, and they would drop it where it is. The public too considering our prospects as at an end, would give up the high expectations with which they had looked to us, and send their youth elsewhere as heretofore. our opinion is therefore that if you cannot get men of the first order, of science, it would be better you should bring the best you can get, altho' of secondary grade. they would be preferable to secondaries of our own country, because the stature of these is known to be inferior to some in other seminaries; whereas those you would bring would be unknown, would be readily imagined such as we had expected, and might set us agoing advantageously, until we could mend our hold.— in your letter of Aug. 13 where you state as a difficulty our having united branches of science which never had been combined in the same person in Europe, such as Chemistry and Natural history (of which last mineralogy is a branch) or Natural philosophy and astronomy (both belonging to Physico-mathematics) it seems not to have occurred to you that altho' we had provisionally, formed the sciences into groupes, associated in their character, we expressly declared them interchangeable among the Professors, to suit their respective qualification.—to the objection of the length of our session we must be unyielding; because holidays for a month or two at a time, and 2 or 3 times a year, requiring nearly as much time after each for the student to recover his lee-way, would never be tolerated in this country. we see no reason why the laborer in the field of Education should require such respites more than those in Law or Medecine; and especially when we require of the first of these only 2 hours every other day.—your letter however of Aug. 27 has quite revived our spirits and reestablished our hopes. a good Professor of modern languages secured a good classical one in view, an able mathematician engaged; nothing more remains of importance but a natural philosopher of high grade. he is truly so. probably one of these will be a chemist. Zoology & Botany we can well supply here; and if you cannot procure a Professor of Anatomy of high qualification, we can suspend that school to a more favorable time. it is the one we are least prepared for, and may best omit for awhile; and you know indeed that we had, at one time, determined to pretermit it in the beginning, and were induced to change our mind merely because of the advantageous opportunity of your mission to obtain a Professor of the highest order of merit, and unless you can do this we will begin without it.—come then with those I have named, and we shall be strong enough. but prefer delay to disappointment for altho' we have counted on opening the 1st of Feb., yet an able and splendid opening at a later day, would be preferred to an early and defective one. for delay we can find excuses, but disappointment would be an abyss to all our hopes.—such names as Ivory and Leslie would indeed set us up at once, if to remain permanently with us. but, leaving us after a short stay, we should be considered by the public as bewidowed, and fallen from our high estate. I am very much pleased by your testimony of the friendly interest Mr. Leslie has taken in your mission. the semibarbarous state of this country, when he was here, was such as might well disgust one of his large views of science. I remember enough of that myself. but I think there are circumstances in our situation now which would engage his approbation and best wishes in our favor.—I received a letter from Mr. Blaetterman saying that if his books were to pay duty he should be obliged to leave them. I immediately stated to the proper department of our general government the peculiar injury it would do us, without books as we are, to be deprived of those of the Professors. they did not see fit to make a general rule, but assured me that they would give, in Richmond, a particular order of exception of their books in this special case, as a part of the baggage attending their persons. I will take care therefore that, if they land *there,* their books shall be passed free of duty. our duties on books in English are almost a prohibition. . . .

I salute you with affectionate friendship and respect.

Th. J.

19. *The Plan of Studies at the University of Virginia, 1824*

WEDNESDAY, APRIL 7, 1824

Joseph C. Cabell attended with the members present on Monday. In the University of Virginia shall be instituted eight professorships, to wit: 1st, of ancient languages; 2d, modern languages; 3d, mathematics; 4th, natural philosophy; 5th, natural history; 6th, anatomy and medicine; 7th, moral philosophy; 8th, law.

In the school of ancient languages shall be taught the higher grade of the Latin and Greek languages, the Hebrew, rhetoric, belles-lettres, ancient history and ancient geography.

In the school of modern languages shall be taught French, Spanish, Italian, German and the English language in its Anglo-Saxon form; also modern history and modern geography.

In the school of mathematics shall be taught mathematics generally including the high branches of numerical arithmetic, algebra, trigonometry, plane and spherical geometry, mensuration, navigation, conic sections, fluxions or differentials, military and civil architecture.

In the school of natural philosophy shall be taught the laws and

---

"Minutes of the Board of Visitors of the University of Virginia during the Rectorship of Thomas Jefferson," A. A. Lipscomb and A. E. Bergh (eds.), *Writings of Thomas Jefferson* (Washington, D.C., 1903), XIX, 433–36, 438.

properties of bodies generally, including mechanics, statics, hydrostatics, hydraulics, pneumatics, acoustics, optics and astronomy.

In the school of natural history shall be taught botany, zoology, mineralogy, chemistry, geology and rural economy.

In the school of anatomy and medicine shall be taught anatomy, surgery, the history of the progress and theories of medicine, physiology, pathology, materia medica and pharmacy.

In the school of moral philosophy shall be taught mental science generally, including ideology, general grammar, logic and ethics.

In the school of law shall be taught the common and statute law, that of the chancery, the laws feudal, civil, mercatorial, maritime and of nature and nations; and also the principles of government and political economy.

This arrangement, however, shall not be understood as forbidding occasional transpositions of a particular branch of science from one school to another in accommodation of the particular qualifications of different professors.

In each of these schools instruction shall be communicated by lessons or lectures, examinations and exercises, as shall be best adapted to the nature of the science, and number of the school; and exercises shall be prescribed to employ the vacant days and hours.

The professors shall be permitted to occupy, rent free, a pavilion each, with the grounds appropriated to it. They shall also receive from the funds of the University such compensation as shall have been stipulated by the agent or fixed by the Board; and from each student attending them tuition fees as hereinafter declared.

The professors shall permit no waste to be committed in their tenements, and shall maintain the internal of their pavilions, and also the windows, doors and locks external during their occupation, in as good repair and condition as they shall have received them.

The collegiate duties of a professor, if discharged conscientiously, with industry and zeal, being sufficient to engross all his hours of business, he shall engage in no other pursuits of emolument unconnected with the service of the University without the consent of the Visitors. . . .

TH. JEFFERSON, *Rector*

20. *John Adams Warns Jefferson against Importing European Professors, 1825*

Your university is a noble employment in your old age, and your ardor for its success does you honor; but I do not approve of your sending to Europe for tutors and professors. I do believe there are sufficient scholars in America, to fill your professorships and tutorships with more active ingenuity and independent minds than you can bring from Europe. The Europeans are all deeply tainted with prejudices, both ecclesiastical and temporal, which they can never get rid of. They are all infected with episcopal and presbyterian creeds, and confessions of faith. They all believe that great Principle which has produced this boundless universe, Newton's universe and Herschell's universe, came down to this little ball, to be spit upon by Jews. And until this awful blasphemy is got rid of, there never will be any liberal science in the world.

I salute your fireside with best wishes and best affections for their health, wealth and prosperity.

21. *Philip Lindsley on the Problems of the College in a Sectarian Age, 1829*

Philip Lindsley (1786–1855), a native of New Jersey and a graduate of the College of New Jersey (1804), returned to his alma mater to study under its distinguished and liberal-minded president, Samuel Stanhope Smith. After some experience in preaching, he became senior tutor at Princeton, and after his ordination in 1817 became vice-president of the college. He declined election to the presidency, as well as to those of three other institutions, until in 1824 he finally agreed to assume the charge of the University of Nashville (until recently called Cumberland College). Lindsley saw great opportunities for the future of higher education in the rapidly developing Southwest, but as these remarks show, he had to cope with great difficulties. The expected public support was never forthcoming, but

Charles Francis Adams (ed.), *The Works of John Adams*, X (Boston, 1856), 414–15.

L. J. Halsey (ed.), *The Works of Philip Lindsley* (Philadelphia, 1866), I, 254–56, 257–59, 260–62. See also Doc. 24, and Part IV, Docs. 20, 22.

Lindsley kept to his task, refusing six more academic presidencies and the provost-ship of the University of Pennsylvania. He was widely recognized as one of the most distinguished educators of his time. The following document is taken from his 1829 baccalaureate address. See John F. Woolverton, "Philip Lindsley and the Cause of Education in the Old Southwest," *Tennessee Historical Quarterly*, XIX (March, 1960), 3–22, and the items cited there in its footnotes.

A principal cause of the excessive multiplication and dwarfish dimensions of Western colleges is, no doubt, the diversity of religious denominations among us. Almost every sect will have its college, and generally one at least in each State. Of the score of colleges in Ohio, Kentucky and Tennessee, all are sectarian except two or three; and of course few of them are what they might and should be; and the greater part of them are mere impositions on the public. This is a grievous and growing evil. Why colleges should be sectarian, any more than penitentiaries or than bank, road or canal corporations, is not very obvious. Colleges are designed for the instruction of youth in the learned languages—in polite literature—in the liberal arts and sciences —and not in the dogmatical theology of any sect or party. Why then should they be baptized with sectarian names? Are they to inculcate sectarian Greek, sectarian mathematics, sectarian logic, history, rhetoric, philosophy? Must every State be divided and subdivided into as many college associations as there are religious sects within its limits? And thus, by their mutual jealousy and distrust, effectually prevent the usefulness and prosperity of any one institution? Why does any sect covet the exclusive control of a college, if it be not to promote party and sectarian purposes?

I am aware that as soon as any sect succeeds in obtaining a charter for a *something* called a college, they become, all of a sudden, wondrously liberal and catholic. They forthwith proclaim to the public that their college is the best in the world—and withal, perfectly free from the odious taint of sectarianism. That youth of all religions may come to it without the slightest risk of being proselyted to the faith of the governing sect. This is very modest and very specious, and very hollow, and very hypocritical. They hold out false colours to allure and to deceive the incautious. Their college *is* sectarian, and they know it. It is established by a party—governed by a party—taught by a party— and designed to promote the ends of a party. Else why is it under the absolute and perpetual management and control of a party? They very eagerly and very naturally desire the patronage of other sects, for the double purpose of receiving pecuniary aid, and of adding to their numbers and strength from the ranks of other denominations.

Let any religious sect whatever obtain the absolute direction of a college—located in a small village or retired part of the country—where their religious influence is paramount, perhaps exclusive—where the youth must necessarily attend upon such religious instructions and exercises and ceremonies as they shall prescribe—where, in fact, they can witness no other—where every sermon and prayer and form, where all private conversation and ministerial services proceed from, or are directed by, the one sect—and, is it possible that youth, at the most susceptible period of their lives, should not be operated on by such daily influences, during a period of two, four or six years? How long will the people be gulled by such barefaced impudence—by such unreasonable and monstrous pretensions?

I do not object to any sect's being allowed the privilege of erecting and maintaining, at their own expense, as many schools, colleges and theological seminaries as they please. But, then, their sectarian views should be openly and distinctly avowed. Their purpose should be specified in their charters: and the legislature should protect the people from imposition by the very act which invests them with corporate powers. Hitherto, almost every legislature has pursued an opposite policy, and has aided the work of deception, by enacting that, in the said sectarian institution, youths of all sects should be entitled to equal privileges. Thus the sectarian manufactory goes into operation under the smiles, patronage and recommendation of the people's representatives. Its friends puff it off, and laud it as the people's school, and plead their liberal charter as the talisman that is to guard the people against every insidious attempt at proselytism; and urge the people to contribute their money to build up their promising and most catholic seminary. The bait is seized—the people are cheated—and the sect has its college. Students of all denominations frequent it. And no man of sense and reflection can doubt the consequences. . . .

A *public* college—that is, a literary and scientific college designed for the public generally—ought to be independent of all religious sectarian bias, or tendency, or influence. And it ought, when practicable, to be situated in a town or city where the several sects, composing the body of the people, have their own places of public worship, to which their sons may have free access; and where the public eye may be constantly fixed on the conduct of the Trustees and Faculty. And where every artful attempt at proselytism would be instantly detected and exposed. Some men are so constituted that they cannot help being partisans and bigots. Such men are not fit to be the instructors of youth, except where it is intended that the dogmas of a sect shall be inculcated.

Science and philosophy ought to know no party in Church or State. They are degraded by every such connexion. Christianity, indeed, if rightly interpreted, breathes a pure angelic charity, and is as much a stranger to the strife, and intrigue, and rancour, and intolerance, and pharisaism of party, as science and philosophy can be. But so long as men are not content to be honest Christians, but will be zealous Presbyterians, Episcopalians, Methodist, Baptist, Quakers or Romanist, we must so organize our *public* seminaries of learning, as that all may intrust their sons to them without fear of danger to their religious faith.

It has been objected to Nashville, as the site of a University for the purposes of general education:—1. That it is the centre of too much dissipation, extravagance and vice. That a residence here might endanger the morals and virtue of youth, and lead them to ruinous indulgence and prodigality. This is a specious objection—but it is merely specious. Small towns and villages are generally more objectionable, in these respects, than cities containing from five to fifty thousand inhabitants. Experience has fully proved in Europe, and in the older States of this Union, that large towns or cities are greatly preferable to small ones for such institutions. All the capitals and most of the second-rate cities of Europe have their universities. And wherever they have been established in small towns, the students are proverbially more riotous and ungovernable in their conduct, more boorish and savage in their manners, and more dissolute and licentious in their habits.

A large town, moreover, always affords greater advantages and facilities for the acquisition of liberal knowledge than a small village. It has comparatively, more literary and scientific men—more individuals skilled in various languages—more eminent professional characters—larger libraries—more ample cabinets and collections of natural curiosities and specimens of the arts—a more enlightened and refined society to polish and restrain youth from vulgar practices and indulgences—a greater variety of churches and other religious institutions to enlarge the mind and prevent the growth of bigotry and sectarism—and, in general, a more powerful and salutary moral influence is exerted and felt than in a small provincial town or country village. The empire of public opinion is recognized and respected. A vigilant and energetic police is ever at hand also to check the sallies and control the *renowning* propensities of the thoughtless, the turbulent, the idle, the reckless and the self-sufficient. . . .

The good people of the Southern States generally, labour under a singular delusion in regard to the benefits which their sons are supposed to enjoy at Eastern seminaries. They have heard much of the steady habits, excellent morals, and religious character of the East; and they presume that their sons, while there, will be precluded from all exposure to vicious temptation. This is a most egregious mistake. The Southern youth, at Eastern colleges, are more exposed to all manner of expensive and ruinous dissipation than they would be at home. They invariably associate together—are always presumed to have plenty of money—are solicited from every quarter to spend it freely—are trusted without hesitation to any amount by those most interested in misleading and in fleecing them—are courted and flattered, and made to believe that they are superior to the natives, whose manners, customs and maxims they affect to despise—are actuated and bound to each other by the lofty and fastidious spirit of provincial clanship, and manifest, to a most ludicrous extent, all the pride and arrogance of aristocratic exclusiveness. Residing among strangers with whom they are never domesticated, and whose peculiarities they are accustomed to ridicule—far removed from the observation and controlling influence of that society to whose tribunal alone they feel ultimately amenable—they assume the port and bearing of independent lordlings and honourable regulators of both town and college—and, provided they manage to escape imprisonment and expulsion, they care not a rush about minor considerations or temporary consequences. In due time, after squandering, in this hopeful career, some two or three thousand dollars per annum, they usually succeed in obtaining—what would seem to have been the sole object of their *literary* ambition—a Bachelor's diploma, certifying to the world that they are accomplished in all the liberal arts and sciences, and "adorned with every virtue under heaven." With this precious trophy of their academic achievements, they return home to gladden the hearts of doting parents, and to receive the gratulations of kindred and friends—but with heads as empty as their purses—and oftentimes with broken constitutions and dissolute habits which totally unfit them for any useful vocation or honourable profession.

This is no exaggerated representation. That there are exceptions, is readily granted. But, like the great prizes in a lottery, they are so few in comparison with the blanks, that nice calculators, who are skilled in the doctrine of chances, would not choose to hazard much upon the issue in either case. On the contrary, at Nashville, no youth from any section of the slave-holding States, will ever dream that he is superior to the common law of public sentiment—that he is above the reach of disgrace from the repulsive and frowning aspect of the society in which he lives—or that his present comfort and future respectability will not depend on the opinion which the good, the wise, the intelligent and the influential may form of his talents, industry, morals and gentlemanly deportment while a college student. In the metropolis of Tennessee, every son of Tennessee will look *up* with deference to the better class of citizens as models for imitation; while at an Eastern village he might look *down* with contempt upon the whole population. And the sneer of a companion at the *Yankees* is, at any time, sufficient to efface from his mind any salutary impression from the rebukes of authority or the counsels of wisdom. . . .

22. *Julian Sturtevant on the Sectarian Background of Illinois College, 1830*

Julian Monson Sturtevant (1805–86) was born in Connecticut and educated at Yale (1826). While a divinity student at his alma mater, he became a member of the famous "Yale Band," whose members pledged to devote themselves to religion and education in the West, and, not long after his ordination in the Congregational church in 1829, he went west and settled at Jacksonville, Illinois, where he became the first instructor at Illinois College. He rose within the institution, where he taught mathematics, natural philosophy, and astronomy, as well as government. In 1844 he became president, a position he held for thirty-two years. Independent in his religious views, Sturtevant fought a long battle to keep Illinois College free

Julian M. Sturtevant (ed.), *Julian M. Sturtevant: An Autobiography* (New York, 1896), pp. 160–61, 178, 181–83, 188–89, 235–37.

from narrow sectarian control. Some of his problems are reflected in these recollec-
tions, edited by his son. See C. H. Rammelkamp, *Illinois College: A Centennial
History, 1829–1929* (New Haven, 1928); see also Part IV, Doc. 10, and Part V,
Docs. 3, 5.

Those were crude times, and the introduction of New England ideas
of education and theology in a community largely southern in its
opinions and prejudices, and accustomed to an uneducated ministry,
could not have been accomplished without some pretty sharp conflicts. There was, however, one special cause of alienation and discord
which was and is a great evil in Christendom. In Illinois I met for the
first time a divided Christian community, and was plunged without
warning or preparation into a sea of sectarian rivalries which was
kept in constant agitation, not only by real differences of opinion, but
by ill judged discussions and unfortunate personalities among ambitious men. . . .

It was to be yet a year and a half before Mr. Beecher would enter
upon the work of instruction. He, however, visited us in December,
1830, for the purpose of becoming acquainted with the situation of the
enterprise and its needs, and to qualify himself to speak and act for
it in the eastern and middle states. Almost immediately after his arrival he was summoned to Vandalia, where the legislature was in session and efforts were in progress to obtain a charter for Illinois College.
The opportunity of meeting the lawmakers of the state and learning
their views in that early day was not lost, but after weeks of trial the
bill was defeated and the hope of obtaining a charter postponed to a
time in the indefinite future. The prejudices that defeated it were so
absurd that we can hardly realize the potent influence they then possessed. The most prominent argument was the alleged discovery that
Presbyterians were planning to gain undue influence in our politics,
and were proposing to control the government of the state in the interest of Presbyterianism. There were only a few hundred Presbyterians
at that time in the entire state. . . .

The early settlers of this entire region were poor. Wealthy emigrants
from the south crossed the "Free State," as Illinois was then somewhat
contemptuously called, and located in Missouri where they could retain
their human chattels. Those who had no slaves preferred to settle in
Illinois where their labor would not be degraded by the companion-
ship of the enslaved negro. From these settlers little help could be expected in the erection and the equipment of a college. Furthermore,

sectarian divisions would have been effectual in depriving us of help from our own community, had the people been far more wealthy. The Presbyterians, from whom alone we could expect co-operation, were but a feeble band. The first of these obstacles time rapidly removed, but the second still hinders the union of the entire community in college building. . . .

By this time we were beginning to feel the early vibrations of that religious earthquake which a few years later divided the Presbyterian Church into two rival bodies of nearly equal strength. That agitation from its commencement exerted a disastrous influence upon our community. One of the principal causes of alienation was the rise and progress of the controversy about Taylorism, or the New Haven Theology. The Presbyterian Church west and south, was composed of two classes of people separated by very marked characteristics. One class was of New England origin. It had been to a great extent brought into the Presbyterian Church under the plan of union between Congregationalists and Presbyterians, negotiated between the General Assembly and the General Association of Connecticut, near the beginning of the present century. The other class was largely of Scotch origin, and adhered very closely to the church of John Knox and the original from which it was copied, the church of John Calvin. These Presbyterians had never been in full sympathy with the "plan of union," and regarded religious ideas imported from New England with peculiar distrust. This suspicion had been greatly intensified by the controversy then in progress in New England. It was perceived that the newly awakened zeal of the East for home evangelization was rapidly swelling the numbers and increasing the influence of the New England party. Active efforts were made to arrest the progress of these ideas and to strengthen the bands of ecclesiasticism against their encroachment upon the Church.

The American Home Missionary Society, with headquarters in New York City, represented in a measure the movement from New England. The advocates of a stronger ecclesiasticism carried on their home missionary operations through the Assembly's Board of Missions which had its seat in Philadelphia. These two missionary organizations, though both endorsed by the Presbyterian Church, were soon brought into sharp rivalry. There is no doubt that the Assembly's board sharply watched those who were commissioned by the Home Missionary Society, and in certain instances made strenuous efforts to abridge their

influence. Nor can it be denied that what was transpiring at Jacksonville was regarded with suspicion at Philadelphia.

The brethren misjudged us. We were not propagandists of Taylorism
or of anything else save the Gospel of Christ. We were not seeking to
gain an influence in the Presbyterian Church. Our only purpose was
to do an earnest and honest work in laying foundations for the kingdom of God. Most of us had then no thought of ever organizing Congregational churches in Illinois. We had no fear that Presbyterians
would oppose such plans as ours. On the contrary we took it for
granted that we should have their sympathy and help. . . .

I cannot leave this painful subject without pointing out one disastrous result of these ecclesiastical and sectarian conflicts which continues to this day. Public opinion in this region was then almost unanimous in favor of intrusting the higher education to institutions
established and controlled by religious people, rather than to those
founded and governed by the state, or by any other political body. In
this respect, the principle upon which our institution was based met
almost universal approbation. Had the Christian people of Illinois
then united to sustain it, or any other college established on like principles, they could easily have given it so much of strength and public
confidence that it would have been above the competition of all non-
Christian insitutions. It was, then, these ecclesiastical and sectarian
rivalries which prevented the religious part of the community from
acquiring a controlling influence on the higher education. After a
time intelligent and patriotic men, seeing the denominations entirely
incapable of uniting for a great undertaking and even weakened by
internal dissensions, began to despair of colleges founded on the voluntary principle, and to turn toward the state as the only hope for
great and well-equipped seats of learning. We still look to our Christian
colleges for an expression of those moral and religious convictions in
which many churches agree. It is a great misfortune that an opportunity was lost and faith in the voluntary principle even temporarily
weakened. It was these divisions, and not any defect in our religion,
which left us like Samson shorn of his strength. . . .

A new obstacle to the progress of collegiate education in this state
had grown up during the last years [1830's] of our supposed prosperity, in the excessive multiplication of institutions of learning. A
mania for college building, which was the combined result of the
prevalent speculation in land and the zeal for denominational ag-

grandizement had spread all over the state. It was generally believed that one of the surest ways to promote the growth of a young city was to make it the seat of a college. It was easy to appropriate some of the best lots in a new town site to the university, to ornament the plat with an elegant picture of the buildings "soon to be erected," and to induce the ambitious leaders of some religious body eager to have a college of its own, to accept a land grant, adopt the institution, and pledge to it the resources of their denomination. These arrangements were entered into righteously, inconsiderately and ignorantly. The righteousness was largely on the side of the land speculator, the religious men engaged in the enterprise having little conception of the resources necessary to found a college worthy of the name, or of the broad co-operation indispensable to its success. They had neglected to count the cost.

It has already been stated that our first application for a charter was defeated. In 1835, the legislature passed a bill chartering four colleges, of which ours was one. This bill, though in other respects satisfactory, contained two illiberal limitations, one forbidding the corporations to hold more than 620 acres of land each, the other prohibiting the organization of theological departments. Both these restrictions were subsequently repealed. After the passage of this act similar charters became very abundant.

This multiplication of colleges was exceedingly disastrous to the interests of liberal education. Every denomination must have its own institution. The small sums of money which could be gathered in a new community for educational purposes and the very limited number of students prepared to pursue the higher branches were distributed among so many so-called colleges that it was impossible for any to attain a position worthy of the name. The far-seeing friends of learning became discouraged in attempting to found institutions in communities so divided. If any fundamental principles have been established by the history of democratic institutions, one of them is, that it is better to rely on voluntary action than on state intervention, whenever the former is adequate to the attainment of the end. The history and the present condition of Harvard, Yale, Williams, Amherst and many other seats of learning both in New England and out of it, afford the most complete demonstration that the voluntary principle will accomplish far better results than can be attained by institutions under political control, and limited in their religious teachings, as such schools must always be. In the valley of the Mississippi we have failed to attain equal success because of our denominational divisions, and have thus unwittingly consented to divorce the higher education from religion. We wisely separate the Church from the State, and then foolishly give over into the hands of the latter the control of our institutions of learning. This is one of the most bitter fruits of our sectarian divisions —a result whose final consequences no man can foresee.

We never sought for Illinois College any ecclesiastical control, and would never have submitted to it. We always desired to place it in the hands of patriotic, religious men, that it might be managed not for a sect in the Church or a party in the State, but to qualify young men for the intelligent and efficient service of God both in the Church and the State. It was never intended to be a Presbyterian or a Congregational institution, but a Christian institution sacredly devoted to the interests of the Christian faith, universal freedom and social order. Would that the Christian people of the state could have united with us in giving it such a character and such a far reaching influence that no institution founded by the state could have equalled it in strength and efficiency.

23. Francis Wayland on Sectarian Support, 1835

On Wayland, see Part IV, Doc. 21.

And if we examine the literary condition of our country, at the present moment, we learn the same lesson, though it can never again be inculcated with the same moral sublimity. Our country, in all its older settlements, is well supplied with colleges and universities, of course, when compared with those in older countries, in an incipient state. But, I ask, by whom were these institutions founded, and endowed, by legislative or by individual benevolence? The answer is, almost universally, by individual benevolence. And whence came that individual benevolence? The answer is equally obvious, it came from the religious. The legislatures of this country have never done for even professional education one tithe of what has been done by the

Francis Wayland, *A Discourse Delivered at the Dedication of Manning Hall, the Chapel and Library of Brown University, February 4, 1835* (Providence, 1835), pp. 20–21.

various denominations of Christians among us. In many cases, the State has done nothing; at best it has generally done but little, and I fear it is too true that even that little has been done badly. The colleges in this country are, in truth, almost strictly the property of the religious sects. You may judge, then, how decent as well as how modest is the intimation, not always too courteously given, that religious men ought not to busy themselves quite so much in the management of institutions of learning. . . .

24. Philip Lindsley on the Condition of the Colleges, 1837

See Doc. 21, and Part IV, Docs. 20, 22. The following document is taken from Lindsley's commencement address of 1837.

In the first place, I will glance at a few objections which are currently urged or insidiously whispered against the University. And, in the second place, I shall endeavour to present a score or two of the many thousand considerations which ought to induce you to sustain it.

I. 1. The first class of objections, which we notice, may be styled *personal.* These refer to, and implicate more or less, the personal character and qualifications of the trustees, president, professors, and other officers of the institution. Of the trustees, I shall say nothing. The Board consists of ex-presidents, governors, senators, members of Congress and of the State Legislature, magistrates, lawyers, physicians and farmers: of men who have filled, or who now fill, the highest and most respectable offices in the nation: whom the people of the Union and of this Commonwealth have delighted to honour, and to whose wisdom and integrity they have confided the dearest interests of their country. If such men cannot be safely trusted to manage the concerns of a university, to whom shall we look for a superior or better superintendence? Probably no other Board of Trustees in the United States can exhibit an array of names so well known, or so eminently dis-

L. J. Halsey (ed.), *The Works of Philip Lindsley,* I, 375–78, 397–98, 412–13, 424–27, 430–32.

tinguished, or so universally popular. And if you are not satisfied with these, you must be hard to please indeed.

I shall pass the Faculty, also, without defence or eulogy. Let each member stand or fall according to his deserts. Let him be judged by his acts and by his peers. A president or professor may be incompetent, physically, morally, intellectually—or he may be culpably negligent and inefficient. But then, he is removable at the pleasure of the Board: and, at the worst, he cannot live always. He will soon be off the stage and out of the way. His incapacity therefore, whether great or small, real or pretended, ought never to be paraded before an intelligent public, as jeopardizing the existence or permanent prosperity of the University itself. He, I repeat, may, at any moment, be got rid of: and at most, he is but an accident, a circumstance—while the University lives forever. You would not denounce your country or your country's Constitution and republican form of government, because you might not happen to approve the existing administration. The latter you may assail and oppose with all your faculties of reason and argument and ridicule; while yet you will stand by your country and the Constitution and the republican system, though a world were to rise up in arms against you. So, in like manner, stand by the University, whatever may be the character of its temporary governors and teachers. If the University be in itself a good thing, or capable of being made good: do not desert or renounce it, merely because some of its non-essential appendages may not be particularly acceptable to your critical judgment or keener sagacity.

2. The second class of objections assume a *party* complexion. Party men, whether political or religious, are apt to regard everything with partial eyes which belongs to their own party; and to frown upon whatever is either neutral or lukewarm or dissentient or adverse. They would have a party college—a political or sectarian college.—A hot-bed for the rearing of political partisans or religious zealots and sectarian bigots. A college which disclaims party attachments is very likely to be repudiated by all parties. Our University occupies a position somewhat peculiar. Its trustees are composed of very decided political leaders and champions of both the great parties which divide our country at the present crisis. Of the precise political creed or bias of the Faculty, the speaker is entirely ignorant. He knows not the politics of any of his colleagues. He has never conversed with them on the subject: and he has never heard an avowal of principles or predilections

from one of them. He cares not what their politics are, or for whom they vote. Thus it is also in regard to religious opinions. Both trustees and faculty belong to different sects and denominations. And the students are left to their own free choice, or to parental guidance, in both religion and politics. Their liberty has never been infringed or interfered with in either respect. No attempt has ever been made to proselyte a single youth to any faith, political or religious. We all profess to be Christians and republicans: and we fain would have our pupils be honest Christians and consistent republicans. This is the utmost of our aim, in all our labours, instructions and exhortations—so far as politics and religion are in question. They may be Methodist, Presbyterians, Baptists, Episcopalians, Roman Catholics, Quakers— Whigs, Democrats, Federalists, Conservatives—we care not—so that they are Christians and patriots. We go for the Constitution of our country and for the religion of Christendom: and we stop not to notice or to inculcate the dogmas of any school, sect or party. Such was the system avowed at the commencement of our connexion with the University and with this community. We gave to the public a solemn pledge to this effect at the outset. Have we ever departed from our system or failed to redeem our pledge? We challenge the severest scrutiny: and we defy contradiction. Our University has never enlisted under the banners of any sect or party, and we trust she never will. The youth of all parties and of all sects are equally favoured, protected and respected within her walls. And when they cease to be so, it will be time enough to complain and to sound the tocsin of alarm. . . .

These objections and a thousand others may be well founded. In some instances, they may be literally true. The university, no doubt, has been perverted and abused. And so have liberty and religion and science and reason, and every human blessing and faculty. The university has never been perfect; neither has any work or attribute or institution of mortal man ever been perfect. The university has been made the engine of error and tyranny and priest-craft and all manner of high-handed iniquity, in some age or country: so have the church and the civil government, divine revelation and human philosophy. Indeed, every *name,* capable of abuse, and of being rendered subservient to the purposes of avarice or ambition or selfish aggrandizement in any form, has been thus employed and dishonoured. If colleges are imperfect and sometimes pernicious, so are common schools and the domestic nursery. And yet, I suppose, we shall not attempt to abolish either families or common schools. Though, it must be confessed, the spirit of *abolitionism* is abroad in our land: and while Eastern *perfectionists* are preaching up the doctrine of the immediate and universal abolition of slavery at the South and the West, and while certain benevolent politicians proclaim the necessity of abolishing the whole banking and commercial machinery of the country, there are also sundry *fair* knights errant boldly enlisted in behalf of the rights of woman, who seem resolved to abolish all family monopolies, and to create a new social arrangement altogether independent of man's lordly and usurped supremacy. Indeed, abolitionism, and radicalism, and agrarianism, and ultraism, and amalgamationism, and Loco-Focoism, and Lynchism, and Fanny-Wrightism, are all the rage: and whether any existing law or usage or institution shall survive the ferment and the struggle, is beyound our prophetic ken to decide or to conjecture. But as our motto is "never to despair of the Republic," we shall proceed with our thesis, upon the presumption that the University, at least, is to endure and to triumph. . . .

If the Legislature of Tennessee will not create and endow a university suited to this Commonwealth, the people must do the work, or it will never be done. Were I a member of that body, and free from all collegiate and clerical connexions, I might possibly attempt an argument or a speech upon this unpopular theme. And I might say some *plain* things about justice and honour and integrity—of indemnification for wrongs inflicted and right withheld—of legislative, as well as individual, obligations to fulfil contracts, to redeem pledges, to pay debts, and to discharge, with a scrupulous and rigid fidelity, all the duties of a responsible and voluntarily assumed trust and guardianship. But as I am not entitled to the floor, I will not address the House at present. If the Legislature, however, will elect me their representative to the Senate of the United States, I will exert my humble faculties to the very uttermost to induce the Government to make a new grant of a few hundred thousand acres of wild land to our hitherto neglected and poverty-stricken colleges and academies; and to absolve the State from all her past iniquities and existing liabilities on this score. I hope the HONORABLE GENTLEMEN will maturely deliberate upon this singularly disinterested and modest proposition of mine, before they proceed to a final choice. They will find me, moreover, a most orthodox, independent, decided, old-fashioned, constitutional politician; who will listen respectfully to all their instructions, and then act just as he pleases.—Always "taking the responsibility," and hazarding the consequences. . . .

I will now briefly advert to certain local habits or conventional usages, which confer on the Northern colleges peculiar importance, and which elevate them greatly in the public estimation.

In the first place: Throughout New England, New York and New Jersey, the office of a trustee is regarded as a most honourable distinction: and it is eagerly coveted by the learned, the wealthy, and the most eminent citizens. No man, in those States, can be so exalted as to feel or fancy himself above or indifferent to this academical trust: and, in general, it is very punctually and faithfully discharged.

In the second place: The office of president and professor is universally looked up to as the highest and most respectable which can be obtained by the aspiring candidates for honourable rank in society. No political or professional station takes precedence of these. Nor would the head of any distinguished or opulent family be ambitious of more creditable vocation or post of honour for a favourite and talented son, than that of a college professorship. Hence it not infrequently happens that a wealthy individual will spare no pains or expense in educating a son expressly for this service. And should no vacant chair seasonably offer, he will perhaps himself endow a professorship in some college on purpose for his son's accommodation. Thus, the present Professor of Greek in Yale College, occupies a chair endowed exclusively by his father—lately a respectable merchant in the city of New York. On all public solemnities and celebrations also, the principals of universities and colleges appear in the first or highest rank. Thus, the people are taught to respect and reverence the literary character, and the literary institution, and the literary professor, and the whole teaching *corps* of the Commonwealth. We have little of this spirit among us at the South and West. The vocation of the teacher is not respected: and hence not many respectable men will seek it as the business of life. Indeed, such is the prejudice, such the ignorance, and such the absurd injustice and impolicy which prevail on this subject, that a man of letters and science is hardly deemed fit for public office of any kind. If he can write a book or deliver learned lectures *ex cathedra,* it is taken for granted that he is good for nothing else. At the East, not only the most accomplished divines, physicians and lawyers, but the most eminent statesmen and judges also, have been *elevated* to university professorships and presidencies. Of the latter class, may be named, among others still living, Duer, Quincy, Butler, Kent, Story, Everett, Adams. During the revolutionary war, the president and a professor of the College of New Jersey were members of Congress—and the first, a signer of the Declaration of Independence. The present Governor of Massachusetts will, no doubt, reach the uttermost goal of his ambition, when he shall be privileged to finish his brilliant career in the University where he first acquired the reputation which attracted the popular notice and demand for his political services. Here, I may remark by the way, that Massachusetts is perhaps the only State which continues to bestow spontaneous honors and unsought offices upon superior talent, learning and integrity. And this is precisely the best educated and most thoroughly democratic Commonwealth in the world. Here, too, have been, from the commencement of its colonial existence, and still are, more and better colleges, academies and common schools than in any other province or State of this continent.

In the third place: The men of the East attend the anniversary commencements of their respective universities. The trustees, of course, are present—the clergy of all sects—teachers of every description—the lawyers and the physicians—the Alumni from every quarter—the governor and suite—the judges and the legislature—the mayor and corporation—the wealth and fashion and beauty of the vicinity—all the world are there. It is a high day—the most joyous and interesting day in the calendar—the grand literary festival of the State. Legislatures and courts, if in session, adjourn to participate in the intellectual banquet and to contribute to its pomp and brilliancy. They will not merely make a *show,* of attendance—march into the church and march out again—but will remain, without moving or fidgeting, to the end of the exercises, or of the exhibition. They will sit it out—nay, sometimes, *stand* it out. I have seen gentlemen, old gentlemen too, literally stand for five successive hours, and listen attentively and respectfully to all the juvenile performances of the occasion. Neither their *dinner bell,* nor a *horse-race,* nor a *cock-fight,* would divert them from the proper duties and proprieties of the day. We, too, may hope for something good and great, when we shall learn to manifest a like sympathy and interest and zeal; and to act a similar part in the periodical celebrations of our literary institutions. . . .

The University will gradually create and collect a literary society among us. Such a society exists in every city and village in our country, where the university has been fairly domesticated, and nowhere else. We have not what may be called a literary society in Tennessee. Nothing like it. The phrase, even, is scarcely understood. Our social parties and intercourse manifest its total absence. We meet together to eat, drink, sing, play and dance; and never to converse as intellectual and intelligent men and women. Now I am no particular admirer of pedants or *blue-stockings*. But I do entertain the fancy that *rational* beings might occasionally assemble at the social fireside for a rational purpose: and where neither the *Grecian* nor the *savant* would be voted a *bore* or a *bear*. I doubt whether it be wise or expedient or creditable to ape the extravagancies and ostentation of a London or Paris, of a New York or Philadelphia. We cannot afford it. We are too poor. Why, I have heard *poverty* pleaded by not a few of our reputed wealthy citizens, as an excuse for not giving a paper dollar, when I have called on them in my official character as BEGGAR GENERAL for the University; and urged, too, with that peculiarly grave and lugubrious expression of countenance which never fails to awaken my tenderest sympathies. And I do intend, by and by, to get up something or other—it may be a musical concert, or a subscription ball, or a benevolent association, or a ladies' fair—for their especial relief and benefit. Alas, the tyranny of fashion is too hard upon them, and upon us all. We sport our dashing carriages and expensive equipments of all sorts, at the hazard, sometimes, of our honesty, and frequently at the sacrifice of all manly independence and domestic comfort and generous hospitality. We give sumptuous entertainments, and squeeze and jam and stuff and *wine* our friends to death or under the table; in order to be envied, or laughed at and ridiculed for our pains. In a word, we imitate the *aristocratic* excesses of the great cities: while we overlook and disregard altogether what in them is most worthy of our emulation and fully within our reach—and withal, vastly more simple and *democratic*. Their literary taste and superior intelligence and refinement, we might aspire to, and successfully aim at, and profitably cultivate. A Parisian or Genevese or Italian *coterie,* or *soiree,* or *conversazione*—where the scholar, the artist, the author, the wit, the ethereal spirits of both sexes, the *beaux esprits* of every *clique* and profession, partake of the "feast of reason and the flow of soul," free from the restraints and pains and penalties of conventional formalities and courtly etiquette—never costs much to the host, and generally proves exhilarating and delightful to the guest. Could we introduce somewhat of the latter custom or fashion into our social arrangements, I think we should be the gainers both in our purses and in our enjoyments. The University will effect the revolution, and infuse the proper spirit, and raise up the requisite elements for the purpose—all in due time. I might expatiate much more largely upon this topic—especially in reference to our children, and to the general welfare of the community—but I forbear.

Part IV

THE QUEST FOR AN ADEQUATE
EDUCATIONAL SYSTEM

Throughout the early nineteenth century American educators were constantly rumbling with protests about the inadequacy of the college system and searching for means to improve it. Many of these complaints were anticipated by Charles Nisbet, who came to Dickinson College from Scotland in 1785. Nisbet found (Doc. 1) that American students were impatient to receive quick degrees but unwilling to work for them and that they received encouragement in these notions from their parents and educational quacks. If learning was to grow in this country, he concluded, "the People must be persuaded that as much time at least is necessary for acquiring it, as is required to serve an Apprenticeship to any Mechanical Profession."

The early nineteenth-century experience of aspiring American scholars at the German universities, then undoubtedly the most rapidly developing and interesting universities in the world, sharpened the American conception of what higher education could be, how lacking American colleges were in freedom of spirit, encouragement to scholars, and even in library facilities (Docs. 2, 3, 4, and 5). George Ticknor, one of the several travelers returned from Germany (Doc. 6), became a relatively successful lecturer in modern literature at Harvard and was consulted by Jefferson in the planning of the University of Virginia. Ticknor also attempted to reform Harvard's curriculum in the 1820's (Docs. 8 and 9), proposing, among other changes, the division of the college into specialized departments in which related studies would be properly grouped. He was a reformer ahead of his time; his colleagues, after partial experimentation, rejected the substance of his proposals, though leaving him free to explore them in his own field of modern languages. After almost fifteen years of agitation for change, Ticknor gave up hope and resigned in 1835.

Yale had even less truck with reform than Harvard. Julian M. Sturtevant, later to become an outstanding educator, found that Yale's power to develop the mind of the student lay in "thorough drill" but that it did nothing more advanced or imaginative. At their best the tutors were "generally excellent drill-masters. They could hardly be said to teach at all. . . ." But Yale held firmly to tradition; and, at a time when criticisms of the required classical curriculum of the old-time colleges were beginning to be heard, its faculty issued a well-stated defense of the classical curriculum, the famous Yale Report of 1828 (Doc. 11), which served as the definitive justification of the college system as it then operated. There were two great things to be accomplished by education, the authors argued—"the *discipline* and the *furniture* of the mind," developing its powers and filling it with knowledge. Of these two, the more important was presumably the first, and therefore the curriculum should put its emphasis on the subjects best calculated to instil mental discipline. For this, it was argued, nothing was superior to the study of the Greek and Roman classics, for these are "especially adapted to form the taste, and to discipline the mind, both in thought and diction, to the relish of what is elevated, chaste, and simple."

Though Yale stood firm, proposals for innovation and for advanced education were constantly being brought forward, and complaints were never lacking about the backwardness of the typical American college. Many earnest promoters of education felt that New York City was a natural site for a distinguished university—a role that Columbia then certainly failed to fulfil (see Part V, Docs. 10 and 11). In connection with the movement that eventually led to the foundation of New York University, a number of teachers were brought together at a convention in New York in 1830 to synthesize the leading criticisms of the college as it then functioned and to formulate proposals that would help in the foundation of a serious center of higher studies. Distinguished teachers weighed the limits of the existing curriculum, the possibilities of graduate study, the status of the professor, the problems of academic government, and the advantages of an urban university (Docs. 12, 13, 14, 15, 16, 17, and 18). Unfortunately, New York University, chartered in 1831, like so many other educational experiments of the period, disappointed its founders. It became a hotbed of controversy, and soon lost a number of its best professors, including Henry P. Tappan (see Part VI, Docs. 2, 4, and 5).

Dissatisfaction with the achievements of the colleges naturally led some critics to question the way in which they were controlled. One of the most formidable of such critiques was that of Jasper Adams, the president of Charleston College, in a notable lecture of 1837 (Doc. 19). Adams felt that much of the blame should rest upon the boards of lay trustees who characteristically had "almost no qualifications which peculiarly fit them for the practical administration of these institutions." He pointed out that colleges tended to improve in proportion as they were allowed by their trustees to be run by presidents and faculties in all matters bearing upon discipline and instruction. Addressing the trustees of Mississippi some years later, F. A. P. Barnard (Doc. 25) echoed the criticism and put it more simply: there was no more sense in trying to displace the professional decisions of educators by those of laymen than there would be in interfering with the decisions of engineers in building a bridge.

Other failings of the colleges were not spared. Philip Lindsley, one of the ablest of the college presidents (Part III, Docs. 21 and 24), pointed out that preparatory education was inadequate (Doc. 20) and that the colleges were doing the work of high schools and academies: "Had we schools of the proper character, and in sufficient numbers, then might our colleges become in fact what they assume to be in name." Francis Wayland of Brown, in his *Thoughts on the Present Collegiate System of the United States,* published in 1842 (Doc. 21), subjected the entire educational system to thorough and unsparing review and argued that it should be candidly re-examined. Wayland questioned everything from the trustee system to the faculties, from the cost of education to the structure of the curriculum. Another New Englander, Edward Everett, emphasized that the colleges were not being supported with nearly enough generosity (Doc. 23) to meet the elementary needs of the libraries, for instance, or to keep them in scientific equipment. When Philip Lindsley, in an address of 1848 (Doc.

22), assessed the American college as a failure and branded the public as remiss in its understanding of and support to education, his estimate sounded like an echo of what Charles Nisbet had said (Doc. 1) over a half-century before.

1. Charles Nisbet Complains of Lazy Students and Educational Quacks, 1793

An erudite and strict Calvinist, Nisbet (1736–1804) came, in 1785, from six years of theological training at Edinburgh to the presidency of Dickinson College, founded two years earlier. The invitation was extended to him by Benjamin Rush (see Part III, Docs. 2, 6) and John Dickinson, trustees of the college, because of his learning and his sympathy with the American Revolution. Nisbet never overcame his initial shock at the low state of American colleges but went on to preside over Dickinson for eighteen years. See James Henry Morgan, *Dickinson College: The History of One Hundred and Fifty Years* (Carlisle, Pa., 1933), and Herbert F. Thomson and Willard G. Bloodgood, "A Classical Economist on the Frontier," *Pennsylvania History,* XXVI (July, 1959), 195–212.

The Rainy Weather by spoiling the Roads, has likeways retarded the Return of our Students, after the Vacation, so that I have waited this Week for them in vain, but must now resume the Fatigues of the Summer Campaign on Monday next with such of them as are already arrived. It is an Affliction to Teachers in this Country, that on Account of prevailing Prejudices among the People, most of their Time and Pains is lost in a vain Attempt to perform Impossibilities, as most of those who attend this Seminary expect to do as much in one Year, as it is possible for any Man to do, with the best Assistance, in four or five. And as they are mostly either at their own Disposal, or have such Influence with their Parents that they can obtain their Consent to any thing they chuse; it is often in vain to oppose their Inclinations. Few Parents take Pains to write us, or to enjoin their Children to submit to our Directions, so that they go away when they please, & sometimes in a very raw & ignorant State, which we cannot help, tho' it may hurt the Reputation of the Seminary. Our Students are generally very averse

Charles Nisbet to Joshua M. Wallace, Carlisle, Pennsylvania, June 8, 1793, A. L. S. Wallace Papers, VI, 28, The Historical Society of Pennsylvania. Reproduced with permission.

to Reading or thinking, & expect to learn every thing in a short Time without Application, & there are Quacks in sundry Parts of the Country, who flatter Expectations of this Nature, & undertake to teach young Men every thing that can be taught, by Way of Amusement, & in a short time. These Quacks are the Bane of Learning, as they flatter the natural Indolence of Youth, & make no Conscience of undertaking to perform Impossibilities. But if ever Learning shall prevail in this Country, the People must be persuaded that as much time at least is necessary for acquiring it, as is required to serve an Apprenticeship to any Mechanical Profession, which is far from being the Case at present. It is only by Time & Perseverance that public Prejudices can be removed especially when they are encouraged by many Quacks in Education, & many Scribblers in the Newspapers & Magazines, whose Nonsense is greedily swallowed by Youth because it flatters their Indolence, & persuades them that Learning may be obtained without Time or Labour. . . .

2. George Ticknor on the Inadequacy of American Libraries, 1816

After graduating from Dartmouth in 1807, reading law for three years, marrying the daughter of a prominent Boston merchant, and seeing America first, Ticknor (1791–1871) resided at Göttingen for twenty months (1815–17) seeking a command of German language and literature. He and his companion, Edward Everett (see Doc. 23), probably were the first two in the long line of American college graduates who attended German universities for advanced training. This letter was written to Harvard's steward, Stephen Higginson. In 1819 Ticknor became the Smith Professor of French and Spanish Languages and professor of belles-lettres at Harvard, a post that had been held for him for three years. He returned from Europe by way of Spain where he studied Spanish literature, met notables, and prepared himself to give the lectures that outlined his famous *History of Spanish Literature* (1849).

On Ticknor's years abroad see Orie William Long, *Literary Pioneers: Early American Explorers of European Culture* (Cambridge, Mass., 1935), pp. 3–31, and Van Wyck Brooks, *The Flowering of New England* (New York, 1936), chap. iv.

George Ticknor to Stephen Higginson, Göttingen, May 20, 1816; partly printed in Thomas Wentworth Higginson, "Göttingen and Harvard Eighty Years Ago," *The Harvard Graduates Magazine,* VI (September, 1897), 7–9.

... I cannot, however, shut my eyes on the fact, that one *very* important and principal cause of the difference between our University and
the one here is the different value we affix to a good library, and the
different ideas we have of what a good library is. In America we look
on the Library at Cambridge as a wonder, and I am sure nobody ever
had a more thorough veneration for it than I had; but it was not necessary for me to be here six months to find out that it is nearly or quite
half a century behind the libraries of Europe, and that it is much less
remarkable that our stock of learning is so small than that it is so great,
considering the means from which it is drawn are so inadequate. But
what is worse than the absolute poverty of our collections of books is
the relative inconsequence in which we keep them. We found new
professorships and build new colleges in abundance, but we buy no
books; and yet it is to me the most obvious thing in the world that it
would promote the cause of learning and the reputation of the University ten times more to give six thousand dollars a year to the Library
than to found three professorships, and that it would have been wiser
to have spent the whole sum that the new chapel had cost on books
than on a fine suite of halls. The truth is, when we build up a literary
Institution in America we think too much of convenience and comfort and luxury and show; and too little of real, laborious study and the
means that will promote it. We have not yet learnt that the Library is
not only the first convenience of a University, but that it is the very first
necessity,—that it is the life and spirit,—and that all other considerations must yield to the prevalent one of increasing and opening it, and
opening it on the most liberal terms to *all* who are disposed to make
use of it. I cannot better explain to you the difference between our
University in Cambridge and the one here than by telling you that
here I hardly say too much when I say that it *consists* in the Library,
and that at Cambridge the Library is one of the last things thought
and talked about,—that here they have forty professors and more than
two hundred thousand volumes to instruct them, and in Cambridge
twenty professors and less than twenty thousand volumes. This, then,
you see is the thing of which I disposed to complain, that we give
comparatively so little attention and money to the Library, which is,
after all, the Alpha and Omega of the whole establishment,—that we
are mortified and exasperated because we have no learned men, and
yet make it *physically* impossible for our scholars to become such, and
that to escape from this reproach we appoint a multitude of professors,

but give them a library from which hardly one and probably *not* one of them can qualify himself to execute the duties of his office. You will, perhaps, say that these professors do not complain. I can only answer that you find the blind are often as gay and happy as those who are blessed with sight; but take a Cambridge professor, and let him live one year by a library as ample and as liberally administered as this is; let him know what it is to be forever sure of having the very book he wants either to read or to refer to; let him in one word *know* that he can never be discouraged from pursuing any inquiry for want of means, but on the contrary let him feel what it is to have all the excitements and assistance and encouragements which those who have gone before him in the same pursuits can give him, and then at the end of this year set him down again under the parsimonious administration of the Cambridge library,—and I will promise you that he shall be as discontented and clamorous as my argument can desire.

But I will trouble you no more with my argument, though I am persuaded that the further progress of learning among us depends on the entire change of the system against which it is directed.

3. Ticknor on Freedom and Advanced Scholarship in Germany, 1815–16

See Docs. 2, 7; O. W. Long, *Thomas Jefferson and George Ticknor: A Chapter in American Scholarship* (Williamstown, Mass., 1933), pp. 14–15, 17; and Richard Hofstadter and Walter P. Metzger, *The Development of Academic Freedom in the United States* (New York, 1955), chap. viii.

OCTOBER 14, 1815

But no man can go far into the body of German literature—above all no man can come into their country and see their men of letters & professors, without feeling that there is an enthusiasm among them, which has brought them forward in forty years as far as other nations have been three centuries in advancing & which will yet carry them

George Ticknor to Thomas Jefferson, Göttingen, October 14, 1815, Jefferson MSS, Vol. CCV, Library of Congress; Ticknor to Jefferson, Göttingen, March 15, 1816, Jefferson MSS, Vol. CCVI, Library of Congress.

much farther—without seeing that there is an unwearied & universal
diligence among their scholars—a *general* habit of labouring from
fourteen to sixteen hours a day—which will finally give their country
an extent and amount of learning of which the world has before had
no example.

The first result of this enthusiasm & learning, which immediately
broke through all the barriers that opposed it, was an universal toleration in all matters of opinion. No matter what a man thinks, he may
teach it & print it, not only without molestation from the government
but also without molestation from publick opinion which is so often
more oppressive than the aim of authority. I know not that any thing
like it exists in any other country. The same freedom in France produced the revolution and the same freedom in England would now
shake the deep foundations of the British throne—but here it passes as
a matter of course and produces no effect but that of stimulating the
talents of their thinking men. Every day books appear on government
and religion which in the rest of Europe would be suppressed by the
state and in America would be put into the great *catalogus expurga-
torius* of publick opinion but which here are read as any other books
and judged according to their literary & philosophical merit. They get,
perhaps, a severe review or a severe answer, but these are weapons
which both parties can use and unfairness is very uncommon. Indeed
every thing in Germany seems to me to be measured by the genius or
acuteness or [of?] learning it discovers without reference to previous
opinion or future consequences to an astonishing and sometimes to an
alarming degree. Some of the examples of this are quite remarkable.
This university, for instance, where there are now above nine hundred
& fifty students to be instructed for Germany and Europe, is under the
immediate protection & influence of the British crown. Its professors—
forty in number—are paid from the treasury of Hanover and appointed by its regency. Yet the principal theologian & most popular
professor here (Eichhorn) has written a very learned and eloquent
book and delivers to a crowded audience lectures no less learned & eloquent to prove that the New-Testament was written in the latter end
of the second century—and another professor of much reputation
(Schultz) teaches that "a miracle is a natural and a revelation a metaphysical impossibility."—If truth is to be attained by freedom of inquiry, as I doubt not it is, the German professors & literati are certainly
in the high road, and have the way quietly open before them. . . .

MARCH 15, 1816

The longer I have continued here, the better I have been satisfied with my situation, and the more reasons and inducements I have found to protract my residence. The state of society is, indeed, poor; but the means and opportunities for pursuing the study of the languages, particularly the ancient, are, I am persuaded, entirely unrivalled. As I have already written you in my long letter on German literature, I was told even in England and by Dr. Parr, England's best and perhaps, vainest classical scholar, that Germany was farther advanced in the study of antiquity than any other nation. This I find to be true. The men of letters here bring a philosophical spirit to the labour of exposition which is wanting in the same class in all other countries. The consequence is that the study of the classicks has taken a new and more free turn within the last forty years and Germany now leaves England at least twenty years behind in the course while before it always stood first. This has been chiefly affected by the constitution of their Universities, where the professors are kept perpetually in a grinding state of excitement and emulation, and by the constitution of their literary society generally, which admits no man to its honours, who has not written a good book. The consequence, to be sure, is that the professors are more envious and jealous of each other than can be well imagined by one who has not been actually within the atmosphere of their spleen, and that more bad or indifferent books are printed than in any country in the world, but then the converse of both is true; and they have more learned professors and authors at this moment, than England and France put together. . . .

4. Joseph Green Cogswell on Life and Learning at Göttingen, 1817

Cogswell (1786–1871) joined Ticknor and Everett (see Doc. 2) at Göttingen in 1817 and struck up a fruitful acquaintance with Goethe in Weimar. He returned to America in 1820 to become, successively, librarian at Harvard, proprietor with George Bancroft of the experimental Round Hill School in Northampton, Massachusetts, and first superintendent of the great New York (Astor) Public Library. See O. W. Long, *Literary Pioneers*, pp. 77–107.

MARCH 8, 1817

I must tell you something about our colony at Göttingen before I discuss other subjects, for you probably care little about the University and its host of professors, except as they operate upon us. First as to the Prof. (Everett) and Dr. Ticknor, as they are called here; every body knows them in this part of Germany and also knows how to value them; for once in my life I am proud to acknowledge myself an American on the European side of the Atlantic, never was a country more fortunate in its representation abroad than ours has been in this instance, they will gain more for us in this respect than even in the treasures of learning they will carry back. Little as I have of patriotism, I delight to listen to the character which is here given of my countrymen, I mean as countrymen, and not as my particular friends, the despondency which it produces in my own mind of ever obtaining a place by their sides, is more than counterbalanced by the gratification of my national feelings, to say not a word of my individual attachment. You must not think me extravagant but I venture to say that the notions which the European literati have entertained of America will be essentially changed by G. and E's [Ticknor's and Everett's] residence on the Continent; we were known to be a brave, a rich, and an enterprising people, but that a scholar was to be found among us, or any man who had a desire to be a scholar had scarcely been conceived. It will also be the means of producing new correspondences and connexions between the learned men of the American and European sides of

Joseph Green Cogswell to Stephen Higginson, Göttingen, March 8 and July 13, 1817; partly printed in Thomas Wentworth Higginson, "Göttingen and Harvard Eighty Years Ago," pp. 9–10, 12–13. Reprinted with the permission of the Manuscript Division, New York Public Library.

the Atlantic & spread much more widely among us a knowledge of the
present literature and science of this Continent.

Deducting the time from the 13th of Dec. to the 27 of January, during which I was confined to my room, I have been pretty industrious
thro' the winter I behaved as well as one could expect. German has
been my chief study, to give it a relief I have attended one hour a day
to a lecture in Italian on the Modern Arts, and to feel satisfied that I
had some sober enquiry in hand, I have devoted another to Prof. Saal-
feld's course of European Statistics, so that I have generally been able
to count at night 12 hours of private study and public instruction. This
has only sharpened not satisfied my appetite; I have laid out for myself a course of more diligent labors the next semester. I shall then be
at least eight hours in the lecture rooms, beginning at six in the morning. I must contrive besides to devote eight other hours to private
study. . . . I am not in the least Germanized and yet it appals me when
I think of the difference between an education here and in America;
the great evil with us, is in our primary schools, the best years for learning are trifled and whiled away, boys learn nothing because they have
no instructors, because we demand of one the full [work?] of ten, and
because laziness is the first lesson which one gets in all our great
schools. I know very well, that we want but few closet scholars, few
learned philologists and few verbal commentators, that all our systems
of government and customs and life suppose a preparation for making
practical men, men who move and are felt in the world, but all this
could be better done without wasting every year from infancy to man-
hood. The system of education here is the very reverse of our own, in
America boys are let loose upon the work when they are children and
fettered when they are sent to our colleges, here they are cloistered,
too much so I acknowledge, till they can guide themselves, and then
put at their own disposal at the Universities. Luther's reformation
threw all the monkish establishments in the protestant countries into
the hands of the Princes, and they very wisely appropriated them to
the purposes of education, but unluckily they have retained more of
the monastic seclusion than they ought.

JULY 13, 1817

I hope that you and every other person interested in the College are
reconciled to Mr Everett's plan of remaining longer in Europe, than
was at first intended, as I am sure you would be, do you know the use

he makes of his time, and the benefits you are all to derive from his learning. Before I came to Göttingen I used to wonder why it was that he wished to remain here so long, & now wonder he can consent to leave so soon. The truth is you all mistake the cause of your impatience, you believe that it comes from a desire of seeing him at work for and giving celebrity to the college, but it arises from a wish to have him in your society, at your dinner tables, at your suppers, your clubs and you ladies, at your tea parties, (you perceive I am aiming at Boston folks), however all who have formed such expectations must be disappointed, he will find that most of these gratifications must be sacrificed to attain the objects of a scholar's ambition. What can men think when they say, that two years are sufficient to make a Greek scholar; does not every body know that it is the labor of half a common life to learn to read the language with tolerable facility; I remember to have heard little Drisen say, a few days after I came here, that he had been spending 18 years, at least 16 hours a day, exclusively upon Greek, and that he could not now read a page of the tragedians without a dictionary; when I went home I struck Greek from the list of my studies, & now think no more of attaining it than I do of becoming an astrologer. In fact the most heart breaking circumstance attending upon human knowledge is, that a man can never go any farther than "to know how little's to be known"; it fills the mind of a scholar with despair to look upon the map of science, as it does that of the traveller to look upon the map of the earth, for both see what a mere speck can be travelled over, and of that speck how imperfect is the knowledge, which is acquired. Let any one, who believes that he has penetrated the mysteries of all science, and learnt the powers and properties of whatever is contained in the kingdoms of air, earth, fire and water but just bring his knowledge to the test; let him for example begin with what seems the simplest of all enquiries, and enumerate the plants, which grow upon the surface of the globe, and call them by their names, and when he finds that this is beyond his limits, let him descend to a single class and bring within it all that the unfathomed caves of ocean and the unclimbed mountains bear; and as this is also higher than he can reach, let him go still lower and include only one family, or a particular species, or an individual plant, and mark his points of ignorance upon each, and then if his pride of knowledge is not yet humbled enough let him take but a leaf or the smallest part of the most common flower and give a satisfactory solution for many of the phenomena they exhibit. But you will ask, is Göttingen the only place for the acquisition of such learning? No not the only, but I believe far the best for such learning as is necessary for Mr E. to fit him to make Cambridge in some degree a Göttingen, and render it no longer requisite to depend upon the latter for the formation of their scholars; it is true very few of what the Germans call scholars are needed in America; if there would only be one thorough one to begin with, the number would soon be sufficient for all the uses, which could be made of them and for the literary character of the country. This one I say could never be formed there, because in the first place there is no one who knows how it is to be done; secondly there are no books; thirdly the habits of desultory study practiced there are wholly incompatible with it; a man as a scholar must be completely upset, to use a blacksmith's phrase; he must have learnt to give up his love of society and of social pleasures, his interest in the common occurrences of life, in the political and religious contentions of the country and in every thing not directly connected with his single aim. Is there any one willing to make such a sacrifice? This I cannot answer, but I do assure you it is sacrifice made by almost every man of classical learning in Germany, tho to be sure the sacrifice of the enjoyments of friendly intercourse with mankind to letters is paying much less dear for fame here than the same thing would be in America. For my own part I am sorry I came here, because I was too old to be upset, like a horse shoe worn thin, I shall break as soon as I begin to wear on the other side; it makes me very restless at this period of my life, to find that I know nothing; I would not have wished to have made the discovery, unless I could at the same time have been allowed to remain in some place where I could get rid of my ignorance; and now that I must go from Göttingen I have no hope of doing that. . . .

5. George Bancroft on the Academic Man in Germany, 1819

At Göttingen the little group that the townspeople called "the new Americans" was composed of Ticknor, Everett, Cogswell (see Docs. 2, 3, and 4), and George Bancroft (1800–91). During his residence (1818–20) Bancroft profited from studies with professors such as Eichhorn and Heeren, from two visits with Goethe, and from his work in oriental languages and biblical literature. In this letter to Andrews Norton (1786–1853), soon to become a renowned Unitarian editor and scholar (see Part III, Doc. 10), Bancroft pointed to some traits of German scholarship that he adopted in a long career as our foremost nineteenth-century historian of American nationalism. On his historical writing, as well as his role in Democratic politics and in diplomacy, see Russel B. Nye, *George Bancroft: Brahmin Rebel* (New York, 1944).

Yet much as I love my country, my home, I rejoice that I am now in Göttingen. I am contented, for I am treated kindly, I am happy, for I am industrious. Yet I know no man in Göttingen, whom I can honour with my whole heart and reason. I know no man, with whom I can actually interchange ideas, no man in whose vicinity I seem to breath purity. The sciences are carried on here as a trade, though an elevating and important one. All that labour, learning, and may I not add acuteness, can effect has been performed. It is wonderful to see how a learned man can look back upon antiquity, how intimately he can commune with her, how he rests upon her bosom as upon the bosom of a friend. He can hear the still feeble voice, that comes from remote ages, and which is lost in the distance to common ears. The darkest portions of history become almost transparent, when reason and acuteness are united with German perseverence. It is admirable to see with what calmness and patience every author is read, every manuscript collected, every work perused, which can be useful, be it dull or interesting, the work of genius or stupidity; to see how most trifling coins and medals, the ruins of art and even the decay of nature is made to bear upon the investigated subject. . . . If the national character of Germany be not amiable, it is at least astonishing; if her literary men are not distinguished for their piety, their example is only so much the more encouraging. It is refreshing to see what man can do, though la-

---

George Bancroft to Andrews Norton, Göttingen, January 9, 1819. Reproduced with the permission of the Massachusetts Historical Society.

bouring under the most unfavourable circumstances; and to think, how nobly all good literature would thrive, if we could transplant it to America, if we could engraft it on a healthy tree, if we could unite it with a high moral feeling, if learning would only go to school to religion.

6. *George Ticknor Describes His Lectures at Harvard, 1823*

See Docs. 2, 3, and O. W. Long, *Thomas Jefferson and George Ticknor: A Chapter in American Scholarship*, pp. 30–31.

When I accepted the place of Professor on the Smith foundation at Cambridge nearly four years since, I determined to devote myself exclusively to the preparation of the two courses of Lectures its Statutes demand, one on French and the other on Spanish Literature, until they should be completed. I began with the French and, in about two years, finished between fifty & sixty Lectures, equal in print to three good sized octavo volumes, to which I have never published a Syllabus, for reasons entirely connected with the state of the Library at Cambridge. Since that time, I have been employed on the Spanish, which I have recently completed in between thirty and forty lectures—equal in amount to two printed octavos; and to this I have just published a Syllabus. They are both in the nature of works on literary History, of which I read portions to my classes without regard to any fixed division into lectures, and as such, they are the first attempt made in this country. For the French portion, my means, compared with those accessible in Europe, were not very ample, though they were by no means deficient:—but for the Spanish portion I believe my collection of books is unrivalled—certainly there is nothing so complete in Spanish belles lettres to be found in the great libraries of England, France, Germany or even Spain itself, where, indeed, the collections have been sadly injured and scattered by the revolutions of the last fifteen years, and where their libraries being hardly an hundred years old were never

Ticknor to Thomas Jefferson, Boston, June 16, 1823, Jefferson MSS, Vol. CCXXIV, Library of Congress.

properly filled. My purpose has been, in each case, to make a course of Lectures more complete & minute than has been delivered before, and to introduce, if possible, a more detailed and thorough mode of teaching, whose object shall be to communicate genuine knowledge, rather than to exhibit the subject in rhetorical declamation. I have succeeded with the students, who have given me their willing attention, in a manner particularly pleasant to me, since I have declined from the first, any attendance on my lectures, which is not voluntary; but the Professors still keep on in the beaten track, and will not probably soon be induced to change. As a specimen of the sort of labour to which I have given the whole of my time, since my return from Europe, I take the liberty to send you with this the Syllabus of my Spanish course of Lectures. Nobody in this country, within my acquaintance, has so much knowledge of this particular subject as you have—nobody has such wide & liberal views of the general principles on which an University should be established and its teaching conducted—and I am, therefore, very anxious to know how you will regard my efforts in the cause, which I know you have so much at heart.

It has given me great pleasure to learn, from some of my friends in Virginia the successful progress of your University. I trust, it will soon go into effective operation and serve as a model to lead all other institutions in the country, just as our imperfect establishment at Cambridge has led all others into an unfortunate imitation of its clumsy system for the last half century. As soon, as I hear it is fairly open, I promise myself the pleasure of visiting it. . . .

7. Jefferson on the Educational Regime at Virginia, 1823

See Docs. 6, 8, and 9, and Part III, Docs. 7, 12, 13, and 17–20.

I am not fully informed of the practices at Harvard, but there is one from which we shall certainly vary, altho' it has been copied, I believe, by nearly every college and academy in the U.S. That is, the holding

---

Thomas Jefferson to George Ticknor, Monticello, July 16, 1823, Jefferson MSS, Vol. CCXXIV, Library of Congress.

the students all to one prescribed course of reading, and disallowing exclusive application to those branches only which are to qualify them for the particular vocations to which they are destined. We shall on the contrary allow them uncontrolled choice in the lectures they shall choose to attend, and require elementary qualification only, and sufficient age. Our institution will proceed on the principle of doing all the good it can without consulting its own pride or ambition; of letting every one come and listen to whatever he thinks may improve the condition of his mind. The rock which I most dread is the discipline of the institution, and it is that on which most of our public schools labor. The insubordination of our youth is now the greatest obstacle to their education. We may lessen the difficulty perhaps by avoiding too much government, by requiring no useless observances, none which shall merely multiply occasions for dissatisfaction, disobedience and revolt, by referring to the more discreet of themselves the minor discipline, the graver to the civil magistrates, as in Edinburgh. On this head I am anxious for information of the practices of other places, having myself had little experience of the government of youth. I presume there are printed codes of the rules at Harvard, and if so, you would oblige me by sending me a copy, and of those of any other academy which you think can furnish any thing useful. You flatter me with a visit 'as soon as you learn that the University is fairly opened.' A visit from you at any time will be the most welcome possible to all our family, who remember with peculiar satisfaction the pleasure they received from your former one. But were I allowed to name the time it should not be deferred beyond the autumn of the ensuing year. Our last building, and that which will be the principal ornament and keystone, giving unity to the whole, will then be nearly finished, and afford you a gratification compensating the trouble of the journey. We shall then also be engaged in our code of regulations preparatory to our opening, which may perhaps take place in the beginning of 1825. There is no person from whose information of the European institutions, and especially their discipline, I should expect so much aid in that difficult work. Come then, dear Sir, at that, or at any earlier epoch, and give to our institution the benefit of your counsel. I know that you scout, as I do, the idea of any rivalship. Our views are catholic for the improvement of our country by science, and indeed, it is better even for your own University to have its yokemate at this distance, rather than to force a nearer one from the increasing necessity for it. And how long before we may expect others in the southern, western & middle region of this vast country?

8. Ticknor on "A General and Well-grounded Discontent," 1825

See Docs. 6, 7, and 9.

I am very anxious to hear from you and know how your establishment is begun,—how far the Professors are such as you desired to find them; how the system itself goes into action; and how many students are arrived, as well as how they come prepared for such instruction as your University proposes to give them. I am the more anxious to know of your progress and success, because I think a general & well-grounded discontent is beginning to prevail in relation to the system pursued at all our colleges in New England, which, being substantially the same, that existed here a century and an half ago, can hardly be suited to our present circumstances and wants. These colleges are now very numerous, & under one pretext or another, are constantly becoming more so. Competition, therefore, is growing more & more active among them, and all are endeavouring to find new and better modes of instruction with which to contend against their rivals. This, however, is very difficult within the limits of the ancient system, & none has yet dared to pass these limits, though Cambridge is now very near it. Of course, we are all looking anxiously towards your new University. It is a case in point for us, & we much desire that the Experiment may succeed according to your wishes, since we shall certainly be able in some way or other to gain instruction from it.

Our own College at Cambridge is not in a better condition than it was when I saw you. There is a good deal of difference of opinion between the different boards that have its management in their hands, & this is likely, I fear to produce more & more bitterness. I am much afraid, that, for a long time, we shall not be able to put things in the condition we desire. . . .

George Ticknor to Thomas Jefferson, Boston, March 28, 1825, Jefferson MSS, Vol. CCXXIX, Library of Congress.

9. Ticknor and the Harvard Reforms of the 1820's

Ticknor had only taught at Harvard for two years when he began to feel urgently the necessity for reform. Disturbed by the idleness of the teachers and the ineffectuality of studies at Harvard, he spoke to the president and some of his colleagues about the need for reform, and, on July 23, 1823, before an interested group of faculty and friends of Harvard, he presented some proposals for change in a paper which is excerpted in the first of these selections. He envisaged a revision of the university laws, a division of the college into departments to group related studies, stricter examinations, an annual increase of studies during the college course, a change to the German classroom lecture system, and other reforms. It was then felt that these proposals should be explained to the public, whereupon Ticknor, at the request of some of the reformers, prepared an article for the *North American Review.* When the editor of that journal decided it would be inexpedient to publish the piece, its sponsors published it separately as a pamphlet, a portion of which is represented in the second of these selections. The *Remarks* were partly in answer to claims by conservative faculty members, who balked at curricular changes, for a seat on the Corporation, something attempted a century earlier by Nicholas Sever (see Part I, Docs. 7, 8). Ticknor's pleas to the Corporation, together with the board's concern over the "Great Rebellion" by the Class of 1823, led to a new code of statutes and laws in June, 1825. But the curricular changes, which included election of courses by students in modern languages and a division of classes based upon "proficiency and capacity" for the more rapid advancement of superior students, were generally ignored by the faculty, for whom application of the laws was finally made only optional. Ticknor, however, did win the elective practice for his own department as well as the departmental system itself within the modern languages, which later flourished at Harvard under President Charles William Eliot and was adopted throughout American higher education. After Ticknor's resignation in 1835, his chair was filled by Henry Wadsworth Longfellow and next by James Russell Lowell.

See Docs. 2, 3, 6, and 8; Samuel Eliot Morison, *Three Centuries of Harvard, 1636–1936* (Cambridge, 1936), pp. 228–38; and Richard J. Storr, *The Beginnings of Graduate Education in America* (Chicago, 1953), pp. 15–24.

It is, I think, an unfortunate circumstance, that all our colleges have been so long considered merely places for obtaining a degree of Bachelor of Arts, to serve as a means and certificate whereon to build the future plans and purposes of life. Such a state of things was, indeed,

---

G. S. Hillard (ed.), *Life, Letters and Journals of George Ticknor* (Boston, 1876), I, 356–59; George Ticknor, *Remarks on Changes Lately Proposed or Adopted in Harvard University* (Boston, 1825), pp. 44–46.

unavoidable at the earlier period of our College, when there was only a President, who sometimes lived permanently in Boston, and a few tutors, who kept a school in Newton; for the number of scholars was so small that it was possible to teach only by classes, and each student, the number being also small, could pass through the hands of every one of them, and receive from every one all the instruction he could give. But now the state of the case is reversed. There are twenty or more teachers, and three hundred students, and yet the division into classes remains exactly the same, and every student is obliged to pass through the hands of nearly or quite every instructor. Of course, the recitations become mere examinations, and it cannot be attempted to give more than the most superficial view of very important subjects, even to those who would gladly investigate them thoroughly, because they must keep with the class to which they are bound, and hurry on from a teacher and subject to which they have, perhaps, important reasons for being attached, to another teacher and another subject, wherein their present dispositions and final pursuits in life make it impossible for them to feel any interest. But at the same time that we at once perceive this system . . . has been carried too far . . . we must still feel that it has in some respects its peculiar advantages. The majority of the young men who come to Cambridge should not be left entirely to themselves to choose what they will study, because they are not competent to judge what will be most important for them; and yet no parent would wish to have his child pursue branches of knowledge which he is sure can never be of use to him in future life.

A beneficial compromise can, however, as it seems to me, be effected between the old system still in operation and the most liberal concessions that would be demanded by one of the merely free and philosophical universities of Europe. . . .

Now if this be the condition of the College, which I do not doubt, or if anything like it exist there, which nobody will deny, it is perfectly apparent that a great and thorough change must take place in its discipline and instruction; not to bring it up to the increasing demands of the community, but to make it fulfil the purposes of a *respectable high school,* to which young men may be safely sent to be prepared for the study of a profession. . . .

Whenever the tribunal of three are satisfied that a young man does not fulfil the purposes for which he came to College, they should be required instantly to dismiss him, for his own sake, for the sake of his friends, and for the sake of the College, since from that moment he becomes a nuisance; for, if it be mere dulness, he is out of his vice, he is continually spreading mischief around him. . . . The longest vacation should happen in the hot season, when insubordination and misconduct are now most frequent, partly from the indolence produced by the season. There is a reason against this, I know,—the poverty of many students, who keep school for a part of their subsistence. . . .

For myself, I will gladly perform all the duties that fall to my office as Smith Professor, and give besides a full twelfth of all the additional common instruction at College, for the three next years, provided this reform may take place, and such branches be assigned to me as I can teach with profit to the school. I am persuaded every other teacher would be equally willing to pledge himself to extra labors in such a cause. . . .

But one thing is certain. *A change must take place*. The discipline of college must be made more exact, and the instruction more thorough. All now is too much in the nature of a show, and abounds too much in false pretences . . . . It is seen that we are neither an University— which we call ourselves—nor a respectable high school,—which we ought to be,—and that with *"Christo et Ecclesiae"* for our motto, the morals of great numbers of the young men who come to us are corrupted. We must therefore change, or public confidence, which is already hesitating, will entirely desert us. If we can ever have an university at Cambridge which shall lead the intellectual character of the country, it can be, I apprehend, only when the present College shall have been settled into a thorough and well-disciplined high school, where the young men of the country shall be carefully prepared to begin their professional studies, and where in Medicine, Law, and Theology, sufficient inducements shall have been collected around and within the College . . . to keep graduates there two years longer, at least, and probably three. . . .

We have now learnt that as many years are passed in our schools, and colleges, and professional preparation, as are passed in the same way, and for the same purpose, in the best schools in Europe, while it is perfectly apparent that nothing like the same results are obtained; so that we have only to choose whether the reproach shall rest on the talents of our young men, or on the instruction and discipline of our institutions for teaching them. Now, as there can be no doubt which of the two is in fault, our colleges, constituting as they do the most important portion of our means of teaching, must come in for their full share of the blame. There may be defects, and there are defects, I know, in the previous preparation of the young men, but the defects at college are greater and graver.

REMARKS

But there is one point that I believe must be made a sort of cynosure, when beneficial changes are undertaken, both at Harvard and at our other colleges; and that is, the principle of thorough *teaching*. On this point, it is desirable to be perfectly plain, and to be very plainly understood. It is a small matter to diminish the unreasonable amount of holidays, or to give the students more and longer lessons, under a division according to proficiency, or to do almost anything else, if the principle of *teaching* is still to be over looked. For the most that an instructor now undertakes in our colleges is to ascertain, from day to day, whether the young men who are assembled in his presence have probably studied the lesson prescribed to them. There his duty stops. If the lesson have been learnt, it is well; if it have not, nothing remains but punishment, after a sufficient number of such offences shall have been accumulated to demand it; and then it comes halting after the delinquent, he hardly knows why. The idea of a thorough commentary on the lesson; the idea of making the explanations and illustrations of the teacher of as much consequence as the recitation of the book, or even more, is substantially unknown in this country, except at a few preparatory schools. The consequence is, that, though many of our colleges may have a valuable apparatus for instruction, though they may be very good, quiet and secluded places for study, and though many of the young men who resort thither, may really learn not a little of what is exacted or expected from them, yet, after all, not one of our colleges is a place for *thorough* teaching; and not one of the better class of them does half of what it might do, by bringing the minds of its instructors to act directly and vigorously on the minds of its pupils, and thus to encourage, enable, and compel them to learn what they ought to learn, and what they easily might learn.

Consider only, that as many years are given to the great work of education here as are given in Europe; and that it costs more money with us to be very imperfectly educated than it does to enjoy the great advantages of some of the best institutions and universities on the continent. And yet, who, in this country, by means here offered him, has been enabled to make himself a good Greek scholar? Who has been taught thoroughly to read, write, and speak Latin? Nay, who has been taught anything, at our colleges with the thoroughness that will enable him to go safely and directly onward to distinction in the department he has thus entered, without returning to lay anew the foundations for his success? It is a shame to be obliged to ask such questions; and yet there is but one answer to them, and those who have visited and examined the great schools of Europe have bitterly felt there, what this answer is, and why it must be given.

In some of our colleges there may be a reason for this state of things. Their means are small; their apparatus incomplete; their instructors few. They do what they can; but they cannot do much more than spread before their students a small part of the means for acquiring knowledge, examine them sufficiently to ascertain their general diligence, and encourage them to exertion by such rewards and punishments as they can command. And in doing this they may do the community great service, and honorably fulfil their own duties. But at Cambridge and at our larger colleges much more than this can be done, and ought to be done. The young men may be *taught,* as well as examined. The large apparatus of Libraries, instruments and collections, and the greater number of Professors and Tutors may be turned to much better account and made to produce much wider and more valuable results. The increasing demands of the community may be here met, and our high places for education may easily accommodate themselves more wisely to the spirit and wants of the time in which we live. And this if done at all, must be done speedily; for new institutions are springing up, which, in the flexibility of their youth, will easily take the forms that are required of them, while the older establishments if they suffer themselves to grow harder and harder in their ancient habits and systems, will find, when the period for more important alterations is come, and free Universities are demanded and called forth, that, instead of being able to place themselves at the head of the coming changes and directing their course, they will only be the first victims of the spirit of improvement.

10. *Julian M. Sturtevant on the Quality of Teaching at Yale in the 1820's*

See Part III, Doc. 22.

The course of instruction in Yale from 1822 to 1826 would now be regarded as very faulty and inadequate; yet it did exert a great and salutary influence over the student. It accomplished admirably certain ends in the development of mind, and those ends cannot be ignored in our present improved methods without irreparable injury. Its power lay in its fixed and rigidly prescribed curriculum, and in its thorough drill. For the first three years of the course the work of instruction was chiefly done by the tutors. These were generally recent graduates who had attained high distinction in their several classes, and had not yet entered on the professional careers to which most of them were destined. Each class was separated by lot into two or three equal divisions, each under the care of a tutor. My own class was the first one thought large enough to require three divisions. Each tutor generally met his division three times daily. Of course if the tutor were thoroughly capable it was no misfortune to pursue all the several branches under one instructor; but if he were incompetent or inefficient his pupils suffered correspondingly.

The tutors were, however, generally excellent drill-masters. They could hardly be said to teach at all, their duties being to subject every pupil three times a day to so searching a scrutiny before the whole division as to make it apparent to himself and all his fellows either that he did or did not understand his lessons. In the course of the recitation the tutor would furnish needed explanations and put those who were trying to improve in a way to do better next time. It was considered no part of his duty to assist his pupils in preparing for recitation. In that task the pupil was expected to be entirely self-reliant. . . .

Certainly the Yale of that day was far from being all it might have been. The tutors were good drill-masters, but they often lacked culture and the true literary spirit. They did not bring their students as they might have done into sympathy with classic authors as models of lit-

Julian M. Sturtevant (ed.), *Julian M. Sturtevant, An Autobiography* (New York, 1896), pp. 84–85, 90–91.

erary excellence. The professor of the Latin and the Greek languages, Prof. James L. Kingsley, seldom lectured, but often instructed his classes in certain favorite authors. He once taught our class, and at the end of the lesson as he closed his book, he said, "Young gentlemen, you read Latin horribly and translate it worse." In another instance he astonished us while closing a series of readings of Tacitus Agricola, by saying, "Young gentlemen, you have been reading one of the noblest productions of the human mind without knowing it." We might justly have retorted to these severe and perhaps deserved rebukes, "Whose fault is it?" In mental, moral and social science our instruction was far from satisfactory. Nor am I sure that we have very greatly improved upon it since then. It seems to me that we yet lack any treatises on these subjects which at all meet the demands of the present time for philosophic inquiry. I confess that I resign my own humble connection with instruction with a painful consciousness of a great unsupplied want. No justice has yet been done to the intuitional nature of the rational soul. In a word, in spite of drawbacks, I am forced to say that from 1822 to 1826 Yale was probably doing better work than any other college in our country. It had an excellent system of drill, which it ought never to relinquish or relax unless it resigns that part of a liberal education to some other equally able and thorough institution. But the Yale of 1826 would by no means meet the present demand for liberal culture and acquisition.

11. The Yale Report of 1828

Yale's leadership in furnishing the largest number of college presidents and, with Princeton, faculty members to the new colleges of the South and West made this the most influential document in American higher education in the first half of the nineteenth century. It was written as the reply of the Yale Corporation and faculty to Connecticut critics of the classical college curriculum who, like exponents of vocational or "practical" studies elsewhere in the 1820's, were specifically opposing the retention of the "dead" languages. The two authors of the Report, which was somewhat shortened for publication in Benjamin Silliman's (see Doc. 17) famous magazine and to which was added a seven-page indorsement by a committee of the Yale Corporation, were President Jeremiah Day (1773–1867) and

"Original Papers in Relation to a Course of Liberal Education," *The American Journal of Science and Arts,* XV (January, 1829), 297–351; quoted from pp. 297–321, 323–25, 328–36, 339–40.

Professor James L. Kingsley (1778–1852). Day, who wrote the first part, was officially connected with Yale for sixty-nine years as tutor, professor, president, and member of the Corporation; his successful presidency was marked by its stability, conservatism, and caution. Kingsley, author of the second part, taught at Yale from 1801 to 1851; his outstanding scholarship made him eminent in the fields of classics, mathematical science, and New England history. Their work quieted the critics of the college and intrenched the classics at Yale for the rest of the century. Not until the 1850's did men such as Francis Wayland (see Doc. 21, and Part VI, Doc. 1) attempt to soften the impact of the Report in some other institutions by their efforts toward curricular change and expansion.

Modern discussions of the Report can be found in R. Freeman Butts, *The College Charts Its Course: Historical Conceptions and Current Proposals* (New York, 1939), pp. 118–25; George P. Schmidt, *The Liberal Arts College: A Chapter in American Cultural History* (New Brunswick, N.J., 1957), pp. 55–58; and Richard Hofstadter and C. DeWitt Hardy, *The Development and Scope of Higher Education in the United States* (New York, 1952), pp. 15–17.

REMARKS BY THE EDITOR [BENJAMIN SILLIMAN]

The following papers relate to an important subject, respecting which there is at present some diversity of opinion. As the interests of sound learning, in relation both to literature and science, and to professional and active life, are intimately connected with the views developed in the subjoined reports, they are therefore inserted in this Journal, in the belief that they will be deemed both important and interesting by its readers.

AT A MEETING OF THE PRESIDENT AND FELLOWS OF YALE COLLEGE, SEPT 11TH, 1827, THE FOLLOWING RESOLUTION WAS PASSED

That His Excellency Governor Tomlinson, Rev. President Day, Rev. Dr. Chapin, Hon. Noyes Darling, and Rev. Abel McEwen, be a committee to inquire into the expediency of so altering the regular course of instruction in this college, as to leave out of said course the study of the *dead languages,* substituting other studies therefor; and either requiring a competent knowledge of said languages, as a condition of admittance into the college, or providing instruction in the same, for such as shall choose to study them after admittance; and that the said committee be requested to report at the next annual meeting of this corporation.

This committee, at their first meeting in April, 1828, after taking into consideration the case referred to them, requested the Faculty of the college to express their views on the subject of the resolution.

The expediency of retaining the ancient languages, as an essential part of our course of instruction, is so obviously connected with the object and plan of education in the college, that justice could not be done to the particular subject of inquiry in the resolution, without a brief statement of the nature and arrangement of the various branches of the whole system. The report of the faculty was accordingly made out in *two parts;* one containing a summary view of the plan of education in the college; the other, an inquiry into the expediency of insisting on the study of the ancient languages. . . .

REPORT OF THE FACULTY, PART I

. . . We are decidedly of the opinion, that our present plan of education admits of improvement. We are aware that the system is imperfect: and we cherish the hope, that some of its defects may ere long be remedied. We believe that changes may, from time to time be made with advantage, to meet the varying demands of the community, to accommodate the course of instruction to the rapid advance of the country, in population, refinement, and opulence. We have no doubt that important improvements may be suggested, by attentive observation of the literary institutions in Europe; and by the earnest spirit of inquiry which is now so prevalent, on the subject of education.

The guardians of the college appear to have ever acted upon the principle, that it ought not to be stationary, but continually advancing. Some alteration has accordingly been proposed, almost every year, from its first establishment. . . .

Not only the course of studies, and the modes of instruction, have been greatly varied; but whole sciences have, for the first time, been introduced; chemistry, mineralogy, geology, political economy, &c. By raising the qualifications for admission, the standard of attainment has been elevated. Alterations so extensive and frequent, satisfactorily prove, that if those who are intrusted with the superintendence of the institution, still firmly adhere to some of its original features, it is from a higher principle, than a blind opposition to salutary reform. Improvements, we trust, will continue to be made, as rapidly as they can be, without hazarding the loss of what has been already attained.

But perhaps the time has come, when we ought to pause, and inquire, whether it will be sufficient to make *gradual* changes, as heretofore; and whether the whole system is not rather to be broken up, and a better one substituted in its stead. From different quarters, we have heard the suggestion, that our colleges must be *new-modelled;* that they are not adapted to the spirit and wants of the age; that they will soon be deserted, unless they are better accommodated to the business character of the nation. As this point may have an important bearing upon the question immediately before the committee, we would ask their indulgence, while we attempt to explain, at some length, the nature and object of the present plan of education at the college. . . .

What then is the appropriate object of a college? It is not necessary here to determine what it is which, in every case, entitles an institution to the *name* of a college. But if we have not greatly misapprehended the design of the patrons and guardians of this college, its object is to *lay the foundation* of a *superior education:* and this is to be done, at a period of life when a substitute must be provided for *parental superintendence.* The ground work of a thorough education, must be broad, and deep, and solid. For a partial or superficial education, the support may be of looser materials, and more hastily laid.

The two great points to be gained in intellectual culture, are the *discipline* and the *furniture* of the mind; expanding its powers, and storing it with knowledge. The former of these is, perhaps, the more important of the two. A commanding object, therefore, in a collegiate course, should be, to call into daily and vigorous exercise the faculties of the student. Those branches of study should be prescribed, and those modes of instruction adopted, which are best calculated to teach the art of fixing the attention, directing the train of thought, analyzing a subject proposed for investigation; following, with accurate discrimination, the course of argument; balancing nicely the evidence presented to the judgment; awakening, elevating, and controlling the imagination; arranging, with skill, the treasures which memory gathers; rousing and guiding the powers of genius. All this is not to be effected by a light and hasty course of study; by reading a few books, hearing a few lectures, and spending some months at a literary institution. The habits of thinking are to be formed, by long continued and close application. The mines of science must be penetrated far below the surface, before they will disclose their treasures. If a dexterous performance of the manual operations, in many of the mechanical arts, requires an apprenticeship, with diligent attention for years; much more does the training of the powers of the mind demand vigorous, and steady, and systematic effort.

In laying the foundation of a thorough education, it is necessary that *all* the important mental faculties be brought into exercise. . . . In the course of instruction in this college, it has been an object to maintain such a proportion between the different branches of literature and science, as to form in the student a proper *balance* of character. From the pure mathematics, he learns the art of demonstrative reasoning. In attending to the physical sciences, he becomes familiar with facts, with the process of induction, and the varieties of probable evidence. In ancient literature, he finds some of the most finished models of taste. By English reading, he learns the powers of the language in which he is to speak and write. By logic and mental philosophy, he is taught the art of thinking; by rhetoric and oratory, the art of speaking. By frequent exercise on written composition, he acquires copiousness and accuracy of expression. By extemporaneous discussion, he becomes prompt, and fluent, and animated. It is a point of high importance, that eloquence and solid learning should go together; that he who has accumulated the richest treasures of thought, should possess the highest powers of oratory. To what purpose has a man become deeply learned, if he has no faculty of communicating his knowledge? And of what use is a display of rhetorical elegance, from one who knows little or nothing which is worth communicating? . . .

No one feature in a system of intellectual education, is of greater moment than such an arrangement of duties and motives, as will most effectually throw the student upon the *resources of his own mind*. Without this, the whole apparatus of libraries, and instruments, and specimens, and lectures, and teachers, will be insufficient to secure distinguished excellence. The scholar must form himself, by his own exertions. The advantages furnished by a residence at a college, can do little more than stimulate and aid his personal efforts. The *inventive* powers are especially to be called into vigorous exercise. . . .

In our arrangements for the communication of knowledge, as well as in intellectual discipline, such branches are to be taught as will produce a proper symmetry and balance of character. We doubt whether the powers of the mind can be developed, in their fairest proportions, by studying languages alone, or mathematics alone, or natural or political science alone. As the bodily frame is brought to its highest perfection, not by one simple and uniform motion, but by a variety of exercises; so the mental faculties are expanded, and invigorated, and adapted to each other, by familiarity with different departments of science.

A most important feature in the colleges of this country is, that the students are generally of an age which requires, that a substitute be provided for *parental superintendence*. When removed from under the roof of their parents, and exposed to the untried scenes of temptation, it is necessary that some faithful and affectionate guardian take them by the hand, and guide their steps. This consideration determines the *kind* of government which ought to be maintained in our colleges. As it is a substitute for the regulations of a family, it should approach as near to the character of parental control as the circumstances of the case will admit. It should be founded on mutual affection and confidence. It should aim to effect its purpose, principally by kind and persuasive influence; not wholly or chiefly by restraint and terror. Still, punishment may sometimes be necessary. There may be perverse members of a college, as well as of a family. There may be those whom nothing but the arm of law can reach. . . .

Having now stated what we understand to be the proper *object* of an education at this college, viz. to lay a solid *foundation* in literature and science; we would ask permission to add a few observations on the *means* which are employed to effect this object.

In giving the course of instruction, it is intended that a due proportion be observed between *lectures,* and the exercises which are familiarly termed *recitations;* that is, examinations in a text book. The great advantage of lectures is, that while they call forth the highest efforts of the lecturer, and accelerate his advance to professional eminence; they give that light and spirit to the subject, which awaken the interest and ardor of the student. . . . Still it is important, that the student should have opportunities of retiring by himself, and giving a more commanding direction to his thoughts, than when listening to oral instruction. To secure his steady and earnest efforts, is the great object of the daily examinations or recitations. In these exercises, a text-book is commonly the guide. . . . When he comes to be engaged in the study of his *profession,* he may find his way through the maze, and firmly establish his own opinions, by taking days or weeks for the examination of each separate point. Text-books are, therefore, not as necessary in this advanced stage of education, as in the course at college, where the time allotted to each branch is rarely more than sufficient for the learner to become familiar with its elementary principles. . .

We deem it to be indispensable to a proper adjustment of our collegiate system, that there should be in it both Professors and Tutors.

There is wanted, on the one hand, the experience of those who have been long resident at the institution, and on the other, the fresh and minute information of those who, having more recently mingled with the students, have a distinct recollection of their peculiar feelings, prejudices, and habits of thinking. At the head of each great division of science, it is necessary that there should be a Professor, to superintend the department, to arrange the plan of instruction, to regulate the mode of conducting it, and to teach the more important and difficult parts of the subject. But students in a college, who have just entered on the first elements of science, are not principally occupied with the more abstruse and disputable points. Their attention ought not to be solely or mainly directed to the latest discoveries. They have first to learn the principles which have been in a course of investigation, through the successive ages; and have now become simplified and settled. Before arriving at regions hitherto unexplored, they must pass over the intervening cultivated ground. The Professor at the head of a department may, therefore, be greatly aided, in some parts of the course of instruction, by those who are not as deeply versed as himself in all the intricacies of the science. Indeed we doubt, whether elementary principles are always taught to the best advantage, by those whose researches have carried them so far beyond these simpler truths, that they come back to them with reluctance and distaste. . . .

In the internal police of the institution, as the students are gathered into one family, it is deemed an essential provision, that some of the officers should constitute a portion of this family; being always present with them, not only at their meals, and during the business of the day; but in the hours allotted to rest. The arrangement is such, that in our college buildings, there is no room occupied by students, which is not near to the chamber of one of the officers.

But the feature in our system which renders a considerable number of tutors indispensable, is the subdivision of our classes, and the assignment of each portion to the particular charge of one man. . . .

The course of instruction which is given to the undergraduates in the college, is not designed to include *professional* studies. Our object is not to teach that which is peculiar to any one of the professions; but to lay the foundation which is common to them all. There are separate schools for medicine, law, and theology, connected with the college, as well as in various parts of the country; which are open for the reception of all who are prepared to enter upon the appropriate studies of their several professions. With these, the academical course is not intended to interfere.

But why, it may be asked, should a student waste his time upon studies which have no immediate connection with his future profession? . . . In answer to this, it may be observed, that there is no science which does not contribute its aid to professional skill. "Every thing throws light upon every thing." The great object of a collegiate education, preparatory to the study of a profession, is to give that expansion and balance of the mental powers, those liberal and comprehensive views, and those fine proportions of character, which are not to be found in him whose ideas are always confined to one particular channel. When a man has entered upon the practice of his profession, the energies of his mind must be given, principally, to its appropriate duties. But if his thoughts never range on other subjects, if he never looks abroad on the ample domains of literature and science, there will be a narrowness in his habits of thinking, a peculiarity of character, which will be sure to mark him as a man of limited views and attainments. Should he be distinguished in his profession, his ignorance on other subjects, and the defects of his education, will be the more exposed to public observation. On the other hand, he who is not only eminent in professional life, but has also a mind richly stored with general knowledge, has an elevation and dignity of character, which gives him a commanding influence in society, and a widely extended sphere of usefulness. His situation enables him to diffuse the light of science among all classes of the community. Is a man to have no other object, than to obtain a *living* by professional pursuits? Has he not duties to perform to his family, to his fellow citizens, to his country; duties which require various and extensive intellectual furniture? . . .

As our course of instruction is not intended to complete an education, in theological, medical, or legal science; neither does it include all the minute details of *mercantile, mechanical,* or *agricultural* concerns. These can never be effectually learned except in the very circumstances in which they are to be practised. The young merchant must be trained in the counting room, the mechanic, in the workshop, the farmer, in the field. But we have, on our premises, no experimental farm or retail shop; no cotton or iron manufactory; no hatter's, or silver-smith's, or coach-maker's establishment. For what purpose, then, it will be asked, are young men who are destined to these occupations, ever sent to a college? They should not be sent, as we think, with an expectation of *finishing* their education at the college; but with a view of laying a thorough foundation in the principles of science, preparatory to the study of the practical arts. . . .

We are far from believing that theory *alone,* should be taught in a college. It cannot be effectually taught, except in connection with practical illustrations. . . . To bring down the principles of science to their practical application by the laboring classes, is the office of men of superior education. It is the separation of theory and practice, which has brought reproach upon both. Their union alone can elevate them to their true dignity and value. The man of science is often disposed to assume an air of superiority, when he looks upon the narrow and partial views of the mere artisan. The latter in return laughs at the practical blunders of the former. The defects in the education of both classes would be remedied, by giving them a knowledge of scientific principles, preparatory to practice.

We are aware that a thorough education is not within the reach of all. Many, for want of time and pecuniary resources, must be content with a partial course. A defective education is better than none. If a youth can afford to devote only two or three years, to a scientific and professional education, it will be proper for him to make a selection of a few of the most important branches, and give his attention exclusively to these. But this is an imperfection, arising from the necessity of the case. A partial course of study, must inevitably give a partial education. . . .

A partial education is often expedient; a superficial one, never. . . .

But why, it is asked, should *all* the students in a college be required to tread in the *same steps?* Why should not each one be allowed to select those branches of study which are most to his taste, which are best adapted to his peculiar talents, and which are most nearly connected with his intended profession? To this we answer, that our prescribed course contains those subjects only which ought to be understood, as we think, by every one who aims at a thorough education. They are not the peculiarities of any profession or art. These are to be learned in the professional and practical schools. But the principles of sciences, are the common foundation of all high intellectual attainments. As in our primary schools, reading, writing, and arithmetic are taught to all, however different their prospects; so in a college, all should be instructed in those branches of knowledge, of which no one destined to the higher walks of life ought to be ignorant. What subject which is now studied here, could be set aside, without evidently marring the system[?] Not to speak particularly, in this place, of the ancient languages; who that aims at a well proportioned and superior education will remain ignorant of the elements of the various branches of the mathematics, or of history and antiquities, or of rhetoric and oratory, or natural philosophy, or astronomy, or chemistry, or mineralogy, or geology, or political economy, or mental and moral philosophy?

It is sometimes thought that a student ought not to be urged to the study of that for which he has *no taste or capacity*. But how is he to know, whether he has a taste or capacity for a science, before he has even entered upon its elementary truths? If he is really destitute of talent sufficient for these common departments of education, he is destined for some narrow sphere of action. But we are well persuaded, that our students are not so deficient in intellectual powers, as they sometimes profess to be; though they are easily made to believe, that they have no capacity for the study of that which they are told is almost wholly useless.

When a class have become familiar with the common elements of the several sciences, then is the proper time for them to *divide off* to their favorite studies. They can then make their choice from actual trial. This is now done here, to some extent, in our Junior year. The division might be commenced at an earlier period, and extended farther, provided the qualifications for admission into the college, were brought to a higher standard.

If the view which we have thus far taken of the subject is correct, it will be seen, that the object of the system of instruction at this college, is not to give a *partial* education, consisting of a few branches only; nor, on the other hand, to give a *superficial* education, containing a smattering of almost every thing; nor to *finish* the details of either a professional or practical education; but to *commence* a *thorough* course, and to carry it as far as the time of residence here will allow. It is intended to occupy, to the best advantage, the four years immediately preceding the study of a profession, or of the operations which are peculiar to the higher mercantile, manufacturing, or agricultural establishments. . . .

Our institution is not modelled exactly after the pattern of *European* universities. Difference of circumstances has rendered a different arrangement expedient. It has been the policy of most monarchical gov-

ernments, to concentrate the advantages of a superior education in a
few privileged places. In England, for instance, each of the ancient
universities of Oxford and Cambridge, is not so much a single institution, as a large number of distinct, though contiguous colleges. But
in this country, our republican habits and feelings will never allow a
monopoly of literature in any one place. There must be, in the union,
as many colleges, at least, as states. Nor would we complain of this
arrangement as inexpedient, provided that starvation is not the consequence of a patronage so minutely divided. We anticipate no disastrous results from the multiplication of colleges, if they can only
be adequately endowed. We are not without apprehensions, however,
that a feeble and stinted growth of our national literature, will be the
consequence of the very scanty supply of means to most of our public
seminaries. . . .

Although we do not consider the literary institutions of Europe as
faultless models, to be exactly copied by our American colleges; yet
we would be far from condemning every feature, in systems of instruction which have had an origin more ancient than our republican
seminaries. We do not suppose that the world has learned absolutely
nothing, by the experience of ages; that a branch of science, or a mode
of teaching, is to be abandoned, precisely because it has stood its
ground, after a trial by various nations, and through successive centuries. We believe that our colleges may derive important improvements from the universities and schools in Europe; not by blindly
adopting all their measures without discrimination; but by cautiously
introducing, with proper modifications, such parts of their plans as
are suited to our peculiar situation and character. The first and great
improvement which we wish to see made, is an elevation in the
standard of attainment for admission. Until this is effected, we shall
only expose ourselves to inevitable failure and ridicule, by attempting
a general imitation of foreign universities. . . .

It is said that the public now demand, that the doors should be
thrown open to all; that education ought to be so modified, and
varied, as to adapt it to the exigencies of the country, and the prospects
of different individuals; that the instruction given to those who are
destined to be merchants, or manufacturers, or agriculturalists, should
have a special reference to their respective professional pursuits.

The public are undoubtedly right, in demanding that there should
be appropriate courses of education, accessible to all classes of youth.

And we rejoice at the prospect of ample provision for this purpose, in the improvement of our academies, and the establishment of commercial high-schools, gymnasia, lycea, agricultural seminaries, &c. But do the public insist, that every college shall become a high-school, gymnasium, lyceum, and academy? Why should we interfere with these valuable institutions? Why wish to take their business out of their hands? The college has its appropriate object, and they have theirs. . . . What is the characteristic difference between a college and an academy? Not that the former teaches more branches than the latter. There are many academies in the country, whose scheme of studies, at least upon paper, is more various than that of the colleges. But while an academy teaches a little of every thing, the college, by directing its efforts to one uniform course, aims at doing its work with greater precision, and economy of time; just as the merchant who deals in a single class of commodities, or a manufacturer who produces but one kind of fabrics, executes his business more perfectly, than he whose attention and skill are divided among a multitude of objects. . . .

But might we not, by making the college more accessible to different descriptions of persons, enlarge our *numbers,* and in that way, increase our income? This might be the operation of the measure, for a very short time, while a degree from the college should retain its present value in public estimation; a value depending entirely upon the character of the education which we give. But the moment it is understood that the institution has descended to an inferior standard of attainment, its reputation will sink to a corresponding level. After we shall have become a college in *name only,* and in reality nothing more than an academy; or half college, and half academy; what will induce parents in various and distant parts of the country, to send us their sons, when they have academies enough in their own neighborhood? There is no magical influence in an act of incorporation, to give celebrity to a literary institution, which does not command respect for itself, by the elevated rank of its education. When the college has lost its hold on the public confidence, by depressing its standard of merit, by substituting a partial, for a thorough education, we may expect that it will be deserted by that class of persons who have hitherto been drawn here by high expectations and purposes. Even if we should *not* immediately suffer in point of *numbers,* yet we shall exchange the best portion of our students, for others of inferior aims and attainments.

As long as we can maintain an elevated character, we need be under no apprehension with respect to numbers. Without character, it will be in vain to think of retaining them. It is a hazardous experiment, to act upon the plan of gaining numbers first, and character afterwards....

The difficulties with which we are now struggling, we fear would be increased, rather than diminished, by attempting to unite different plans of education. It is far from being our intention to dictate to *other* colleges a system to be adopted by them. There may be good and sufficient reasons why some of them should introduce a partial course of instruction. We are not sure, that the demand for thorough education is, at present, sufficient to fill all the colleges in the United States, with students who will be satisfied with nothing short of high and solid attainments. But it is to be hoped that, at no very distant period, they will be able to come up to this elevated ground, and leave the business of second-rate education to the inferior seminaries.

The competition of colleges may advance the interests of literature: if it is a competition for *excellence,* rather than for numbers; if each aims to surpass the others, not in an imposing display, but in the substantial value of its education....

Our republican form of government renders it highly important, that great numbers should enjoy the advantage of a thorough education. On the Eastern continent, the *few* who are destined to particular departments in political life, may be educated for the purpose; while the mass of the people are left in comparative ignorance. But in this country, where offices are accessible to all who are qualified for them, superior intellectual attainments ought not to be confined to any description of persons. *Merchants, manufacturers,* and *farmers,* as well as professional gentlemen, take their places in our public councils. A thorough education ought therefore to be extended to all these classes. It is not sufficient that they be men of sound judgment, who can decide correctly, and give a silent vote, on great national questions. Their influence upon the minds of others is needed; an influence to be produced by extent of knowledge, and the force of eloquence. Ought the speaking in our deliberative assemblies to be confined to a single profession? If it is knowledge, which gives us the command of physical agents and instruments, much more is it that which enables us to control the combinations of moral and political machinery....

Can merchants, manufacturers, and agriculturists, derive no benefit from high intellectual culture? They are the very classes which, from their situation and business, have the best opportunities for reducing the principles of science to their practical applications. The large estates which the tide of prosperity in our country is so rapidly accumulating, will fall mostly into their hands. Is it not desirable that they should be men of superior education, of large and liberal views, of those solid and elegant attainments, which will raise them to a higher distinction, than the mere possession of property; which will not allow them to hoard their treasures, or waste them in senseless extravagance; which will enable them to adorn society by their learning, to move in the more intelligent circles with dignity, and to make such an application of their wealth, as will be most honorable to themselves, and most beneficial to their country?

The active, enterprising character of our population, renders it highly important, that this bustle and energy should be directed by sound intelligence, the result of deep thought and early discipline. The greater the impulse to action, the greater is the need of wise and skilful guidance. When nearly all the ship's crew are aloft, setting the topsails, and catching the breezes, it is necessary there should be a steady hand at helm. Light and moderate learning is but poorly fitted to direct the energies of a nation, so widely extended, so intelligent, so powerful in resources, so rapidly advancing in population, strength, and opulence. Where a free government gives full liberty to the human intellect to expand and operate, education should be proportionably liberal and ample. When even our mountains, and rivers, and lakes, are upon a scale which seems to denote, that we are destined to be a great and mighty nation, shall our literature be feeble, and scanty, and superficial?

REPORT OF THE FACULTY, PART II

. . . The subject of inquiry now presented, is, whether the plan of instruction pursued in Yale College, is sufficiently accommodated to the present state of literature and science; and, especially, whether such a change is demanded as would leave out of this plan the study of the Greek and Roman classics, and make an acquaintance with ancient literature no longer necessary for a degree in the liberal arts. . . .

Whoever . . . without a preparation in classical literature, engages in any literary investigation, or undertakes to discuss any literary topic, or associates with those who in any country of Europe, or in this country, are acknowledged to be men of liberal acquirements, immediately feels a deficiency in his education, and is convinced that he is destitute of an important part of practical learning. If scholars, then, are to be prepared to act in the literary world as it in fact exists, classical literature, from considerations purely practical, should form an important part of their early discipline.

But the claims of classical learning are not limited to this single view. It may be defended not only as a necessary branch of education, in the present state of the world, but on the ground of its distinct and independent merits. Familiarity with the Greek and Roman writers is especially adapted to form the taste, and to discipline the mind, both in thought and diction, to the relish of what is elevated, chaste, and simple. . . .

But the study of the classics is useful, not only as it lays the foundations of a correct taste, and furnishes the student with those elementary ideas which are found in the literature of modern times, and which he no where so well acquires as in their original sources;—but also as the study itself forms the most effectual discipline of the mental faculties. This is a topic so often insisted on, that little need be said of it here. It must be obvious to the most cursory observer, that the classics afford materials to exercise talent of every degree, from the first opening of the youthful intellect to the period of its highest maturity. The range of classical study extends from the elements of language, to the most difficult questions arising from literary research and criticism. Every faculty of the mind is employed; not only the memory, judgment, and reasoning powers, but the taste and fancy are occupied and improved.

Classical discipline, likewise, forms the best preparation for professional study. The interpretation of language, and its correct use, are no where more important, than in the professions of divinity and law. . . .

In the profession of medicine, the knowledge of the Greek and Latin languages is less necessary now than formerly; but even at the present time it may be doubted, whether the facilities which classical learning affords for understanding and rendering familiar the terms of science, do not more than counterbalance the time and labor requisite for obtaining this learning. . . .

To acquire the knowledge of any of the modern languages of Europe, is chiefly an effort of memory. The general structure of these languages is much the same as that of our own. The few idiomatical differences, are made familiar with little labor; nor is there the same necessity of accurate comparison and discrimination, as in studying the classic writers of Greece and Rome. To establish this truth, let a page of Voltaire be compared with a page of Tacitus. . . .

Modern languages, with most of our students, are studied, and will continue to be studied, as an accomplishment, rather than as a necessary acquisition. . . . To suppose the modern languages more practical than the ancient, to the great body of our students, because the former are now spoken in some parts of the world, is an obvious fallacy. The proper question is,—what course of discipline affords the best mental culture, leads to the most thorough knowledge of our own literature, and lays the best foundation for professional study. The ancient languages have here a decided advantage. If the elements of modern languages are acquired by our students in connection with the established collegiate course, and abundant facilities for this purpose, have for a long time, been afforded, further acquisitions will be easily made, where circumstances render them important and useful. From the graduates of this college, who have visited Europe, complaints have sometimes been heard, that their classical attainments were too small for the literature of the old world; but none are recollected to have expressed regret, that they had cultivated ancient learning while here, however much time they might have devoted to this subject. On the contrary, those who have excelled in classical literature, and have likewise acquired a competent knowledge of some one modern European language besides the English, have found themselves the best qualified to make a full use of their new advantages. Deficiencies in modern literature are easily and rapidly supplied, where the mind has had a proper previous discipline; deficiencies in ancient literature are supplied tardily, and in most instances, imperfectly. . . .

Such, then, being the value of ancient literature, both as respects the general estimation in which it is held in the literary world, and its intrinsic merits,—if the college should confer degrees upon students for their attainments in modern literature only, it would be to declare *that* to be a liberal education, which the world will not acknowledge to deserve the name;—and which those who shall receive degrees in this way, will soon find, is not what it is called. A liberal education, whatever course the college should adopt, would without doubt continue to be, what it long has been. Ancient literature is too deeply inwrought into the whole system of the modern literature of Europe to be so easily laid aside. The college ought not to presume upon its influence, nor to set itself up in any manner as a dictator. If it should pursue a course very different from that which the present state of literature demands; if it should confer its honors according to a rule which is not sanctioned by literary men, the faculty see nothing to expect for favoring such innovations, but that they will be considered visionaries in education, ignorant of its true design and objects, and unfit for their places. The ultimate consequence, it is not difficult to predict. The college would be distrusted by the public, and its reputation would be irrecoverably lost. . . .

No question has engaged the attention of the faculty more constantly, than how the course of education in the college might be improved, and rendered more practically useful. Free communications have at all times been held between the faculty and the corporation, on subjects connected with the instruction of the college. When the aid of the corporation has been thought necessary, it has been asked; and by this course of proceeding, the interests of the institution have been regularly advanced. No remark is more frequently made by those, who visit the college after the absence of some years, than that changes have been made for the better; and those who make the fullest investigation, are the most ready to approve what they find. The charge, therefore, that the college is stationary, that no efforts are made to accommodate it to the wants of the age, that all exertions are for the purpose of perpetuating abuses, and that the college is much the same as it was at the time of its foundation, are wholly gratuitous. The changes in the country, during the last century, have not been greater than the changes in the college. These remarks have been limited to Yale College, as its history is here best known; no doubt, other colleges alluded to in the above quotations, might defend themselves with equal success.

12. Henry Vethake Proposes Curricular and Teaching Changes, 1830

Documents 12–18 are portions of addresses made to the Convention of Literary and Scientific Gentlemen in New York City in October, 1830. The convention was called partly to criticize the spirit of the Yale Report in 1828 (see Doc. 11) and partly to lay the foundation of what was to become New York University. Some of the leading men of letters in the country attended or sent their advice. Although their discussions were far-ranging and lacking in central agreement on all matters having to do with higher learning, there did emerge from them a clear idea of the necessity for a university, rather than a college, in a great metropolis. Secretary of the convention, and the man responsible for publishing its proceedings, was John Delafield (1786–1853), New York banker and Columbia College graduate. See Richard J. Storr, *The Beginnings of Graduate Education in America,* pp. 33–43.

Born in British Guiana, Henry Vethake (1792–1866) taught mathematics and philosophy at several colleges. When he submitted this first paper read at the convention, Vethake was teaching at Princeton. Thereafter he held a professorship in the University of the City of New York, the short-lived institution that was the direct result of this convention; he won membership in the American Philosophical Society, served a brief term as president of Washington College, Virginia, then was connected with the University of Pennsylvania from 1836 to 1859. Dyspeptic and peppery in his later years, Vethake made his reputation as a thoroughly orthodox political economist. He did much to further the idea of economics as a separate academic discipline, but by the 1850's he doubted the wisdom of graduate and popular instruction and reversed the sentiments he expressed in 1830.

On Vethake see Joseph Dorfman and Rexford Guy Tugwell, *Early American Policy: Six Columbia Contributors* (New York, 1960), pp. 155–204.

The students of our colleges, it is well known, are almost universally divided into four different classes, viz: the Freshman, Sophomore, Junior, and Senior Classes. The course of study in each of them endures for a year, and is the same for every student, whatever may be his capacity or tastes. A candidate for admission to the Freshman or lowest class, besides possessing a competent knowledge of various branches of what is usually styled an *English* education, such as English Grammar, Geography, &c. must come prepared to be examined on a certain number, or on portions of a certain number of the classical (Greek and

Journal of the Proceedings of a Convention of Literary and Scientific Gentlemen, Held in the Common Council Chamber of the City of New York, October, 1830 (New York, 1831), pp. 21–42.

Latin) authors; and the Greek and Latin languages are also usually the principal subjects of study during the first two years of the collegiate course, the sciences only becoming predominant objects of the students' attention in the Junior and Senior years. The instruction in the different sciences, Mathematical, Physical, and Moral, is, generally speaking, conducted almost entirely by recitation from a text book, with remarks, less or more extended, on the part of the teacher. At certain stated periods *distinctions* or *honours* are awarded to a certain number of the students who excel in scholarship; and, at the close of his college career, every individual receives the first degree in the Arts. These are all the different circumstances which involve the points that will present themselves for my animadversion.

It is clear that our colleges are not institutions which are engaged in diffusing the blessings of knowledge among the community as generally as they have it in their power to do. They do not say to parents, send your children within our walls to make such acquirements in science, or letters, as their previous education may fit them to make. A young man desirous of obtaining a knowledge of Mathematics, Natural or Moral Philosophy, Chemistry, Natural History, or Political Economy, and who may possess all the preparatory information requisite for attending with advantage the course of instruction in any of those branches of knowledge, will yet find himself debarred from admission to college, if he have not provided himself with a certain stock of Latin and Greek. Our colleges do in fact say to such an individual, whatever your aspirations after knowledge may be, to you *we* are not the dispensers of it. It is true that we have it in our power to make you more useful members of society, and to exalt you in the scale of being; but, nevertheless, we condemn you, as far as lies with us, to comparative ignorance and a lower sphere of usefulness; and we reserve our instructions for those only who have the wealth necessary to enable them to consume many years of their lives in the exclusive, or nearly the exclusive, occupation of learning two complicated and difficult languages, very imperfectly, in most cases, after all. That the learned or dead languages should, some two or three centuries ago, have been made the study of every one having in view scientific information as his ultimate end, as well as by those whose lives were to be devoted to literary or philological pursuits, was natural enough; since at that period almost all useful knowledge was contained in books written in those languages, which for that reason then

hardly deserved the epithet of dead. But that, at the present day, when
men of science, with very few exceptions, and those chiefly among the
Germans and the other northern nations of Europe, make use, in re-
cording their speculations, of their vernacular tongues,—when every
thing which antiquity has left us worth the perusal, for the sake of
acquiring information, has been translated into the modern dialects,
the English among the number,—when the progress of knowledge,
more especially of mathematical and physical science, has been such
as to render the older authors of no value, except in so far as the gratification of the curiosity of those who are interested in tracing the gradual
advances made by the human mind gives them one,—and when, more
particularly in the United States, the number of individuals desirous
of gaining useful information, vastly exceeds that of those who have
the time and money to enable them to go through the *whole* course
of education prescribed by our colleges,—it does seem to me that the
very general persistance of those institutions, in the *restricted* system
above mentioned, is one of the most remarkable instances with which
I am acquainted, of a persistance in error, merely because it has been
long established. . . .

While I thus fully acknowledge the value of classical literature, I
see no reason why an *artificial* preference should be given to it in our
systems of education, and why young men should be told, that unless
they learn Latin and Greek, they shall not be permitted to learn any
thing else. Whilst I would have ample provision made in our colleges
for instruction, and able instruction, in these languages, as well as in
every branch of literature and science, I would leave the *supply* of instruction in all to be regulated by the proportional *demand* of the
public for each. . . .

That the courses of instruction would become superficial if opened,
as is proposed, to all who are *sufficiently* prepared, by their age and
previous education, to attend them with advantage, is an assumption
which seems to me, to be quite gratuitous. In the present state of
things, as every one knows, a few of our colleges, in order to attract
such students as are more anxious to get a degree, than an education,
degrade their instruction below what is furnished by many of our
gymnasiums, or academies of reputation, which, having no foreign
or adventitious support from the power of operating on the imagina-
tions of the public, and more particularly of the younger portion of it,
by the magic of degrees and diplomas, are dependent for patronage

on merit alone. So, no doubt, would this continue to be the case under the system of which I am an advocate. Some institutions would still think it for their interest to teach more superficially than others, or would not have it in their power to furnish as extensive and thorough an education as others; but I do not hesitate to assert, for reasons to be presently stated, that the fact would be found to be, that the changes proposed would have a tendency to elevate rather than to lower the scale of education. This is, indeed, implied in the next objection to be considered, and which is in direct contradiction with the one of which we have been speaking. . . .

The remark, so often made, that the object of that education which is communicated by one mind to another, is not intended to make men masters of any one science, but rather, in addition to the expanding and invigorating of their faculties, to give them an encyclopedic outline of human knowledge, to be afterwards filled up, by their own unassisted efforts, in such parts as they may then select for their particular provinces of intellectual labor, is one which I am not disposed to controvert; but I cannot but think its application to the case under consideration to be somewhat strained, and out of place. I presume it can hardly be intended by the friends of the new University scheme, to undertake to produce annually a number of *finished* scholars, and *accomplished* men of science. They will still leave the eminences of knowledge to be slowly attained by the strenuous and persevering efforts of the student, long after he shall have quitted the walls of the University. The several courses of instruction will certainly not be of a nature to require the whole time and attention of those who attend them; the students, with the exception of a few, of inferior capacities, or of inefficient habits of intellectual exertion, will have ample leisure to engage in the study of more branches of knowledge than one. The numerous relations, too, which apparently the remotest of the sciences bear to each other, and the frequent points of contact which many of them present, have a constant tendency to withdraw the mind from a limited field of study, and to induce it to waste its energies in ranging fruitlessly over too wide a surface. Hence there is no room for apprehending that young men at college will confine themselves, from inclination, to the acquiring of a single science alone. I see no objection, however, to render it obligatory on them to attend at the same period of time, a certain number of courses, unless specially exempted for sufficient reasons, as is now the arrangement in the University of

Virginia. Such a regulation would, indeed, be highly expedient in reference to the *discipline* of an institution, by securing, as much as possible, a full employment of his time for every student. But independent of any measure of the kind, there will be no difficulty in acquiring an *outline* of human knowledge. Besides the effect naturally resulting from the discursive disposition of the mind above mentioned, the tendency of the present age, more especially in our own country, for reasons which it is unnecessary to adduce, since the fact will hardly be questioned, is to produce a state of things in which the most educated men are, in general, acquainted, to a certain extent, with all things under the sun, rather than with any one branch of knowledge thoroughly, so as to be able to be of much practical service to their fellow men, or to contribute in any striking degree, to the progress of invention or discovery. And it would be well, perhaps, for the interests of education, if our literary institutions were to administer some check to this prevalent evil, instead of encouraging it by teaching, as some of them do, a mere smattering of many things. . . .

The fact is that the existing state of things, which I am anxious to see altered, is the necessary result of the arrangement of the students into regularly organized bodies, and of the distribution among them of the usual distinctions and honors. The student who would frequently visit his instructer, or even exhibit, unasked for and unnecessarily in any way before his class, his information, or his desire to obtain information, would at once become an object of suspicion and jealousy. He would be charged by his fellow students with an intention to curry favor in order to obtain unfairly an honor. He is condemned by their esprit du corps to content himself with such displays of his knowledge or talent alone as can be fairly made in reply to the questions put to him, in the class by his teacher. For the confirmation of this statement I appeal to the professors and students of colleges generally. . . .

I am persuaded that the error is as frequently committed in this country of teaching almost entirely by hearing recitations from a text book, as in Europe by trusting to the delivery of lectures alone. Both these methods I regard as extremes to be avoided. The proper system seems to me to be a combination of lectures, on all the branches that admit of them, with close examinations on their subject, and on the correspondent parts of a text book to be put into the hands of the students. With these accompaniments I do think that lecturing is not only the most agreeable mode of communicating instruction but that there is no other public mode in which a taste and an enthusiasm for knowledge can be so readily excited. There is something peculiarly impressive in the tones and aspect of a public speaker which we can fully realize by reflecting on the very different effect produced by a written discourse read in the closet, and the same discourse delivered from the pulpit or the rostrum by a man of even ordinary powers of elocution. I would, therefore, oblige every professor to read a course of lectures, or to lecture without note if he pleased, on the subjects embraced in his department: if he can do the latter *well,* so much the better. There is, indeed, one case, and one case only, in which I would allow him to hear recitations from a book, and comment upon the text, to wit, when he is himself the author of the text-book; for there would then be evidently very little use in repeating to his hearers what they have before them in print; and there would be no danger of his comments being either spiritless or sparing.

13. *Francis Lieber on the Purposes and Practices of Universities, 1830*

Francis Lieber (1800–1872) was well versed in the spirit of eighteenth-century science, or German *Wissenschaft,* implying rational and total understanding as well as systematic learning, which he praised before this gathering of intellectuals (see Doc. 12). He received his Ph.D. at Jena after fighting in the German War of Liberation, and he was trained in historical method and outlook by Barthold Niebuhr, the great historian of Rome. As a political refugee from Germany, he arrived in the United States in 1827. Gaining many academic friends, he turned his outstanding scholarship to editing an encyclopedia, writing on prison reform, and producing our first systematic treatises on political science. He taught at South Carolina College (1835–56) and at Columbia University (1857–72). See Frank Freidel, *Francis Lieber: Nineteenth Century Liberal* (Baton Rouge, La., 1947), and Part V, Doc. 12.

It would lead me beyond the limits of the present subject; were I to give my views respecting that word *useful,* so popular in our time, and, in my opinion, so often misunderstood, so vaguely applied, a word,

Journal of the Proceedings of a Convention of Literary and Scientific Gentlemen . . . in . . . the City of New York, October, 1830, pp. 60–67.

which indicates something so powerful in respect of all the lower branches of human concerns, and is so devoid of meaning, wherever we elevate ourselves above that point. But, it is necessary for me to state, that utility, in the meaning in which it is taken most commonly, that is, as turning directly to account, ought by no means to be the sole standard in establishing a university, nay not even the highest. It is the very character of utility, that common life itself provides for it, but it does not, and cannot provide for things or objects, whose effects, though the most noble, are the more distant. Science is always useful in a higher sense. It ennobles the mind, and the most abstract sciences which at first glance may appear the most useless, are the least excepted from this assertion. I ask simply and plainly, who is able to give a definition of the word *useful,* with regard to sciences? Certainly some are more important for a university than others, because they answer certain purposes, for which a university is established, more fully than others; but all are useful, and to determine their degree of usefulness, by the number of students who attend the lectures, in which they are treated, would be, in my opinion, somewhat like judging the *usefulness* of christianity by the small number of persons, who in some countries, and in some ages, attend divine service. . . .

It seems to me, that it is the very duty of a university to provide for branches which by the natural course of things—as in every country they take a certain course—are left unprovided for. I will give an instance. Every one in this country studies the constitution, and is naturally led to do so. It would seem to me not necessary, then, to appoint a Professor for the history of the United States alone; perhaps even some evils would be connected with such a chair, as he must necessarily view it in the light of one or the other party of his time; whilst I would urge strongly the establishment of a professorship of general history, (perhaps connected with some other professorship,) because the ordinary course of things in this country, or in fact any where, does not naturally lead to that salutary, noble study, that truly republican and religious study, which unfolds to us the great book of experience, teaching us wisdom from the experience of extinct races, from what they had gained or lost, enjoyed or suffered, and offering a warning from the grave in the lessons of past times, and giving warmth and expression to religious feeling by showing how He, who appears in every leaf and insect, in the eternal laws of nature, and the fine construction of physical man, manifests his godlike wisdom still more to the adorer of his greatness in the moral construction of man, and the great ways on which He conducts nations and ages through apparent disorder to His own great ends. . . .

The principle of making a Professor almost entirely dependent upon his pupils, is objectionable also on another account. To refer a Professor solely or chiefly to his popularity with the students for his support, would be dangerous in all branches, which are not of a very positive and distinct nature, as for instance, anatomy. A Professor of history might make his lectures popular, nay, he might treat generally parts of history, which are more entertaining than others; but whether he would thus most contribute to the purpose of his appointment is a very different question. The best is not always the most popular. Indeed, I have seen students fill a lecture room for the mere sake of entertainment, because the Professor interspersed his lecture (by no means the best of the university) with entertaining anecdotes. I recollect two such instances. However, taking the principle generally, would it not be making the students judges of the professors? Competition is excellent, and the vital agent in all things, where the people interested are proper judges of the subject which interests them. . . . But what would be the case in universities established on that principle? *youths* would judge of *men,* and in regard to that very matter, which they have still to learn; in which they, therefore, are incompetent, else, they would not need the instruction. I do not deny, indeed, that the intense study found in the German universities is owing in a great measure to the liberty of choice left to the students, because liberty produces activity; but I do deny that it would be safe, to let the support of the Professor depend upon the judgment of the students. Have the greater men always been the most popular among the students? By no means. . . .

What, however, has given such excellence to the German Universities? What maintains such a truly scientific spirit among their Professors? I answer—the scientific spirit of the whole nation; a consequence of its entire want of a public political life, the destruction of its political existence as a nation for centuries, and the liberty of thinking produced by the reformation; in one word, it is a consequence of the fact, that the German's life is entirely within him; a good, bought dearly enough. It seems to me, that were you even to give to a German a settled annuity, as those of the English fellows, he would nevertheless be found active and ambitious in the cause of science; because almost the only field of ambition of a German, I mean that ambition which looks beyond the life of the individual and seeks for another distinction than that of titles and wealth, is science. . . .

The student ought to be left more at liberty, and time ought not be wasted in *recitations*. Certainly I would not advise the following entirely [of] the German system, which leaves the student totally without control in respect to his studies, no examinations ever taking place; but it must be remembered how severe in most States, particularly in Prussia—how very severe are those examinations established by government, without which no person can begin to practice medicine, law, or can become ministers, or teachers at a *gymnasium,* or receive an employment in the administrative branch. As government here does not ordain such examinations, it would be best perhaps to adopt somewhat the French system, viz: to have semi-annual examinations, real, thorough examinations, connected with prizes, etc. as in the *Ecole Polytechnique.* In Germany, Professors often appoint hours, in which they receive questions from their pupils respecting the lectures they have heard from him, and talk over the different subjects. . . .

14. Jared Sparks on Professorial Appointments at Harvard, 1830

Graduate of Harvard in 1815, Unitarian clergyman in Baltimore (1819–23), and vigorous editor of the *North American Review* (1823–29), Jared Sparks (1789–1866) was beginning his greatest work, the publication of the writings of George Washington, when he addressed the convention in New York City (see Doc. 12). Later at Harvard he became the first professor of secular history in any American university (1838–49) and served as president (1849–53).

See Samuel Eliot Morison, "Jared Sparks," *Dictionary of American Biography,* XVII (New York, 1935), 430–34, and H. B. Adams, *The Life and Writings of Jared Sparks* (2 vols.; Boston, 1893).

As to the topic now before the convention, respecting the mode of choosing Professors, they are all chosen at Harvard College in the first instance by the corporation, or rather nominated by that body for the approval or rejection of the overseers. But as a case has rarely, if ever

Journal of the Proceedings of a Convention of Literary and Scientific Gentlemen . . . in . . . the City of New York, October, 1830, pp. 82–83.

been known, in which such a nomination has been rejected by the overseers, the election of all the Professors and immediate officers may be said to pertain in practice to the corporation alone. It is probable, however, that this is seldom done without consulting the members of the faculty into which a Professor is to be chosen. No good policy would introduce an efficient member into a small body, where such a step would be likely to endanger harmony of feeling and action. For this reason, it may be well worthy of consideration, whether, in the scheme of a new constitution, it is not better to provide for the nomination of a Professor by the members of the faculty, with whom he is to be associated. Such a body would be as capable as any other, to say the least, of judging in regard to the requisite qualifications of a candidate, and much more capable of deciding whether his personal qualities, traits of character, and habits of thinking, would make him acceptable in their community. It seems evident, therefore, that something is lost, and nothing gained by referring this nomination to another body of men, who have no interests in common with the party chiefly concerned. It is enough that the electing, or sanctioning power, dwells in a separate tribunal.

15. Bancroft on the Nature of an Urban Academic Community, 1830

See Docs. 5 and 12.

A University is not devoted exclusively to any one department of knowledge. It opens its gates wide to the reception of all valuable truth; and sustaining no particular branch of science by the sanction of prescription, by the continuance of favoritism, or by the dead letter of intellectual mort mains, it allows to each division of human knowledge that degree of prominence, which its intrinsic merits can obtain. In the true social spirit, it receives and takes an interest in every thing that belongs to the human understanding.

Journal of the Proceedings of a Convention of Literary and Scientific Gentlemen . . . in . . . the City of New York, October, 1830, pp. 46–52.

Neither is it a mere system of lectures adapted to the curious and the idle. It is designed not to afford pastime but to excite and encourage severe industry; not to furnish amusement, but to diffuse and to advance science.

Nor does it attach itself to any sect in religion. God forbid, that the day should ever arrive, when there should be a separation of pure morality and deep religious conviction from our public places of education; but the character of a University requires, that it should be subordinate to no religious party, subservient to no religious sect. It must be established independently, on its own merits.

The idea of a University, liberally constructed, precludes rivalry or jealousy. Competition between literary corporations does not produce the same excellent results as competition between literary men. The very nature of a University implies, as we have seen, so extensive co-operation, so enlarged a liberality, that it cheerfully receives within itself all the genuine friends of science.

But as between man and man, there is nothing so salutary as that healthful competition, which ensures the greatest success of the most industrious and most powerful efforts, in a University, a *career* must be opened, not *places* established. Things must be so arranged, as to have exertion a natural result of causes always in operation. No board of directors, no examining committee, no legislative precautions, can effect the results, which come spontaneously from the free development of talent under the excitement of emulation, and stimulated by the prospect of emolument and fame. The scholar should, indeed, himself, prefer his vocation to every thing, and will never attain eminence, unless his unbiassed inclinations are heartily engaged in his pursuit; but the interest of the public requires that honors and rewards should be commensurate with practical exertions; for the public in its nurseries of science needs to foster, not the indolent gratification of a favorite taste, but a hardy perseverance in a course of active usefulness.

The establishment of a University, calls for an effort, proportioned to the dignity and importance of the design. Its perfect results can at best be realized but slowly. A very few years ago the government of Bavaria opened a University in Munich, a city not much more than one third as large as New York; but as former ages had already collected there, hospitals, a very valuable museum, a magnificent library, and other fixtures, the establishment within a year after its formation, went into successful operation. So, too, at Berlin, a city by far the largest in Northern Germany, yet much inferior to New York, in wealth and business, and population; a palace, a royal library, hospitals, a most admirable cabinet of natural history, were at once given to lend a lustre to the rising University, and its growth into celebrity was sure and rapid. But it took nearly a century to bring Göttingen to its present high distinction; the genius of a Haller was needed, to expand its means of instruction in Natural History: the marvellous perseverance of Heyne, to impart correct views on the subject of its library; and now the talent of a Gauss to give perfection to its observatories.

In New York there is no public library of any very considerable value. No scientific collections in the various departments which need them. But the study of medicine and surgery is favored by the very condition of being in a metropolis; and a learned, intelligent and active bar, courts of all kinds, the natural attractions of a large city, and a lucrative profession, would seem suited to invite the youthful aspirants after eminence in the law. At Göttingen seven hundred is no unusual number to belong to the law department alone. And the profession is with us, a more crowded one, than it is in Europe. The pursuits of philosophy and the arts, on the contrary, may have a harder struggle. Our countrymen profess, many of them, to strive to see, how much of the learning of former ages may be dispensed with, rather than how much may be retained. In the absurdly boasted march of mind, they would propose to throw away the accumulated stores of preceding ages, as useless baggage, forgetting that all knowledge is but an accumulation of facts, and of reasonings, based upon them. The rejection of the wisdom of the past, does not awaken originality, but produces poverty of intellect by the loss of the materials, on which originality should be exercised.

Finally, the question recurs, whether the country in its present condition, demands a University, and whether any responsibility rests upon New York with relation to it.

With respect to the wants of the country, the answer must be found in the *numbers of our people,* already surpassing that of any protestant kingdom or state in the world, excepting England; in the *character of our government,* which can never interfere with free inquiry and the pursuit of truth; in the *relative age of our population,* which, in its rapid increase furnishes a larger proportion of persons to be educated than is found in older countries; in the *basis of our social system,* which regards intelligence as a conservative not less than as a productive principle in the body politic; in the *forming character of all our institutions,* which are as yet hardly fixed, but remains yet to receive the impress which they are to bear forever; in the *period of our history,* when the old states are in truth rapidly becoming the mothers of new ones; *in the condition of our strength,* since the weakness of to-day becomes to-morrow, the confidence and admiration of the world; and lastly *in the character of our population,* proverbially ambitious, and inquisitive, where elementary education is already universally diffused, and where under the auspices of our political equality, the public walks of honor and emulation, are crowded with throngs from every class of society.

If attention recurs to New York, the mind readily recals [*sic*] the *extended relations of this city with the foreign world.* Where can the wisdom of former generations, the intellectual inheritance bequeathed by the old world to the new, where can it so readily be gathered and received as in the city, which has its agents under every zone, and is connected by the closest bonds with every part of the civilized world?

The subject gains a deeper interest, when we consider the influence which New York must necessarily exert upon the country. The emigrant in the remotest settlements looks to this city as the place that connects him with the active world. Whether we give attention to it or not, New York, the mistress of the sea, holding also in her hands the keys of the interior, is the very heart of the business community; and its pulsations are felt throughout the land. The christian philanthropist, the advocates of religious liberty, and the advocates of intelligence, have to decide, whether this extensive power shall be felt only through the markets and the exchange, or whether it shall be the means of fostering that great communion, which exists among all the friends of humanity.

On New York itself a successful University might not only reflect a brilliancy of reputation, but also confer inestimable benefits. . . .

On men of letters the great commercial city would exert a favorable influence. The habit of the place is industry; and the literary man, partaking of the general excitement, is led to form habits of profound application. So, too, the varied intercourse with men of all nations, stirs the stagnant pool of superstition and prejudice. The immense movements in business, the daily spectacle of crowds of sail from every quarter of the world, the frequent presence of minds, which have been developed in the most different pursuits, or ripened under every sky, gradually yet surely tend to promote intellectual freedom, and to do away that narrow mindedness which is the worst enemy of improvement.

16. Henry E. Dwight on the Low Status of Teachers, 1830

Eighth son of the elder President Timothy Dwight of Yale, Henry Edwin Dwight (1797–1832) was the earliest American registered at the University of Berlin. His *Travels in the North of Germany* (1829) lauded the German academic system. At the time of this convention (see Doc. 12), he and his brother, Sereno, were operating a gymnasium at New Haven on the order of the Round Hill School at Northampton, Massachusetts. Just before his premature death he declined a professorship in the newly founded university in New York City.

The want of competent teachers is one of the principal reasons, why the classics have been studied with so little enthusiasm in our country. Teaching with us, is in most instances a secondary employment, one which the graduates of our colleges embrace for a few years, and then abandon forever. Even while thus occupied, their professional studies are the most interesting objects presented to their view, engrossing most of their thoughts. Their limited resources compel them to devote several years to this employment, and when they have learned a little of the art of teaching, which, in truth, is one of the most difficult arts ever acquired, they resign their places to those who are still younger, and who have had less experience than themselves. Education has consequently never become a distinct profession in the United States, but a stepping-stone to one of the learned professions. In consequence of this, instructors are less respected in our country than in any other, and few men of talents are willing to devote their lives to teaching, or even to pursue it longer than their necessities compel them, unless there is a prospect of obtaining a place in some of our colleges. . . .

Journal of the Proceedings of a Convention of Literary and Scientific Gentlemen . . . in . . . the City of New York, October, 1830, p. 135.

17. Benjamin Silliman on the Government of Yale, 1830

The following remarks were made by Benjamin Silliman (1779–1864) on the first and third days (October 20, 22) of the convention in New York City (see Doc. 12). Silliman served Yale for fifty-one years (1802–53) as professor of chemistry and natural history. In that time he became our outstanding academic scientist, lectured widely on geology, mineralogy, and chemistry, and founded and edited *The American Journal of Science and Arts* (see Doc. 11), a great scientific journal that is a monument to his eminence.

See John F. Fulton and Elizabeth H. Thomson, *Benjamin Silliman, 1779–1864: Pathfinder in American Science* (New York, 1947).

The faculty of Yale College have no voice in the appointment of Professors, by law—as the appointments are made by the board of Trustees called the "President and Fellows"—that in fact however their opinions and wishes are regarded, and it is very rare that an appointment is made except in accordance with them:—that the President of the College being the presiding officer both in the corporation and in the faculty, the wishes of the latter readily find, through him, a passage to the former, and a nomination by the faculty, or at least an expression of their views is always expected; that the faculty ought always to be men in whose heads and hearts unlimited confidence can be reposed, and that this being the fact, a board of trustees could rarely be safe in disregarding their suggestions,—that there is in Yale College, besides the corporation, a "Prudential Committee", consisting of the President and three other gentlemen, members of the corporation, of whom one is regularly the Governor or Lieut. Governor of the state,— who meet at least four times in a year and deliberately settle the accounts, and in conjunction with the faculty devise the various plans, and mature the reports which are to be made to the corporation. The latter board generally sit but once in a year, and on common occasions finish their business in one day: this they are enabled to do, because the business is prepared and digested by the Prudential Committee and the faculty—and although the corporation is an independent body, it rarely acts in important cases, without the concurrence of both the faculty

Journal of the Proceedings of a Convention of Literary and Scientific Gentlemen . . . in . . . the City of New York, October, 1830, pp. 79–80, 156–57.

and the Prudential Committee—and as great confidence always prevails, between these respective bodies, the business of the institution
proceeds harmoniously. . . .

It would be happy if parents would frequently resort to the institutions in which their children are members, and ascertain in person
their condition; that they should go into their recitation and lecture
rooms, and into their chambers, and thus ascertain their habits, opportunities and prospects; that the government of a college should be efficient, and should have power to remove any injurious member, after
suitable efforts to produce reformation; that the government is crip-
pled and will not be respected by the students, provided it is obliged to
depend upon a higher board to confirm its decisions; that the government should, however, be held amenable to a higher board to revise its
decisions, and that this board should have power to revise them if they
should appear erroneous, but until this is done, their decisions should
be final:—that the government should, however, itself, be governed by
fixed laws, which should of course be made public, as well as those
that govern the students; that all may know their duties; that the *spirit*
of the government should be entirely parental—the intercourse of the
officers with their pupils, mild, affectionate, and winning, like that of
parents with their children; and that if students were disobedient, and
unworthy in their conduct, the tone of their instructers should still be
calm although firm, never harsh or menacing.—It was observed that,
as good parents are familiar with their children, enter into their feelings, and even mingle occasionally in their amusements, so, as far as it
is practicable, the college government ought to imitate the parental,
but that in both cases there *must be* obedience, and the authority of the
parent or instructer should not be questioned by the child or pupil, although both are held amenable to moral sanctions, to public opinion,
and to the laws.

18. J. Leo Wolf on the Advantages of German Academic Freedom, 1830

Little is known of J. Leo Wolf, whose remarks on the organization of a university were published as an appendix to the journal of this convention in New York City (see Doc. 12). He is identified as coming from Hamburg and as having studied at Marburg, Göttingen, and Berlin. He spoke with the pride of a new citizen of the United States.

The students of the German Universities are under no literary control. They may pursue their studies as they please, although a general plan is recommended to them; they may attend the lectures regularly or not; they are under no control of this kind. Only in cases, where they attend to no lectures at all, which is soon observed, they receive an admonition from the Dean of the Faculty, to which they belong, not to lose sight of the object for which they stay in the University. Nor are the students ever examined by their Professors, excepting they desire them to do so, and engage them for it purposely.

The semi-annual examinations, as recommended by some of the gentlemen of the Convention, lower the student to the rank of a school boy, while, being a man, as he ought to be, they are useless, for he will know that it is for his own good, to be assiduous in his studies. Moreover, the result of his studies is proved at the time, when he desires to graduate and to be licensed for the practice of his profession. Then he must pass a strict, rigid and public examination; and this I should warmly recommend. In Prussia these examinations are particularly severe, but quite impartial, and recorded. . . .

All restrictions upon the moral and literary freedom of the students, are injurious to the free development of science. The heroes of German science and literature, as Kant, Kaestner, Leibnitz, Ernesti, Haller, Gronovius and others, were all educated in the German Universities, when they enjoyed the greatest freedom. The despotism of the German governments, for centuries past, suffered and sanctioned this unbound liberty of the students, while all other classes of society were chained, for they were sensible of its importance to themselves, as the means to

---

Journal of the Proceedings of a Convention of Literary and Scientific Gentlemen . . . in . . . the City of New York, October, 1830, pp. 247–256.

be provided with able men to fill their offices. Experience proves this. Austria has for some time past confined the moral and intellectual liberty of her students, and has turned her Universities almost into schools[.] What is the result? her seats of science are barren of all, which has recourse to speculative branches of knowledge and philosophy; the exact sciences only continue flourishing there. . . .

The feeling of liberty and independence in youth, is a prominent feature and an admirable characteristic of this country; and if this feeling is with difficulty controlled in boys, as has been stated by several gentlemen of the Convention, and has been intimated to me by some of my friends; how much more difficult will this be in young men of eighteen or twenty years of age, who will constitute, I hope, the greater number of our students in the New University. All kinds of restrictions in this age have a tendency to defeat themselves. Moreover those, who enter the University, must be expected to come, from love of science, and as love for any subject whatsoever is a feeling, which rises voluntarily, and cannot be enforced, so neither ought love for science to be enforced, nor would it be of any avail.

I am persuaded, that the flourishing state of the German Universities has its origin in this liberty. If you think the natives of that country to be partial or prepossessed in their statements, ask those of your own countrymen, who have been there; compare what they have seen of the state of science in Germany to that of other countries, and see the result. . . .

Why is the political state of this our country, the most flourishing on the globe? but because we enjoy the most unbound liberty of the press. We see the proof of liberty in this; why not allow the same to science in its fullest extent, and admit freedom to teach or to be taught in whatever the human mind may incline to?

The German students have their own court and tribunal, formed in every University by the professors: they are not under the control of the police or state laws, excepting in criminal cases. I am in possession of the laws of the Universities of Marburg, in Hesse-Cassel, of Gottingen and of Berlin, in which places I performed my studies, from which I furnish some of their particulars. But here, where the students would necessarily stand under the common law, many of those laws would not be applicable.

There are, besides, two other great causes of the flourishing state of the German Universities, and of sciences there in general.

The first is, that those who desire to be matriculated as students of theology, law, or medicine, must prove their ability for the pursuit of these professions, and that they have attained a sufficient classical education. This is ascertained either by testimonies, if they are issued by well known and good colleges, or in want of these, by an examination, previous to the matriculation. Only the pursuit of those sciences, which are embraced in the faculty of philosophy, as history, geography, mathematics, languages, belles lettres, philosophy, natural sciences, &c. should be permitted to all, without further difficulty.

The second cause of the flourishing state of the German Universities consists in the great literary rivalry between the professors of a University, and particularly between those of the same line. For every principal branch of science there are in every good University at least two lecturers, in order that their ambition may be excited by a noble competition. If there be but one professor for a branch of science, and the students be compelled by necessity to attend his lectures, he is very apt to become careless in his zeal. I know of instances of this kind in some of the German Universities, although generally there are several lecturers on the same subject. . . .

In our institutions, where the professors are neither appointed nor paid by government, but are obliged to rely chiefly on their private efforts and the emoluments received from the sale of their tickets, a larger number of teachers would cause no additional expense, but would be beneficial as well to the students as to the cause of science. I would therefore suggest, that every one who thinks himself competent to teach, should be permitted to do so, and should have the free use of the halls of the University, provided he proves, that he has passed through a regular course of professional education, and has gone through a strict examination for the degree or license of his profession. The result and success of his professorship should entirely depend upon himself, and in order to create a noble literary, but no pecuniary competition, a certain rate of charges for every kind of lectures should be established, from which no one should be permitted to deviate.

I have a catalogue of the lectures of the Berlin University for 1823, and another of the same University for the last winter course before me, which contains 24 courses of lectures on theology, 40 on jurisprudence, 86 on medicine and surgery, 29 on natural sciences, 15 on philosophy, 13 on mathematics, 17 on politics, 11 on history and geography, 5 on the fine arts, and 38 on languages, making a total of 278 courses of lectures, all of them to be delivered during one winter course, in the building of the University. This extent cannot at once be given to the new University, nor can it be expected, but we ought to aim at it, and if the right course be pursued, we shall attain it. As the soil of this, our land, is bountifully blessed by nature before many others, and wants but the hand to cultivate it; so is the mind and natural talent of its people, and wants but a spot to be fostered in. I sincerely, therefore, wish success to the new University, and hope to see it soon established . . . .

19. *Jasper Adams on the Relation between Trustees and Faculty, 1837*

Jasper Adams (1793–1841) was a graduate (1815) of Brown University who presided successfully over Charleston College in South Carolina from 1824 to 1836, except for an eighteen-month interim as president of Geneva (Hobart) College, 1826–28. At Charleston he raised the standards, reputation, and enrolment of the college. The American Institute of Instruction, where Adams delivered his address, was one of the principal societies of educators and laymen in the 1830's that propagandized for educational reforms.

See Richard Hofstadter and Walter P. Metzger, *The Development of Academic Freedom in the United States*, pp. 236–38.

At the close of the Revolution which severed these United States from Great Britain, the number of our universities and colleges was eight only;[1] the number now organized is nearly a hundred. Many of these institutions are feeble, as the original eight all were, during and at the close of our colonial existence, but their establishment is good proof of a spirit on the part of the people of this country, worthy of all commendation and encouragement. They have been planted with the original settlement of the country itself, and they may be expected to grow with its growth and strengthen with its strength. They must continue to be, as they have hitherto been, the foundation of our honor

Jasper Adams, "On the Relation Subsisting between The Board of Trustees and Faculty of a University," *American Institute of Instruction, Lectures . . . at Worcester, Mass., August 1837* (Boston, 1838), pp. 139–158.

[1] Pitkin's Civil and Political History of the United States, Vol. I, p. 153.

and renown, the prime sources of our moral prosperity and welfare; the fountains whence are to flow, the fertilizing waters of literature, of science, of philosophy, and of religion. Our country, too, is blessed with very numerous institutions designed for the study of law, medicine and theology, which have attained to various degrees of strength and stability. Besides these several classes of institutions for the attainment of liberal and professional learning, we have hundreds of academies, a considerable number of which have attained to much distinction and usefulness. The permanent success of these institutions, essentially involves, as has been suggested, the great cause of the literature, the science, the morals, the religion and the education of the country. Every thing which we are accustomed to esteem most valuable, must sooner or later take its moral and intellectual tone from the character of these institutions. The magnitude of the interests, therefore, which they involve, cannot fail to render whatever pertains to their structure, character and usefulness, an object of superlative importance to every American patriot and citizen. I could not fail, therefore, to be justified in inviting the attention of the American Institute of Instruction, to *any feature* in their organization, which, on the one hand, might promise to enhance their efficiency and promote their usefulness; or which, on the other, might threaten to paralyze their energies, and impair or destroy the hopes and confidence reposed in them by the country which has founded and cherished them.

Our universities, colleges, academies,—our institutions too for the study of law, medicine and divinity, are, with very few exceptions, established on essentially the same plan. They consist of a corporate board of trustees, whose number varies from seven up to fifty or sixty persons, in whom the legal interest of the institution is vested. The beneficial interest belongs to the public. Besides this corporate board of trustees, there is sometimes attached to the institution a board of oversight, or superintendence, who have the power of affirming or exposing the proceedings of the inferior board, who have the right of interference when they think proper, and who are entitled to be consulted on extraordinary occasions. Such is the constitution of Harvard University. The common law right of visitation resides in the founder, his heirs, or his representative. This right is, therefore, sometimes in the state, sometimes in an individual, or several individuals, and sometimes in a select body of men, to whom the right of visitation has been transferred by the founder. The right of visitation in Harvard University is said to reside in the Board of Overseers.[2]

A faculty of which these institutions further consist, is a select body of learned men, to whom the instruction and the administration of the discipline are, generally with some qualification, entrusted. It is, too, a body perfectly well recognised as distinct from the board of trustees. The administration of the discipline comprises the judicial and executive authority of the institution. The faculty customarily assemble by themselves to transact the business of the institution, they are governed by their own rules, they act by their president, or by a committee of their own body, they usually have their own secretary, and keep a record of their own proceedings. The faculty, moreover, are the body, which is held by the public, to be chiefly responsible for the good conduct of the institution. It is the department through which it is practically known to the community, and on which it must principally depend for character and usefulness. The pupils and the parents communicate almost entirely with the faculty, scarcely at all with the trustees. And it is a part of the history of the literary institutions of this country, that they have been chiefly built up by the sacrifices, the exertions, and the wise management of their faculties. The presiding member of the faculty, often, though by no means always, holds his office during good behaviour, and sometimes, though not often, the professors hold theirs by the same tenure. The presiding member of the faculty is usually a member (*ex officio*) of the board of trustees.

This rapid statement of the manner in which our universities, colleges, academies, and schools of the professions of whatever kind, are usually constituted, has not been made without a special object in view. It is preliminary to the examination which, on this occasion, I propose to make, into the nature of the relation which subsists between the trustees and faculties of these institutions, and into the chief reciprocal duties which spring from this relation. Unquestionably, it is the duty both of the trustees and faculties of the important institutions entrusted to them, to co-operate with each other harmoniously and energetically in building up their institutions, in providing them with every thing necessary to successful instruction, in conciliating public

---

[2] Mr. Webster thinks, that the visitatorial power in Harvard University belongs to the fellows, or members of the corporation; though he admits, that "some power of inspection is given to the overseers." Wheaton's Reports, Vol. IV, p. 567.—Letter to John Lowell, Esq., ascribed to Edward Everett. Boston, 1824, pp. 91–93.

favor to them, and inspiring public confidence in them. It is very manifest, that all this is their duty; but it is equally the duty of every good citizen to do the same thing, as opportunity permits and occasion is presented. This view and this language, then, are too general and too indefinite to be instructive; and to be really and practically informed on this subject, we must descend to particulars. The inquiry must be narrowed down to the nature of this relation, and the peculiar duties arising from it. To this end, and with a view to secure to myself the advantages of order and arrangement, I propose,—

I. To inquire into the legal character of the relation, and to state the legal principles and doctrines, which have a bearing on it, so far as I have been able to collect them.

II. To draw aid and illustration from the reason of the thing, and from the analogies furnished by other kindred relations.

III. To examine it by the light of experience drawn from the history of our colleges and other literary institutions.

I. The corporate character of the board of trustees has already been adverted to. "Corporations for the advancement of learning, (denominated by us colleges,) were entirely unknown to the ancients, and are," says Chancellor Kent, "the fruits of modern invention. In the time of the later Roman Emperors, however, the professors in the different sciences, began to be allowed regular salaries from the government, to become objects of public regulation and discipline. By the close of the third century," continues he, "these literary establishments, especially the schools at Rome, Constantinople, Alexandria and Berytus, began to assume the appearance of public institutions; and privileges and honors were bestowed upon the professors and students, who were subjected to visitation and inspection, by the civil and ecclesiastical powers. It was not, however, until at least the 13th century, that colleges and universities began to confer degrees, and to attain the authority and influence which they now enjoy. The University of Paris was the first which assumed the form of our modern colleges."[3]

The board of trustees is designed to give the institution perpetuity of existence, and along with this, a stability and permanence, which could not be secured by a private institution depending on the life, talents and resources of one or more individuals. This feature in their struc-

---

[3] Kent's Commentaries on American Law, Vol. II. p. 218. Angel and Ames on Corporations, pp. 29, 30.

ture, to wit, the permanence and stability secured by a perpetual existence, is extremely valuable, and even essential, because large funds, extensive libraries, and a variety of philosophical and other apparatus,
must, beyond what can ordinarily be collected in a single age, is indispensable to any considerable success and usefulness. In the board of
trustees resides the legislative power of the institution. The trustees,
too, manage the funds and appoint the faculty. It will hereafter be
seen, in what way, and with what qualifications, it is their duty to exercise these important powers. A board of trustees, moreover, selected
from various professions, composed of men of eminence, sharing
largely of the public confidence, and having a commanding influence
with the government and in private society, is generally supposed to
command a more extensive patronage for the institution, and to give
it a more advantageous connexion with the public, than it could otherwise enjoy.

The inquiry next presents itself,—what is the *Faculty* of a college
or university; and what is its constitution in contemplation of law?

The idea of one corporation being engrafted on another, seems to be
familiar to the law, and those engraftments on their original corporations, are called, in reference to them, *quasi corporations.* Thus, the
supervisors of a county in the state of New York, have been decided to
be a corporation for certain special purposes pertaining to the country
which they represent.[4] So too, the overseers of the poor, and the loan
officers of a county, are quasi corporations, invested with corporate
powers, limited, indeed, but co-extensive with the duties imposed upon
them by statute or by usage.[5] School districts are included in the same
class of corporations. It has been decided by the Supreme Court of
Massachusetts, that a school district may sue as a corporation and by
its corporate name.[6] "These corporations," says Chief Justice Parker,
"possess by necessary implication, the authority which is requisite to
execute the purposes of their creation."[7]

Such is the true nature, as I understand it, and constitution of the
faculties of our colleges in contemplation of law. They seem to be that

---

[4] Jackson v. Hartwell, 8 Johnson's Reports, 422.

[5] 2 Kent's Commentaries, 221.—North Hempstead v. Hempstead, 2 Wendell's Reports, 109.

[6] Angel on Corporations, p. 16.

[7] 4th School District v. Wood, 13 Mass. Reports, 192.

"kind of assembly in corporations," which Mr. Kyd denominates "administrative," while the boards of trustees comprise the "legislative and electoral assemblies in corporations," spoken of by the same learned author. This view of the rightful constitution of the Faculties of our colleges, is highly important, as it tends to give them the stability and independence essential to the successful discharge of the duties of instruction and discipline, which ought always to be committed to them. The law pertaining to the relation between the trustees and faculty, is scanty and rather indefinite, as the nature of the relation, and the relative positions, rights, duties, privileges and responsibilities of the respective parties, have never, so far as I know, been submitted to judicial examination in this country. It is much to be wished, that the analytical mind of a Mansfield, a Parsons, a Scott, or a Marshall, might be brought to bear on this entire subject.

The adjustment of many questions pertaining to this relation, belongs, it seems, to the person or body of men, in whom the visitatorial power resides. The visitor has a special jurisdiction, and his tribunal is recognised by the law of the land. Lord Mansfield, in commenting upon the convenience of the tribunal of a visitor, says,—"it is a *forum domesticum* calculated to determine *sine strepitu* all disputes that arise within learned bodies. This power being exercised properly and without parade, is of infinite use."[8] A visitor may administer an oath, or require an answer upon oath. He ought always to proceed, whether upon a general visitation, or a particular appeal, summarily, simply, and entirely without the noise and parade of a court, "for herein consists the whole excellence of his tribunal."[9]

II. The reason of the thing, and the analogies furnished by the kindred relations, will be found much more instructive on this subject, than the law of the land, which, it seems, has not yet been fully declared and illustrated by our judicial tribunal.

Guided, then, by the reason of the thing, in what position does the faculty of a college naturally stand in reference to the board of trustees? Does the circumstance, that the faculty are appointed by the trustees, of itself place the former in an inferior situation in respect to the

---

[8] The King vs the Bishop of Ely, 1 Blackstone's Reports, p. 82.

[9] Ibid. 7 Pickering's Reports, 303.—Angel and Ames on Corporations, 410–419. Allen vs. McKeen, 1 Sumner's Reports, 276.—Auburn Academy vs. Strong, 1 Hopkin's Chancery Reports, 278.

latter? Is a faculty naturally subordinate to a board of trustees? If so, in what respects? A correct answer to these questions is highly important to the interests of many literary institutions in the country.

It may be observed, that an act of incorporation is, in all cases, to be regarded as *a means* devised by the legislature, to accomplish some particular *end* or *ends*. A corporation always has reference to something beyond itself. It always looks to the attainment of some *end,* which it was designed to accomplish. The incorporation is of no importance, any further than it serves to secure the desired *end*. This is the nature and essence of all incorporations, and will serve as a key to the right understanding of the powers and privileges, with which the boards of trustees of our literary institutions are invested. They always look to something beyond themselves. Thus, a college is not founded, that it *may be incorporated,* but it is incorporated, that it may the better accomplish the end for which it was founded,—that is, the incorporation is subordinate to *the end* for which the institution was founded. In other and plainer terms, a board of trustees is to be looked upon as *a means* devised by the legislature to accomplish certain *ends*. The chief of these ends, and the end too, in which all the minor objects are included, in the establishment of a college, is, the organization of a learned and effective faculty, qualified to impart such instruction in literature and the sciences as is called for by the wants of the community. Again, the means are always subordinate to the end, and are of themselves comparatively unimportant, except as they serve to accomplish the end designed. To make, then, the faculty of a college subordinate to the trustees, is to reverse the usual order of things, to subvert first principles, to exalt the means above the end, instead of making them subordinate to the accomplishment of the end.

But the argument arising from the nature of the case and the reason of the thing, may be pursued still further. It has before been said, that public opinion, which is much stronger than laws and charters in this country, is accustomed to hold the faculty of a college chiefly responsible for the manner in which it is conducted,—in other terms, for its success or failure. If it is successful, they have the credit; if unsuccessful, the discredit, in like manner, whether deserved or undeserved, falls on them. Now no principle is plainer, than that when a person, (or body of men) is responsible for the issue of any business or enterprise, he ought to be permitted to select his own means, and to appoint his own agents and associates. This he may rightfully claim, nay, he ought to claim it, and it is but the merest justice to award it to him, in its fullest measure. There is no case to which this principle is more applicable, and with less restriction, than to the case of faculty of a college in their relation to the board of trustees. For the latter to undertake to advise, and to insist upon directing the former in regard to the instruction and discipline of a college, is completely reversing this well settled principle, as well as the natural and well established order of things.[10]

This conclusion obtained by consulting the nature of the relation and the reason of the thing, is amply confirmed by adverting to several kindred cases embraced within the very comprehensive relation of the employer and the person employed. The general principle which governs this familiar relation unquestionably is, that the employer advises, instructs and directs the person employed; but to this, there is a considerable number of well established and familiar exceptions. Whenever the employer engages and pays for, the manual labor, the mere physical strength and the time of the persons employed, he is accustomed to superintend and wholly to *direct* their labors. But in every case, in which *peculiar skill, knowledge and experience* are required in *the party employed,* he is entitled, in consequence of such peculiar knowledge, skill and experience, *to advise and direct his employer.* This distinction runs through every department of labor, and every profession and pursuit of life. The relation of the lawyer and his client, furnishes a familiar illustration of this distinction. The lawyer, although he is the party employed, advises, and directs his employer, in his own business. The case of the physician and his patient is another of these well established exceptions to the general rule, that the employer instructs and controls the employer. The physician *employed* advises and prescribes for the patient who is his *employer.* The case of the clergyman and his congregation is another instance of the same distinction,

---

10 I understand, it is a principle of law as well as of morals, that whenever a man is made responsible for a *result* in the course of business, it is not competent for his employer *to direct* him, in respect to the manner in which he is *to obtain such result.* He is entitled to act upon the dictates of his own judgment and independently of any interference on the part of his employer. Thus, it is stated to me, that the teller of a bank, being strictly responsible for *accurate results* in paying out and receiving money, is not subject to the instruction of his superiors, in regard to the manner in which his part of the business is transacted.

equally familiar and unquestionable. The preacher is always the rightful judge of the doctrines and morals which he is to preach to the congregation which employs him. In like manner and for the same reasons, the faculty of a college, university or other institution of learning, are entitled to advise the board of trustees which employs them, in respect to *the literary department* of the institution. And on the other hand, the trustees are bound in reason and conscience to consult the faculty, to receive their advice, and in all ordinary cases to act upon it, in the discharge of their duties, so far as the same department of the institution is concerned. The successful instruction of a college, and the wise administration of its discipline, require qualifications as high and as peculiar as those which are called into exercise by the classical office, or by the duties of the lawyer and the physician. In truth, it will not be arrogating too much to affirm, that few situations require more skill, knowledge and experience, than the wise administration of the affairs of a college.

If any thing is wanting to confirm this view of the nature of the relation which I am examining, it may be found in the absurd consequences which flow, in abundance, from the doctrine, that the trustees of a college are entitled by virtue of their office, to advise, instruct and direct its faculty in respect to its instruction and the administration of its discipline. I can but touch on this part of the subject. The trustees of our colleges have, with few exceptions, almost no qualifications which peculiarly fit them for the practical administration of those institutions. They are not often selected for their situation, by reason of any peculiar fitness. They consist without much discrimination, of eminent lawyers, clergymen and physicians; successful agriculturists, manufacturers, merchants, and other substantial classes of the community. But assuredly, the qualifications which have given them eminence and success in the professions and branches of business, which it has been their choice to pursue, have imparted to them no peculiar fitness to gain the ascendancy over young men, and to inspire them with the love of virtue, and the enthusiasm of learning. It is too manifest to require argument, that such men, however worthy and excellent they may be, in their personal characters, and however distinguished in the line of their several pursuits and professions, are no more qualified and entitled to advise and direct a college faculty within their peculiar department, than the client is to advise and direct his lawyer, or the patient his physician.[11]

III. I am now prepared to examine this subject by the light of experience, drawn from the history of our colleges and other literary institutions. From a personal experience of more than twenty years, from conversing with a great number of college officers, from perusing all the printed histories of our colleges, and various documents[12] respecting the administration, I feel justified in considering several particulars fully established.

1. No college in this country has permanently flourished, in which the trustees have not been willing to concede to the faculty, the rank, dignity, honor and influence, which belong essentially to their station. There has been much and just cause of complaint in this particular. Cases have not been very unfrequent, in which the trustees of our colleges have been willing to impose the most burthensome duties upon a faculty, to leave them to struggle unaided amidst every variety of discouragement, and at length, to claim to themselves, all the honor of a wise and successful administration of its affairs. It has not been very unusual, even to call the faculty of a college, "the servants of the trustees;"—but surely such language does not correspond to the nature of the relation, nor to the state of things that ought to exist in a literary institution. "In a literary institution," says a late college officer, "there should be no offices of more honor or dignity than those given to the literary men who are its instructers. They indeed," continues he, "should be the servants of the public, but not of any other body of men." Again, "the reputation of a college cannot be unappropriated, nor attach itself to the abstract idea of the institution; it belongs, in

---

[11] Every profession and employment of life, has a greater or smaller portion of *the peculiar skill and knowledge* of which I have spoken, and on which I have insisted. But there is this difference. In some professions, the peculiar skill and knowledge which pertain to them, is manifest to all. This is true of law, medicine and the mechanic arts. In other professions, the existence of such peculiar skill and knowledge, though not less real, is much less manifest. The administration of our colleges is an example. But nevertheless, skill in their management, as Lord Coke says of the law, comes from "long studie, often conference, long experience, and continuall observation." (Co. Lit. 232, b.)

[12] The most instructive and valuable of the documents here referred to, is, "A Narrative of the Embarrassments and Decline of Hamilton College, (N. York) by Henry Davis, D. D. President." The volume contains 158 pages closely printed and in fine type, and a copy of it ought to be in the hands of every trustee of a literary institution in the country.

the nature of things, to individuals; and the more clearly and definitely it attaches to certain individuals, the better. But the faculty are
marked out by every circumstance as the proper representatives of the
college; with whose offices all the honor due to the institution ought
to be associated. No other body of men ought to intervene, to obscure
them from public view; and to take from their offices, the rank, respectability and dignity which should be connected with them. They
perform the labor and bear the burthens of the institution, its honors,
therefore, in the nature of things, rightfully belong to them."[13]

2. It is a part of the history of our literary institutions, that those
colleges have been most flourishing, in which the instruction and discipline have been most exclusively committed to their faculties. This
fact, the result of the experience of the country, may be easily explained.
"To render a college in the highest degree prosperous and useful, the
first step is, to secure as its instructers, men of the first talents, the
soundest learning, the purest morals, and the deepest sense of religion.
To this end its offices must be such, that men of the character described
will be willing to accept and willing to retain them. They must be
offices of dignity and trust, affording to those who hold them, full opportunity of making the best use of their abilities for the good of the
institution. Again, the instructers thus secured, must not be subjected,
as mere ministerial officers, to the direction of other individuals, who
are in comparison, but remotely connected with the college, and imperfectly acquainted with its interests. An institution will flourish then
and then only, in the best sense of that term, when such men as have
been described are made responsible to the public for its prosperity,
and enjoy all the power, dignity and honor, which ought to accompany this responsibility."[14]

Instead of this encouraging, this inspiriting condition of things,
many a faculty of a college, who felt themselves qualified, not only
to sustain their institution, but to raise it to usefulness and renown, and
gain for it the favor, confidence and patronage of the public, have
found all their efforts discouraged, embarrassed, and finally defeated
by the conduct of their board of trustees. Plans of improvement, after
having been matured by much labor and careful consideration, have
been presented for acceptance and approbation, only to be retained

[13] See Professor Norton's Speech before the Overseers of Harvard University, p. 17.

[14] Professor Norton's Speech. Introduction, p. xxii.

with coldness and indifference, treated with neglect, and finally rejected, after a hasty examination, for want of a competency to understand them. Favorable times and seasons have been permitted to pass by unimproved, and have been lost never to return, because the faculty had not power to act on the subject, and the trustees could not be induced to seize the favorable moment, and turn the occasion to the benefit of the institution. Under these circumstances, the faculty have been compelled to remain inactive, and let things take their course, or to resign their offices in discouragement and disgust. In either case, the institution has been ruined.

3. It is settled by the experience of our colleges, that whenever the trustees have interfered in the instruction and discipline, they have acted without tact, without address, without knowledge, without firmness, without perseverance, and with such a mixture of rashness and indecision, that they have signally failed. Some amusing as well as instructive cases to this effect might be cited, if the time at my command permitted. "After nearly thirty years *personal* experience," says President Davis, "in the government and discipline of five colleges, this measure" (to wit, interference in the administration of discipline by a committee of the trustees) "was entirely new to me. Motives of delicacy alone prevented me, when it was proposed before the board, from an open and decided resistance to it. I then viewed it, as I ever since have, as a direct and dangerous encroachment upon the appropriate and exclusive province of the faculty; and as tending in no small degree to impair their authority and influence with their pupils. It was too apparent from the appearance of the young gentlemen before the committee, not to be perceived, that they had a similar view of it. For, there was something in their every look, and word, and gesture, which insinuated beyond the power of misapprehension, *you are off your ground; this is the business of the Faculty, not yours.* Never, in any case, have I known the faculty of a college treated with such marked disrespect by scholars, as were the committee on this occasion. Some of the officers, if not all, spoke of it among themselves as a matter of surprise, that gentlemen of their standing should be treated by our young men with such a palpable want of deference. It was remarked by one of the committee, soon after the commencement of their investigation, 'I am astonished at this insolence; this spirit must be broken down:' and it was subsequently remarked by them, 'we must go through with this thing, or the college is ruined.'

"Several of the young gentlemen," continues he, "have, since they were graduated, mentioned to me, as a palliation of their conduct, that the general feeling and sentiment among them was, that the corporation was meddling with that with which, *properly,* they had no *immediate* concern: and they have also remarked, that the proceeding tended much, in the estimation of the thinking part of the students, to weaken and degrade the government of the Faculty. Neither the corporation, nor their committee, it is presumed, intended any such thing. But how could the effect be otherwise? That such must be the necessary and inevitable tendency of such a measure, cannot, it appears to me, but be perfectly obvious to every man of only common knowledge of human nature, who will for a moment consider the subject."[15]

In truth, how can an interference of this kind prove otherwise than a signal failure? The trustees are not instructers, they have not, with very few exceptions, the habits of instructers, they are unacquainted with the habits, the dispositions, the prejudices, and the peculiar modes of thinking which prevail among students;—how can they, then, be successful in dealing with them? The instruction and discipline of a college are the appropriate business of the faculty, and not of the trustees. Besides, the faculty and not the trustees supply the place, perform the duties, assume the responsibilities, and enjoy the rights of the parents, so far as the education of their sons is concerned. The trustees leave their appropriate sphere of duty, dignity and usefulness, when they interfere with the instruction and discipline of a college. The students, too, are sagacious enough to perceive this, and seldom fail to let trustees know, that in undertaking such an interference, they are out of their proper element, and engaged in a business which they do not understand. There are some remarkable instances of this kind, besides the one mentioned above, among the records of the difficulties which have existed in our colleges.

4. It is easy, too, for any one practically acquainted with the management of a college, though, perhaps, for no other person, to understand, that any *direct interference* made with a view even *to sustain* a faculty will be injurious to, if not destructive of discipline. I say, all *direct* interference, for *indirect* interference may, under certain circumstances, be useful. For instance, *after* a crisis in the discipline, of

---

[15] A narrative of the embarrassments and decline of Hamilton College, by Henry Davis, D. D., President, p. 19.

more than ordinary difficulty, a resolution approving the measures of the faculty, may be useful. Again, after an investigation into the actual condition of an institution, a resolution founded on the result of the previous inquiry, if favorable, and commending the institution to the public, may serve to invite confidence in its claims to public patronage. But it may be well to sustain the position now under discussion, by authority, as well as by argument.

"Let the trustees of a college," says President Davis, "only suggest to the scholars (I care not in what way) that the officers, in the opinion of the board, are not able to govern them; that the aid of the board is deemed necessary in enforcing these regulations, and in securing the performance of those duties which are prescribed in the by-laws for the faculty, and although their influence and authority, provided they are discreet men, may not be at an end, yet they are directly and essentially impaired. The father of a family may, with equal wisdom call in his neighbors or the civil magistrate to his aid, in the government of his children. Let this be done, and what becomes of the cordial respect and obedience which are naturally due to every parent? What becomes of his authority?"[16]

In this connexion, I take leave to advert to a misapprehension to which I am exposed, and against which I am anxious to guard myself. I have spoken freely of the errors and mistakes into which our boards of trustees have too frequently fallen. In speaking thus freely of them and their mistakes, however, I have not intended to speak reproachfully of them. Far otherwise. I have intended to speak of them with a true respect. Their characters generally entitle them to respect, and their intentions may be presumed to be as upright as those of other bodies of respectable and honorable men. The duties which they have been accustomed to perform, have always, I believe, been performed without other reward, than the honor conferred by the station, and the consciousness of doing good. If I am not mistaken in respect to the good motives and good intentions which I have ascribed to them, they will, I am sure, be the last to complain of me for an unreserved expression of my sentiments respecting the important duties with which they are charged. If any good is to come from this discussion, it was indispensable, that the nature of the duties of our boards of trustees,

---

[16] A Narrative of the embarrassments and decline of Hamilton college, by Henry Davis., D. D., President, p. 19.

arising from the relation in which they stand to their faculties, should be carefully and candidly inquired into, and that the mistakes into which they have been accustomed to fall, and to which they are always liable, should be fully brought to view. There is no fault in *the construction* of our colleges,—I am convinced they are admirably *constructed,* and they cannot fail to be eminently successful, if the trustees and faculties which are the constituent parts of them, *will study and understand their respective positions and duties,* and, each acting within its rightful and appropriate sphere, *will mutually abstain from encroaching on each other's rights, duties and privileges.* In case of such encroachments, the trustees are most likely to be the aggressors. This tendency to encroachment on the rightful sphere of the faculty, is indeed, the besetting sin into which our boards of trustees have fallen, and to which they are always exposed. They usually consist of men of talents and influence, and such bodies of men are always too apt "to feel might and forget right." They are accustomed to trust in the sufficiency of their own wisdom, and are too much inclined to despise and reject advice of whatever kind. Such mistakes, however much they are to be regretted, may cause the less surprise, as the situation in which our trustees stand, is unknown to the country from which we derive most of our institutions, as well as most of our knowledge.

With the way prepared, as it is, by the preceding discussion, I will conclude by summing up very briefly, what I understand to be the respective duties of a board of trustees and a faculty growing out of the relation in which they stand to one another.

1. To the trustees belongs of right and necessity the original organization of the college under its charter. This document is to be the fundamental law of the college, and it usually names the original trustees, and sometimes the faculty. When the faculty are not named in the charter, it is the duty of the board to appoint them. When, however, the faculty has once been filled up, it is the duty of the board, in supplying vacancies, to be governed chiefly by the advice and wishes of the faculty. This is necessary to preserve that harmony among the members of a faculty, without which no literary institution can be successfully conducted. Nothing tends more to disturb this harmony so indispensable to the usefulness of the institution, than the introduction of a member into a faculty, to whose admission the other members are opposed. The adjustment of any disputes and controversies which may arise between members of the faculty is an essential part of the

duty of the trustees. The right, too, of assigning to the members of the faculty, their salaries and their respective departments and duties, of instituting an inquiry into the state of the institution, of calling the instructers to account if unfaithful, and of removing them for just and adequate cause, is, from the necessity of the case, vested in them.

2. Again, to the trustees, the right of managing the funds of their institution seems to belong, exclusively of the faculty. For this department of the business of a college, they are ordinarily much better qualified, by their experience in pecuniary affairs, and their knowledge of men and things, than the members of a learned faculty living the secluded life of the professed scholar. Still, even in this department, so far as respects appropriations of money for the enlargement of the library and the increase of the apparatus of the institution, a marked respect ought to be shown for the opinions and wishes of the faculty.

3. It is the duty of the trustees of a literary institution, to sustain the faculty by their countenance and encouragement, to conciliate public confidence and favor towards their institutions, by availing themselves of the opportunities which are continually occurring, to give correct information, to draw attention towards them, to remove unjust prejudices against them, and to use, for their benefit, their personal influence in the various ways in which it may be used,—or in more general terms, to assume the character and act the part of patrons towards them. This is the most dignified and honorable, as well as the most advantageous attitude in which they can place themselves, in respect to the institution whose interests they have in trust. The countenance, encouragement and influence of a respectable and honorable body of men, such as our boards of trustees usually are, standing in this relation to their institution, shielding it from unjust prejudices, connecting it advantageously, by their intervention, with the public, and conciliating for it general favor and esteem, will be felt, imparting life, spirit and animation to every department. To take an illustration from Holy Writ, such influence and patronage in favor of an institution, is like the descent of the dew of heaven, and of the refreshing rain, upon the dry and thirsty ground.

4. The nature of the relation in which the faculty of a college stands to a board of trustees, makes it the duty of the latter to be governed by the advice of the former, in every case and branch of the collegiate business, which requires for its suitable transaction, the peculiar skill, knowledge and experience, which the faculty alone can, from the

nature of the circumstances, be presumed to possess. From this principle many important results immediately flow. Among them are two that are most worthy of attention. 1. That the regulation of the course of study, including the choice of text-books, ought to be committed to the faculty. 2. That the mode of instruction, the discipline of the college, and the internal administration of its affairs, ought to be exclusively committed to them. It may well be admitted, that the suggestions of a respectable body of men, like a board of trustees, especially in their private capacity, may sometimes be useful. But any direct and palpable interference, especially in the instruction and discipline, is beyond their rightful province, and will infallibly ruin the institution. Without a sphere of duty, in which freedom and independence of action are secured to them, no faculty, whatever may be their talents and virtues, can be useful or successful. I repeat, that whenever the measures of an institution are to depend on the peculiar knowledge and experience alone possessed by the faculty, it is as absurd for the trustees to act otherwise than by their advice, as it would be for a patient to reject the advice of his physician and prescribe for himself; or for a client to advise and direct his lawyer in the management of his cause. The patient would be likely to lose his life, and the client his cause, by his rashness and presumption. In the same way, more than one board of trustees has ruined, and every board will ruin its college, which shall interfere with the province rendered appropriate to the faculty by the peculiar skill, knowledge and experience, which their education, greater attention to the subject, and practical opportunities, have naturally, and as matter of course, given them.[17]

I have thus, Gentlemen of the Institute, brought to your notice, the relation, upon the right understanding of which, and the duties growing out of it, I am convinced, the success of our literary institutions essentially depends. As far as I know, it has never before been made

---

[17] It is true, the charters of our colleges generally, if not always, give to the trustees the right of regulating the instruction and discipline. But they ought always to regulate both the one and the other, *through the faculty, and through the faculty only.* They can never exercise this right successfully in any other way. I trust, the true doctrine is gaining ground in this country. "The immediate government of the several departments (of the university) must necessarily be entrusted to their respective faculties. The Regents (trustees) shall have the power *to regulate the course of instruction,* and prescribe, *under the advisement of the professorships,* the books and authorities to be used in the several departments."—Report, (respecting a university) of the Superintendent of Public Instruction of the State of Michigan, made to the Legislature, January 5th, 1837, p. 36.

the subject of special investigation. It is in some respects, I admit, a dry and uninviting discussion. Still, I hope the Institute will, by reason of its utility, consider me justified, in claiming for it, a share of their attention. Every faculty of a college must, I am sure, be anxious to secure to itself, a more independent and unrestricted sphere of duty, enterprise and usefulness, than those bodies have usually been permitted to enjoy. The subject is worthy, I am persuaded, of still further attention, and of being still further unfolded and elucidated. For, whatever pertains to the success of our universities, colleges, academies, and schools of the learned professions, pertains, it may be said with the most perfect truth, to the vital interests of the country.

20. *Philip Lindsley on the Inadequacy of Preparatory Schools, 1825*

See Part III, Docs. 21, 24, and Doc. 22 of this Part. The following document is part of Lindsley's inaugural address at Nashville in 1825.

It is very questionable whether the existence in a community of a small number of learned men be, on the whole, advantageous, where the body of the people are doomed to absolute ignorance. They then constitute a privileged order—seek their own aggrandizement—and control the destinies of the State. Some such men have been, and still are, in every civilized kingdom. They may be found at the court of the Grand Turk, and in the most despotic empires of Asia. They are essential to the political machinery of their masters. But from the people, science is as effectually excluded, as if it were hermetically sealed up. Upon them its light never flashes except to blast and to consume.

A free government, like ours, cannot be maintained except by an enlightened and virtuous people. It is not enough that there be a few individuals of sufficient information to manage public affairs. To the people our rulers are immediately responsible for the faithful discharge of their official duties. But if the people be incapable of judging correctly of their conduct and measures; what security can they have for

L. J. Halsey (ed.), *The Works of Philip Lindsley* (Philadelphia, 1866), I, 74–75, 78–79, 80–83, 101–4.

their liberties a single hour? Knowledge is power, by whomsoever possessed. If the people would retain in their own hands that power which the Constitution gives them, they must acquire that knowledge which is essential to its safe keeping and rightful exercise. Otherwise, they will soon be at the mercy of the unprincipled aspiring demagogue —who, for a time, may court and flatter them—but who will assuredly seize upon the first favorable crisis to bend their necks to his yoke and compel them to hail him as their lord and sovereign. . . .

It is evident, as I before remarked, that the rich, at least, the very rich, could easily educate their children at distant or foreign seminaries. And it would be greatly to their advantage to do so, at any expense, were there no seminaries at home, or within every one's reach. Suppose there were no college in Tennessee—and but twenty individuals wealthy enough to send their sons to a college out of the State—it would then be in the power of a score or two of persons to monopolize all the liberal professions and all the avenues to wealth and honour in the commonwealth. But raise colleges among yourselves, and you reduce the charges of a liberal education so considerably that hundreds and thousands can immediately avail themselves of their aid. Not only all the middling classes of citizens, but enterprising youth of the poorest families may contrive to enter the lists of honourable competition with the richest. As is done every day in the Northern and Eastern States; where, indeed, the poor, more frequently than the rich, rise to eminence by their talents and learning. Such is the peculiar genius and excellence of our republican institutions, that, moral and mental worth is the surest passport to distinction. The humblest individual, by the diligent cultivation of his faculties, may, without the aid of family or fortune, attain the most exalted stations within the reach or gift of freemen. What an encouragement to studious effort and enterprise? What an incentive to the generous aspirings and honourable amibition of our youth? Why should not the door be opened wide for their entrance upon this vast theatre of useful action and noble daring? . . .

But there is another prevailing heresy on this subject which deserves exposure and condemnation. It is, that superior learning is necessary only for a few particular professions and situations—such as we have been contemplating. Now, I affirm, in opposition, it may be, to all the learned faculties of all the learned professions, and to all vulgar prejudices, that every individual, who wishes to rise above the level of a mere labourer at task-work, ought to endeavour to obtain a liberal

education. I use the term *liberal* in a liberal sense; without necessarily
including every branch of literature or science which usually constitutes a college course. The farmer, the mechanic, the manufacturer,
the merchant, the sailor, the soldier, if they would be distinguished in
their respective callings must be educated. Should it be objected, that
well-educated youth will not *labour* for their support; that, if they
become farmers or manufacturers, they will, at most, merely superintend and direct the labours of others, I answer—1st. That we, at this
moment, need thousands of such men. Would not every planter who
cultivates the soil by slaves, and every farmer who does the same by
hired labourers, be the better, the happier, the more useful with a
good education than without it? May not the same be said of the directors of printing, mercantile, and manufacturing establishments:
and, indeed, of every man who is above, or aspires to be above, the
meanest drudgery of manual labour? Here then are thousands in the
community who, or whose children at least, might be liberally educated without diminishing the number of actual labourers. So that
any increase of seminaries, upon any plan, is not likely very soon to
affect the common concerns of productive industry, except by bringing
to bear upon them the salutary influence of more light and knowledge,
and so far greatly to improve and meliorate the character and condition
of all classes of citizens.

But, in the second place, were it possible to give, what might be
styled a liberal education of a suitable kind to every child of the Republic, so far from proving detrimental to industry and enterprise, it
would produce a directly contrary effect. Differences in rank, station,
and fortune would still exist. The pulpit, the bar, the healing art, the
army, the navy, the legislative hall, the bench of justice, and all posts
of honour and emolument, would, of course, be occupied then as now
by men of comparatively superior talents, learning or address. While
the remainder would be compelled, according to their abilities or
necessities, to do what they best could for a livelihood. Though all
would be learned to a certain extent, yet there would be various grada-
tions of excellence. The competition for honourable distinction would
range on a higher scale, and among men of greater intellectual attainments, than is now the case; but in reference to the whole body of the
people, the principle and the result would be the same. All would find
their level, and every individual his appropriate place and sphere. Even
supposing then, what is not likely soon to happen, that all were edu-

cated—and educated in the best manner, we need not apprehend that a famine would ensue from lack of industry.

In the third place, so far as the experiment has been made, we find that the educated poor do in fact become, in the same proportion, more industrious, useful and happy. I appeal to the school at Hofwyl—to history, and to the actual state of the world—to every fact which can be adduced as bearing upon the argument. Three centuries ago, it was considered dangerous for the common people anywhere to be taught even the art of reading. And a mechanic who could then read his Bible was a greater rarity than would be, in our day, a mechanic who could read Homer in his native tongue. . . .

A leading defect in the American system of education, is the want of good preparatory schools. This evil is felt and acknowledged, in a greater or less degree, in every part of our country. Colleges complain, and with abundant reason, that very few of their pupils come to them well taught even in the few elementary branches which their statutes require, as qualifications for admission. I should be within bounds, were I to affirm, that, during my connexion with one of our most respectable colleges, not one youth in ten entered it thoroughly prepared. It cannot be supposed that the grammar schools are on a better footing in the Western than in the Middle States. The truth is, that no regular efficient system has as yet been adopted anywhere. This matter is left too much to chance, or to individual enterprise. Sufficient encouragement is not usually given to classical teachers to render their profession lucrative and honourable—so as to command the services of men of talents and learning. Without this inducement, such men will seldom consent to teach; except, it may be, for a season, as a matter of convenience or necessity, and as the means of rising to some other and better occupation.

In England there are several hundreds of richly endowed grammar schools—the head-masters of which receive a much larger pecuniary compensation than the Presidents of our richest colleges. The superiority of her scholarship need not therefore occasion any surprise. The cause is obvious. I am no blind admirer of the English school system—unrivalled as it has ever yet been; nor do I wish to see it introduced into this country without very considerable modifications. Still, we have nothing that deserves to be compared with it. Nor need we expect similar excellence until merit in the teacher be adequately rewarded.

If there be one vocation more important to the community than any other, or than all others, it is that of the instructer of youth. And yet it is regarded and treated, in many places, as scarcely above contempt; and its emoluments barely suffice to preserve a family from beggary. Physicians, lawyers, merchants, farmers, mechanics, may all become rich; but whoever heard of a schoolmaster's making a fortune by his profession in our country? And yet, who will pretend to say that his profession is less useful, necessary or meritorious than any other in the nation? Why then should it be less profitable or less respectable? I fearlessly put the question to any man of liberal feelings and sound judgment; and I challenge him to assign even a plausible pretext for thus degrading a teacher to the level of a drudge, or for employing none but those who are content to be drudges, and who are fit for no higher rank in society? I again repeat, regardless of all prejudices and defying all rational contradiction, that, in a Republic, where knowledge is the soul of liberty, no profession ought to be more generously cherished, honoured and rewarded, than that of the worthy instructer of youth.

Our country needs seminaries purposely to train up and qualify young men for the profession of teaching. Though the idea perhaps may be novel to some persons, yet the propriety and importance of such a provision will scarcely be questioned by any competent judges. The *Seminarium Philologicum* of the late celebrated Heyne at Göttingen, though a private institution in the midst of a great university, furnished to the continent of Europe, during a period of nearly half a century, many of its most eminent and successful classical professors and teachers. We have our Theological Seminaries—our Medical and our Law Schools—which receive the graduates of our colleges, and fit them for their respective professions. And whenever the *profession* of teaching shall be duly honoured and appreciated, it is not doubted but that it will receive similar attention, and be favoured with equal advantages.

At present, the great mass of our teachers are mere adventurers—either, young men, who are looking forward to some less laborious and more respectable vocation, and who, of course, have no ambition to excel in the business of teaching, and no motive to exertion but immediate and temporary relief from pecuniary embarrassment—or men, who despair of doing better, or who have failed in other pursuits—or who are wandering from place to place, teaching a year here and a year there, and gathering up what they can from the ignorance and credulity of their employers. That there are many worthy exceptions to this sweeping sentence, is cheerfully admitted. That we have some well qualified and most deserving instructers, we are proud to acknowledge—and as large a proportion probably in this section of our country as in the older States. Still, the number is comparatively small: and the whole subject demands the most serious attention of the good people of this community. We have no system—no regularly and judiciously organized schools for classical instruction; where the teachers feel themselves comfortably, honourably and permanently established; and where the pupils are duly trained and disciplined as candidates for the college or university. We have taken the liberty to name the evil; and we appeal to the good sense of the public with confidence that the time has arrived for its correction or removal. Should these remarks meet the eye of any faithful instructer in this vicinity, he will regard them as proceeding from a friend, who feels for his situation, who respects his office and character, and who will never fail to afford him all the countenance, and to render him every service that may be in his power. Every such man deserves well of his country—and is more justly entitled to her lasting gratitude than multitudes of those whom she most delights to honour.

In consequence of the unfortunate state of our schools generally, colleges are compelled to fix their standard of qualifications for admission so low as necessarily to remain themselves but grammar schools of a rather higher order. Had we schools of the proper character, and in sufficient numbers, then might our colleges become in fact what they assume to be in name. Then might be learned in the former, so much of the classics and mathematics, of history, chronology, antiquities and other branches, as that a college would be a fit residence for young men, and its liberal pursuits adapted to their previous attainments. Then philosophy and science and elegant literature might unfold their richest treasures to minds prepared to receive and to relish them. And, until then, we must be content to pursue the humble course which has been already marked out.

But let us not despair of ultimately reaching the very *maximum* of our wishes. Let us commence where we must—with such youth as our country can furnish. Let us diligently cultivate, improve and polish the materials at hand—in the best manner we can. Let us not seek to make children youth, and youth men, and men lawyers, physicians, clergymen or politicians, too fast. Let us keep our pupils at their proper work—and carry them as far as they can safely and surely go, and no further. Better teach them one thing well than twenty things imperfectly. Their education will then be valuable as far as it extends. Some will leave us able and willing to teach others upon our own plan. Every year, perhaps, we may advance a little—demand something more for admission—and that something in better style—send forth more and abler instructers—in return, receive still more accomplished pupils —and thus proceed, year after year, slowly but surely, until we elevate our schools and our college to a rank and standing worthy of a free, enlightened and magnanimous people.

21. *Francis Wayland's Thoughts on the Present Collegiate System, 1842*

In this searching appraisal of the aims and services of American colleges, Francis Wayland (1796–1865) displayed his anxious concern for the whole pattern of American college life. As president of Brown University (1827–55) it led him to propose a radical expansion of the Brown curriculum in 1850 (see Part VI, Doc. 1) in order to fill the educational needs, as he saw them, of merchants, farmers, and manufacturers (see also Part III, Doc. 23). The last thirteen years of his presidency were, in effect, an answer to the Yale Report of 1828 (see Doc. 11). Through his memorable personality, energetic administration, impressive teaching, textbooks, preaching, and reform activities, Wayland ranks as one of the great figures in nineteenth-century American education.

Influential upon his career were two other leading educators of the century: Eliphalet Nott (1773–1866), venerable president (1804–66) of Union College where Wayland graduated in 1813, and Moses Stuart (1780–1852), famed biblical scholar at Andover Theological Seminary with whom Wayland studied (1816–17) before entering the Baptist ministry.

On Wayland see Walter C. Bronson, *The History of Brown University, 1764–1914* (Providence, 1914), pp. 204–316; William G. Roelker, "Francis Wayland: A Neglected Pioneer of Higher Education," *American Antiquarian Society Proceedings,* LIII, Part I (April, 1943), 27–78; Theodore R. Crane, "Francis Wayland and the Residential College," *Rhode Island History,* XIX (July, October, 1960), 65–78, 118–28, and the same author's unpublished doctoral dissertation on Wayland (Harvard University, 1959).

Francis Wayland, *Thoughts on the Present Collegiate System in the United States* (Boston, 1842), pp. 22–75, 108–12, 132–60.

CHAPTER II

THE PRESENT SYSTEM OF COLLEGIATE INSTRUCTION

IN THE UNITED STATES

1. *Of the Visitorial Power*

It is obvious that if a large amount of public property, or of property which has been contributed or bequeathed by private charity for a public purpose be intrusted to special agents for the accomplishment of that purpose, some individual or corporation must exist, to whom these agents must be held responsible for the due discharge of their duties. In the case of a College, to this visitorial power properly belongs the oversight of the property of the institution, the appointment and removal of officers of instruction, the establishment of laws for the government of the society, and the general duty of ascertaining from time to time whether the ends desired by the founder or the State are accomplished. Sometimes a part of these duties are, by the terms of the foundation, differently appropriated, and the members of the college exercise, or are supposed to exercise, visitorial powers over themselves. This is evidently an abuse and is inconsistent with the well being of the institution. In this case, the visitorial power proper is more limited in its authority. It cannot then originate statutes and can do nothing more than see that the statutes, whatever they may be, are enforced. This is commonly the case with the English colleges. Every college has its visitor appointed by the statutes of the foundation, commonly the King, a Nobleman or Bishop, and his duty, if he really have any, is merely to see that the injunctions of the founder are obeyed. I need scarcely add that in this case the authority is in general merely nominal.

In this country the visitorial power is almost universally vested in a corporation commonly denominated the Board of Trustees. Sometimes there are two or more boards and the visitorial power is divided between them. On this corporation, whether simple or complex, devolve the duties to which I have alluded in a preceding paragraph. They hold the property of the Institution, appoint and remove all officers of instruction and government, fix and alter their salaries, enact all laws, and see that these laws are carried into effect, or at least they assume the responsibility of performing all these duties. This corporation is created in the first instance by the Legislative act which grants the charter to the college, and they have the power, in most cases, of filling their own vacancies. The office is commonly for life. For the discharge of its duties these corporators are responsible to no one. If they do well they receive no praise, and if ill, no censure. They make no report of their proceedings, for there is no power to which they are amenable. They are wholly independent of all authority. They receive no payment for their services and are remunerated for their labors merely by the personal consideration which may be supposed to attach to their office.

I have said that the members of the Board of Trustees, in an American college hold their offices for life, and fill their own vacancies. This is generally the fact. In a few cases they are appointed for a term of years by the Legislatures of the State by which the college is established, and in some other cases they are composed in part of the officers of government. These however are the exceptions. The general rule is as I have stated.

So far as I know, this corporation meets about once a year, at the time of the annual commencement. Their meeting commonly occupies but a portion of a day. In this time, vacancies in the Board of instruction, and in their own board are filled, the salaries of instructors are voted, they receive a general account of the condition of the college, attend to a few items of miscellaneous business, and their duties are discharged for the year. Every thing else appertaining to the working of the system is carried on by the officers of instruction. I ought to have added that all degrees are conferred by the Board of Trustees.

I have said, that occasionally, their [sic] exist two boards instead of one. I may add that to one of these not unfrequently, a more direct influence over the course of instruction is confided. In such a case, it sometimes happens that this board meets oftener, and that to it are occasionally referred matters of serious discipline, or proposed regulations in the course of study. This is however a modification of the form rather than of the fact. The corporators do not consider it necessary in this case more than in the other, to make themselves familiarly acquainted with the subject of education. They are generally men of high professional standing, deeply immersed in business; and, relying, in the main, upon the superior practical knowledge of the senior officer of college, in general, yield an assent to his suggestions, and assist him more by dividing with him the responsibility than in any other manner.

2. Of the Executive Officers of Colleges

These consist very generally of a President, Professors, and Tutors. The first two offices are held during good behavior, that is, unless some serious disqualification be proved, for life. The office of tutor is annual, and the incumbent generally holds it for two or three years, for the purpose, mainly, of perfecting himself in his classical and mathematical studies, previously to entering upon the immediate preparation for his profession.

On these officers devolves the whole labor of the instruction and government of the college. The president, besides being the principal executive officer, is generally charged with some department of instruction. To each professor is committed a particular department, although it is not uncommon, when the necessities of the college demand it, for one to take a share in the labors of another. The instruction given by the tutors is generally confined to the two lower classes. It is however commonly understood, in theory at least, that the professor is responsible for the instruction in his department whether that instruction be given by himself or by a junior officer. It is therefore his duty to superintend the labors of the tutor and give to him all the advantage of his superior knowledge and experience. The care of the collegiate discipline is generally devolved upon the whole body of the faculty. Sometimes however the reverse is the case and a part of the officers of instruction have no other duty than that of teaching, while the discipline is confided to the others, or to persons specially appointed for this purpose.

These officers are all appointed by the corporation or Board of Trustees, or that body, by what name soever it may be called, which exercises visitorial power. Their salaries are, I believe, generally the same during their continuance in office, and are rarely if ever either increased or diminished in consequence of the success or the insufficiency of the incumbent. If the number of students in college increases, the additional receipts are devoted to the erection of buildings, the employment of other professors, or the reduction of the price of tuition, and not to the augmentation of the salaries of the present instructors. And as these salaries are commonly so small that to reduce them would oblige all the officers to resign, if the number of students becomes so far diminished that even the present salary cannot be paid, an appeal is at once made to the charity of the public to sustain the

institution. This appeal is commonly made on the ground of the necessity of educating young men for the office of the christian ministry;
and it is commonly successful. A whole college faculty is thus sometimes for a considerable period supported in part by charity; their fees
for tuition being sufficient to pay but a portion of their salary.

The assignment of the duties of the different officers, is, I believe,
generally either left to themselves; or is adjusted by usage. No one has
any supervision over any other, except in the case of junior officers
already mentioned. The number of pupils attendant upon a particular
professor is never influenced by his peculiar merits; inasmuch as every
student is a candidate for a degree, and every candidate for a degree
must attend the instructions of every teacher. Here is of course the
smallest possible encouragement to individual exertion, and to elevated
attainment since whether the teacher do much or little, whether he be
successful or unsuccessful his emolument and the number of his pupils
will remain almost unchangeably the same.

It might be supposed that when the system has thus removed all the
ordinary stimulants to professional effort, it would supply their place
by increased vigilance in the visitorial power. But this I believe is never
done. The connexion between the visitorial and executive branches of
instruction is, in this respect, so far as I know, almost a nullity. For all
practical purposes it might almost as well never exist. A Board of
Trustees too frequently neither knows, nor provides itself with the
means of knowing any more about the internal working of the college, over whose destinies they are chosen to preside than any other
men. . . .

CHAPTER III
OF THE DEFECTS OF THE SYSTEM OF COLLEGIATE EDUCATION
IN THE UNITED STATES, AND THE MEANS BY WHICH IT
MAY BE IMPROVED

Sect. 1. *Of the Visitorial Power*

The first question that here presents itself for discussion is the following:—Whence arises the necessity for the exercise of visitorial power
in a system of collegiate instruction. The answer to this question will
immediately present itself, when we have considered the difference
between an establishment for public, and one for private education. A
private school or academy is established by the instructor on his own

responsibility, and solely for his own benefit. Like any other producer, he asks what is the product most in demand in the market, and having answered this question satisfactorily to himself, he offers to furnish the product to those who may desire and can pay for it. If he and his employers agree, his business prospers. If they differ, his business fails, and he must either abandon or modify it. If his employers are satisfied, his end is accomplished. If he be incompetent or unfaithful, the thing speaks for itself, and in a very short time works its own remedy. The public is in no manner interested in the result. Beyond the parents who pay the teacher, the success or failure of the experiment is no man's concern. No immunities are granted to the instructor. The public supports him by none of its funds, and therefore the public has no right to interfere with his affairs, or to inquire whether he manage them well or ill.

In the case of a public institution, however, all this either is or ought to be reversed. This will appear from several considerations.

1. A collegiate establishment is *supported* in part by the public. Either the whole State, or a large number of individuals in the State have advanced a considerable amount of funds which are devoted exclusively to the support of the institution. Not unfrequently legislative grants are annually made for the same purpose. The amount of capital thus invested in New England alone, would amount, I presume, to more than a million and a half of dollars. This sum having been invested for a particular purpose, it is evident that the public has a right to visitorial power, in order to ascertain whether the income arising from it be appropriated according to its original design. Boards of Trustees or Corporations, are the agents to whom this power is committed, and they are bound to exercise it according to the design for which they were appointed.

2. To these institutions is committed the power of conferring academical degrees, or publicly recognised certificates of a certain amount of literary and scientific acquirement. These degrees were formerly to a great degree, necessary to entrance upon the study of either of the learned professions. The rules in these professions have of late been in this respect, greatly relaxed, yet the desire even at present manifested to obtain a degree, shows whatever may be said to the contrary, that this form of testimonial has not by any means lost its value. It is always understood to mean that a man has passed through that course of liberal study, which, in the judgment of the community in which

he lives, is necessary to a well educated man. It is obvious that such a testimonial, if conferred with any thing like a strict regard to merit and attainment, must be of material value to any young man just entering upon the duties of active life. It creates a presumption in his favor, which is no contemptible advantage. It is the guarantee to the public, without examination of the candidate, that a certain portion of his life has been devoted to liberal studies. And it is manifest that the general literary and intellectual character of a community must be greatly affected by the degree of attainment which this testimonial is made to represent. What would be the intellectual condition of a community if nothing were required of the candidate for a degree but a knowledge of English Grammar and Geography; that is, if this amount of knowledge were all that was required of him who was recognised as a liberally educated man. The exclusive power of conferring this testimonial being thus given to collegiate institutions, it constitutes a second difference between them and private establishments for the purpose of education.

Let us next observe the reason for which these privileges are conferred.

I think it will be admitted without controversy, that this capital is not invested and these privileges are not conferred for the purpose of supporting instructors in Colleges. They deserve nothing more for laboring in this vocation than in any other. A man can no more claim a salary from the public as a matter of right, because he teaches Greek and Geometry, than because he teaches English Grammar and Arithmetic. A man who teaches the former branches of education may incidentally derive benefit from the arrangements which the community may make with regard to this subject, but this is not the reason for which the community has made them.

Nor is it, I think, the object of the public, in the encouragement which it gives to collegiate education, simply to multiply the number of professional men, whether Lawyers, Physicians, or Divines. This is a matter which may very well be left to individual preferences and individual talents. In all intelligent communities, the supply of professional labor will commonly be at least equal to the demand for it. The demand, as in other cases, creates the supply. If this mode of labor be lucrative, it will attract producers in sufficient numbers to meet the exigencies of society. With respect to two at least of the professions, there is more reason at all times to apprehend a glut, than a scarcity.

3. Nor is it the object of these encouragements to fix a general standard of acquisition, and then induce as large a number as possible to attain to it. For, in the first place, it would be difficult if not impossible, to hit upon such a standard as would meet the wants of those who desire a valuable education, and be at the same time within reach of all who wished to attain to it. And, besides, the only method by which all who desired to make this acquisition could be reached, would be to give it away altogether. If this were done, it would greatly increase the number of those who would make this modicum of attainment, but to a large portion of them the gift would be worse than useless. It would unfit them for more active pursuits, and would not enable them to procure a sustenance by intellectual exertion. It would produce a large amount of very moderately educated talent, without giving any real impulse to the mental energy of the community.

4. The object then for which I suppose these encouragements to a liberal education are given is, to furnish means for the most perfect development of the intellectual treasures of the country. In order to the [*sic*] most perfect condition of any society, it is necessary that, whenever unusual talent of any kind exists, it be so cultivated as to be able to accomplish the highest results of which it has been made capable. This talent is very equally distributed among the various orders of society, least of all is it limited to the rich. But the means for the thorough and radical training of a human mind are very expensive. They involve the cost of libraries, philosophical apparatus, laboratories, and a formidable array of teachers of distinguished ability. Were these to be provided by individual enterprise, the expense would be so great that none but the rich would be educated and by far the larger part of the talent of a country must perish in useless obscurity. Hence arises the reason why a large portion of these means, all that which involves the outlay of considerable capital, should be the property of the public, and why it should be open to the use of all who might by the use of it be rendered in any way benefactors to the whole. The design therefore of university establishments, so far as the public is concerned, is not to furnish education to the poor or to the rich, not to give away a modicum of Greek and Latin and Geometry to every one who chooses to ask for it, but to foster and cultivate the highest talent of the nation, and raise the intellectual character of the whole, by throwing the brightest light of science in the path of those whom nature has qualified to lead.

From these remarks, we may easily learn the nature of that responsibility which devolves upon the Trustees or Corporation, or in general, upon the visitorial power of a college. The visitors are entrusted with all the capital appropriated by the public, or by individuals, for carrying forward this specific purpose. They have the power of appointing and removing all college officers. They alone confer degrees, and they determine the course of study which shall be pursued by the candidate for a degree. They have a general power of visitation, and may, within legal and constitutional limits, alter or amend or modify the course of liberal education as they please, and thus to a considerable extent, cause the intellectual character of the community to be what they wish. And when we consider that the Trustees of the Colleges in New England alone are intrusted with more than a million and a half dollars, expressly set apart for the accomplishment of this purpose, and that they have the authority to direct the energies of a large body of able and industrious men whose lives are devoted to the labor of instruction, I think it will at once appear that few offices can be held of greater importance than theirs; and that, if our system of education and general improvement fail, on them by far the greater portion of the responsibility, and of course the disgrace of that failure must rest.

Supposing these principles to be correct, let us proceed briefly to inquire what are the proper qualifications for that office in which the visitorial power resides.

1. The members should be capable of fulfilling their duties. One of these duties is that of appointing teachers, another that of removing them, for incompetency, another that of prescribing the course of studies proper to be pursued. Now all this supposes a considerable amount of knowledge, and an acquaintance with the theory, if not the practice of education. A school committee is considered incompetent to its trust, if it cannot decide correctly on the merits of the candidate for the mastership of a district school. But it is to be remembered that the school committee are exactly visitors, and they sustain to the school precisely the same relation that a Corporation does to a College. Besides, the weight of character of such a board depends much upon its known learning and ability. I remember to have heard when a boy, of a Trustee of a College who attended an examination in Greek, and for two hours used his book upside down. Were these instances frequent, but little respect would be paid to the decisions of such a Corporation.

2. They should be from station and character elevated above the reach of personal or collateral motives. A College, in order to succeed

well, must be governed by its own principles. Its object is the intellectual cultivation of the community. So long as this is made the governing principle of all its arrangements, it will prosper; for it will accomplish the object which men of sense desire to see accomplished, and its works will speak for it. But if it be made subservient to any other end, it will and it ought to fail. Its Corporation should therefore be men who are incapable of acting from fear, favor, or affection. In all official acts, they should look with equal eye upon the merits of the nearest relative, and upon those of a stranger. They should know no parties either in politics or religion; and knowing nothing but the duties and obligations of their office, should appoint and remove solely and entirely for the good of the institution of which they are the appointed governors.

3. They should be few in number. That corporations have no conscience I would by no means assert, but I believe it will generally hold true that their conscience is inversely as their number. In large bodies responsibility is too much divided. The overawing power of majorities is greater. Party spirit is more readily excited and perpetuated, and intrigue is much more successfully carried forward. A few men who look each other directly in the face, and every one of whom feels that he is personally responsible to his equals for his acts and his opinions, is a safer repository of an important trust than a larger, and of course more miscellaneous assembly.

4. They should be chosen for a term of time, and not for life. A body chosen for life is peculiarly liable to attacks of somnolency. Every thing in such a society tends in a remarkable degree to repose. Inefficient men, like Jefferson's office holders, "rarely die and never resign." Yet the period of office should not be so brief as to interfere with the steadfastness of plan and comprehensiveness of design. It would probably be wise to construct a board in such a manner that a portion should go out of office every two or three years. In this manner a majority would always remain acquainted with the affairs of the institution and able to resist any premature and unadvised changes. It is no small advantage to be able to drop an inefficient member of any corporation.

5. They should, if possible, be elected by some body out of themselves to whom they should be responsible. This would do much to secure efficiency and would leave opportunity to apply suitable correctives whenever they became necessary. If this cannot be done, they

should annually make a report of their doings; so that their acts may in some way come under the supervision of the public.

I think it manifest that, in a collegiate system, the visitorial power in order to discharge its duties with efficiency, in other words, to perform the functions for which it is created, should be chosen for the reasons, and somewhat in the manner that I have here indicated. When, however, I speak of their efficiency, I do not suppose it necessary that they should be always present, superintending every act, and directing every recitation. Much less do I intend that they should usurp the powers and functions of the faculty of instruction. These last have their own proper office, and their peculiar responsibilities and duties; and these are no more to be incroached upon by the board of visitors, than by any one else. A system, in order to work well, must be pervaded in every member by vital energy, each part performing in its own appropriate functions in harmony with the rest, but yet not interfered with by them. It is the business of the visitorial power so to construct the system, so to arrange its various stimulants and so to bring then [*sic*] to bear upon every department, that the machine will go of itself without perpetual tinkering. The principles must be laid down and the laws enacted, but these laws must be executed by the faculty, and in the execution of these, their appropriate duties, they must be free and independent. But they should be free and independent within law; and should be so situated that every man shall receive the result of his own actions, whether that result be success or failure.

Let us now examine the visitorial power as it exists among us, and observe how far it corresponds in its organization with the above principles.

1. Are the boards of colleges chosen simply in view of their qualifications, for this peculiar office? Are they, in general capable of judging of the qualifications of the persons whom they appoint, or of their success after they have been appointed[?] Are they specially interested in the subject of education? Do they, in consequence of their appointment to this office, make the subject of education their particular study? Do they as a matter of duty devote any portion of their time to this particular labor? Are they chosen for political, or sectarian, or other reasons, instead of those which have been here suggested? The answer to these questions it is not necessary that I should suggest. Every one acquainted with the practical working of our collegiate system, can answer them as well as I.

By these remarks I hope it will not be supposed that I am capable of the least feeling of disrespect towards those of my fellow citizens who hold this office. I know them to be frequently chosen from the best men in the land; and I believe that they will be the last to take offence at any suggestions which are necessary to a full discussion of this subject. I speak not of the men but of the system. They have rarely if ever sought the places which they occupy; and have generally accepted them at the wish of the friends of the institutions which they represent. They were not expected to perform any labor, and they have not supposed that it was their duty to perform any. It is the error not merely of boards of visitors, but of the community. The importance of the subject has been forgotten, and hence every one of its departments has suffered the effects of that forgetfulness.

2. With regard to personal honor, our Boards are I believe as unexceptionable men as could any where be found. They could not easily be induced from personal considerations to deviate from what they believe to be the course best adapted to secure the good of the institutions which they govern. That when appointed by Legislatures they have not sometimes been influenced by political considerations I would not be so ready to affirm. The temptation to error in this respect arises sometimes from differences in religious belief. Almost every college in this country is either originally, or by sliding from its primitive foundation, under the control of some religious sect. Hence it is in matters of this kind taken for granted that the predominance of that sect, if not its exclusive occupation of office, is at all events to be maintained. This, according to the circumstances of the case may be just or unjust, and the Board may be as they frequently are, tied down by enactments of the founder; but from what principles soever it may proceed, it of course limits competition; and instead of placing an institution on its proper basis that of a seminary of learning, it places it in a complicated position in which a part of its energies are wasted upon an extraneous object. I do not say that this alliance of two objects is unnecessary or unwise. I am fully aware of the aids which religion has extended to learning. This union may prevent greater evils than it engenders; nay it may be that without the aid of religious sects, our colleges would scarcely have existed. I refer to the subject merely as a matter for consideration and in order that it may be suitably weighed. If it be a necessary evil let us have no more of the evil than is necessary to the attainment of good.

I say that our error arises, in part, from this source. But it is only in part. The feeling which pervades us on this subject, I think, is, that a college requires to be patronized, that it must be recommended to the public by an array of names of such distinguished persons as are understood to countenance it. A list of such names at the head of its catalogue of officers, is supposed to add dignity to the institution, and at the same time to offer a guaranty to parents that the institution will be well conducted. It is understood that the duties to be discharged, are merely nominal, and the honor of the place is a full compensation for the appearance of responsibility which it imposes. It is given and received and held as a ceremony. It stands between the public and the College; I had almost said, depriving both of the influence which each would exert on the other. If it attempt to carry out the wishes of the public, acting with imperfect knowledge of the subject, it is very liable to act wrong. If it act not at all, it still serves as a shield to protect the faculty from observation, and from the just result of negligence in office. Said Jeremy Bentham on one occasion, "I do not like Boards, for," added he, punning upon the word, *"Boards are always fences."* That they are liable to be, is evident. That it need not to be so I believe. That it would not be so if the gentlemen who hold this office, were aware of the responsibility which really rests upon them, I confidently trust. It is for the honest purpose of setting before them this responsibility, that these pages are written. They ought not to allow themselves to be used by way of guaranty, unless they really act as guarantees. If they allow a college to rely upon their names, instead of relying upon its own ability and skill, they will injure instead of benefit the cause of Education.

3. The number of persons composing our boards of trustees is various. It rarely if ever falls below twelve, and sometimes rises as high as fifty. Where there are two Boards composing the Corporation, it is, I think, sometimes even larger than the latter number. Where important responsibility is confided, and efficient action is contemplated, I imagine that twelve is the greatest number compatible with success. Our Boards are, therefore, if I mistake not, by far too large.

4. The offices in our Boards of trustees are held almost universally for life. The vacanc[i]es which occur are filled by themselves. Hence they are responsible to no one. Their proceedings are rarely published. In such a case the large majority having been in office from time immemorial, the tendency is almost irresistable [*sic*] to allow things to con-

tinue as they have been. In this respect our organization is as defective as it can be.

So far as we have proceeded, it will, I think, appear evident that this part of our collegiate system was originally formed without any reflection upon the duties which these officers were called to discharge and without any inquiry into the mode in which the discharge of those duties could be most successfully secured. The plan first adopted has been somewhat servilely followed, and no attention has as yet been directed to the question how it might be changed for the better. And yet I think it must be evident that upon this part of the system more than any other, the improvement and perfection of any plan of education mainly depends. The reader who wishes to see this subject discussed with great learning and ability, will find much to interest him in an article on University Patronage, in the Edinburgh Review, No. 119, for April, 1834; I presume from the pen of Sir William Hamilton, Professor of Logic, in Edinburgh University.

But perhaps it may be said that although the organization of our system be defective, yet its duties are faithfully performed. It may be the case that the members of our collegiate boards in New England are deeply impressed with the fact that the intellectual character of the nation depends for its elevation and development emphatically upon themselves, and that under the full impression of this solemn conviction they are seriously engaged in discharging the duties of their high vocation, that our higher seminaries owe that portion of success which they have attained to the efforts and labors of the visitorial power. I say all this may be, but I think it is not commonly so understood. I fear that the public does not expect, nor do the boards of trustees generally perform any labor of this kind. Nor are they greatly to blame for this. It arises from a want of attention directed seriously to the subject.

Or again it may be said that our colleges are so organized as to need no such supervision as that of which I have spoken. I here say nothing of the individual officers composing the College Faculties in our country. More amiable, intelligent, and upright men could rarely be selected; but I say that the system of our colleges more than almost any other, requires a special supervision. The officers are paid by salary, their remuneration in the same college is generally equal, good or ill success has but a small and indirect power to increase or diminish it; there is involved in the system no appeal to pecuniary interest or love of distinction. In this absence of all the usual stimulants to effort, it is manifest that the motive arising from the knowledge that their labors are seen and appreciated by those in whom the community has reposed this high trust, must be in the highest degree salutary, if not absolutely indispensible.—There are no men in our country from whom important labor is expected whose position is so artificial and so at variance with the ordinary principles of human action as the officers of American Colleges. Were they not honorable and virtuous men, they would not accomplish the tenth part of what they do.

If the above suggestions be well founded, it will appear evident that one step, not to say the very first step, in the improvement of American Colleges will be the improved organization of the Boards of Trustees or of Visitors. It seems to me that either they have a real and most important duty to discharge, or else they have none at all. If no duty really devolve upon them, then the office which they hold had better be abolished, since by standing between the Instructors and the public, it diminishes the responsibility of teachers, and is thus injurious to the system. If the office which they hold be really and vitally important, then it follows that those who hold it should be so organized as to be able to discharge its duties in the best possible manner. They should be placed under such responsibilities as will best stimulate them to labor in their appropriate office with zeal, efficiency and honor.

To all this I well know that many objections may be urged. For instance, it may be said that Colleges commonly, are eleemosynary corporations, bound by the law of the founder, and that the present arrangements are frequently a part of that foundation. This is true, and so far as it is true, I see not how amendment can take place, except by intrusting the whole visitorial power to a small and responsible committee. It may be said again, that colleges are frequently endowed by a sect for the particular purpose of educating men for the gospel ministry, and that they would not consent to throw open the whole system on the simple grounds which I have mentioned. Here again may be an insuperable obstacle. Or again it may be said that the plan of appointing Boards of Trustees for a term of years by Legislatures, has failed in consequence of the malign influence of party politics. All this I admit. If politicians, like Virgil's harpies, will insist on defiling what they cannot eat, I know of no remedy that can be anticipated from that source. Or again, it may be said that there is not interest enough on this subject in the community to carry forward any change in this respect; or that if the theory of the system were changed, it would inevitably fail in practice, inasmuch as it would be impossible to find men competent to such a trial, or that if found competent they would not give to it the time and labor necessary for the successful discharge of its duties. If this be so, I grant the case to be hopeless. The other obstacles might be surmounted. Where there is a will there is a way. But for indifference on such a subject, there is no cure; and we must wait until the community attain to a higher sense of social and moral obligation.

Supposing however, all this to be so, two conclusions will follow. If there exist not in the community, sufficient energy and self denying effort to carry forward institutions of learning, let the blame be laid at the right door. Let not colleges be blamed for not doing what the apathy of the community renders impossible to be done. Instead of changing college courses, and trying experiments on college discipline, let us strive to arouse the nation to a conviction of the importance of the subject. Let us strive to cure the ailing member. If the heart be diseased, let us not persist in blistering the head. If the community will take an intelligent interest in the subject, all the other disorders will easily remedy themselves.

But, if we despair of this, and whether or not it must be dispaired [sic] of, every man must judge for himself; then another idea suggests itself; the system must be changed. The present system rests fundamentally on the power of visitation. The board, as I have said, is really in the place of the public. If it cannot be so constructed that it shall be able to discharge its functions, then let it be abolished, and let the rest of the system be so constructed that this deficiency may be supplied in some other manner.

Sect. 2. *Of the Faculty, or Officers of Instruction*

In speaking of the nature of a private school, in the preceding section, I have remarked that such an establishment is simply an arrangement between the parent and the instructor. The parent ascertains for himself the character of the instructor, and acts accordingly. If he find that he has been deceived, he seeks another teacher. Any other instructor may be employed to perform the service, no one having any prescriptive privileges more than another. But, in the case of a public institution, the circumstances are changed. Here, the community have granted a special privilege, that of conferring degrees, and this degree can be obtained no where else but from a College or University. Besides, the public having undertaken to superintend such institutions, have endowed them with the public money, and have virtually promised to take care that this money be well appropriated; and that the education there given shall be as perfect as the circumstances of the community shall render practicable.

Such being the case, it is clearly necessary to such a system, that the best teachers be appointed, and that they be placed under such conditions that all the motives to diligence and success which ever impel men to their duty, shall be called into action here.

And first, as to the mode of securing the best men for instructors. In order to accomplish this result, the appointing power should most properly reside with the visitorial corporation. They have no interest to subserve, and if they are able and willing to perform their duty, all that is needful can be done. But supposing this be the case, how shall they ascertain the desert of the candidate[?] In Scotland, elections to professorships depend I believe, mainly on family, or political, or ecclesiastical interest. In England, Professors are generally appointed by such persons as the statutes of the founder may have ordained, and their offices are generally bestowed as the reward of successful scholarship, and are not considered as a part of the working system of the university. In France, all appointments in most of the departments, are made to depend upon a rigorous and searching examination of the candidates by a competent board; and on the examination, which the candidates conduct, of each other. In Germany, as every graduate may obtain a license to teach in the University, every one has an opportunity of showing to the public his ability, and of thus enforcing his claim to the honors of a vacant chair. What mode should be adopted with us I pretend not to decide, but that it should be such as to secure the highest amount of talent and skill, is, I think, evident. It should therefore be such as to allow free competition, and it should involve such tests as would inevitably secure the public against imposition, and it should be conducted with perfect impartiality. Were professorships in all our colleges open to competition, and were every candidate sure that the election would be decided upon the merits of the case, the stimulus to intellectual cultivation in this country would be greatly increased, and the honor of an academical appointment immeasurably augmented.

Secondly. The tenure and the emoluments of office should, as far as possible, be made to depend upon the labor and the success of the incumbent. A small salary might properly be guaranteed to him, and the rest should depend upon himself. This might be accomplished by authorizing him to receive payment for tickets. This would however be of no avail if every person were obliged to take a ticket who was a candidate for a degree, unless parallel professorships were appointed in case the regular incumbent failed to satisfy just expectation. Were professors appointed in the manner I have suggested, they would be placed under the same motives to labor as any other man. Every one knowing that his emolument and distinction would be increased in proportion to his exertion, would throw his whole soul into his work, and the public would thus derive the benefit of his full and concentrated mental effort. Were this the case also, there would be no difficulty in equalizing labor. Where labor brings its appropriate reward, it is rather sought after than declined. Every man, in such a case, is desirous of doing all in his power, and of doing it as well as he can. In this most important point, therefore, the necessity of visitation is to a considerable degree removed, since the system is so arranged that it will go of itself.

If these are the true principles on which officers of instruction in colleges should be appointed and continued, our system in this country is defective in several particulars.

The whole power theoretically rests with the Corporation, or Board of visitors. This requires no alteration. But let us inquire how are appointments generally made? Is any competition invited or even admitted? Are the candidates ever examined as to their fitness for the office to be filled? Are any means taken to enable the board to secure the best man that the office will command? So far as I know, this is very imperfectly done, if it be done at all. In some of our Southern Colleges I know that vacancies are announced and candidates are invited to send in their testimonials. Upon the strength of these testimonials elections are generally made. But no one who has any practical acquaintance with the manner in which testimonials are commonly procured, would rely upon them in any matter of importance. The testimonials of a candidate, if procured by himself, are too frequently evidence of his perseverance, rather than of any other qualification.

But it may be asked, if this method is not adopted, how are appointments made[?] I answer, generally, I believe, upon the recommendation of the Faculty. The Faculty have in theory no voice in the appointment of their colleagues, but inasmuch as the Board to which this duty specially appertains, is unable to devote to it the attention which its importance demands, they are commonly obliged to perform an office which does not properly belong to them. They generally from the persons within their knowledge select one who in their opinion is best suited to the office, and their wishes, are acquiesced in by the Corporation. Thus they really nominate and the corporation appoint. But since where there is a good understanding between the parties, their nomination is almost always confirmed, they may be considered as in fact filling their own vacancies, and making their own appointments.

As the system is at present constructed, this probably is the best method which could be devised. When Boards having no deep interest in education, and unaware of their responsibility, make appointments without consulting the officers of instruction, they are liable to influence from motives from without, either political, or sectarian, or personal. I have known instances in which most unsuitable candidates have thus been elected, and imposed for life upon a college faculty. This is a case of most aggravated injustice. It is not only a sacrifice of the great interests of education to the most contemptible selfishness, but it obliges a number of industrious and worthy men to support an inefficient, nay sometimes an injurious colleague, out of their own honest earnings. I do not say, that any honorable men would be guilty of so great a wrong, if they would pause to reflect upon the consequences of their action; but honorable men, when associated together, not unfrequently, by reason of thoughtlessness, are responsible for wrongs which individually they would be the last to justify.

But it must be evident that the officers of instruction themselves must be greatly embarrassed in the selection of the candidate whom they would recommend for appointment. In the first place, the situation is by no means easily to be filled. It requires a great variety of qualifications, which do not always meet in the same person. A teacher, in addition to learning in his particular department, must have ability to communicate knowledge. He must also be a disciplinarian, competent to control his classes and excite them to diligence, and prompt to bear his share of labor in maintaining the good order of the College. Besides this, as officers in an American college are so intimately associated together, he must be a man of amiable manners, and sufficiently well endowed with radical good nature and spontaneous fellow feeling. Now all these are not always associated in the same person.

In the next place, the Faculty have but little range of selection. They are restricted in a considerable degree within the list of their own graduates. Those who have left the institution for several years are commonly deficient in the habits and the peculiar learning necessary to the successful discharge of professorial duty; and moreover, but few of them if well established in an active profession could be induced to return to the confinement of a college; specially by such remuneration for their labor as a college would be able to offer. The tutorial office constitutes a good school for professors, but then it is held for a short time, and is commonly relinquished before the incumbent has attained to sufficient age and reputation to render him a prominent candidate for a professorship. In this manner, the choice of a faculty, when a vacancy in their number occurs, is commonly much restricted as well as embarrassed. As no competition is offered, they know not who will take office. As no examination is ever sustained they have but imperfect means of ascertaining either the present ability or the future promise of the candidate. Hence they are obliged to feel about in the dark, and after balancing the various points in the case, recommend the person who, upon the whole, promises to succeed the best.

But suppose now an officer appointed who is well adapted to the discharge of his duties. The emolument which he receives is perhaps greater than he would receive for the first few years of his life in another profession, but vastly less than he could ordinarily receive after he became well established in it. It is by salary, and it is commonly unchanged during his whole continuance in office. At first he labors assiduously to prepare himself for success in his department. He in a few years attains to all the knowledge which, owing to the fixed nature of our system, he is able to communicate. Beyond this his calling presents to him no reason for advancing. Were he ever so much distinguished, his compensation would be no greater nor his field of scientific labor more extensive. Beyond his own associates and his small class of pupils, no one is aware either of his labors or of their success. Under these circumstances one of these results will commonly ensue. Either he will settle down into a willingness to be satisfied with that to which he has already attained, or he will devote himself to writing for the press, and thus employ his most valuable energies, while the College receives only the remainder, or else he will engage in part in some secular or professional pursuit from the emolument of which he may meet his increasing expenses.

But suppose the case to be reversed. Suppose that an unsuitable man has been appointed, and that he is unable from want of talent, learning, or industry to discharge with effect the duties of his office. His instruction is known to be almost worthless. He goes through his routine of duty mechanically and every student in turn is obliged to attend upon his appointed exercises. He performs the least possible amount of labor consistent with physical obedience to the law. The College suffers. The indolence originating in his department either spreads into all the others, or must be counteracted by the increased effort of his associates. In the mean time the number of students in consequence of his inefficiency diminishes, and the means of the institution are impaired. He is not only supported by his associates, but they are, by his failure rendered less able to support either him or themselves. Suppose all this, and what, I ask, is the remedy[?]

It may be said that the corporation has the power of removal. True, but for what cause except incompetency? And who does not know that this is one of the most difficult things to be proved? Where is the standard of competency, and how is it to be applied in this case[?] That he does not do his duty, every body knows. That the College is suffering from this incompetency, no one doubts. But is he so incompetent that he must be dismissed, and his living taken away? What can he do if he is removed? These are the questions that would be asked at once, instead of the question whether it be right for a man to get his living by wasting the time and ruining the intellectual habits of all the young men who are so unfortunate as to come under his charge.

But suppose that a deficiency be palpable and capable of proof sufficient to satisfy any reasonable man. How is action in the premises to be commenced[?] The matter belongs wholly to the Corporation, or Board of visitors. It is essentially a part of the visitorial power and one of the special purposes for which that power was created. But, in the first place, this Board as I have said never attends the recitations, lectures or examinations; or, if they do, they never attend for this purpose. They are not always qualified to judge. And again who is to be the prosecutor[?] In such a case men almost always throw the burden of an unpleasant duty upon each other, that is, throw it off entirely. Here then but little relief is to be expected. The only remaining hope is in the Faculty. But is it their duty? Ought it to be in honor or consistency devolved upon them? Should they be obliged to make known the deficiencies of each other? Suppose that urged by conscience and necessity they represent the case to the corporation, at once there will be raised the cry of persecution; and those who yesterday complained most loudly of the deficiency in instruction, will, today, be loudest in the denunciation of the only means by which it can be remedied.

But suppose all this to have been overcome, and the case to be honestly brought before the visitorial power. The incumbent is incompetent. But he was appointed without examination. Is he more incompetent than he was when appointed? His sins are sins of omission, how shall these be proved[?] If then he be a man destitute of honor and public spirit and determined to hold fast to the emoluments of an office while incompetent to the discharge of its duties, it may be very difficult to relieve the institution of the incubus. In the face of all these obstacles, is it remarkable if a Faculty bear for life an infliction of this sort, and see their labors rendered comparatively useless, and the young men committed to their charge wasting a large portion of their time, and look on in hopeless despondency because they know of no practicable method of relief. I have myself known of a case in which a gentleman utterly unfit for his office was appointed to preside over a very important department of college education; for more than twenty years he kept that department down under the intolerable pressure of his own inefficiency; and thus more than twenty classes of young men were sent out into the world without any adequate instruction in one branch of their education; without the mental discipline which this portion of study ought to have afforded; by so much unfitted for the study of a profession, and prepared only to depress the standard of education whenever they were employed as instructors. I think that any sober man will agree with me that this is a serious evil. But, I ask, where in our present collegiate system, shall we find the remedy? And is it not time that a remedy be provided?

How often cases of this kind occur, it is not for me to say. In showing that they are liable to occur, I have shown the defect of the system. Its tendency is to offer a bounty for indolence and incapacity, for it rewards them as well as industry and talent. Things always follow their tendencies. Hence, in so far as the system has any effect, that effect is to depress the energy of the laborious by obliging them to bear a gratuitous and unreasonable burden. Nor is this by any means the worst point of the case. Its tendency is to keep down the standard of education, and expose the best portion of a young man's life to shameful and ruinous waste.

But it may be asked, have not our colleges on the whole, done well for the country, and are they not deserving of the public patronage[?] I answer most sincerely in the affirmative. They are in the main well officered; and the incumbents are generally able and industrious men. But what they accomplish is done not in any manner through the co-operation of the system, but in defiance of it. If they do so much when laboring at every disadvantage, what might they not accomplish were their energies uncramped, and a free field of professional enterprise opened before them[?] The fact is that in this country every one must labor, or be supposed to labor. The whole College Faculty as a body must perform the labor necessary to a respectable discharge of their duties, or the whole system would go down. What one will not or can-not do, must some how or other be done by some one else; and besides this, there is, with every high minded and public spirited man, a love for the labor in which he is engaged, and a willingness to make sacri-fices of personal ease, and even of personal reputation, to support the character of an institution of which he forms a part. These high quali-ties have conspired in no small degree to maintain our colleges at the point of respectability to which they have attained. I can with the most delightful recollections bear witness to their existence; and I do from my soul mourn that they are obliged to be exerted in so unfavorable a field and under so many and almost intolerable discouragements. These however are as we shall see but a part of the difficulties under which the instructors in American colleges are obliged to labor.

From what has been advanced I think it will be sufficiently obvious that our system in these respects is susceptible of important improve-ment. It requires to be so constructed that every man shall receive the result of his own actions, and not of the actions of another. In order to accomplish this one of two things as it seems to me must be done, either the appointment to office must be made by examination, and be subject to strict and impartial supervision, including removal from of-fice at the judgment of the Board of Visitors; or else every officer must be so situated that his emolument will in the nature of the case depend upon his desert, so that if his instruction be worthless, no one will be obliged to pay him for it, and if it be valuable, it may attract pupils according to its value. In this manner, a remedy will be applied by the system itself, and thus the machine will, so far as this point is con-cerned, go alone. Suppose that this plan had been adopted from the first commencement of our literary institutions, no one can conceive the change which would have been effected in their power. A professional career would have been opened to every collegiate instructor as wide, and as far reaching as to men in every other department of intellectual exertion. Talent of the highest rank would have been attracted to our colleges. Emulation of the loftiest character would have been awakened. Instead of a great number of small and ill supported Colleges, we should have had a small number of real and efficient Universities. I believe that this change alone would have increased the learning and intellectual vigor of the nation an hundred fold. . . .

Sec. 3. *Of Collegiate Education*

And now supposing a change of this kind to have been made; there are three modes in which our present system might be modified.

First, the number of studies pursued during the College course, might be limited in such manner that whatever is taught may be taught thoroughly. The College would in this case be open only for persons who are candidates for degrees. The standard of attainment may be as high as is considered desirable. The difference aimed at would be this, that, instead of learning *many* things *imperfectly,* we should learn a *smaller* number of things *well.* I am sure that every man in active life would, on retrospection, wish that his education had been thus conducted. By learning one science well, we learn *how to study,* and how to master a subject. Having made this attainment in one study, we readily apply it to all other studies. We acquire the habit of thoroughness, and carry it to all other matters of inquiry. The course of study at West Point Academy is very limited, but the sciences pursued are carried much farther than in other institutions in our country; and it is owing to this that the reputation of the institution is so deservedly high. The English University course is, in respect to the number of branches pursued, limited, and yet it is remarkably successful in developing the powers of the mind. Observe the maturity and vigor which the young men there frequently obtain. They sometimes go from the University, as for instance, Pitt, Fox, and Canning, directly to the House of Commons, and are competent at once, to take an important part in the labors of that august assembly. And yet more, I apprehend that the acquisition of the habit of thoroughness is the true method of arriving at the most extensive attainments. A few years since I had the pleasure of meeting one of the most learned German scholars who has visited this country. I asked him how it was that his countrymen were able, at so early an age, to obtain the mastership of so many languages. He replied "I began the study of Latin at an early age. Every book that I studied I was made thoroughly acquainted with. I was taught to read and re-read, translate forwards and backwards, trace out every word and know every thing about it. Before I left a book it became as familiar to me as if written in German. *After this I never had any difficulty with any other language.*"

2. But secondly. Suppose a course so limited does not find favor, and it be contended that as the branches of knowledge are multiplied, a greater number must be included in the course of liberal education. If this be thought preferable, let us do this. But let us not attempt impossibilities, nor let us be contented with superficial education. Let us extend the term. It was originally in fact, seven years. Let us make it five, or six. If the requirements of admission were greater, and the College course increased by the addition of one or two years, a great gain would be made to the cause of education. I think that there is but small fear of our doing too much, if we only do it well.

3. The third plan would be to make a College more nearly to resemble a real University; that is, to make it a place of education in all the most important branches of human learning. This might properly include instruction in all professional, as well as ante-professional science. It should comprize teaching in Latin, Greek, French, German, and Hebrew languages, Mathematics, Mechanics, and all the branches of Natural Philosophy, Moral Philosophy, Intellectual Philosophy, Physical Science in all its departments, Rhetoric and its kindred literature, History, as well as instruction in Law and Medicine.

Of these branches, those might be selected which should be required of the candidate for the degree of Bachelor of Arts, and his graduation might depend not on time of residence, but on proficiency to be determined by examination. Another course embracing other studies might be made requisite to the obtaining of another degree. If one is Bachelor of Arts, the other might be Bachelor of Science, or of Literature. And still more, in order to bring the whole course of study within the scope of University stimulants, the degree of Master of Arts, instead of being conferred without additional attainment, as it is at present, might be conferred only on those who have pursued successfully the whole circle of study marked out for the candidates for both degrees. The degree of Master of Arts would then designate a degree of positive attainment, and would be a valuable and efficient testimonial. As it is now, to all practical purposes, we throw this degree away. It exerts no power of motive whatever. The best and the worst scholars are equally entitled to it on the third year after graduation. It might be made, as it seems to me, to subserve a valuable purpose in a system of education. . . .

It may be a question which of these plans is best suited to the purposes of our country. Either would I think be preferable to our present system. One may answer better in one place and another in another. I merely suggest these as topics for consideration to those who are interested in the cause of Collegiate education. I am desirous at least of laying the case before the visitors and officers of Colleges among us for candid consideration. If they should contribute in even so small a degree to direct the public attention to the points to be aimed at, or even to be avoided, I shall receive a full reward. In this country, if a movement can only be but commenced in the right direction, it will soon make ample progress. I say a movement in the right direction, for I have no idea that any change of value can be made instantaneously. If however the learned and able and self-sacrificing men who are now engaged in the profession of teaching can be led to act wisely and in concert on this subject, and the public can be brought into harmony with their action, I believe that a mighty impulse might be communicated to the cause of education among us. . . .

CHAPTER IV

OF SOME PREVALENT ERRORS IN REGARD TO
COLLEGIATE EDUCATION

I have thus far considered the system of Collegiate education by itself, and have endeavored to point out those of its defects which seem to me to stand most in need of correction. I beg leave now to direct the attention of those who have had the perseverance to follow me thus far, to some prevalent misconceptions on the subject, which need only to be understood, in order to be abandoned.

The first of these which I shall consider, is the cost of Collegiate education in this country. It is by many persons believed to be dear. We are continually reminded by all the friends of Colleges that it will never do to increase our expenses. College education, it is said, must be cheap, or a College cannot be sustained. If a new branch of study is to be introduced, or an additional instructor to be appointed, or any improvement is suggested, we are told to go on by all means, if the change would be advantageous, only taking care that the education shall not cost any more. And I think that I do not greatly mistake in asserting that in the larger number of instances parents decide upon the institution to which their sons are to be sent, rather by the cheapness of the education, than by any other fact in the case. And hence it is that to most of the annual catalogues of Colleges is appended a statement of expenses including not only the cost of tuition, board and lodging, but also of fuel, lights, washing, and I know not how many other *et ceteras*. By a comparison of these, a parent or student can easily learn which is the cheapest College; and as all lead to the same degree, that is, all confer the right to attach the same letters to the graduate's name, that which is the least expensive, has the best prospect of success.

Let us then inquire what is meant when we affirm that an article is cheap.

If we turn our attention to any article but education, we can answer the question in a moment. When a product is brought into the market, and we know the cost of its creation, and ascertain that the price merely pays the cost of investment, labor and interest, and yields to the producer the ordinary rate of remuneration, we say that it is as cheap as it can be afforded. If it be sold for a less price, the producer must be ruined. If it yield an extravagant remuneration, it is dear, and we know that so long as capital and labor are free, it will be by competition brought down to the average profit of other investments.

And still more, every one is aware that by no possible shrewdness can we permanently keep an article below the cost of its production. We may, if we choose, declare that we will not give more than half the price which we have formerly given. But this will not in any manner alter the case. The producer cannot be induced to give away the half of his product. If it cannot be brought to market at our price, he will cease to produce it and we must do with out it; or else, as is more probable, he will make use of a cheaper and less valuable material, employ less skillful workmen, and produce an article which will afford him a reasonable profit at our arbitrary prices. We get it for a less sum, but we get it no cheaper; we pay a low price for a poor article, and have laid out our money in spite of ourselves at a decided disadvantage.

These principles are exceedingly obvious, and they apply as truly to the case of College Education as to any other. The natural price of such education would be estimated as follows. We should first estimate the amount of capital invested in buildings, libraries, apparatus, and charge upon this sum the ordinary rate of interest. We should add to this, the salaries of professors and other teachers at the rate of remuneration ordinarily earned by persons employed in similar labor. These two items added together, would form the cost of College education; and if nothing more were charged, the article would be furnished at its natural price. It would be cheap just in proportion as the sum charged fell short of these amounts.

What now are the facts in this case? The whole amount invested in grounds, buildings and libraries, is almost actually sunk; that is, it is either given to the public outright, or else it is made to pay but a very small rate of interest. In a College, for instance, with which I am acquainted, the property of the Institution, in lands, buildings, &c., is probably worth one hundred and fifty thousand dollars. The interest of this sum would be nine thousand dollars per year. The whole amount paid for the use of it by the students is about eighteen hundred dollars, or less than two per cent. And it is to be remarked that out of this sum is to be deducted all the expenses necessary for important repairs. I presume that the College does not receive for this property much more than the nett sum of one per cent. This is certainly as cheap a rate as could be demanded. For the use of this property and the labors of its professors, the College receives of the students about seven thousand five hundred dollars. That is, for the use of its buildings and means of education, together with the labors of eight officers, it receives fifteen hundred dollars less than it could obtain from this property alone at the ordinary rate of interest. In fact were the property to be sold and the purchase money invested, it could pay a larger salary than present to its officers, and give away their labors without a cent of remuneration.

Were this all, it would be sufficient to establish the truth of what I have asserted. But this is not all. Most Colleges are in possession of funds to a considerable amount. In some cases the funds are large. But whether large or small they are commonly given to the public, that is they are appropriated either to the support of indigent students, or else they are applied to the several purposes of the institution, that is, to the payment of instructors. In this latter case they reduce the price of tuition to the whole public to precisely the amount of their value. In the College to which I have alluded, fifteen hundred dollars annually are appropriated to this purpose. To how great an extent these remarks apply to other Colleges I am not competent to say, but I know that in spirit they apply to all. Whatever means the College may possess are always appropriated upon the same principle, and with the same design, to reduce, as far as possible, the price of tuition. I ask any one in the least acquainted with political economy whether there be any thing in the market as cheap as College education.

But this is not all. I have thus far only stated that the investment in College education is almost entirely given to the public. The next item of cost is the salaries of teachers. I will now add that I believe that the instructors of Colleges in this country, are remunerated, at a lower rate than almost any other professional men. I know but very few who are competent to their situation, who might not earn a larger compensation in any other profession. That this is the case, is manifest from the fact that few young men with fair prospects before them can be ever induced to leave their profession for any office that a College can offer. It is my impression that professorships in New England Colleges vary from six hundred to twelve hundred dollars per annum. And I ask, what inducements could such an income offer to a lawyer, physician, or a clergyman, who had only even begun to take rank in his profession[?] And besides this, it is to be remarked that this salary can very rarely be increased by any efforts of the incumbent. As it is in youth so must he expect it to be in age. It holds out before him the cheerless prospect of circumstances becoming with every year narrower, terminating at last in death which leaves his widow and children, pennyless.

But the officers of Colleges are not only underpaid, if we compare them with men of other professions; they are underpaid if compared with private instructors. In any of our large towns a private instructor who is competent to his place receives a handsome remuneration; a remuneration I presume frequently twice as great as that received by the professors in the nearest College in his vicinity. The price of tuition in a classical day school, in any of our cities is twice or three times as great as that demanded by Colleges. That is, for the labors of six or eight competent men, you pay but half or one third as much as you pay for the labors of one man. In the one case you require the instructor to be responsible for the conduct of the pupil for the whole four years; in the other you require of him attendance only during the hours of study and assume the other responsibility yourself. In the one case you have the advantage of a very large investment almost for nothing, in the other no investment is required except the rent of a convenient room or two for the purposes of study and recitation. If this be the case it must appear evident either that the instructors of Colleges are greatly underpaid or else that they are exceedingly unfit for their offices. But whether fit or unfit, whether the article which they furnish be good, bad or indifferent, no one reflecting on these facts can for a moment doubt of its cheapness. It is, I have no doubt, afforded to the public at from half to one third of its cost, while the cost itself is reduced from twenty-five to fifty per cent. below the ordinary wages of similar labor.

To a person whose attention has not been attracted to this subject, all this may seem strange; but I am persuaded that I have not spoken in the language of exaggeration. I have never conversed on this subject with a gentleman at all acquainted with active business, who was not surprised at the low rate of College expenses. Parents have assured me that they were obliged to send their sons to College because they could not afford to bring them up in a good counting house. For the reasons which I have given, a liberal education for a son, is much less expensive than a corresponding education for a daughter. And in a word, it not unfrequently happens that a young man of industrious and frugal habits, who enters College, with nothing more than one or two hundred dollars, by laboring in vacations, and sometimes by devoting an intermediate year to teaching, will graduate without being in debt, and will in a year or two obtain a situation more lucrative than that of most of his instructors. Where this is the case I think there can no complaint be made of the dearness of a Collegiate education.

I have treated this part of the subject at greater length than I intended, because I think it needs to be understood. I am desirous that this whole matter should be examined; and I am satisfied that such an examination will result in the general conviction that Collegiate education is not only cheap, but that it is too cheap for the good of education. I am sure that every one who reflects upon the subject, will be convinced that the instructors of Colleges should be remunerated with a larger salary, or else be placed in circumstances in which they may be more able to benefit themselves by the exercise of their talents. If we pay for nothing but moderate capacity, we shall employ nothing but moderate capacity. And woe be to the cause of Collegiate education when it falls into the hands of third or fourth rate men. I hope that I have made it evident that College education in this country is cheap enough, so cheap that no one can reasonably complain of it on that score. I proceed then to examine another opinion intimately connected with this idea of cheapness.

It is frequently said that this is a republic, here we are all equal, the avenues to distinction are, and of right ought to be, open to all; every man whether poor or rich, of whatever occupation, should have the opportunity of improving himself to the utmost; this is demanded by the nature of our institutions, and it is important to success in the arts as well as necessary to the full development of the universal mind. To all this I fully agree. It is the expression of my own long cherished sentiments. I would foster these ideas to the utmost of my ability, and I wish that they were universally diffused and universally acted upon. I have here only to remark upon the bearing which they have upon the present question.

1. It is granted that it would be very desirable to establish means, for the improvement in science and the arts, of all classes of the community. I think it desirable that it should be furnished, in many cases, I care not if in all, gratuitously. But I ask if you are about to make a present to your neighbor, is this any reason why you should not pay for it[?] If you wish to give away education, is this any reason why instructors should not be as well recompensed as other men[?] It would certainly be an ambiguous charity to oblige your neighbor to furnish you with his goods at half price because you intended to give them away. Or on the other hand, if you really desire to afford the means of improvement to every citizen, is it wise to pay for his instruction so small a price that the education which he receives is worthless; so worthless that he will not receive it as a gratuity[?] Look at our common school system in New England. Here we offer to all the means of obtaining a common English education. It is all, in some sense, given away. But is this ever considered as a reason why the instructors should be underpaid[?] And still further; where instructors in our schools have been poorly paid, it has been universally acknowledged to be bad economy; the schools have been badly attended, badly taught, and in ill favor with the public; on the contrary, where instructors have received sufficient remuneration, good men have been without difficulty employed; schools by a change of this kind, have been doubled and almost trebled in numbers, and the system has at once received the favor of the public. If therefore, it be granted that the good of the whole requires the means of education to be open to all, it by no means follows either that teachers should be underpaid,

or that the education should be rendered of but little value, by driving from the profession those who are by talent and discipline, capable of conferring the greatest benefits upon the community.

But let us examine this argument in another point of light. It is asserted that it is important to present to all men in every rank of life the means of full mental development—and therefore, that *Collegiate* education must be reduced to the extremest degree of cheapness. I grant the premises but I deny the conclusion.

If it be desirable to furnish the means of intellectual development to all, and I believe it to be so, then it follows that we should provide the means of this intellectual culture, either by private munificence or public endowment. I know of but one instance in this country in which this has been done, and that is the instance of the Institution in Boston so nobly endowed by the late Mr. Lowell. By the will of that distinguished benefactor of his native city, a provision has been made for the gratuitous delivery of courses of Lectures to the citizens of Boston on the most important branches of Science. The design has been carried out according to the intention of the testator, and with the most triumphant success. The ablest talent of New England, and even of Europe, has been secured for this service, and the lectures have been attended by thronged audiences which have filled one of the largest rooms in the city. The benefit which this charity will confer upon the citizens of Boston in awakening the slumbering intellect, in stimulating the active mind to more zealous inquiry, and in binding together in one, all the different classes of society will be incalculable. And I think I may add that the success of this experiment has arisen in no small degree from the fact that the institution has been conducted on principles analogous to those which I have suggested. Instead of frittering away the means at his disposal by creating a large amount of tolerably good instruction, the gentleman under whose control the bequest has been placed, has determined to render it as valuable as this or any other country could supply. The lecture room has become a centre of universal attraction. How different would have been the result, had courses of inferior lectures been delivered in every school district in the city. No one would have accepted the gift, for no one would have thought it worth his acceptance, and the whole charity would have been a failure.

I say then that granting the importance of providing means of intellectual cultivation for all the community the only inference from the assumption is that such means ought to be provided. I hope the time will come when all our large towns as well as our cities will be thus endowed. But I say that Colleges are not at present such institutions; they are at present *merely schools preparatory to entrance upon some one of the professions.* Whether therefore tuition be cheap or dear, the argument stated above can have no reference to them. Whether it be cheap or dear, the College as at present constituted, can be of no service to those classes of the community referred to in the argument.

I say a College with us is not an establishment for the instruction of any one in whatever he pleases, but for instruction in a particular course, and that in consequence of its forming an isolated society it naturally repels from its association all who are not engaged in similar pursuits. Now this being the case the question at once arises, is there any reason why the public should make a special effort merely to increase the number of professional men. If a man wishes to pursue one profession rather than another, or to change the profession which he has already chosen, he has a perfect right to do so. But is he therefore an object of charity? Are we in special need of recruits to fill the ranks of the professions? Or still more, because he wishes to enter a profession is it desirable in order to accommodate him that we reduce the price of tuition in such a manner as to render the tuition itself of small value not only to him but to all the rest of the community.

But it will doubtless be asked why should not these means of general improvement be connected with Collegiate establishments. Why should not professors in Colleges deliver courses of lectures which would be attractive to the whole community; and why should not the means which are at present available to a part be made available to the whole? I answer at once, I see no reason whatever why it should not be so. I think that such an arrangement would be a great benefit to the officers, the College, and the community. It would open to the instructor a wide and attractive field of professional exertion. It would enlist in favor of the College all the sympathies of the public, and it would spread before the whole people such means for intellectual improvement as the necessities or tastes of each individual might demand.

I am aware that in order to accomplish this result some changes must be effected in our College system, and if this instruction is to be gratuitous, additional professorships must be endowed. The professor must be relieved from much of the police duty which devolves upon him at present. A variety of courses of instruction must be provided for, which do not enter into our present arrangements. But I see no insuperable difficulty in devising a plan which might meet the exigency, specially if such changes should be introduced into our system as I have elsewhere suggested. It is not, however, my intention to enter upon the discussion of this subject. My object is merely to show that the importance of the diffusion of valuable knowledge only teaches us that means for accomplishing so desirable an object should be provided; that it does not apply to Colleges which are merely professional schools; or that if it apply to them at all, it merely goes to prove that they might confer a much wider benefit upon the community were they enabled to modify their present system and greatly enlarge their foundations.

But it will here be asked, what is to be done for our students for the ministry, if the expenses of Colleges are increased[?] How shall the churches of our land be supplied with pastors[?] I answer first, if the ministry be adequately supported, and duly sustained, there will be no difficulty in this respect. We shall surely confer no benefit on the ministry by hiring men to enter it, by the promise of an education, and then keeping them in poverty for the rest of their lives. I answer again, this is a question respecting general education, and is therefore to be judged of upon its own merits. If our arrangements for the education of the ministry are at variance with the general advancement of the community, our arrangements must be changed. If we wish to educate a young man for the ministry, there is no reason why we should not pay that price for his education which shall secure the best instruction both to him and to every one else. To do otherwise would be to inflict an injury both upon ourselves and upon the public. In a word, when we are deliberating upon a plan for the intellectual improvement of the whole community, let us keep that object simply and steadily in view, and we may be assured that if the good of the whole be promoted the good of the part cannot be neglected.

I had intended in this place to inquire into the tendencies of the present system of ministerial education and trace out the probable results of creating a general fund, (as is the case with education societies,) for the use of all persons who are willing to prepare for the sacred office; and also to inquire into the expediency of multiplying Colleges, as they have of late been multiplied by all the religious sects. I have supposed it easy to show that from this latter cause, the supply of professional education has far outrun the demand, and, as in every similar case, led to what may be called, for the want of a better name, underbidding each other; and that it has thrown the responsibility of their support, not on the results of their own labor, but on the charities of the sect by which they have been established. But all this I willingly waive. I fear that many of these benevolent efforts will prove monuments rather of the charity than the wisdom of the present generation. As however this topic does not fall directly within the range of the present undertaking, I cheerfully leave the discussion of it to others.

In answer to all that I have said, I am perfectly aware that it may be urged that I am recommending dear instead of cheap education; that I wish to restrict the number of educated men; and that all this is at variance with the nature of our institutions. To the suggestion I can only reply that I can conceive of no motive which should induce an American citizen either to entertain or to promulgate such an opinion. As to the charge of wishing to render education dear. I reply in the first place that nothing that I have said is, so far as I know, chargable with this inference. It has been commonly taken for granted that our *first* and most important business is to make education *cheap*. This assumption I have denied and on the contrary have asserted that our most important business is to make it *good;* that its *goodness* is our *first* concern, and its cheapness only secondary; and that by seeking first of all to render it cheap we were in danger of rendering it useless.

But this is not all; I have endeavored to show that by multiplying Colleges, and spending so large an amount of our funds in buildings, we have rendered our means for the reduction of the price of tuition almost useless. I also believe that another system might be adopted which by attracting a greater number of students, and stimulating teachers to greater energy and efficiency, would attract higher talent to the professional chair; without in the least increasing the expenses of each individual pupil. What I propose then in this respect, may be briefly summed up as follows: Let the education in our Colleges and Universities be exact, generous and thorough; let it be rendered capable of improvement, and let it be for the interest of all connected with it to improve it, whether it cost more or less than at present; And secondly let it be rendered as cheap as is consistent with goodness; and still more, let provision be made either in connexion with Colleges or independently of them, for the wide dissemination of knowledge in science and the arts; and let this knowledge be of the very best description which American scholarship can supply. Such are in few words my sentiments on this subject, and I hope that I have not uttered any thing at variance with them.

I close this chapter with one other remark; it is upon the commonly received notion that a course of education must be popular. If by being popular it is meant that it must follow every whim of the day, and introduce or discard studies because for the time being they may be in vogue or out of it; if it be meant that our course of discipline must change at the will of every popular convention which may endorse the theoretical notions of an educational reformer, I must be permitted to live a little longer in doubt of the assertion. If it however be meant that it must commend itself to the good sense and patriotism of the American people, I assent to it most cordially. Nothing which is not popular in this sense can be or ought to be sustained. But in order to secure this kind of popularity, we must strive to render education good. We must adopt our plans not only for the present but for the future; we must honestly strive to render our whole course of higher education as valuable and as universally available as possible. We must not only do this but we must spread before the public our reasons for so doing and explain the manner in which we intend to accomplish it. I do most honestly believe that by so doing we shall carry the whole community with us. If we would be popular let us remember that we can never attain our end by aiming at it directly. The approbation of our fellow citizens will in the end be conferred not on those who desire to please them, but on those, who honestly do them good. Popularity is valuable when it follows us, not when we run after it; and he is most sure of attaining it, who, caring nothing about it, honestly and in simplicity, and kindness earnestly labors to render his fellow men wiser, and happier, and better.

CHAPTER V

CONCLUDING REMARKS

I have thus considered at considerable length, some of the most important points of our present Collegiate system. Unless I have been greatly deceived I have shown that this system calls for serious revision; if we desire that it should be adapted to the existing wants of the community.

I propose in these few concluding remarks to review briefly the points which I suppose to call most loudly for attentive consideration.

I beg leave, however, to repeat what I have often stated before, that I only present these topics as matters for consideration. I by no means suppose it practicable, or even wise were it practicable, to transform all our Colleges at once, in order to conform them to the plans which I have indicated. There is a demand for a change in our Collegiate system. Changes are from time to time effected, without as it would seem, any great practical improvement. My object is simply to point out the objects at which we should aim in our attempts at change. If it should seem that in any respects I have indicated the direction in which we should move, let us move in that direction. If I have illustrated the evils under which we labor, let us strive to remove them. If I have totally failed in this attempt, let some one better qualified accomplish the task more successfully. But at any rate, let us have the object which we desire to attain placed full in our own view, and in the view of the whole community; and let us all labor for its accomplishment, sincerely, earnestly and harmoniously. In this manner alone, can we hope to improve the condition of higher education throughout our country.

1. *I begin then with the Corporations, or Boards of Visitors, in our Colleges.* On them devolves, in truth, the incipient action which shall effect this whole subject. They are the appointed guardians of education. In them is vested the whole power of ordering, directing and governing the institutions of higher learning. They hold all the funds appropriated either by private or public munificence to the purpose of elevating the standard of knowledge in the youth of our country. They appoint and remove officers, fix the rate and manner of their compensation, ordain the studies to be pursued, and on them it is devolved to see that the designs of the public or the founder are carried into effect. This power can be exercised by no other person whatever. So long as they hold their office, no one else can act in the premises, without usurpation. If they do not act according to their solemn promises, no action can be had. Such being their power and their responsibility, I beg leave most respectfully to remind them of their duty. Unless they make themselves acquainted with the subject of education, unless they will devote to the proper duties of their office a portion of their time, unless they will assume the responsibility which must be incurred by efficient action, unless in a word they will make an earnest effort to improve the present system of education, on them a charge of grave dereliction of duty will rest. If, as is doubtless in many instances the case, their organization is imperfect, it may be modified. If the duties

to be discharged are onerous, they may be divided among them. In the officers of Colleges, they will, I am convinced, find ready and active coadjutors. If these two principal agents in the Collegiate system seriously undertake a revision of its fundamental principles, I am convinced that they will confer a most important benefit on the community. It is in their power to extend the blessings of higher education very widely among all classes of our fellow citizens, and also render education incomparably more valuable than it has ever been in this country. But the work must commence with the visitors. To them it properly appertains. They owe it to the public to whom they are responsible. They owe it to the rising youth of our country, who in this respect, are placed specially under their pupillage. They owe it to their God who has committed to their charge so solemn a responsibility, and placed in their hands in no small degree, the destinies of this great republic. I cannot believe for a moment that they will be recreant to so grave and important a trust.

2. *Of the Organization of our Colleges.* Our Colleges as I have already remarked are at present scarcely any thing more than schools for the education of young men for the professions. So long as we continue the present organization they can be no other. While we construct our system for this purpose and adhere to a regular gradation of classes and prescribed studies for each, we may make what changes we please, but the regular course will control every other. But while we have made our College course a mere preparation for professional education, we have so crowded it with studies as to render it superficial and probably less valuable for its particular purpose than it was originally. I am not sure that we are not already suffering from the effect of the course which we have pursued. I rather fear that the impression is gaining ground that this preparation is not essential to success in professional study. A large proportion of our medical students are not graduates. The proportion of law students of the same class is, I rather think, increasing. The proportion of students for the ministry who resort to College is much larger than formerly. This is owing in no small degree, to the aid of education societies. What would be the case if this aid were out of the question, I am unable to determine. If these things be so, it would seem that while we have been restricting our Collegiate education to one class, its value by that class is less and less appreciated.

But while this is the case, in consequence of this unintentional restriction, a very large class of our people have been deprived of all participation in the benefits of higher education. It has been almost impossible in this country, for the merchant, the mechanic, the manufacturer, to educate his son, beyond the course of a common academy unless he gave him the education preparatory for a profession. This was not the education which he wanted, and of course, his son has been deprived of the cultivation which the parent was able and willing to bestow. Now the class of society that is thus left unprovided for, constitutes the bone and sinew, the very choicest portion of this or of any community. They are the great agents of a production, they are the safest depositories of political power. It is their will, that, in the end, sways the destinies of the nation. It is of the very highest importance, on every account, that this portion of a people should possess every facility for the acquisition of knowledge and intellectual discipline. Nothing would tend so much to the progress of wealth among us as the diffusion throughout the whole people of a knowledge of the principles of science, and the application of science to the arts. And besides, a knowledge of moral and intellectual philosophy, of the fundamental principles of law, of our own constitution, of history, of vegetable and animal physiology, and of many other sciences is just as necessary and just as appropriate to the merchant, the manufacturer, the mechanic, and the farmer, as to the lawyer, the clergyman, or the physician. Why should it be supposed that all higher knowledge should be engrossed exclusively by the professions[?] If a man wishes to give his son a good education why should he be obliged to make him a lawyer, a physician, or a clergyman[?] Why should not the highest intellectual endowment, cultivated by the best preparatory discipline be found in every mode of occupation[?] And if this be so why has this whole subject been so long neglected among us[?] Is it not time that our system should in this matter undergo a complete and radical revision[?]

What I would propose on this subject then is briefly as follows. In the first place let the course preparatory to a profession be distinctly marked out and let it be generous and thorough. Let it embrace such branches of study as are particularly necessary for fitting men for the professions, and let it be carried on to such an extent as shall communicate enlarged and generous knowledge, and vigorous mental discipline. But while this is done let our system be so enlarged in its provisions that the means of education in other branches may be open to all who choose to avail themselves of them. Let there be established courses of lectures on all the subjects which I have specified, and as many more as may be necessary, to which men of all classes may resort. Let there be no compulsory residence, let every man come by ticket, and let him be admitted to every privilege which the nature of the case demands. In a word let the College be the grand centre of intelligence to all classes and conditions of men, diffusing among all the light of every kind of knowledge, and approving itself to the best feelings of every class of the community. Let it, besides being a preparatory school to the professions, be a Lowell Institute to the region in which it is placed. I know of nothing that would tend so strongly to promote the growth of wealth and civilization and refinement among us. Nothing would so surely annihilate that division of the community into classes, which, already, in spite of our democratic institutions, threatens the direst evils to our republic.

3. *Of the Officers of Colleges.* I have in the preceding pages endeavored to set forth the evils of our present organization in this respect. I would suggest the importance of opening our professorships to a freer competition, so that the College may have the benefit of a choice from all the talent that is willing to employ itself in the profession of instruction. Besides this I would have the emolument of every professor so adjusted that he shall feel directly the results of his diligence and ability, or of his indolence and inefficiency. There can be no reason why a teacher in College should not be placed under the same inducements to labor as any other man. In no other way can we expect him to devote his whole talent with earnestness to his profession. On no other principles can we expect the cause of education to be sustained with the vigor and efficiency which its importance so clearly demands.

If it be said that this is impracticable, then there are other means which must be resorted to. The College must be placed under close and active supervision. The board of visitors must annually examine its condition, and without fear, favor or affection, remove from time to time, every unsuitable incumbent. This would accomplish the same result in another way, but it would be an onerous, an unpleasant and an odious duty. It is better to construct the system in such manner, that an inefficient officer would have no desire to remain, than to make the place desirable for him and then displace him by an arbitrary act.

4. *Of the Discipline of our Colleges.* I have endeavored to show that our discipline is too lax for the young, and unnecessarily strict for the older students. Two methods would present themselves for relieving

this embarrassment. The one is to admit no student until he had attained to the age of self government, and then leave him to his own responsibility. The other would be to admit the young, but place them under stricter supervision. I think that either plan would have advantages over our present system. How far such a change could be carried into effect, I must leave to the judgment of the officers of each particular institution. I am however well convinced that our Colleges would be greatly improved by raising the requirements of admission to the regular or professional course so high that the student might be obliged to spend a year or two years longer in the grammar school. The studies of most of our Colleges during the first year, might be more successfully pursued in school under the eye of the instructor, than within the walls of an University. A change of this kind would be greatly for the advantage both of the College, and of the grammar school. And if the plan which I have suggested were carried into effect, that is, if the advantages of the institution were thrown open to every class of society, this extension of the requirements might the more easily be enforced. There would be no crowding into the regular course, of those who enter merely for the sake of the benefit of particular studies, and who wish to graduate at the earliest practicable age. Their object could be accomplished more successfully in another way. Each course of instruction would stand on its own merits, and the object of the institution would be to render each one as perfect as the nature of the case would permit.

On the subject of residence in College, I have already suggested an opinion. It seems to me that in investing so large a portion of our funds in erecting dormitories, we have committed an error. The funds have however been thus appropriated, and they cannot be recalled. Were the system of residence abandoned, these buildings could be of no use except for the residence of professors. If this part of our plan be injudicious, we can however cease to repeat our error. We can refrain from spending any more of our money in this manner. And we can, as opportunity occurs, try the experiment of allowing residence out of College. If it be found on a fair trial to succeed, it will at least demonstrate the important fact that a College or University can be established, with all the means of instruction which we now possess, at half or one third of the expense which it now involves. This will certainly be an important addition to our knowledge on the subject.

5. *Of Premiums.* I have alluded to the importance of this mode of

stimulants in a course of education. I will only add that I would extend the benefit of this incentive to every branch of knowledge taught by a College, not merely to the regular preparatory course, but to every other. Were this done, I am persuaded that a keen and honorable emulation would be excited among all classes of students. Prizes would be borne away by young men in every occupation. Mechanics, Farmers, Merchants and Manufacturers, would vie with their fellows preparing for the professions, and would as often be entitled to the distinction conferred upon merit. The effect of this upon all classes of the community would be incalculable, and I can conceive of no case in which it would not be beneficial. In this manner also, deserving young men of narrow means might be most advantageously assisted. The prize, if in money, would materially relieve their wants, while instead of being bestowed as an alms, it would be conferred as a reward of merits; instead of depressing the recipient by proclaiming his poverty, it would distinguish him in the eyes of the community as one who had deserved well. I believe that if a large part of the funds appropriated in our Colleges for the support of the indigent were distributed in this manner, it would have the most beneficial effect upon the cause of education.

Here I close these remarks which have, I fear, been already too far extended. It has been my lot to speak chiefly of the defects of our system of education. It would have been much more agreeable to treat of its excellencies, which I believe to be great and manifold. To speak of these however, did not come within the scope of my design, which was merely to take notice of those things which need to be improved. The motive with which I have written, so far as I am conscious of it, has been to contribute my mite towards the improvement of higher education in our country. I offer it to the consideration of the public with unfeigned diffidence, in the humble hope that it may in a small degree contribute to the wider diffusion of intellectual cultivation among all classes of the community.

22. *Philip Lindsley on the Failure of the American College, 1832 and 1848*

See Part III, Docs. 21, 24, and Doc. 20 of this Part. This document is taken from Lindsley's baccalaureate address of 1832 and from his commencement address of 1848.

1832 BACCALAUREATE

I care as little about names as any man. If the *name* of college or university be unsavoury in the ears of the people or of the people's guardians and conscience keepers, let it be cashiered. Let our colleges and universities be called academies, lyceums, gymnasia, common schools, or popular intellectual workshops—or by any other republican appelation, if any more acceptable or less invidious can be invented. It is the thing—the substance—the knowledge—the mental enlargement and energy and power—that I would give to the people in as ample measure as possible. That they may be sovereign in fact as well as in name. That they may be capable of knowing and guarding and asserting their own rights and liberties, without the second sight of any political juggler or officious bankrupt Solomon. . . .

I have been pleading the cause of farmers and mechanics for some ten or a dozen years past. Because upon them, as enlightened, judicious, independent, patriotic citizens, depend the destinies of this Republic. The question is, shall they lead or be led? Shall they arrest and put down the factious spirit of unprincipled ambition, or shall they tamely lend themselves as the instruments and the victims of its desperate and treasonable purposes? The crisis has arrived when the people must speak and act wisely and resolutely, or their ability to speak and to act, with decisive efficiency, will be lost forever.

The lawyers are now our sole political guides and instructors. They engross the learning of the country; I mean all that learning which is brought to bear on government, legislation and public policy—for the physicians rarely intermeddle in these affairs; and the clergy ought forever to be excluded by law, if not by a high sense of duty. Our farmers and mechanics therefore, who constitute the great body of the people, are governed by the lawyers. Now it is not in human nature, that in

L. J. Halsey (ed.), *The Works of Philip Lindsley,* I, 345, 349–50, 557–59, 570–71.

such a country as ours, there should not grow up a sort of professional aristocracy, which in time may become irresistible. Wherever there is a privileged order, no matter how constituted—whether like the *patrician* of ancient, or the *ecclesiastic* of modern Rome—it will, if not duly checked and counterbalanced, in the long run, become overbearing and tyrannical. I look to the college for a seasonable supply of countervailing agents. I look to a well educated independent yeomanry as the sheet anchor of the Republic. I look forward to the period when it will not be deemed anti-republican for the college graduate to follow the plough; nor a seven days' wonder for the labourer to be intellectual and to comprehend the Constitution of his country.

1848 COMMENCEMENT ADDRESS

Colleges confer degrees upon unworthy candidates.—I admit the fact. I wish it were otherwise. Of honorary doctorates, perhaps the least said the better. Happily, with one exception, they do but little harm, even if they do no good I think that colleges, in this great model Republic, might, with manifest propriety, cease to grant the doctorate altogether. I see no reason why American preachers, and schoolmasters, and authors of spelling books and grammars, should not assume the D.D. or LL.D. at pleasure, according to their taste or self-appreciation; just as our whig and democratic loafers and politicians contrive, by some process or other, to become entitled or accustomed to the prefix or suffix of Colonel, General, Esquire, Honorable, or His Excellency. Why not? The exception just alluded to, is the doctorate of medicine. This, whether conferred *causa honoris* or *in course* upon ignorant or unprincipled persons, is a grievous injury to the public.—Because an M.D. is a passport to popular confidence and practice. Here the people cannot judge for themselves. They rely on the testimonials thus dishonestly furnished by learned and responsible corporations. And hence irreparable wrongs may be inflicted and endured before the *Doctor's* utter incompetency can be detected and exposed. That a reform is needed here and everywhere, in the Medical Schools and in reference to medical practice, I believe, is the opinion of the enlightened profession generally, on both sides of the Atlantic.

But the objection relates chiefly, I suppose, to the first degree—the degree, namely, of Bachelor of Arts. Very true: this degree is conferred by all the colleges in the Union every year upon some unqualified—perhaps, in the aggregate, upon many unqualified and very unworthy individuals. This arises from several causes. 1. From the fact, that a portion of the youth who enter our colleges are deficient in intellect. They do not possess minds capable of high and liberal cultivation. Here the native or raw material is wanting. "Non ex quovis ligno Mercurius fit." No college professors can work miracles, or convert a blockhead into a Solomon.—"Though the ass may make a pilgrimage to Mecca, yet an ass he will come back." 2. From idle habits—from lack of industry and application. No brilliancy of talent will master any science or language without labour. While persevering labour will ultimately triumph over all difficulties, and insure success to even comparatively humble genius. 3. From a defective school education—the want of the requisite qualifications for a college life—or from the extreme youth of the party when admitted. . . .

When this college was revived and reorganized at the close of 1824, there were no similar institutions, in actual operation, within two hundred miles of Nashville. There were none in Alabama, Mississippi, Louisiana, Arkansas, Texas, Middle or West Tennessee—and none in Kentucky, nearer than Lexington. There are now some thirty or more within that distance [of 200 miles;] and nine within fifty miles of our city.* These all claim to be our superiors; and to be equal at least to old Harvard and Yale. Of course, we cannot expect much "custom," or to command a large range, of what is miscalled, patronage. With so many formidable rivals and opponents at our very doors—eager to welcome pupils of all ages, and of every and no degree of literary qualification—with capacious preparatory departments for A, B, C—*darians* and Hic, Haec, Hoc-*ers*—promising to work cheap; and to *finish off* and graduate, in double quick time, and in the most approved style, all who may come to them—it is wonderful that the regular classes of our humble "concern" should be maintained in a state of even *quasi* vitality. Or that a frugal, sagacious, dollar-loving public should condescend to remember us at all.

Besides, the several religious denominations have colleges of their own. And it is right, natural and proper, that they should sustain them. As we belong to no sect or party, we have no sect or party to

---

* I have a list, now before me, of twenty-five colleges or universities in Tennessee alone.—Several of these belong exclusively to individuals; and are bought and sold in open market, like any other species of private property. They are invested with the usual corporate powers, and may confer all university degrees at pleasure. This is probably a *new* thing under the sun: but Solomon's geography did not extend to America.

stand by and befriend us; to praise, puff, glorify, and fight for us. This is, perhaps, the worst possible position. To be neutral—of no side, of no party, of no creed—why neither politician nor pedagogue, church or school, would be regarded or trusted by any class. The *just milieu* is a paradox—an anomaly—not to be tolerated in this fair land of religious freedom and equal rights.

Nearly all the preachers, teachers, editors, demagogues, and other friends of the people, are hostile to us and to Nashville. They give us a bad name. Our goodly city they represent as a very dangerous place for youth. And even some of our own grave citizens, occasionally, admit the charge and confirm the imputation. I offer no defence or apology, and make no complaint. Let time do its appropriate office: and the millennium will arrive at last—in spite of colleges and croakers.

23. Edward Everett on Harvard's Need for State Funds, 1848–49

Edward Everett (1794–1865) was president of Harvard for only three years (1846–49). The brevity of his tenure was due to poor health, to his dislike for the role of college disciplinarian, and to the way he conscientiously attended to petty administrative details. He took as many pains in persuading faculty members to attend chapel services as he earlier had taken, while ambassador at London (1841–45), in corresponding with Lord Aberdeen on international boundary problems or in conducting the gubernatorial affairs of Massachusetts (1836–39). During Everett's presidency the Lawrence Scientific School at Harvard was opened. His respect for the sciences was exhibited in his first plea to the Massachusetts legislature (1848) for state funds for Harvard, partly reproduced as the first section of this document. The state, however, did not contribute funds to Harvard after 1823. In his second plea to the legislature (1849), partly reprinted here, Everett included his idea of the social function of higher learning. It reflects his own experience, for he had risen from modest circumstances, by virtue of his learning, through the Unitarian ministry and literature to eminence in Massachusetts society and Whig politics.

On Everett see Paul Revere Frothingham, *Edward Everett: Orator and Statesman* (Boston, 1925), and Part III, Doc. 13.

Edward Everett, *Orations and Speeches on Various Occasions* (Boston, 1850), II, 544–50, 607, 619–20, 622–25.

II. The next object to which the legislative bounty, if granted us, might be advantageously applied, is the procuring of apparatus in the various scientific departments, the increase of the mineralogical and other scientific cabinets and collections, and the completion of the set of instruments required at the observatory. It will readily be understood, that objects of this kind are of prominent importance in a place of education. The departments of science to which they pertain are progressive. New truths and facts, requiring new experimental illustrations, are constantly discovered in natural philosophy. Without taking into account deterioration by use, antiquated apparatus in the lecture-room is as useless as antiquated machinery in a manufacturing establishment. The advancement which has been made within thirty years in spinning and weaving, is not greater than that which has taken place in physical science. Hence the necessity, in a well-provided lecture-room, for a constant supply of new and often expensive apparatus. This remark applies with equal force in chemistry, with the additional consideration, that of the apparatus and the substances required for experiments in chemistry, a considerable portion is consumed and destroyed in the using. In like manner, constant accessions must be made to a mineralogical and a geological cabinet, to keep it up to the standard of the science. We have an ample mineralogical cabinet at Cambridge, formed chiefly within the last twenty-five years, containing, also, very valuable articles belonging to the geological branch. We have, however, nothing that can be called a systematic geological collection, and the formation of such a collection will be one of the first objects to engage the attention of the professors in our new scientific school. For this purpose, and to make those additions to the cabinet of minerals which are required for the illustration of a progressive science, a moderate fund is needed. If these additions are not made, the value of the collection is soon impaired. It sinks by degrees into a scientific toy-shop,—a mere exhibition. A collection of minerals formed and arranged a century ago, would have but little more value, for the illustration of the present state of the science, than a collection of porcelain. As for geological systems, they are the growth of the last fifty years.

The wants of the observatory for the present will be less urgent than those of the other scientific establishments, but will be constant. New and improved instruments will be from time to time required. Our observatory is amply furnished for almost every description of celestial observation, but astronomy is as much a progressive study as any other branch of science. Although we had at Cambridge, before the new observatory was built and the new instruments procured, a good many instruments, mostly presented from time to time by the friends of the institution, during the period which has elapsed since the burning of Harvard Hall in 1764,—instruments some of them of considerable cost, and deemed at the time of value,—there was not one of them with which an observation of the heavens of any scientific value could be made.

Now, for the purposes I have enumerated, we have no funds at Cambridge whatever. However great may be the necessity for adding an article of philosophical apparatus, a series of minerals, a new astronomical instrument, we have no means of doing it but those furnished by the general funds, or by a separate appeal to the liberality of our friends. It is in this last way that a magnificent mastodon was procured two years ago, at an expense of three thousand dollars, and still more signally, it is in this way that we have been provided with our great telescope, at an expense of twenty thousand dollars. But these are efforts of liberality not often to be repeated. Recourse ought not to be had to *extra* bounty for the supply of regular wants. Establishments kept up by casual supplies of this kind will inevitably be stinted; particularly in matters which, though important, are too small to warrant an appeal to the liberal friends of the university. Besides this, the persons actively engaged in government and instruction, being those who are best acquainted with the wants of the college in all these respects, have full occupation for their time, and no leisure for the work of habitual solicitation. Finally, there is such a thing as wearing out one's welcome.

III. Another very important object of expenditure is the library. I would call it the *most* important, if I knew degrees in these matters, all of first-rate interest and necessity. Our library, it is true, is large; at least it seems so in this country. It exceeds fifty-three thousand volumes, which is one tenth part of the estimated size of the library of the British Museum,—one twentieth part of the reported size of the Royal Library at Paris. Still it may be asked, are not fifty-three thousand books enough? Can any mortal man read fifty-three thousand volumes? To which I readily reply, no one can read a tenth or a fiftieth part of that number of books, to any advantage; at least if they are of the size of many of the mighty folios that adorn our shelves. But a

public library is not for the use of any one man, or any one class or set
of men, having the same tastes, objects, and range of study. It is for our
numerous body of instructers in their several departments; for four or
five hundred students, graduates, and undergraduates; for a long list
of other persons, having, by the standing laws, the right of borrowing
books from the library; and it is for the public at large; for no individual having occasion to consult it, for any serious purpose, literary or
scientific, is ever refused.

Again, of the fifty-three thousand volumes, a portion are of no great
value. Many volumes are given to public libraries, because they are
hardly worth the room which they occupy on the shelves of private
collections. Then the value of books is changeable, as of most other
human things. Hundreds of volumes in every department, once useful,
or thought so, cease to have any value for present use; except as they
illustrate the history of the human mind, or incidentally establish a
date or a fact. There is, I admit, a real use, in this way, even of the poorest book. Public libraries reject nothing that is not abominable. It may
sometimes be important, in literary history, to prove that a book is
worthless,—to show that the doctrines it teaches have no foundation,
or that it teaches them in an unprofitable manner. It is valuable in the
library, because it may be important, for some purpose, to prove that it
is valuable nowhere else.

This, however, is but a very subordinate object in what may be called
a *working library,* such as we wish ours to be. Such a library must be
well provided with books of direct, positive utility. These are of two
classes—the great standard works which are never antiquated, and the
valuable new books which are constantly appearing in every department of science and literature. Our library is amply supplied with
many of the books belonging to the first class; thanks to the bounty of
the Hollises and other noble benefactors in earlier or later days. But it
is surprising how small the number is of books which are of unchang-
ing value,—I mean, sir, in reference to the wants of a library. . . .

And then, sir, the progressive portions of science and literature properly so called. Take the great modern science of geology, which may
be said, in its systematic form, to date from Cuvier and the close of the
last century,—a science which comes so near to the interests of the
miner, the agriculturist, and the engineer, and in reference to which
thousands of volumes have already been published, and hundreds are
annually appearing. There is not a work a hundred years old of any

systematic value in this department. I do not say there are no old books which contain valuable hints and facts; but that there is no elementary treatise of earlier date, which has a present scientific value. The modern science of chemistry is a little older, but not much. It dates from the last quarter of the eighteenth century. You cannot have a bleachery, print-works, or a dyeing establishment, without knowledge, and that in the most recent form, derived from this science. The books of a hundred years old will not give it to you; they have no other than an historical value. The whole fabric of science is of later date; many of the most important discoveries have been made within a very few years. Similar remarks may be made of almost every branch of natural philosophy. Electricity, galvanism, magnetism, crystallography, optics, pneumatics, must be all studied in very recent books. The most brilliant discoveries in almost all of them are the product of the present century. It would be unjust to bring the date of modern astronomy lower down than the time of Newton; but a man might know the *Principia* by heart, and not be able to lecture to a village lyceum on the present state of the science. Although he discovered the great law by which the motion of the heavenly bodies is regulated, six only of the primary planets were known to him. Ten more have since been discovered, and five within the last two years. In most branches of intellectual and moral science, the really useful books—I mean those of most practical utility—are comparatively recent. All which have been contributed by Germany to the general stock are of this description. So, too, of voyages and travels, statistics, ethnography,—departments in which the modern press has been unusually prolific. This class of books contains many new publications of great cost and value; we have but very few of them, even of those which pertain to our own continent, though our collection of books relative to America is said to be larger than that of any other public library.

Now, sir, for new books in all the departments of art, literature, and science, we have barely eight hundred dollars a year,—a sum inadequate to the purchase of the new works of value which annually appear in any one department. What is the consequence? It is twofold; —first, all who have studies which must be pursued, are obliged to have private libraries of their own, a steady drain on small incomes; and, secondly, they are obliged to endure at every turn the mortification and disadvantage of remaining in ignorance of the present condition of the sciences, or to take it at second hands from the reviews.

There can be no cheerful progress, no first-rate scholarship, under such circumstances.

Nor is it for the immediate benefit of the university or its members that the library is useful. Although of necessity they are most directly benefited, yet we strive to make it generally useful to the public and the country. It is at all times open to the studious and inquisitive. Our books and the appliances for using them are always at their command. In special cases, books are sent to remote parts of the country. We have, since I have been connected with the university, permitted them freely to be sent, not merely to distant parts of our state, but to New York and Washington. I believe this has always been the practice. This favor would never be refused, unless the rarity and value of the book were so great, as to make it improper to take the risk of transportation to a distance. We should be glad to make the library still more useful, by making it regularly accessible to larger numbers. It must be considered, however, that this implies an increased number of attendants; and that the support of the establishment to the amount of more than three thousand dollars per annum, is a charge upon the university, which, for want of funds, is necessarily assessed on the students. . . .

1849

What is the prayer of the colleges? It is, in a word, that the legislature would allow the revenue from the public lands—*after* the limit of one million of dollars assigned by law to the school fund has been reached—to accumulate for the formation of another fund, one half as large as the school fund, to be appropriated in some fixed proportion for the benefit of the colleges. . . .

I know, Mr. Chairman, before this audience it cannot be necessary to argue the cause of higher education, scientific and literary, forming as it does the best preparation for all the departments of professional life; for enlightened statesmanship; and for an efficient application of philosophical principles to the great industrial interests of the community. Who does not know, sir, that there is not a yard of cotton cloth bleached or printed in the commonwealth, without assistance from the last results of chemical research; that you cannot construct a turbine water-wheel but by the aid of the highest mathematics; nor establish a uniform standard of weights and measures, without building upon a series of geometrical operations which began with Hipparchus? The tables by which the navigator—perhaps the illiterate navigator—finds

the ship's place at sea, are written in the very depths of the starry heavens; and the most learned eyes for ages have strained themselves dim,
through glasses of wondrous mechanism, in deciphering the mysteri-
ous characters. The electric telegraph, which brings you the daily news,
is the last achievement of a department of physical science in which
some of the brightest intellects of the last hundred years, from Franklin to Morse, have concentrated their powers of observation and analy-
sis. This step and that may be taken by an uneducated man,—may
even be the work of chance,—but the grand result is the product of
cultivated mind, strained to the highest tension of its powers. . . .

But it is still said, The schools are for the many; the Colleges for
the few; the legislature must take care of the many, the few may take
care of themselves; let those who want college education—the few—
get it as they can.

To this there are two answers. In proportion as you cheapen college
education, more will be able to avail themselves of it. You thus answer
your own objection, by granting the prayer of the memorial. It will
become the interest of the many, if you will let it. That is one answer,
although I must say, in point of fact, I cannot think even now, that
college education is unreasonably high. The charge for tuition at Cambridge, where it is somewhat higher than at the other colleges, is seventy-five dollars a year. This pays for thorough and accurate instruction given by fifteen or sixteen able and accomplished men in the ancient and modern languages, in the exact, the critical, the applied, and
moral sciences, in addition to general supervision three fourths of the
year. For the instruction of a day school in Boston, five hours in the
day, one hundred dollars per annum are paid. Gentlemen in practical
life can say where else, for seventy-five dollars per annum, they can
procure such an amount of intellectual labor to be done, requiring
equal talent and preparation, and involving equal responsibility. The
sum of seventy-five dollars per annum is, moreover, not quite half
what the service costs the university. Some things, I know, are dear,
however low the price. But when we give you, as you admit we do,
the true thing, and that at half cost, you cannot say you have had a
hard bargain.

But to the objection that school education is the interest of the many,
and college education the interest of the few, my main answer is, that
it is founded in a great fallacy. The man who makes that objection has
not formed even a distant conception of the grounds of the duty which

devolves upon an enlightened state, to educate its children. He is thinking of individuals. He forgets that it is the public, as such,—the State,
the great, complex, social being, which we call Massachusetts, the gen-
ial mother of us all,—that it is *her* interest in the matter which creates
the duty, and which gives all its importance to education, as an affair
of public concernment, whether elementary or academical. It is not to
teach one man's boy his A B C, or another man's boy a little Latin and
Greek, for any advantage or emolument of their own, that the Pilgrim
Fathers founded the college, or required the towns to support each its
school. As far as individuals, many or few, are concerned, I have just
as much natural right to call on the state to pay the bill of the tailor
who clothes, or the builder who shelters my children, as of the schoolmaster or schoolmistress, the tutor or professor, who instructs them.
The duty of educating the people rests on great public grounds,—on
moral and political foundations. It is deduced from the intimate connection which experience has shown to exist, between the public welfare and all the elements of national prosperity on the one hand, and
the enlightenment of the population on the other. In this point of view,
—I say it confidently,—good college education for those who need it
and want it, is just as much the interest of the many, as good school
education. They are both the interest of all,—that is, the whole community. It is, of human things, the highest interest of the state, to put
the means of obtaining a good school education, and a good college
education, within the reach of the largest number of her children.

In the nature of things there will not be so many who desire a college education, although it is a popular error to think that every one
goes to college who can afford it; that the *few* who go to college are
exclusively those who are sometimes invidiously called the "few." Very
many sons of the wealthy are not sent to college. Of those who go to
college, the majority are the sons of parents in moderate, narrow, and
even straitened circumstances. The demand here, as elsewhere, regu-
lates supply. All have not the taste or talent, are not intended for pursuits which require academic training. But I maintain that, for the
limited number required to meet this demand, it is just as much the
interest of the community that it should be adequately and honorably
supplied, as that the wider demand for school education should be
adequately and honorably supplied.

It is not for the rich that the public aid is wanted. They will obtain
good education, if they desire it, in one place if they cannot in another;

although it is a serious evil to have to seek it abroad. As far as individuals are concerned, it is the poor student that needs cheapened education. If he cannot get that near home, he cannot get it at all. It is not that you expect to breed up every one who goes to college into a man of eminence,—an Adams, a Channing, a Bushnell, a Webster, a Prescott, a Bancroft. The lottery of life is not all highest prizes. But you do wish to train up even minds like these in a healthy, fruitful nurture; and you wish to prepare for future usefulness in church and state the mass of average intellect. I suppose there are not above five hundred young men, natives of the commonwealth, now at college; but it is as much for the interest of Massachusetts that they should have a good education, as cheap as possible, as that the two hundred thousand who wish for it should have a good school education. It is one great interest; but if we must draw distinctions, the son of the poor man, whose life is cast in some obscure interior village, or in some laborious walk of city life, has a deeper personal interest in the matter than the son of the affluent in town and country.

24. F. A. P. Barnard Describes the Ideal College Officer, 1855

Frederick Augustus Porter Barnard (1809–89) presided with distinction over Columbia University from 1864 to 1889. He kept Columbia in step with the changes of the 1870's toward an expanded and elective curriculum. Although the old ideal of mental discipline was giving way in academic opinion to the ideal of a great university as the heart of metropolitan culture serving the people's needs, Barnard always insisted that disciplined learning and scholarship were the core of academic life. The memorial to his persistent efforts for the higher education of women is Barnard College.

In his earlier career he graduated from Yale (1828), taught there and at two institutions for the deaf and dumb, then went south to hold professorships in the University of Alabama (1837–54) and the University of Mississippi (1854–56). He was president and chancellor at Mississippi (1856–61). His *Letters on College Government* first appeared in *The Mobile Register* and were continued in a Montgomery newspaper. They expressed Barnard's sympathy for the classical curriculum es-

Frederick A. P. Barnard, *Letters on College Government* (New York, 1855), pp. 44–50; quoted in John Fulton, *Memoirs of Frederick A. P. Barnard* (New York, 1896), pp. 156–61.

poused in the Yale Report of 1828 (see Doc. 11) and for strict student discipline at a time when the University of Virginia's elective plan was being proposed for the University of Alabama.

The first trait of character which I regard as essential to the success of a college officer, under our present system of government, is one in which few are found to fail; but which rather from its occasional predominance over the milder traits, gives sometimes something like a tone of harshness to the manner, which it were better to veil; and that is *firmness.* No government can succeed which fails to command respect, and no respect can be felt for a vacillating, timorous, or irresolute superior. The hand must be at once strong and steady which holds the rein over the giddy impulses of heedless or undisciplined youth; nor will any one be found more ready to admit this necessity than those, or at least the majority of them (for most young men are ingenuous) who themselves need the restraint. But upon this point it is unnecessary to multiply words, since the absence of the quality under consideration is rarely one of the faults of an American college officer.

It may be occasionally otherwise in regard to the quality of which I am next to speak, and of which the importance is always most felt in connection with the last. I mean a *mildness of manner,* which divests the firmest government of every appearance of sternness, and clothes the severest decrees of justice with the exterior of kindness. The popular appreciation of the value of such a union of qualities is manifested in the frequent application of the maxim, which, with aphoristic brevity, associates them, as the *"suaviter in modo, fortiter in re."* . . .

Much, also, of the success of college government depends upon the exercise of a *wise discretion* by the officer, in regard to the use he may make of his own powers. Because he may punish, it does not follow that he always should punish, whenever occasion arises. It does not even follow that he should always betray his knowledge of the offense, farther than to the offender himself. By privately admonishing the individual of the impropriety of his conduct, and pointing out to him the danger to which he has exposed himself, much more good may often be accomplished, in the way of prevention and reformation, than by all the disgrace attendant on public rebuke and censure. When such a course is possible, it is obviously the wisest, as it is the kindest and most forbearing. But such a mode of proceeding may not always answer the purpose; and on this account it is, that no quality of mind is of higher value in the officer than a clear and discreet judgment. Censures, penalties, punishments of all kinds, are unavoidable necessities arising out of the imperfection of human nature; but as their main design, in human institutions, is the prevention of offences, so the less these are resorted to, consistently with the attainment of this end, the better.

It is not an unfrequent occurrence that a young man in college feels himself aggrieved by something which has occurred between him and his instructor. He may imagine that a fair hearing has not been given him in the recitation room; or he may interpret in an injurious sense words addressed to him in the hearing of his class; or he may believe that he has not been rated as high on the record as his performances merit; or some other cause of dissatisfaction may arise, to induce him to remonstrate or complain. Nor should the instructor turn from such representations contemptuously away. *Patience* should be one of his marked characteristics; and he will probably never find it more thoroughly tried than on occasions of this kind. For if he possess the qualities I have already enumerated, especially the last two named, he will have been steadily laboring against the very errors which he sees thus imputed to him, and he must feel that his intention is certainly wronged, whatever impression his words or acts may have conveyed. But this must not provoke him to listen any the less patiently, or to explain any the less circumstantially, the occurrences out of which the dissatisfaction has grown, nor if he pursues such a course will he usually fail to dispel the momentary chagrin and re-establish the feeling of confidence and kindness which it had temporarily disturbed.

I need not say how important it is that the college officer, whether in dispensing censure or praise, should be actuated by no feeling of favor on the one hand, or of prejudice on the other. There exists no higher necessity in the civil courts, that justice should be meted out with severe *impartiality,* than that the same principle should preside over all the awards of college authority. No more frequent charge is advanced against the officers of our literary institutions than that they are partial. The partiality alleged to exist is more commonly one of favor than the contrary; but we hear it sometimes asserted, nevertheless, that the prejudices of officers blind them to the merits of certain individuals, or lead them to exercise toward such an undue severity. As a general rule, it may be said that these imputations are unfounded. . . .

It may be observed that the most cautious wisdom will not always preserve to the most judicious college officer the invariable and unfailing good-will of those whom it is his duty to control. Sudden ebullitions of temper on the part of excitable young men may prompt them to hasty words or acts, well suited to subvert the equanimity of any one however by nature imperturbable. Yet the *imperturbability* of a college officer should be superior to all such provocations. He should tranquilly suffer the moment of excitement to pass by; and allow the offender, under the influence of the self-rebuke usually consequent upon reflection, to make the reparation which the case demands. To allow himself to become excited, is but to widen the breach and render it irreparable; when but a single consequence can possibly follow. He who has set at defiance the authorities of the college, or treated its representative with gross disrespect, can no longer remain a member of the institution. The necessity, therefore, of *great power of self-command* on the part of a college officer is obvious; for though the occasions which may severely try it can never be frequent, yet the want of it, whenever they occur, is a misfortune for which nothing can adequately compensate.

I have but one thing more to add. To a wise college governor, *the word* INEXORABLE *will be unknown*. The faults of youth are usually faults of impulse rather than of deliberate purpose. They evince not so much settled wickedness as thoughtless folly, or giddy recklessness of disposition. Few so immature in years as are the majority of college youth are already entirely abandoned; while it is a fact almost without exception, that those among every body of students who have passed the climacteric which separates them from boyhood, have ceased any longer to require the restraining influence of college governments. The culprits, then, who are brought to the bar of college justice, are almost invariably boys whom vice has not had time utterly to subjugate, and whose consciences are not yet callous to every appeal. From such, when they repent, a considerate governor will be slow to turn unfeelingly away; nor while there remains room for pardon will he hesitate to extend it to them. He will remember that on his decision perhaps hangs the entire destiny of the offender for this world, if not for another; and no considerations but such as involve the highest interests of the entire community over which he is placed as a guardian will prevent his accepting the evidence of sincere repentance as an expiation of the most serious fault.

But were all college officers gifted in the highest degree with the qualities which I have enumerated, I do not know that it would follow that troubles would be impossible. I only know that the non-existence of these endowments, to at least a pretty large extent, leaves open a wide door for their entrance. It is true, therefore, that the existing college system is dependent for its successful operation, in a very eminent degree, upon the kind of men to whom its administration is entrusted; and this fact, if it inheres in the system only in consequence of the existence in the same system of features which are inessential to the great purposes of education and which admit of easy removal, is an evil the more to be deplored because it is unnecessary. . . .

25. Barnard Argues for Enlarged Faculty Powers, 1856

These remarks are the gist of Barnard's argument before the trustees of the University of Mississippi for putting the practical matters of instruction into the hands of the faculty. See Doc. 24.

Gentlemen, . . . you have undertaken the construction of a railway to connect the town of Jackson, Mississippi, with the town of Jackson, Tennessee. You have employed a corps of engineers. You have fixed the termini of your road and the general line of its course; but do you attempt to prescribe the details of the work of construction? You do not undertake to tell the engineers how they shall cross this river, or build that embankment, or cut that hill; that is the engineer's business. You employ engineers because they understand that business better than you. If you let them alone, they will do it judiciously. If you were to follow them mile by mile and compel them to make bridges and embankments and tunnels according to your ideas, the work would probably be spoiled. Just so in the University. You have asked us to educate the young men of Mississippi; you have appointed us because we are professional teachers and you believe we understand our business; you have prescribed the broad outlines of our work, and we have undertaken to do the work on those lines. Now, if you are to direct the details of the work at every step, you will succeed no better than you would succeed if you were to direct the engineers of the Mississippi Central in the same way. Our professional knowledge and experience will be set aside and rendered useless, and our whole work will probably be badly botched.

John Fulton, *Memoirs of Frederick A. P. Barnard*, p. 205.

Part V

FREEDOM AND REPRESSION

IN THE OLD-TIME COLLEGE

Among the most conspicuous limitations of the old-time college was the absence of institutional safeguards to the intellectual freedom of the presidents and faculties—the absence, even, of a well-formulated ideal of academic freedom. From the earliest days it had been clear that sectarianism would be one of the most powerful enemies of freedom of thought and, hence, of the development of first-rate academic work. Jefferson had warned against sectarianism, for instance, in a notable letter of 1822 (Doc. 1) to his friend Thomas Cooper. Cooper was to feel the force of these observations some years later. Having come to the United States from England in 1794 with a personal history of controversy and dissent, Cooper had become president of South Carolina College (later the University of South Carolina). In spite of his distinguished record of achievement at the college, Cooper was frequently in contention with the Presbyterian clergy, chiefly for his attacks on Calvinism, his materialist views, and his criticisms of the principle of a hired clergy. In 1831 an attempt was made in the state legislature to secure his dismissal, and in the following year Cooper presented an eloquent defense (Doc. 2) of his opinions and conduct before the trustees of the college, which was perhaps the most imposing statement for freedom of thought made by an academic man between the Revolution and the Civil War.

The notion, expounded by Cooper, that the rights of teachers were in fact an extension of an age-old struggle for freedom of thought won increasing recognition, and President Josiah Quincy incorporated an argument to this effect (Doc. 7) in the closing passages of his *History of Harvard,* published in 1840. The following year, the Michigan regents warned against "the morbid prejudices of sectarians" and affirmed that "the establishment of a collegiate institution in a free state, and the conducting of its interests, should ever be on liberal principles, and irrespective of all sectarian predilections and prejudices" (Doc. 8).

Sectarian prejudice was the cause of one of the most sensational of college controversies—the one aroused at Columbia in 1854 by the proposed appointment of the distinguished chemist Wolcott Gibbs to a newly vacated professorship. Gibbs, as a Unitarian, excited the prejudices of the clerical members of the trustees and some of their more conservative lay allies—to the growing outrage of the great diarist George Templeton Strong, who recorded almost daily his reactions (Doc. 10) to their views and stratagems. With another liberal trustee, Samuel B. Ruggles, Strong co-operated in the writing of a pamphlet, published under Ruggles' name (Doc. 11), which cogently indicted the bigotry of the old-fashioned trustees and linked this bigotry to the backwardness of the college. Both Ruggles and Strong were interested in making Columbia into a genuine university, and their dissatisfaction over the Gibbs decision must be considered not merely as a consequence of their concern for intellectual freedom but also of their desire to see Columbia provide New York City with the great university it needed. In this respect, their protest must be considered a part of a growing literature of discontent with the entire state of American higher education (see Part VI) that led to the university movement.

With the rise of sectional estrangement (Docs. 6 and 15), the slavery controversy also became a threat to freedom of thought. True, some northern institutions like Oberlin (Doc. 4) became committed to the abolitionist point of view—in itself not a desirable development, for academic freedom implies that there shall be no binding corporate commitment on controversial issues. Others, like Illinois College (Doc. 5), were endangered by their insistence on propagating abolitionist views in the face of a hostile community. In the South such agitation was hardly possible, for that section quickly closed its mind on the question of admitting open debate on slavery after 1830. Few southern academic men spoke out on the issue, but when they did they were likely to be in trouble. The mere suspicion of incorrect sentiments helped to drive Francis Lieber (Doc. 12) out of South Carolina College in 1855; and in the following year Benjamin S. Hedrick was dismissed by the trustees of the University of North Carolina for announcing his support of the Republican John C. Fremont in the presidential election (Docs. 13 and 14). Northern teachers were not immune on this count. The Michigan regents, for example, despite their noble statement on sectarian prejudice, had enough political prejudice to dismiss the Reverend D. D. Whedon from his professorship (Doc. 9) because he espoused the doctrine of "the higher law" to which most abolitionists appealed when their demands came into conflict with man-made law. In the same way Nathan Lord at Dartmouth resigned as president and trustee of Dartmouth in 1863 (Doc. 17) because of the hostility aroused toward him by his pro-slavery views.

1. Jefferson on the Effects of Religious Intolerance on Education, 1822

—Your favor of October the 18th came to hand yesterday. The atmosphere of our country is unquestionably charged with a threatening cloud of fanaticism, lighter in some parts, denser in others, but too heavy in all. I had no idea, however, that in Pennsylvania, the cradle of toleration and freedom of religion, it could have arisen to the height you describe. This must be owing to the growth of Presbyterianism. The blasphemy and absurdity of the five points of Calvin, and the impossibility of defending them, render their advocates impatient of reasoning, irritable, and prone to denunciation. . . . [The] ambition and tyranny [of the Presbyterians] would tolerate no rival if they had power. Systematical in grasping at an ascendency over all other sects, they aim, like the Jesuits, at engrossing the education of the country, are hostile to every institution which they do not direct, and jealous

Thomas Jefferson to Thomas Cooper, Monticello, November 2, 1822, Jefferson MSS, Vol. CCXXIII, Library of Congress.

at seeing others begin to attend at all to that object. The diffusion of instruction, to which there is now so growing an attention, will be the remote remedy to this fever of fanaticism; while the more proximate one will be the progress of Unitarianism. That this will, ere long, be the religion of the majority from the north to south, I have no doubt.

In our university you know there is no Professorship of Divinity. A handle has been made of this, to disseminate an idea that this is an institution, not merely of no religion, but against all religion. Occasion was taken at the last meeting of the Visitors, to bring forward an idea that might silence this calumny, which weighed on the minds of some honest friends to the institution. In our annual report to the legislature, after stating the constitutional reasons against a public establishment of any religious instruction, we suggest the expediency of encouraging the different religious sects to establish, each for itself, a professorship of their own tenets, on the confines of the university, so near as that their students may attend the lectures there, and have the free use of our library, and every other accommodation we can give them; preserving, however, their independence of us and of each other. This fills the chasm objected to ours, as a defect in an institution professing to give instruction in *all* useful sciences. I think the invitation will be accepted, by some sects from candid intentions, and by others from jealousy and rivalship. And by bringing the sects together, and mixing them with the mass of other students, we shall soften their asperities, liberalize and neutralize their prejudices, and make the general religion a religion of peace, reason, and morality. . . .

2. *Thomas Cooper's Defense of His Views before the South Carolina Trustees, 1832*

Thomas Cooper (1759–1839) was born in England; he attended Oxford but never received a degree, perhaps because of his unwillingness to meet the religious qualifications. After a controversial career as a scientist and philosopher, he came to the United States in 1794 with his friend Joseph Priestley. He was soon deeply involved in American politics on the Jeffersonian side, and he was among those

Dr. Cooper's Defense before the Board of Trustees, from the Columbia [South Carolina] *Times and Gazette,* December 14, 1832.

convicted under the sedition law in 1800; he served six months in prison. After some years as a state judge, he re-entered learned life as professor of chemistry at Carlisle (later Dickinson) College, from which he went to the University of Pennsylvania in 1815 after four years of service. Jefferson, who had long since been friendly with him (see Doc. 1), wanted him for the University of Virginia, but clerical opposition and the delay in the opening of the university interfered with this plan. In 1820 Cooper became professor of chemistry at South Carolina College (later the University of South Carolina) and shortly afterward became president. His anticlericalism aroused the hostility of the influential Presbyterians of the state, and his support of nullification offended unionists. An attempt to remove him from his post led to this eloquent defense of intellectual freedom. See Dumas Malone, *The Public Life of Thomas Cooper* (New Haven, 1926), chapter xi, which states (p. 355 n.) that the *Defense* "was based upon notes and recollections of the editor, verified by consultation with others present and with Cooper himself," and that Cooper's trial was held on the evenings of December 4 and 5, 1832. See also Daniel W. Hollis, *South Carolina College* (Columbia, S.C., 1951), chapter vi.

IN drawing up a brief account of this interesting trial, we have aided our own notes and recollections, by consulting others who were present, as well as Dr. Cooper himself.

After a series of incessant attacks on Dr. C.'s presumed infidelity, during the whole of the year 1831, this case was first brought before the Board of Trustees, in Dec. 1831. To insure a full attendance of the Board, it was deferred to the 16th of May, 1832. It was then put off until the regular meeting of the Board, in Dec. 1832. At the meeting of 16th May, Dr. Cooper moved that his trial and the proceedings relating to the charges against him, should be held in public. This was agreed to by the Board.

On the 3d of December, 1832, the Trustees met, but not in full Board: the Trial was again put off to the evening of the 5th, and adjourned to the Hall of the House of Representatives; on which, and on the succeeding evening, Dr. Cooper made and closed his defence. The proceedings occupied altogether about four hours, including both evenings.

The charges, in number three, brought against this gentleman, were in substance, that by various publications, such as his *Political Economy,* his *Letter to any Member of Congress,* and his translation of *Broussais on Insanity,* he had unnecessarily advanced opinions respecting religion, offensive to the parents of Students committed to his care, and to large classes of citizens, and injurious to the interests of the College: AND, that he had at lectures, and on other occasions, in-

terfered unnecessarily with the religious opinions of the students, and
inculcated upon them doctrines contrary to those in which he knew
they had been educated, and offensive to their parents and guardians.

In support of these charges, the books above mentioned, were at a
former meeting produced and passages read; and a letter also was
read from one of the students, containing averments of the last part
of the charge. This letter was, not on oath, nor was any examination
had of the writers; and it was furnished by Dr. C. himself, on the
evening of the 5th. Dr. Thomas Taylor, who sent this information, did
not make his appearance to support it, and he was positively contra-
dicted by six several witnesses present on the occasion referred to.

The evidence of students, summoned by the Trustees in support of
the charges, and by Dr. Cooper in his defence, having been taken on
oath before Judge Martin, and Col. Preston; and being sealed up when
taken, was read on the evening of the 5th December, 1832. When the
reading of the testimony was finished, Dr. Cooper was called on to
make his defence.

He began by stating that this was a new scene in Republican America—and would furnish a new page in the history of South-Carolina.
He stood there an accused person, before a court of ecclesiastical inquisition, sitting under legislative authority, to inquire into all false
doctrines, heresies, and schisms, of which the President of the College
might have been *vehemently suspected*—(the usual expression of the
Courts of Inquisition—prototypes of the present.) This inquiry took
place, in the middle of the 19th century; in South-Carolina—a State
at this moment tremblingly alive to the usurpations and infractions of
our national compact by Congress, and the substitution of discretionary
jurisdiction, in lieu of the express authority of the Constitution, and
in defiance of its wholesome limitations. The Trustees (said Dr. C.)
are now called on by my accusers, to commit the very same usurpations, that they complain of in Congress.

This was not the case 150 years ago, when JOHN LOCKE of England,
in 1669, was appointed to draw up a Constitution for the colony of
South-Carolina, containing a clause "that no one should be molested
on account of his religious tenets; or prohibited, on that account, from
any office under the civil government of the colony." This Constitution, was deliberately confirmed after 20 years experience, in 1689, and
declared to be the constitutional law of the colony forever. He stated
that the Test act of England had passed in 1678, and the revocation

of the edict of Nantes in 1688. The liberal constitution of South-Carolina, attracted hither those who revolted at religious persecution in England, as well as very many of the oppressed Huguenots of France; greatly to the advantage and prosperity of the colony. In 1690, John Archdale, a quaker, was chosen Governor of the colony, and served with exemplary fidelity and reputation.

Dr. Cooper hoped, that no descendant of the Huguenots, who had hitherto ranked among our most respectable citizens, would disgrace himself and his ancestors, by appearing among the persecutors on the present occasion.

Far different, however, was the case now: the march of mind had been retrograde; and he now appeared before a court of ecclesiastical inquiry, to defend himself for holding opinions which the evidence that accompanied them had forced upon his conviction, and which the constitution of the United States and of this State, had guaranteed the right to profess and avow. He then enumerated briefly, the substance of the arguments on which he proposed to rely; but which, not having time during that evening to dwell upon so fully as his case required, he craved time till the succeeding evening for that purpose, which was acceded to.

On the succeeding evening, in the hall of the House of Representatives, which was crowded with members, and townsmen, and citizens from the country, Dr. Cooper about a quarter past 6 began his defence in chief. The arguments he dwelt upon were substantially as follows, to wit:—

That the charges brought against him, must be proved as laid: that accusation was of itself no proof; that, if convicted, he must be convicted on the testimony produced; that the two facts, of his opinions being offensive to large classes of people, and to the parents of the young men; and that, these, his opinions, had been injurious to the college, were facts, not to be assumed, but to be proved. He appealed to every trustee who had heard the testimony read, whether there was one syllable of evidence, that had the least bearing on either of these two facts, or any attempt to shew that the publications referred to, had been circulated in this State. The only substantial point of inquiry for the Trustees, was, had Dr. Cooper's opinions lessened the number of the students? He stated it as a fact officially known to every Trustee at the Board, that, during the year 1831, when the presses teemed with pamphlets against him, and the papers throughout the State with weekly invective, a greater number of students had applied for admission into college than had ever been known before, except on one occasion. He called upon every man who had heard that testimony read, to say, whether it was not, in every part of it, and from every student examined without exception, one continued and ample panegyric on his caution, his impartiality, his faithful discharge of duty, and his total abstinence from all interference with the religious opinions of the young men under his care; every one of whom when examined, declared upon oath, that Dr. Cooper was accustomed, on all occasions, to direct the students that it was their duty, while at college, to abide by the religion of their parents; and that he never did interfere in any manner, with their religion, nor had they ever heard that he had done so. He concluded this head, by calling on any Trustee, to point out one sentence in the whole of the evidence thus taken, that could be adduced in support of the accusations, or any of them. He denied that any court of law would send such evidence to a jury; and he demanded of the Trustees, as his matter of right, a judgment, as in case of non-suit.

2dly. He denied the jurisdiction of the board over publications not made in South Carolina. He contended that, whether these publications were issued at London, or Constantinople, or Pekin, or New York, or Washington, was immaterial. The board had no jurisdiction beyond the State. And he proved from evidence formerly given before the board, coupled with the declarations of Gen. Blair, and a member of the board, that the "Letter of a Layman," and "Broussais," had never in point of fact, been published by Dr. Cooper in South Carolina. That, as to the passages referred to in his Political Economy, they related not to religion, but the ministers and dispensers of religion; not to doctrines, but preachers; and the question was not a theological, but a statistical one, connected with the subject of political economy, and related to pecuniary expedience alone. At any rate, every Quaker throughout the Union, had held during 150 years, and do now hold, the same opinions with Dr. Cooper, on this express point.

He went on to give a history of the numerous attacks on him without the least provocation, and without reply, from the very time when he first came to South Carolina, to the present day. He showed, also, that the present accusations had already been made before the Legislature some years ago, on presentment of a grand jury; referred to a committee; considered and dismissed, as without foundation. That the accusations, therefore, now prepared, had already passed *in rem judicatam,* and he was entitled to be free from them; unless it was intended to harrass him with annual applications to the legislature, on charges already decided.

He stated that all these attacks were manifestly and on the face of them the attempts of the Calvinistic Clergy and their adherents, to monopolize all the seminaries of education in the United States, and to advance beyond the power of opposition, the political predominance of that class of Sectarian Clergy. All this was too manifest to be doubted. It was the same kind of attempt, to monopolize for that sect, the home market of ecclesiastical dominion over, and the supply of teachers to schools and colleges, which the manufacturing monopolists had succeeded in establishing.

He appealed to every trustee, whether it was not notorious to the public, that all the opinions now complained of, were held and avowed by Dr. C. at the time when he was elected president. His previous publications, his connection with Dr. Priestly, and with Priestly's opinions, were known to every Trustee, when he came here. His defence of Materialism was published as early as the year 1789.

He contended that every opinion complained of, as held by the President of the College, had long been held by large classes of the most respectable citizens of the United States, and were not novelties introduced by himself.

His opinions as to a *salaried Clergy and public prayer,* were held by Wm. Penn and the whole body of Quakers; by your own John Archdale, the subject of Dr. Ramsay's panegyric in the history of South Carolina.

His opinion as to *Materialism,* by all the fathers of the christian church, for some centuries after Christ; by all the Priestleyans and Unitarians in England and this country; some of the most eminent of modern divines of the Episcopal Church; by Law, Bishop of Carlisle; by Watson, Bishop of Landaff; and this doctrine is, at present, a subject of controversy between Mr. Balfour, of Charlestown, (Mass.) and Professor Steuart of Andover. That it is the opinion of those eminent physiologists; Cabanis and Broussais of Paris; Lawrence, of London; and McCartney, of Dublin. That it was the opinion avowed also by Thomas Jefferson. It is known to have been held by Dr. Rush; and must of necessity in a very few years, become the prevailing opinion of every physiologist, if it be not so at this moment.

That the *Sabbath is not a day of religious observation under the*

Christian dispensation, is well known to be the opinion of almost every Divine of eminence in England and this country; and is so held by Dr. Paley, whose works are text books in this College, under direction of the Trustees.

That as *to the Pentateuch,* of which the discussion was rendered unavoidable by Professor Silliman, no man who has duly attended to the scriptural and historical arguments, on both sides of this question, can possibly believe that the Pentateuch, *as we now possess it,* was the writing of Moses. Dr. Cooper went so far as to declare, that, he would scruple to give credence to the oath of any man, who would, after full examination, deliberately say that it was so.

6. Dr. Cooper then proceeded to shew, that all these obnoxious opinions were, in fact, propagated by the Legislature of South Carolina as well as by Dr. Cooper; in as much as they are all to be found in the Rev. Dr. Channing's panegyrical view of the theological tenets of the poet and republican John Milton; to be found (as it ought to be) in the Legislative Library.

Suppose a Legislator were to ask me, (said the Dr.) "who propagated among the people the dangerous Heresies? They are laid at your door." My reply would be, *mutato nomine de te fabula narratur.* As Nathan said unto David, thou are the man! They are your own Heresies, propagated under your authority, recommended by your sanction, found in your own library.

He then read from that review, the opinions of Milton—
Denying the creation out of nothing.
Denying the immateriality and separate existence of the Soul.
Denying the propriety of a separate order of men, like the Clergy.
Denying the propriety of pecuniary pay given to the Clergy.
Denying the obligation of public prayer; and of the modern sabbath.
Insisting on the *right* of free discussion.

Dr. Cooper referred also to the very strong argument of Dr. Channing against the calvinistic principles of the class usually stiled *orthodox,* and the elaborate defences of Unitarianism in that book. He stated, that Dr. Channing was, by common acknowledgment, one of the most eloquent, able, and learned divines of the United States. He asked then, whether these were not accusations against Wm. Penn, John Archdale, John Milton, Benjamin Franklin, Thomas Jefferson, Dr. Rush, Dr. Priestly and Dr. Channing, as much as against Dr. Cooper? and whether it was a crime in the President to hold opinions in common with such men? He declared that he did not pretend to advance his own opinions as true, but as the opinions which, whether true or false, had been forced upon him, by the evidence to which he had been subjected; he had no doubt his adversaries were equally honest and justifiable in holding their own opinions, which must of course, be the result of the evidence to which they had access. They had as much right to their opinions as he had to his own; but neither of them had any right to be offended with the other, for opinions which did not depend upon the will, but were forced on our conviction, by the evidence which accompanied them. In proportion as that evidence was complete, the decisions and the opinions would approximate to truth. If imperfect in material points, the result would be error. But every person was irresistibly compelled to decide according to the balance of evidence actually presented to his understanding. Error of opinion therefore, could be no crime; for it was involuntary; and for the same reason, no cause of offence to others. If a man differs in sentiment, from his neighbour, his neighbor differs from him; and it is a subject of mutual amnesty, not of mutual complaint, or anger, or hostility.

This matter (says Dr. C.) has been misunderstood. A man can utter what he pleases: his organs of speech are under his control: he can *say* that an apple is an oak tree, or that the propositions of Euclid are all false; but he cannot *believe* this. Belief is the result of evidence addressed to the *understanding;* the WILL has no control over it; a Jury may deliver a false verdict knowing it to be so, but it is not in their power to believe it true. In belief or unbelief therefore, there is neither merit or demerit, for no man can avoid the result of evidence actually presented.

Dr. Cooper then took occasion to descant on the Charge that his opinions were offensive, to large classes of the community; and on Judge Huger's assertion in the Legislature, that unpopularity was of itself a sufficient cause of removal from office.

He asked who could point out any Reformer, against whom the same objection had not been made? Aristides was banished, Socrates was put to death, because their opinions were offensive and unpopular with the populace and the clergy of the day. Jesus Christ was crusified at the instigation of the clergy, on a charge of blasphemy; the apostles were accused of having turned the world upside down; Wickliffe and the continental reformers were persecuted, because their opinions were unpopular. Biddle was imprisoned, Servetus was burnt, Gallileo immured in a dungeon, his disciple, the Baron de Linck, was condemned to death at Turin, Locke was driven in exile, Buffon and Laurence were interdicted; all, because their opinions were, not untrue, but unpopular. They were heretical and heterodox. Thinking with the wise, they rejected the fashionable system of prudent falsehood, and would not stoop to profess with the vulgar. They uttered boldly what they honestly believed to be true, and therefore useful to their fellow men.

Christendom was once Pagan: it is now now [*sic*] what writers are pleased to call Christian. In the Popish part of it, Protestantism is unpopular, and a crime; in the Protestant part of it, the Roman Catholics are equally obnoxious.—England was once Pagan, then Papist, then Protestant, then Papist, then Protestant again. Each party, when uppermost, committed acts of murderous cruelty on their opponents, because their opinions were offensive and unpopular.—England was once Independent, Presbyterian and Calvinistic; in a year or two, it became Episcopalian and Arminian; it is now in a great part Unitarian. Massachasetts was once Puritan, Calvinistic and Orthodox; it is now Unitarian and Heterodox. Who can tell what sectarian variety will be the predominant and popular doctrine in South Carolina, five years hence?

Popularity at one time believed in ghosts, in witchcraft, in miracles, in apparitions, and the second sight. Such was the popular belief with Lord Hale, Sir W. Blackstone, Dr. Johnson; who believes them now? The geology of the Plutonians, now universally adopted in Europe, was extremely unpopular, a few years ago, at Edinburgh, as it is now at Yale. The Manchester rail road had to contend with unpopularly [*sic*] for some years. Navigation by steam, was in his time, denounced before the American Philosophical Society as chimerical, so was the modern doctrine of combustion in England.

When I wrote and published *Consolidation,* (said Dr. C.) I became so unpopular, on that account, that two public proposals were made, to remove me from the Presidency.—When in my speech at the Anti-Tariff meeting at Columbia, in June, 1827, I asserted, that if the system so popular at the North, of making the South a tributary, was persisted in, we should, by and bye, be driven to *calculate the value of the Union* to our section of the country. You all know the torrent of abuse thrown on me, for that prophetic expression, from one end of the United States to the other.

Look at your own proceedings. Is Nullification even yet a popular measure? Is not the abuse thrown on you, unmeasured and unqualified? Have you yet persuaded your enemies, that a law enacted by incompetent authority is null and void, and is no law binding upon others? That any man may, and honest men ought to oppose it? But will South Carolina be deterred from what is right, through dread of its being offensive or unpopular with the ignorant and interested? No: her march is onward; and the abuse heaped on her by the men who vociferate *"unpopularity,"* will be unneeded and forgiven; for those who abuse her, like the populace at Jerusalem, know not what they do.

I am not ignorant that cautious and experienced men of the world, who look exclusively to their own successful standing with the public, regard as imprudent, dangerous and unwise, all those persons who brave public prejudice, and render themselves, by so doing, unpopular. It is a serious misfortune to run half a century ahead of the knowledge of the day; and if a man is bent on doing this, he should make up his mind to meet the consequences, and count the cost. Men of moderate intellect disapprove, the timid are alarmed, foes are excited, and friends stand aloof. A man, so determined to abide by Truth, through evil report and good report, must be content to brave the pity of some, the sneers of others, and the rancerous hatred of all who live and prosper by existing error. I am not blind to all this; but the prospect of becoming the instrument of good to mankind, and the cheering of a man's own conscience, are of no small value when honestly earned. The pamphlet entitled *Consolidation,* was, in this point of view, an act of imprudence; an accusation which has been, and still is brought against every proceeding of the State Rights Party, by their more cautious opponents. This therefore is a dart, that my political fellow laborers are not entitled to cast at me.

That no one ought to oppose existing error, but those who are able to afford the risk, is an established maxim of worldly prudence; most sedulously inculcated by every one who profits by existing error, because it withdraws from opposition nineteen-twentieths of their opponents. Is it a maxim for the *People* to adopt?

Let me now suppose a case: that you have a President of the College, of known talents and extensive acquirements; who possesses the difficult art of communicating knowledge to others; whose literary reputation is established; whose manners are conciliatory; whose morals are unexceptionable, and his long tried course of conduct, unimpeachable—

would you reject these qualifications, because some of his speculative opinions were unpopular to a portion, and that not a large one of his fellow citizens? If he has a right to claim popularity for qualifications useful and substantial, will you reject him on account of *"the color of his mule, or the cut of his cravat?"* I should hope the gentlemen appointed to preside over the highest literary institution of the state—whose duty it is, not to follow public prejudice, but to counteract the tendencies of ignorance, and to lead public opinion to enlarged and liberal views of the prospect before us—would hardly condescend to make such a sacrifice on the altar of popularity. Offensive? Who has a right to be offended at the speculative opinions of Dr. Cooper? Dr. Cooper asks such a man, "what right sir, have you to be of a different opinion from me? By the same right, I differ from you." Offensive! Are the Constitutions of the United States and of our own State, to be sacrificed to the ignorant prejudices of men who have never taken the trouble to read them? Of men who know not what spirit they are of? Dr. Cooper takes no offence at their differing from him; he would feel himself degraded if he did: why should they be offended because he does not see sectarian questions in the same light that they do? Is not the press open to both sides, and is not the tribunal of the public, the proper court to try these questions? Those only resort to obloquy and abuse, and call in the aid of the civil power, who feel themselves in the wrong—who are angry, because their cause is weak; and being unable to conquer by argument, call aloud upon the civil authority for pains and penalties on their opponents. But the public have learnt at last, that their own interest requires discussion, wherever there is doubt; that persecution makes no converts; and that a cause which trembles at the slightest breath of inquiry, may be safely permitted to stand or fall as unworthy of support, if it cannot support itself.

If I am (says Dr. C.) to avoid unpopular and offensive opinions, which change their character and costume almost every year, give me, if you please, under the authority of the Board, an index expergatorius for the year; furnish me with a chart of my annual voyage, so that I may avoid the rocks, and shoals, and breakers of what is called heterodoxy. Orthodoxy means always the opinions of those who hold their own opinions to be true. Orthodoxy, said Bishop Warburton to Lord Sandwich, is my Doxy: Heterodoxy, is another man's Doxy.

8. Dr. C. then proceeded to state, that it was the universal law of every civilized community, that all contracts deliberately settled and

agreed upon, should be punctually performed; that no party had a right to add clauses, conditions, or provisoes, of which no notice was given when the contract was entered into. No party can, at his own good will and pleasure, make a new contract, in despite of the other: or add, alter, or interpolate any clause or proviso, to serve his own temporary purpose, and force it on the other. 1 Kent's Comment. 393.

Does the contract of Dr. Cooper with the Trustees contain any prohibition as to uttering or publishing, or avowing, defending, or professing, any speculative opinion whatever? Would the Trustees have had any right, under the Constitution, to have insisted on such a condition, or to have made any discrimination or preference? Most certainly, if any such clause or condition had been proposed, Dr. Cooper would have rejected it at once. He would not, in such case, have been here now. The very proposal, by the Board, or by any member of it, would have been a crime.

9. To make that an offence now, which was no offence when Dr. C. accepted of his present situation, amounts to the enactment of an *ex post facto* law; do the Trustees claim the right of constituting new offences, at their own good will and pleasure, and of punishing them as they see fit?

10th. Dr. Cooper then proceeded to deny the right of the Board to make discriminations and differences, as to the religious opinions which the faculty of the College had a right to profess and avow. If any section or description is peculiarly fostered or sanctioned, every other is prostrated and proscribed. Where can the Trustees find their authority to institute in College an established religion, or to make *any* discrimination? If they had, as they have not, the right, it would be highly expedient to use it. We have, in College, sons of Calvinists, and Universalists, Trinitarians and Unitarians, Arminians and Anti-nomians; sons of Jews, and of persons of no particular religion. What is the rule of justice and expedience in such case? Interfere with none of them: leave every opinion to fall or rise by its own value. Dr. Cooper's advice has been constant, reiterated, and uniform to the students, *as every witness examined has testified*—"follow, while at College, the religion of your parents."

It savors of unfair dealing with the Students of the College, to conceal from them, differences of opinion which they are sure to meet, when they leave it; and prohibit all insight into views and arguments, which are necessary to be known and considered, before any man can

honestly determine, where truth is to be found. This system of management, the offspring of sectarian timidity, is not to be approved.
Would it not be a fraud on the students, to teach them one side of a
question, and to prohibit or conceal all arguments on the other side?
Is this the system of Ethics that this Board will venture to avow? Do
you require a student who comes here, to commence his studies under
this organized plan of authorized deception?

11th. Dr. Cooper had intended to suggest, that this was, in fact, a
political attack of the party who now form the minority of the State.
But the voice of the people has spoken; and those who formerly
doubted will be inclined to obey. For this reason, he would urge no ir-
ritating remarks, or unnecessarily wound the feelings of those whom
he hoped to see united with the people of this State, lending their aid
to a common cause, and joining to resist a common oppression. His
inclination was, to convert, if possible, foes into friends.

12th. Dr. Cooper took occasion to examine the act of 1802, which
gave origin to this Institution. In that act, the only cause of removal
permitted to the Trustees, is *misconduct in office. Expressio unius, est
exclusio alterius.* Conduct is one thing, opinion is another thing. The
usual meaning of language must not be changed, confounded and rejected, in the construction of an enacting clause. Who ever pretended
before, that opinion meant conduct, or conduct opinion? Or how can
the profession of opinion be misconduct, if the right to profess it be
guarantied (as it is) by the paramount law of the land? To convert
opinion into misconduct, you must shew your right to control opinion; whence do you derive it? Had the Legislature committed to this
Board the charge of investigating whether Dr. C. had been guilty of
misconduct in office, (the only question which they had a right to give
in charge) it might have been determined, by an appeal to the testimony of witnesses; and all the rest of the present discussion saved; but,
as it is; charges are brought forward, which involve the religious rights
of the whole community; and compel Dr. C. to feel that he is not now
pleading the cause of the President of the College, but the cause of religious liberty, and the rights which the Constitution has guarantied to
every citizen without exception. This cause he will defend at all risks,
faithfully and fearlessly.

That the opinions objected to, as used by Dr. C. in his lectures, were
intimately connected with the subjects treated, and the doctrines necessarily advanced, or were unavoidably elicited by the occasion, *has*

been fully shewn by the testimony. They were *not* extraneous to his duty, or uncalled for by the subject and the occasion. They cannot therefore amount to misconduct, in any possible sense of the word.

13th. Dr. C. alluded, very briefly, to the very strange opinions advanced, and the objections taken, at a former meeting. But, as the gentlemen from whom they proceeded, were not present, he forbore to consider them.

14th. He then proceeded with his argument drawn from the Constitution of the U. States and of this State, to establish his right to entertain, profess, and avow, and in public or private to defend, any opinion whatever, on the subject of religion.

He said, the liberties of the American people depend on the principles that will govern the present case. If the Trustees may construe the Constitution, so as to serve a present convenience—if they may substitute their own discretionary construction, and indirectly contravene the plain meaning of the constitutional expressions—if they are at liberty to supply, at their own will and pleasure, any supposed *casus omissus,* among the constitutional provisions—if they are at liberty to mould the national compact into any form that may suit the present notions of the present Board—and make the constitutional rights of the citizen to bow down before the decisions of a temporary tribunal— if *they* may do all this, on the present occasion, why is *Congress* to be prohibited from doing the same? The same legal principles may apply to a case, where a dollar is at issue, as where a million is at stake.

Let us examine then, first the Constitution of the United States, and next, the Constitution of our own State. But before I enter into detail (the Dr. said) I would willingly make some preliminary remarks.

All sound politics, and all sound morality, like all sound science of every kind, must be built, not on any *a priori,* innate, or intuitive knowledge; but on the results of actual experience. Wisdom must be bought, and sometimes at a high price. It is well founded only, when it is founded on experience. But experience is not innate and intuitive. Many an experiment must be made and fail; many a fanciful and deceitful theory must be brought to the test of fact and trial, before we can be convinced that it is worthless. Such is the case peculiarly with the science of government. Truth is a slow traveller. It has taken mankind three thousand years to get a glimpse of one political conclusion which long and dear bought experience has pointed out, viz: that all governments ought to be instituted and constructed for the good of the many who are governed, and not of the few who govern. Theoretical writers of modern times seem, for the most part, to adopt this conclusion; but it is a truth *practically* rejected throughout Europe, and it cannot be said to be put in practice even here.

In all the Revolutions that the abuse of power have driven the people to engage in, they have changed their tyrants, but they have not changed the tyranny. Despots have been sacrificed to popular vengeance; but the despotism remained. Rays of light, gleaming through the darkness of past ages, gave birth to the Cortes of Spain, the Parliaments of France, the Magna Charta of the English Barons, the Bill of Rights under Charles the 1st. and the Revolution of 1688. But no great and leading principles, in favor of the many, were deliberately penned as the documentary charter of the *people's* rights. In England, the farce of a Constitution, much talked of, no where to be found, has at length been reduced to one principle, the *Omnipotence of Parliament;* a principle anxiously enforced, and strenuously urged, by the present abandoned majority in the Congress of the United States. This principle was distinctly laid down, as constitutional law, in Mr. Cooke's late speech; and listened to, with great complacency, by the House. It is in fact based upon the doctrine of *general welfare,* introduced by Mr. J. Q. Adams, and received with infinite satisfaction by all the federalists and consolidationists of the day. Men, with whom the government is every thing, the people nothing.

The first effectual attempt to give origin to political power, by express delegation, and to limit the extent and define the bounds of entrusted authority by a written constitution, was among ourselves. This was the result of reflection on past experience; and a measure it was, full of wisdom and happy omen. Unluckily, as no human effort is ever perfect, at the first trial, the imperfection of language has rendered our experiment defective. The ingenuity of verbal quibble has contrived to throw doubts on a part of our Constitution, where common sense and plain popular feeling would see no difficulty. Moreover, instead of making all implied powers *indispensible* to the powers expressly delegated, we have most injudiciously admitted the words *useful and proper;* affording a latitude of interpretation to perversity of construction, not foreseen by the men who penned our national compact.— Hence the door has been thrown open for discretionary interpretation; and Congress now considers a written constitution as a nose of wax—a theory to be treated civilly, but disregarded practically. Your government is now the discretion of a majority, exercised under the omnipotence of Congress; and the rights of the States, as well as of the citizen, are now held by that tenure, and by that alone. Discretionary construction adopted to suit temporary expedience, has converted this federal union of independent States, into one despotic, consolidated government: and limitations of power and jurisdiction deduced from the Constitution, are openly laughed to scorn.

I ask of you, gentlemen, is it not so? I ask of you, whether, at this moment, this be not the sum and substance of the complaints of South-Carolina? and whether congressional descretion, usurped and enforced to promote the purposes of sectional plunder, has not prostrated the Constitution through the very men who have taken a solemn oath to preserve it inviolate? And again I appeal to you, as republicans and Carolinians, and I ask, whether my accusers have not called upon you deliberately to commit the same grave offence on the present occasion, which you have so long complained of, and so steadily opposed, when committed, by Congress against yourselves? You are asked, by people who pretend to take umbrage against all those who do not adopt their sectarian theology, to set aside the Constitution of the United States and your own State; to substitute your discretion, in lieu of the Constitution; and forfeit your characters for the sake of their religious prejudices. But I know you better than my accusers do: and I have no fears while I have wise and honorable men to appeal to as my judges.

Let us take up the Constitution of the United States: if not as authority strictly technical and legal, yet as demonstrative evidence of public opinion.

By art. VI, sect. 2, this is made the supreme law of the land.

By amendment 1. *Congress shall make no law, respecting an establishment of religion: or, prohibiting the free exercise thereof: or abridging the freedom of speech, or of the press.*

Let us analyse these clauses and their expressions,

Respecting: That is, about or concerning, or relating to religious preference.

An establishment of Religion: That is, giving one set of opinions, respecting religion, a preference, by law, over another. No such law shall be passed.

Well then, if you may not enact such a law directly, can you bring about such a result by indirect legislation, by management or implication? For instance: no tax shall be paid on any article of export; but, says the majority in Congress, we will lay such a tax on the imported article, which pays for the export, that one half of the value of the export shall be forced into the public treasury, or into the pocket of the home monopolist.

In imitation of this manoeuvre, my opponents say, we will not establish by law any form of religious worship; O! no! God forbid: but we will expel from office all men who express religious opinions not conformable to our own. For all such are offensive and unpopular. This may be a clerical mode of superceding the limits imposed by the Constitution: is it an honest one?

Or, abridging the freedom of speech, or of the press; That is, nothing shall be punishable by law, which the plain meaning of the Constitution permits. It does not permit slander or libel.—Punish them: it does permit every freedom concerning religion; you cannot punish that. In my own case, whom have I libelled? the clergy? Is not the press open to them and to me? Have I libelled religion? Whose? Not my own:—there *is* no true religion but mine. Every man says so of his religion; I have the same right to say so of mine: that is Truth, which is Truth to me.

The Constitutions of our sister States recently adopted, may be considered as popular, constitutional comments on that of the United States. Here Dr. Cooper read, and referred to the Constitutions of Maine, 1819, Indiana, 1816, Mississippi, 1817, Illinois, 1818, Alabama, 1819, Missouri, 1820, and recently Mississippi, in all of which it is substantially declared, that no man whatever shall be hurt or molested, or in any manner damnified on account of his tenets respecting religion; and presenting altogether a body of testimony conclusive against all kind of legislation respecting or concerning religion. This general, this anxious, sedulous exclusion of religion from legislation, furnishes a fair comment, on the part of the people of the United States, on the Constitution of 1787, and a reasonable rule for construing it. Whether this prohibition to Congress is of itself a prohibition also to each particular state within its boundary, may admit of a doubt; but it is important to shew the perfect coincidence of opinion and feeling, throughout our continent, on these subjects.

From these premises, Dr. Cooper deduced the conclusion, that every kind of restraint on the profession, avowal, or discussion of religious tenets, was in manifest hostility, not only to the letter and spirit of the Constitution of the United States, but of the people in general, in every

State. They had furnished a commentary on that Constitution, and a canon of construction for the amendment above quoted, by which its real meaning might be reasonably and fairly settled. If so, by what authority could the trustees, as agents of the Legislature, legislate on the subject of religious opinion at this board; and frame a constitution for the government of the College, in direct hostility with public sentiment?

Proceed we now to the Constitution of our own State, 1790. It says that *"The free exercise and enjoyment of religious profession and worship, without discrimination or preference, shall forever hereafter be allowed within this State to all mankind."* Const. S. C. Art. 8.

Free exercise and enjoyment. That is, unfettered, untrammelled unchecked, uncontrolled, unlimited, unforbidden. If otherwise, is it free? Can a man be said to have the free exercise and enjoyment of his religion, if he is liable to be turned out of office for professing it? Can a man have the free enjoyment of that, which he is forbidden to enjoy under pain of punishment? Have the ignorant people who have instigated these accusations against me, ever read the Constitution of their own State; or are they aware that every legislator takes a solemn oath to protect, support, and preserve that Constitution? If a choice is to be made between the College and the Constitution, far better is it to prostrate the first than the last. The religionists have rights but they have no right to ask that the constitution shall be surrendered to be mangled at their sectarian discretion. They have no right to require of their representatives to commit perjury in support of orthodoxy.

Religious profession and worship. That is open, public avowal, at all times and every where. What is profession but *public* avowal? or worship but public worship?

Without discrimination or preference. So you may be a Presbyterian, Episcopalian or Baptist, but not a Quaker, Unitarian, Jew, or Deist. You may profess with John Calvin, or John Knox, or John Wesley, but not with John Milton, John Archdale, or John Adams. You may hold with Archbishop Laud, or Bishop Horsley, but not with Benj. Franklin, or Jos. Priestley, or Thos. Jefferson. You may believe and profess that three units added together make *one;* but if you should miscalculate and call them *three,* you are a dangerous man—begone! And this is called making no discrimination, giving no preference! And your President must conform in submissive silence to this grave mockery of the Constitution, or he is "turned out to grass!"

To all mankind. Does all mankind include Dr. Cooper? I have heard
of a classification in England, of the human race, into the men, the
women, and the Herveys; is it here, the men, the women and Dr.
Cooper? Is Dr. Cooper excluded from the expression, "of all mankind"?

In South-Carolina. So, I may profess whatever I please in South-
Carolina, but not in the South-Carolina College! Where is it laid
down, that the boundaries of South-Carolina, do not include the College? Or is it like the District of Columbia, an extraparochial locality?
The climate, in this insulated district, being essentially and exclusively
orthodox!

Remember the great and leading truth of republican policy. All assumption of undelegated, unauthorized authority, is Usurpation—to
enforce it, is Tyranny; to assume it and enforce it in plain and manifest violation of a solemn oath, is what? Not a drop in the ocean; not
the small dust of the balance; it is something more weighty and more
serious; something that one would suppose a religious man would not
hastily rush upon, even in support of what is called Orthodoxy.

Remember, this is not a country of legislative omnipotence, or uncontrolled discretion; but of defined and limited jurisdiction. You are
not permitted to act on dubious implication, or discretionary latitude
of construction. The authority you assume is unjustifiable, if it be not
plainly delegated, in words not to be misunderstood and void of all
ambiguity. Where there is reasonable doubt—room for hesitation—you
are bound not to act. *Quod dubitas ne feceris.* Is there any thing like
doubt, or any latent or any patent ambiguity in these liberal expressions of constitutional right? Can any honest man put two meanings
upon them? If not, you are conscientiously bound by the plain words
of our national compact, to their fullest extent.

When the people of this State, by their constitutional representatives, met to form a political community, and to make with each other
a mutual compact, on terms of liberal equality, they met, not as Calvinists or Arminians, as Trinitarians or Unitarians, as Christians,
whether Papist or Protestant, as Jews or Deists—but as *Men*. They met,
not to form a religious, but a political community. They met, not to
regulate their expectations in another world, but their interests, as men
and as citizens, in this. They purposely excluded all religious distinctions and considerations, and agreed to permit full licence to each
other to agree or disagree on the contentious questions of theology. All

this is manifest from the expressions of the Constitution. The mutual compact thus entered into, is binding upon us; but if any legislature or any board of trustees can set it aside, because it may be convenient to do so, a national compact of citizen with citizen, is a farce; and constitutional rights are words without meaning. If the ignorance of the people, will not permit you to support your College, without annulling the Constitution, there is no hesitation which should be saved. But, in fact, your College is quite as flourishing as the difficulties of the times and surrounding competition, will permit it to be. You have no reason for complaint, in this respect; and I take for granted you will furnish no reason for complaint in any other.

Such is the defence on which I, for my own part, chuse to rest this case. I take this ground, because I am not now fighting my own battle. Every citizen of the State is as much concerned in this defence, as I am. The questions are, whether the free exercise and enjoyment of religious profession and worship, without discrimination or preference, shall forever hereafter in South Carolina be allowed to all mankind, or shall it not? Are our religious rights in whole or in part, within the power and jurisdiction of the legislature, or any agent appointed by the legislature? Are we bound by the Constitution or are we not? I contend that the Constitution—that contract made on terms of perfect equality, by every citizen with every other, has withdrawn from the legislature all consideration of religious questions. Is it so or not?

Compared to these great questions, my office and its emoluments, are the mere dust of the balance. I desire it distinctly to be understood, that, having fully and faithfully performed my duty, I have no favour to ask of the Legislature or of this Board. I am contending for objects, of higher moment than my own—for the rights of every inhabitant of South Carolina; nor will I, from any risk of what may happen, yield one iota of the great trust which an ignorant and ill-judging coalition of politicians and religionists have thought fit to throw upon me.

I go further: if the Constitution by which you are bound, had not included one syllable touching the religious rights of the people, they would have been as sacred and as binding, as they are now: for they were so, before a Constitution was thought of. Can any man whatever, possess the right of sacrificing to another, for any consideration under Heaven, his obligations to his Creator, his rights of conscience, his duty to promulgate whatever he believes to be useful to his fellow men and true in itself? Can any man voluntarily contract with his fellow men, for any consideration under Heaven, that he will live on, a time-serving hypocrite, and a deceiver of those who put confidence in his declarations? His religious obligations, are anterior to, and independent of all social compact; and profligate and immoral must that contract be, that would annihilate them. The declarations of the Constitution therefore, are not enactive, but declaratory; and every honest and wise man, must feel the honesty and wisdom that dictated them.

Sir, this Board is acting as the agent of the Legislature in this affair: and I claim from them and from you, for myself and all other citizens of this State, the right of entertaining in private, and professing and defending in public, peaceably, by all fair and reasonable argument, any opinion whatever on any subject whatever without exception, within the illimitable extent of human inquiry. I claim it as one of the *rights of man,* before political constitutions were invented or proposed. I claim it as a right clearly and fully guaranteed by the Constitution of the United States, and of this State in particular. A right, that cannot be refused or withheld without prostituting the Constitution of the Country at the foot of undelegated, discretionary authority.

Sir, this is not a day when the right of free discussion is to be submitted to a licenser. This is not a day when the human intellect may be required to bow down before the presumptuous ignorance of civil authority, as the sufficient Judge of all possible controversies. No sir: the *tribunal of the public,* is the only Court of Appeals in the last resort; and fact and argument, with full freedom of discussion to all the parties before that court, are the means by which Truth seeks to obtain its decision in her favor. The tide of public opinion long checked by the ignorance of past ages, is returning with irresistible force toward the vast ocean of unlimited inquiry; and no puny effort of civil despotism or religious fanaticism can turn it from its course, or set bounds to its progress. To this Board, Sir, of well informed and honorable men, I can safely state this feature of the 19th century; for you are well able to appreciate its correctness, and prepared to act according to your honest judgments, on these most manifest signs of the times. Experience has settled the rule, *where there is doubt, let there be discussion.*

I have now, in this great question, done my duty, faithfully I hope, and fearlessly, to my fellow citizens and myself. I leave you, gentlemen, to do yours.

During the course of Dr. Cooper's speech, the plaudits of the multitude who attended as auditors and spectators, threatened to interrupt the business of the evening: but they were checked and silenced by a remonstrance from the President of the Board.

On the evening of Saturday the 8th, the Board of Trustees met in the College Library, and

Resolved, That no charge against Dr. Cooper, shewing that his continuance in office defeats the ends and aims of the institution, or authorizing his removal, has been substantiated by proof; and that the charges against him, be therefore dismissed.

3. Julian Sturtevant on the Anti-intellectualism of the Evangelicals in Illinois in the 1830's

Sturtevant (see Doc. 5, and Part III, Doc. 22) fought consistently to loosen the grip of sectarian control upon Illinois College.

At the time of which I am writing the only congregations sustaining regular Sabbath services in Jacksonville [Illinois] were the Presbyterian and Methodist Episcopal. The Methodists, who were far the more numerous, worshipped in a large private house. The third Sabbath after my arrival the Presbyterians expected to use the court house instead of the school-house then undergoing repairs. The Methodists generally occupied the court house for their quarterly meetings. Hence there arose a collision of appointments for which no one in particular was to blame. On Sabbath morning I found the court room in which I expected to preach already occupied by the celebrated Peter Cartwright and a large congregation of Methodists. Of course I had no alternative but to take my seat with the congregation and join in the worship. As it was a quarterly meeting the Lord's Supper was to be observed after the discourse. Under such circumstances one would naturally have expected a tender evangelical sermon, full of those truths which commend themselves to every Christian heart. Judge my astonishment at hearing instead a bitter attack upon Calvinism, or rather a caricature of that system, held up now to the ridicule and then to the indignation of the hearers. It must have been known that there were many Presbyterians present. Mr. Cartwright could hardly have been ignorant of

Julian M. Sturtevant (ed.), *Julian M. Sturtevant, An Autobiography,* pp. 161–63.

the fact that the man who had come here to lay the foundations of a college was one of his congregation, and yet he took particular pains to ridicule collegiate education, repeating the already stale and vulgar saying: "I have never spent four years in rubbing my back against the walls of a college." Mr. Cartwright himself must have greatly changed his views when, thirty years later, he accepted with apparent satisfaction the title of D. D. and was generally called Dr. Cartwright.

I left the court house at the close of the service with many sad thoughts. Is it true, I asked myself, that in the field where my life is to be spent the Church of Christ is a house divided against itself? Am I to find the bitterest enemies of my work in a separate camp of the Lord's professed followers? Here where ignorance is so prevalent am I to find eminent ministers of the Gospel disparaging and ridiculing my humble efforts in the cause of education?

The same somber religious aspects presented themselves wherever I turned my eyes. The community was perpetually agitated by sectarian prejudices and rivalries. It was deemed wise to omit our service on a certain Sabbath for the accommodation of a few Cumberland Presbyterian families who desired to hear a minister of their own order. Of course I was in the congregation. The speaker was not "apt to teach." He was without even average intelligence or culture, and commenced his sermon with much hesitation and evident uncertainty. After speaking fifteen minutes, without any trace of connected thought, so far as I was able to perceive, certainly with no distinct propositions, he suddenly began to rant. His words were spoken so rapidly and in so high a key that few could be understood. Nothing seemed clear but the frequent repetition of cant words and phrases void of connection, all accompanied by a vehemence of tone and gesture that astonished and distressed me. He suddenly ceased, announced a hymn, prayed and dismissed the congregation. The house being densely filled and the air stiffling it was an inexpressible relief to escape into the open air. To my amazement I was assured on the way home by a lady of our own congregation, from whom I had hoped for better things, that we had heard a most excellent sermon. My cup was full! Was this woman a fair type of the people among whom my future life was to be spent? Was sect so strong that in order to prevent our community from being further divided religiously we must listen on Sabbath morning to such a shower of emptiness and stupidity? These were queries, however, to be communicated only to the one who could perfectly sympathize with me.

4. J. H. Fairchild on the Antislavery Commitment of Oberlin, 1833–34

James Harris Fairchild (1817–1902) was born in Massachusetts and taken to the Western Reserve of Ohio in his first year. He entered the first Freshman class at Oberlin in 1834 and graduated four years later. Subsequently, he studied theology and served as a tutor, then (1858) as professor of moral philosophy, and finally (1866) as president. See A. T. Swing, *James Harris Fairchild* (New York, 1907), and Robert S. Fletcher, *A History of Oberlin College* (2 vols.; Oberlin, 1943).

The plan of Oberlin originated with Rev. John J. Shipherd, in the year 1832, while he was pastor of the Presbyterian church in Elyria. Associated with him in the development of this plan was Mr. P. P. Stewart, formerly a missionary among the Cherokees in Mississippi, and at that time residing in Mr. Shipherd's family. They and their wives prayed and talked together, and prayed alone, until the work lay out before them with such distinctness that Mr. Shipherd in after years was wont, with due modesty, to refer to this conception as the pattern shown him in the mount; and it is remarkable that the "plan," brought out in his first published circular, might be taken in all its leading features, for a description of the college as it stands to-day— not that all his ideas have been realized minutely, but the prominent characteristics are here before us.

The plan involved a school, open to both sexes, with various departments, Preparatory, Teachers, Collegiate, and Theological, furnishing a substantial education at the lowest possible rates, and with such facilities for self-support as the "Manual Labor System" was supposed to present. The school was to be surrounded by a Christian community, united in the faith of the gospel and in self-denying efforts to establish and build up and sustain the school. Families were to be gathered from different parts of the land to organize a community devoted to this object. No new principle of organization or of social arrangement was proposed; but those who were ready to volunteer in the enterprise were asked to indicate their consecration to the work by subscribing to the following articles of agreement, called the Oberlin Covenant:

"Lamenting the degeneracy of the Church and the deplorable con-

---

J. H. Fairchild, *Oberlin, Its Origin, Progress, and Results. An Address . . . 1860* (Oberlin, 1871), pp. 3–15, 17–20, 22–29.

dition of our perishing world, and ardently desirous of bringing both under the entire influence of the blessed gospel of peace; and viewing with peculiar interest the influence which the Valley of the Mississippi must exert over our nation and the nations of the earth; and having, as we trust, in answer to devout supplications been guided by the counsel of the Lord; the undersigned covenant together under the name of the Oberlin Colony, subject to the following regulations, which may be amended by a concurrence of two-thirds of the colonists:

"1. Providence permitting, we engage as soon as practicable to remove to the Oberlin Colony, in Russia, Lorain county, Ohio, and there to fix our residence for the express purpose of glorifying God in doing good to men to the extent of our ability.

"2. We will hold and manage our estates personally, but pledge as perfect a community of interest, as though we held a community of property.

"3. We will hold in possession no more property than we believe we can profitably manage for God, as his faithful stewards.

"4. We will, by industry, economy, and Christian self-denial, obtain as much as we can above our necessary personal or family expenses, and faithfully appropriate the same for the spread of the gospel.

"5. That we may have time and health for the Lord's service, we will eat only plain and wholesome food, renouncing all bad habits, and especially the smoking and chewing of tobacco, unless it is necessary as a medicine, and deny ourselves all strong and unnecessary drinks, even tea and coffee, as far as practicable, and every thing expensive that is simply calculated to gratify the palate.

"6. That we may add to our time and health, money, for the service of the Lord, we will renounce all the world's expensive and unwholesome fashions of dress, particularly tight dressing and ornamental attire.

"7. And yet more to increase our means of serving Him who bought us with his blood, we will observe plainness and durability in the construction of our houses, furniture, carriages, and all that appertains to us.

"8. We will strive continually to show that we, as the body of Christ, are members one of another; and will, while living, provide for the widows, orphans, and families of the sick and needy as for ourselves.

"9. We will take special pains to educate all our children thoroughly, and to train them up in body, intellect and heart for the service of the Lord.

"10. We will feel that the interests of the Oberlin Institute are identified with ours, and do what we can to extend its influence to our fallen race.

"11. We will make special efforts to sustain the institutions of the gospel at home and among our neighbors.

"12. We will strive to maintain deep-toned and elevated personal piety, to "provoke each other to love and good works," to live together in all things as brethren, and to glorify God in our bodies and spirits which are his.

"In testimony of our fixed purpose thus to do, in reliance on divine grace, we hereunto affix our names."

These articles were thought to serve the purpose of bringing together families, devoted not only to a common end, but agreeing in their views of practical duty and in the means of promoting religious education. After a few years, however, the Covenant was mainly laid aside, being found to be too specific to serve as a general pledge of Christian purpose, and too general to be a guide to specific duty. It was often more difficult in a particular case to decide what the "Covenant" required, than what were the requirements of Christian benevolence. It seemed more wholesome and more conducive to Christian unity to shorten rather than lengthen either the creed or the covenant.

The plan arranged, a *name* was required for the school and the "colony." This was borrowed not from Oberlin the elegant scholar, but from Oberlin the Swiss pastor, representing in his self-denying and efficient life that love toward God and that sympathy with man which the founders of this school desired to establish and cherish here.

The school, although sufficiently grand in its conception to be called a university, according to the modern western fashion, was named the "Oberlin Collegiate Institute," which remained its legal designation until the name was changed upon application to the legislature in 1850. . . .

To this wilderness the original colonists gathered, embracing families from several of the New England States, and from New York and Ohio—all of New England origin. The first season "Oberlin Hall," the first college building, was erected, and in December of that year [1833] the school was opened under the temporary care of a student of Western Reserve College, J. F. Scovill. . . . The school during this introductory term, not yet permanently organized, numbered forty-four pupils, from the States of New Hampshire, Vermont, Massachusetts, New York, Pennsylvania, Ohio, and Michigan—not children of the colonists, but young people who on their own account had made their way to the school in the wilderness.

In May of the next year, 1834, the school was regularly organized under permanent teachers—Rev. S. H. Waldo from Amherst and Andover, James Dascomb, M. D., from New Hampshire and the Dartmouth Medical School, and Daniel Branch from some eastern college, with their wives, all just entering upon active life. The number of pupils the first year reached one hundred. In October the first college class was organized, and the first commencement held, or rather a "Senior Preparatory Exhibition," as the performers were commencing Freshmen instead of Bachelors. The exercises of that first commencement afforded Greek and Latin orations, a colloquy in which the vexed question of the study of the "dead languages" was settled upon an orthodox basis, and sundry disquisitions treating of various matters of literature, taste and practical duty—not one allusion to slavery or politics. Coming events do not always cast their shadows before.

In the winter of 1834-5 the Trustees first took their position upon the admission of colored students, and in the spring the Theological Department was organized, and the Board of Instruction enlarged by the accession of President Mahan and Professors Finney, Morgan, and Henry Cowles. Theological students came in considerable numbers from Lane Seminary, and the college department received large additions from Western Reserve and other colleges. Thus suddenly did the Institution spring into complete and vigorous action, outgrowing even the sanguine hopes of its founder, although his expectations were too broad to command the confidence of careful and considerate men until he had imparted to them his own enthusiasm. . . .

"THE COLONY"

To many, these were days of poverty and some times of misgiving; but in general, faith in God, and zeal in a new enterprise and satisfaction with results, saved even the weary from despondency. The aim of the founder in planting the colony was that it should always remain a quiet and retired Christian community, embracing the school, sustaining it in all its arrangements, and admitting nothing inconsistent with its interests. Such a community he believed was necessary, not only for the prosperity of the school, but to illustrate gospel principles in practical life. To some extent these ideas have doubtless been realized. The school has been established and has attained prosperity, because the colony has sustained and upheld it. Such a school, under the circumstances, or under any circumstances, would have been an impossibility without the support of a sympathizing community. . . .

The retirement of Oberlin in the wilderness may have been essential to its early growth, and was doubtless providential. It was certainly secluded, by its position, from the public gaze. At the outset no carriage-road reached it, and for two years or more the devious tracks through the forests which were called roads, were often impassable to carriages. There are probably ladies among us to-day who were obliged, in coming to the school from their Eastern homes, to walk the last two or three miles through mud and water to the ankle. Some ladies even walked from Elyria, because the road was thought impassable, or there was no conveyance at hand. But this seclusion was long since broken up. Students gathered here by hundreds from the East and the West, the North and the South. The colony advanced gradually but steadily, until it has become a wide-spreading village of three thousand inhabitants; and one of the great thoroughfares of the country, finding its track ready graded along the clay belt of Northern Ohio, has taken Oberlin in its course. Thus Oberlin has become linked to the world, and must share its fortunes.

The policy of Oberlin, too, whatever may have been "the pattern shown in the mount," has been from the outset any thing but seclusive. Those who wish the world to let them alone, must let the world alone. This Oberlin has not done, and never intended to do. The first Summer the students showed their aggressive tendencies by going out in scores three or four miles to *temperance raisings,* and by gathering Sabbath-schools in destitute neighborhoods. The first Winter the Oberlin Church sent out deputations to visit neighboring churches and stir them up to love and good works, and the students taught the district schools throughout the region. The next Summer the "Big Tent" was brought on, and a campaign of protracted meetings was commenced in the region by the President, aided by Theological students. The next Winter a bevy of anti-slavery lecturers was let loose upon the State. The world, thus rudely disturbed, in turn intruded upon our quiet, and the idea of seclusion passed away as a dream. The period of rest has not yet come.

THE OBERLIN CHURCH

A church was organized in September, 1834, upon the usual basis of churches in Northern Ohio, Congregational in structure, but connected with Presbytery. . . . In 1836 the church united with several others on the Reserve, in a movement to form a Congregational Association, and the connection with Presbytery was terminated. Several of the prominent men here, President Mahan, and Professors Finney and Morgan, had always been Presbyterian in their associations, and, with the exception of President Mahan, were not specially zealous in this movement. The movement of the church too was not the result of any sectarian impulse, but of the practical want of a freer Christian action in the performance of its work. At this very time a change was made in its Confession of Faith to adapt it to meet the approbation of all evangelical Christians. The doctrines of Election and Perseverance were omitted, and those of Future Reward and Punishment, and the Christian Sabbath were added. The Covenant was also amended so as to give liberty in reference to Infant Baptism. This change was made, not because there were many here who objected to those controverted doctrines, or to infant baptism, but to preclude the necessity of the multiplication of churches, and in obedience to a prevailing conviction that any basis for a church less catholic than Christianity itself was unscriptural. Upon this basis the church has stood and prospered until the present time, its members coming from all the evangelical denominations, and never experiencing any want of harmony from this diversity of early prepossessions. . . .

EARLY SPIRIT OF THE PLACE

From the earliest days of Oberlin there has been an earnestness and an energy of religious life in the Church which has been the secret of its power. This energy and activity were shown not merely in outward works and special revival efforts, but in deep heart-searchings and personal endeavor for higher spiritual attainments. Oberlin was the offspring of the revivals of 1830, '31 and '32. The aggressive missionary spirit which resulted from the great religious movement was the impulse which led to the establishment of the institution and the place. . . . Those great revivals were often spoken of as the dawn of the millenium, and the conviction was fastened upon the minds of those who gathered here that there was a special call for faithful labor and special encouragement in its performance. To this conviction the particular type of truth brought out in those revivals—man's moral agency, and his immediate responsibility for his own salvation and the salvation of others, had greatly contributed. This truth, then fresh and new in the churches, gave birth to Oberlin among its other results, and was at the foundation of the energy which characterized it. . . . All this tended to an intensity of religious life which the world has witnessed only at rare intervals. The churches abroad looked on with misgiving, with suspicion, with derision, and with here and there a manifestation of sympathy. The phenomenon was too startling to invite to a close examination. Good men kept their distance and called it fanaticism and heresy, and looked with confident expectation for the usual fruits of so corrupt a tree, the immoralities which heresy and fanaticism produce. Men not so good, not only anticipated but discovered these outbreaking evils, and the echoes of the reports of all sorts of enormities perpetrated here have scarcely yet died out in the land. Bad men framed the stories and good men believed them, always with sorrow, we would hope; but often the sigh was followed with the self-consoling observation, "just as we expected." One not entirely unwholesome result of this was that Oberlin was held under strict surveillance by friends and foes. Every careless or hasty expression of religious truth uttered at home or abroad, every instance of immorality transpiring within the original three miles square, every outbreak of youthful indiscretion in the school, was trumpeted and misrepresented and exaggerated until at last it crystalized in the columns of the infallible New York Observer as "the latest Oberlinism," all the natural outcome of Oberlin fanaticism. This fanaticism, when calmly looked at, was no spirit of bitterness, cursing those who held different views, no claim of spiritual illumination, setting aside the sure word of prophecy and uttering its own dreams as authoritative; it was an earnest spirit of inquiry in reference to the teachings of God's Word, a self-denying application of these truths to practical life, and a hearty recommendation of them to the acceptance of others. It was a fanaticism that sent preachers of good tidings to scattered and shepherdless flocks on the western prairies— teachers of colored schools to Southern Ohio and to Canada, where the labor was abundant and the pay was scorn—missionaries to the Indian tribes of the frozen North, and of the Rocky Mountains, to distant islands and to Western Africa. . . .

With all the intensity of thought and action in reference to religion and practical morality, the various fanaticisms which have cursed the land during the last twenty-five years have scarcely reached us here. Perfectionists as Oberlin men were *supposed* to be, the fanaticism of Perfectionism prevailed elsewhere—not here; nor did it go out from among us. Abolitionists as they *were*, the anti-slavery fanaticism and infidelity found their head-quarters elsewhere and cursed Oberlin at a distance. The prophets of Second-Adventism set Oberlin off to destruction, because there were not ten righteous to save the city. All these and seven other spirits, thought to find here a place for themselves, "empty, swept and garnished." These all had opportunity to show their claims, but they preached "another gospel." They were not received into the house, nor bidden God-speed. . . .

It may be supposed by those who were not in the midst of these early scenes, that the piety of Oberlin was specially noisy and demonstrative, as it was fervid and engrossing. Such an impression would be a mistake. There were instances indeed when the forest or the college hall echoed to a prayer which was over-loud, but these were exceptions. If the voice of prayer fell continuously upon the ear of one who traversed the hall at the morning or the evening hour, it was because the low pleading was repeated at every door. The power invoked was not that appealed to by the prophets of Baal; it was the Lord God of Elijah. . . .

There has been a somewhat general impression abroad that the religion of Oberlin in those days was ascetic in its character, and that Oberlin must have been a dim and gloomy place, somewhat after the style of the religious institutions of the middle ages. No impression could be farther from the truth. Even the *Grahamism* which prevailed at one time was not asceticism. It was merely an attempt at applied physiology—a blunder, probably; but one sustained at the time by such authorities as Professor Hitchcock at Amherst, and Dr. Mussey at Dartmouth. The whole constitution of the place, and its varied interests and occupations, precluded the prevalence of the ascetic type of religion. It is difficult to introduce practical asceticism into an institution embracing five hundred young people of both sexes, taken from the middle classes in American society, with aggressive energy pervading their very bones and all the hopes and plans of life leading them on. . . .

THE ANTI-SLAVERY MOVEMENT

The anti-slavery element was not incorporated into the original constitution of Oberlin, except as it is implied in the very idea of a Christian colony and school in a land where slavery exists. . . . The original Oberlin men, like all good men at the North, were opposed to slavery, but they did not dream that this would be one of the first topics which would disturb their quiet in the wilderness. The Colonization Society was supposed to present the only practicable means of operating against slavery; and in a discussion which took place in the Oberlin Lyceum during the first Summer, it appeared that teachers, students and colonists were all colonizationists, with the exception of Mr. Shipherd himself, and two or three students who had learned the doctrine of abolition at Mr. Monteith's school at Elyria. The prevailing sentiment was that it would never do to "let the slaves loose among us." . . . The men who undertook such an enterprise were strongly impressed with the conviction that the world was capable of improvement, and they had strong faith that they should live to see it move. It was almost necessary that such a place should become anti-slavery, when once the issue was fairly made and presented. This actually occurred in the winter of 1834–5, under the following circumstances: Lane Seminary, a Theological school near Cincinnati, had been in existence two or three years, and had collected a class of students of unusual ability and energy. Many of these were from Oneida Institute, a school which enjoyed a few years of vigorous life in Central New York. They were manual labor students, energetic and self-relying. As an indication of their spirit, it may be stated that, in going from Oneida to Lane, some of them went down the Allegheny and Ohio as hands on flatboats, and pocketed a handsome purse to begin their studies upon at Cincinnati. Among these Oneida students was Theodore D. Weld, a young man of surpassing eloquence and logical powers, and of a personal influence even more fascinating than his eloquence. I state the impression which I had of him as a boy, and it may seem extravagant; but I have seen crowds of bearded men held spell-bound by his power for hours together, and for twenty evenings in succession. Besides these Oneida students, there were others at Lane, prominent actors in the scenes to which I refer, some of them sons of slaveholders, and linked to slavery in all their worldly interests. The whole number of students there at the time was above one hundred. Many of these were not theological students, but were connected with a literary department in preparation for theology, under the charge of our own Professor Morgan. The theological Professors were Dr. Lyman Beecher, Professor Stowe, and another gentleman unknown to fame.

About this time (as early, at least, as 1833) the quiet of Boston and New York, and some other Eastern cities, had been disturbed by the startling utterances of Wm. Lloyd Garrison and his Liberator. He took issue at once with the Colonization Society, and called on all honest men to stand aloof from it, as false in principle and pernicious in its results. He enforced the duty of immediate and unconditional emancipation, as the only right and safe course. "Slavery is a sin, and ought to be immediately abandoned," was in those days the burden of his message. Men of strong anti-slavery feeling were at once brought over by his facts and his logic. Weld, too, in the quiet of Lane Seminary, was moved, and others moved with him. The students requested of the Faculty the use of the public room occupied as a chapel, for the discussion of slavery. The Faculty recommended quiet—rather discountenanced the discussion, but did not prohibit it. The students gathered in the chapel, and for eighteen successive evenings continued their debate. At the outset there was great diversity of sentiment, but in the end the anti-slavery view prevailed almost unanimously. We may well suppose that the discussion would be earnest and thorough, for there were men there whose course for life was to turn upon the result. . . .

As a result of the anti-slavery movement in the Seminary, the young men were stirred up to do something for the colored people in the city. They gathered them in Sabbath-schools, and established day schools among them, and made use of all the means at hand to elevate and advance them. . . . Movements like these disturbed the quiet of the Trustees of the Seminary, some of whom were wholly men of commerce, and understood better the pork market than the management of a literary institution. Others sympathized in the general apprehension of evil from the anti-slavery excitement.

The Summer vacation of twelve weeks came on, and the Professors, with one exception, had left for the East. The students, too, were mainly scattered. The Trustees held a meeting at this juncture, and passed a law, without any consultation with the Faculty, except the single member who remained, prohibiting the discussion of slavery among the students, both in public and in private. They were not to be allowed to communicate with each other on the subject, even at the table in the Seminary commons. At the same time the Trustees dispatched a message to Professor Morgan, in New York, that his services were no longer required. No reason was assigned him for so abrupt a termination of his relations. Perhaps they already apprehended what they soon realized, that his occupation was gone. But in the Seminary it was well understood that he was sacrificed on account of his sympathy with the anti-slavery movement. The other Professors returned to swallow, as best they could, the bitter pill which had been prescribed for them. The students returned to enter their protest against the oppressive gag-law of the Trustees, and to ask dismissions from the institution. Four-fifths of them left in a body, and Lane Seminary has to this day scarce recovered from the blow. . . .

Arthur Tappan, of New York, sent them an offer of $5,000 for a building, and the promise of a professorship, if they would establish a school under anti-slavery influences.

In December of this year, 1834, Mr. Shipherd, who was then the principal financial agent of the Oberlin Collegiate Institute, visited Cincinnati for the purpose of soliciting funds. There he met Rev. Asa Mahan, who was at the time pastor of the Sixth Presbyterian Church in the city. He had been one of the Trustees of Lane Seminary—had protested earnestly against the action which had been taken, and had resigned his place when he saw that the majority would pass and sustain the odious law prohibiting the discussion of slavery. He was in sympathy with the protesting students, and between him and Mr. Shipherd the plan was devised of adding at once a Theological Department to Oberlin, and bringing on the seceding students from Lane to constitute the first theological classes. Mr. Shipherd's anti-slavery zeal was quickened by contact with the exciting influences there; and under date of December 15, 1834, he writes, urging the appointment of Rev. Asa Mahan as President, and Rev. John Morgan, Professor of Mathematics. He also writes: "I desire you, at the first meeting of the Trustees, to secure the passage of the following resolution, to-wit: 'Resolved, That students shall be received into this Institution irrespective of color,' This should be passed because it is a right principle, and God will bless us in doing right. Also because thus doing right, we gain the confidence of benevolent and able men, who probably will furnish us some thousands. Moreover, Bros. Mahan and Morgan will not accept our invitation unless this principle rule. Indeed if our Board would violate right so as to reject youth of talent and piety because they were *black,* I should have *no heart* to labor for the upbuilding of our Seminary, believing that the curse of God would come upon us, as it has upon Lane Seminary, for its unchristian abuse of the poor slave."

This letter was addressed to the acting Secretary, and of course was communicated to the officers and teachers on the ground. The doctrine proposed was a new one, and the people of Oberlin were not prepared to embrace it at once. There were no precedents in its favor. No such thing had been heard of in the land, nor, so far as they knew, in any other land. There was earnest discussion, and intense excitement. It was believed by many that the place would be at once overwhelmed with colored students, and the mischiefs that would follow were frightful in the extreme. Men who afterwards stood manfully in the anti-slavery ranks, when the battle was hottest, and whose lives had shown that they could face duty in its most forbidding aspects, were alarmed in view of the unknown and undefined evil which threatened. Young ladies who had come from New England to the school in the wilderness—young ladies of unquestioned refinement and goodness, declared that if colored students were admitted to equal privileges in the Institution, they would return to their homes, if they had to "wade Lake Erie" to accomplish it. These same young ladies, afterward, showed their New England spirit, not in wading Lake Erie, but in stemming a torrent of abuse and reproach, which they encountered in their fearless advocacy of the cause of the oppressed. . . .

President Mahan and Professor Morgan were appointed, according to the request of Mr. Shipherd, although the platform on which they had placed themselves was not adopted.

This action of the Board was not satisfactory to Mr. Shipherd, and another meeting was called, about six weeks later, at Oberlin. . . .

When the question was finally taken the division of the Board was equal, and Father Keep, as the presiding officer, gave the casting vote in favor of the admission of colored students. The resolution which at length passed was not simple and direct, like the one proposed originally by Mr. Shipherd, but it seems the expression of timid men who were afraid to say precisely what they meant. It is as follows:

"Whereas, there does exist in our country an excitement in respect to our colored population, and fears are entertained that on the one hand they will be left unprovided for, as to the means of a proper education, and, on the other, that they will, in unsuitable numbers, be introduced into our schools and thus in effect forced in to the society of the whites, and the state of public sentiment is such as to require from the Board some definite expression on the subject; therefore, resolved, that the education of the people of color is a matter of great interest, and should be encouraged and sustained in this Institution."

The logic of the resolution is not very luminous, nor is the conclusion entirely unambiguous, but the effect was decisive and unequivocal. It determined the policy of the Institution on the question of slavery, and no other action has been needed on the subject from that day to this. It was a word of invitation and welcome to the colored man, as opposed to the spirit of exclusion which was then dominant in the land. That this decision was regarded as involving grave consequences, is manifest from the intense excitement which existed here at the time. There were no colored students at the door seeking admittance. Indeed there was but one colored person at the time resident in the county; but they were very generally expected as the result of this decision, and when, at length, a solitary colored man was seen entering the settlement, a little boy, the son of one of the Trustees, ran to the house, calling out, "They're coming, father—they're coming!"

At the same meeting of the Trustees, when the anti-slavery action was taken, Rev. Charles G. Finney, of New York city, was appointed Professor of Theology—an indication that the Institution was not about to devote itself to the single idea of opposition to slavery, but to prosecute this as one more part of the comprehensive work of Christian labor.

In the Spring of 1835—twenty-five years ago—Oberlin received the accession from Lane. The place was already *full,* and a building was extemporized for the accommodation of the "rebels" as they were called. . . .

The effect of this accession upon the Institution and the place was, of course, decided and manifest. The school was at once transformed from a Collegiate Institute—as it had been modestly called—to a University, embracing the same departments as at present, with students in every stage of advancement. Hence, the mistake has often been made abroad, of attributing the origin of Oberlin to the explosion at Lane Seminary. The Collegiate Department received considerable accessions about the same time from Western Reserve College, the Trustees of which had been exercised somewhat after the manner of the Trustees of Lane, by the anti-slavery zeal of Professors and students. Thus Oberlin incurred odium not only by its anti-slavery position, but by becoming an asylum for discontented students. If these students had been such as could well be spared by the schools from which they came, the case would have been far different; but the "glorious good fellows" of Lane, as Dr. Beecher called them, were well matched in the earnest and thorough-going young men from Hudson.

Such an amount of anti-slavery material thrown together, still warm from the crucibles where it had been elaborated, of course involved some vigorous effervescence. There was no inert matter present upon which to act. Within the circle of the forest which bounded the vision, all was life and animation. Anti-slavery principles and facts were then fresh and new. They took a strong hold upon the hearts of old and young. They were the theme of private thought, of social conversation, and of public discussion—the burden of song and of prayer. Fourth-of-July celebrations were transformed into anti-slavery meetings; and the whole ground of slavery, in its relations to morals and to political economy—to the Constitution and the Bible—was traversed again and again.

In the autumn of this famous year, just before the winter vacation, Weld came among us to lay open the treasures of his anti-slavery maga-zine—to equip the young warriors for their winter campaign; and more than twenty long, dark November evenings he illuminated with the flashes of his genius and power. Under such influences, Oberlin became, of course, thoroughly "abolitionized." . . . It was not uncom-mon for our students, as they went abroad into neighboring towns, to be assailed with abusive words, even when passing quietly along the street; and when they ventured to address a public meeting on the subject of slavery, they sometimes encountered rougher arguments than bitter words. Several of the more advanced students devoted the winter vacations to lecturing on slavery, under the auspices of the original American Anti-Slavery Society. The mobs which they were called to encounter were sometimes amusing and sometimes terrific. They found warm friends wherever they went—friends whose fidelity was often proved in the hour of peril. There are those among us who could tell some startling tales of anti-slavery campaigns. The ruffianism and malignity of the Missouri border at a later day, scarce exceeded the bitterness and mean hatred which anti-slavery men encountered in many portions of Ohio, and of which Oberlin and its students received a double portion. The terrible mobs which sometimes occurred, were, perhaps, less annoying than the low and contemptible abuse, which was matter of almost daily experience. The schools which our students taught were characterized as "nigger" schools—the churches where they preached were "nigger" churches. At length, this expressive adjective was exchanged for the prefix "Oberlin," as embodying all that was odious in abolitionism, and pernicious in religious heresy. . . .

5. Antislavery Sentiment at Illinois College, 1837

See Doc. 3, and Part III, Doc. 22.

The events just recorded placed Mr. Beecher and his immediate friends at Jacksonville in imminent peril. Our friends far and near were greatly alarmed. There was evident danger that a ferocious mob would make an immediate attack upon the head of the institution and upon the college buildings. For me and the other instructors only one course of action was now possible. Though President Beecher was the immediate object of hostility, all of us were threatened, and the very existence of the college was endangered. It was no time to discuss the action of the convention, the death of Mr. Lovejoy or the expediency of Mr. Beecher's course. He had committed no crime, and had only advocated the freedom of the press and exercised the right of free speech which belongs to every citizen of a free country. It was our duty to stand by him at whatever hazard. In this we were unanimous. Threats were abundant but no actual violence was attempted, and the excitement gradually subsided. But it left in many minds a feeling of intense hatred, not only toward Mr. Beecher but toward us all. And it should be borne in mind that these hostile feelings were not confined to such persons as generally composed the mob, but affected many individuals of wealth and social standing and even of religious reputation.

This feverish state of the community was a great obstacle in the way of the college. It greatly limited the number of our students. The secular newspapers of St. Louis were widely circulated in all the southern portion of Illinois, and were intensely hostile in their utterances concerning us. The prejudices thus excited could not be argued away, though in the progress of a generation they have been lived down. For

Julian M. Sturtevant, An Autobiography, pp. 224–26.

many years we were constantly exposed to annoyances in the immediate vicinity of the institution.

As has already been intimated, there was much anti-slavery sentiment among the more thoughtful and earnest of our students. At our public exhibitions, which occurred two or three times a year, the young men were often disposed to give free utterance to their convictions on such subjects, and neither our tastes nor our principles permitted us to repress them by any stringent restrictions. On the other hand these exhibitions were generally supervised by certain men of ruffianly habits and pro-slavery prejudices who wished to act as the self-constituted guardians of the moral and social proprieties of the occasion. The consequence was that the trustees of churches not otherwise unfriendly were reluctant to grant the use of their places of worship for our exercises, lest these gentlemen might express their feelings in such a way as to injure the buildings. The history of our town in those years is a sad story. "My soul hath it in remembrance and is humbled."

6. Emerson's Opinion of Southern Students, 1837

The *Journals* of Ralph Waldo Emerson (1803–82) here reflect the persistent hostility between the ethos of the South and that of educated New Englanders. Compare with it the reaction of Henry Adams to the southern students at Harvard in chapter iv of his *Education* (Boston, 1918, and later editions), and that of the southerner in Doc. 15.

SEPTEMBER 28

I hope New England will come to boast itself in being a nation of Servants, and leave to the planters the misery of being a nation of served. . . .

OCTOBER 8

The young Southerner comes here a spoiled child, with graceful manners, excellent self-command, very good to be spoiled more, but good for nothing else,—a mere parader. He has conversed so much

Edward Waldo Emerson and Waldo Emerson Forbes (eds.), *Journals of Ralph Waldo Emerson*, IV (1836–38 [Boston, 1910]), 298, 312–13.

with rifles, horses and dogs that he has become himself a rifle, a horse and a dog, and in civil, educated company, where anything human is going forward, he is dumb and unhappy, like an Indian in a church. Treat them with great deference, as we often do, and they accept it all as their due without misgiving. Give them an inch, and they take a mile. They are mere bladders of conceit. Each snipper-snapper of them all undertakes to speak for the entire Southern States. "At the South, the reputation of Cambridge," etc., etc., which being interpreted, is, In my negro village of Tuscaloosa, or Cheraw, or St. Mark's, I supposed so and so. "We, at the South," forsooth. They are more civilized than the Seminoles, however, in my opinion; a little more. Their question respecting any man is like a Seminole's,—How can he fight? In this country, we ask, What can he do? His pugnacity is all they prize in man, dog, or turkey. The proper way of treating them is not deference, but to say as Mr. Ripley does, "Fiddle faddle," in answer to each solemn remark about "The South." "It must be confessed," said the young man, "that in Alabama, we are dead to everything, as respects politics." "Very true," replied Mr. Ripley, "leaving out the last clause."

7. Josiah Quincy's Plea for Educational Freedom, 1840

Josiah Quincy (1772–1864), member of a family prominent in Massachusetts affairs since the seventeenth century, graduated from Harvard in 1790, served in the Massachusetts state legislature and in Congress, won fame for improving living conditions in Boston while mayor (1823–28), and presided over Harvard (1829–45) as the first lay president since John Leverett. More successful as an administrator than as a leader of undergraduates, Quincy put the law school and the library on solid foundations. His *History of Harvard,* from which this document is taken, illustrated his Unitarian viewpoint: it emphasized the university's tradition of free and liberal learning.

In Europe, after the lapse of what are called the dark ages, the means of education were directed by the Catholic clergy, who applied agents to the mind, and treated it in a manner more suited to the purposes

Josiah Quincy, *The History of Harvard University* (Cambridge, 1840), II, 444–46.

of the Church, than to its own nature. Religion and learning were taught by the same masters. They enforced the dogmas of the former by the terrors of a future life, and taught the rudiments of the latter by corporeal terrors in the present. The object and effect of this system were not so much to excite, although it had incidentally that effect, as to control the action of the intellectual principle, and so to bring it into subjection, that all its energies should be exerted in prescribed paths and directed by authorized influences. Under this system, the mind was taught just as man teaches those inferior animals, which, though possessed of muscular powers far superior to his own, he renders subservient to his purposes; making fear the chief principle of instruction, as being the best means of keeping the subject in ignorance of its own inherent strength.

After the Reformation, a more liberal system was introduced. It made its way slowly, however, in the ancient schools and colleges, even of the States which had concurred in the principles of the Reformation. The interests of the Church of Rome were not annihilated, but only transferred. The States and hierarchies, which succeeded, adopted very much the old principles, as to the mode of bringing the general mind into subjection through the instrumentality of education.

The labor of the last and the present age has been efficiently directed to soften the rigors and break the shackles of ancient discipline; to remove obstacles from the path of intellect, and to supply it with aids and encouragements. The principle of fear has been almost wholly banished from systems of education, and that of hope and reward substituted. The duty of considering science and learning as an independent interest of the community, begins to be very generally felt and acknowledged. Both in Europe and in America attempts are making to rescue the general mind from the vassalage in which it has been held by sects in the church, and by parties in the state; giving to that interest, as far as possible, a vitality of its own, having no precarious dependence for existence on subserviency to particular views in politics or religion; and, for this purpose, to place it like a fountain opened in regions far above those in which the passions of the day struggle for ascendency,—to which all may come to gain strength and be refreshed, but whose waters none shall be permitted to disturb by their disputes, or exclusively to preoccupy for purposes of ambition.

Great improvements have been made in respect to modes of education, yet the question is daily raised, whether those now in use are the best for exciting the immaterial principle into action. Many points of conduct in our public institutions of learning are made the subjects of controversy; and this will probably continue to be the case, so long as men are free to take different views of the same subject, and reason concerning it with different proportions of intellectual power and practical knowledge. Upon all the points on which this diversity of opinion occurs, the true course seems to be, to adopt changes with great deliberation; and, when adopted, to proceed with them in a just spirit, and with a fixed intent to give them a fair trial; remembering, that man is often able to conceive of a perfection, which he is not able to attain, and that many things appear plausible in theory, which, on trial, prove fallacious. . . .

8. The Michigan Regents Warn against Sectarianism, 1841

George Duffield (1794–1868), the first signer of this committee report of the Michigan regents to the state superintendent of public instruction, was a Presbyterian clergyman. He graduated from the University of Pennsylvania in 1811, served a pastorate (1816–35) in Carlisle, Pennsylvania, then went to a notable ministry for thirty years in Detroit.

The history of all collegiate institutions in this country dependent immediately on the State has shown that they have never prospered, as long as they have been subjected to the influence of desultory legislation, of the uncertainty from year to year whether any system adopted by one Legislature might not be changed the next, and of the want of an efficient Board of Trustees or Regents, of sufficient permanence, and possessed of adequate power for the responsible care and management of their interests, both literary and pecuniary. The establishment of a collegiate institution in a free state, and the conducting of its interests, should ever be upon liberal principles, and irrespective of all sectarian predilections and prejudices. Whatever varieties of sect exist in these United States, the great mass of the population profess an attachment to Christianity and, as a people, avow themselves to be Christian. There

I. N. Demmon (ed.), *University of Michigan Regents' Proceedings, 1837–1864* (Ann Arbor, 1915), pp. 210–11.

is common ground occupied by them, all-sufficient for co-operation in an institution of learning, and for the presence of a religious influence, devoid of any sectarian forms and peculiarities, so essential, not only as the most efficient policy, but also for the development and formation of the most valuable traits of youthful character, and of qualifications for future usefulness. Experiments made in other States, by catering to the morbid prejudices of sectarians, have only embarrassed the institutions of the State, and matured the growth of numerous and rival colleges avowedly sectarian. Attempts made to exclude all religious influence whatever from the college, have only rendered them the sectarian of an atheistical or infidel party or faction, and so offended and disgusted the majority of the population agreeing in their respect for a common Christianity, that they have withdrawn their support, confidence, and patronage, and left them to drag a miserable existence, till they invoked the presence and influence of the Christian religion in them. The only security that can be had for the avoidance of sectarianism, and the necessity and desirable influence of Christianity, in the conduct of a collegiate institution, intended to be the common property of the State, is to be sought in the character and principle of the men who are placed over it, and held responsible for its administration. There are men to be found in all different Christian sects of sufficiently expanded views, and liberal spirit, and enlightened minds, devoid of the spirit of bigotry and narrow prejudices of sect and of party, that can be selected and deputed to such a work, whose public spirit and philanthropy and whose love of country and attachments to the interests of their State and its entire population, will always furnish the best and only true guarantee against the evils of sectarianism. The Board are happy to state the fact, without meaning in the least to commend themselves, that while they consist of gentlemen from almost, if not all, the principal Christian sects in our State, there has nothing occurred in their individual intercourse, their deliberations or debates, or any of their official acts, which have ever elicited occasion for the expression, or even the existence of jealousy and suspicions growing out of sectarian prejudices or attachments.

All of which is respectfully submitted,

(*Signed*) GEO. DUFFIELD,
J. OWEN,
MARTIN KUNDIG,

Detroit, December 20th, 1841   *Committee*

9. *Professor Whedon's Dismissal for Advocating "The Higher Law," 1851*

Daniel Denison Whedon (1808–85), Methodist Episcopal clergyman, editor, and teacher, graduated from Hamilton College in 1828. During his professorship of ancient languages and literature at Wesleyan in Connecticut (1833–43), he opposed the radical abolitionist movement within the Methodist church, only to be dismissed, ironically, from his chair of logic, rhetoric, and philosophy at Michigan (1845–51) for opposing the extension of slavery. He later became widely known for his popular commentaries on the Bible.

See Wilfred B. Shaw, *The University of Michigan* (New York, 1920).

DECEMBER 31, 1851

Justice Pratt . . . offered the subjoined preamble and resolution:

WHEREAS, The great primary object of establishing "the University of Michigan" as clearly expressed by the people through the Act of their Legislature was, "to provide the inhabitants of the State with the means of acquiring a thorough knowledge of the various branches of Literature, Science, and the Arts," that as such Institution it is worthy of the pride and fostering care of every citizen of the entire State and whose duty it should ever be to watch and guard it assiduously [*sic*] and to see that it is not by any means perverted or directly or indirectly used for any other purpose, and especially that it is not used for the inculcation of political or religious dogmas; and,

WHEREAS, It is represented and is undoubtedly true, that the Rev. D. D. Whedon, one of the Professors of said Institution, has during a period of time past not only publicly preached but otherwise openly advocated the doctrine called, "The Higher Law," a doctrine which is unauthorized by the Bible, at war with the principles, precepts, and examples of Christ and His Apostles, subversive alike of Civil Government, civil society, and the legal rights of individual citizens, and in effect constitutes in the opinion of this Board a species of moral treason against the Government; therefore;

Resolved, That the Rev. D. D. Whedon for the reasons aforesaid be and he is hereby removed.

I. N. Demmon (ed.), *University of Michigan Regents' Proceedings, 1837–1864,* pp. 501–3.

For which Maj. Kearsley offered the following as a substitute:

Resolved, That in the view of the duty devolving upon the Board of Regents-elect to reorganize the Faculty of Arts in the University and to appoint a President, it is expedient that this Board provide for that contingency by determining the terms of the existing members of said Faculty, therefore:

Resolved, That the terms of office of the present Professors of Natural Philosophy and Mathematics, of Logic, Rhetoric, and History, and of Greek and Latin Languages in the University respectively terminate and expire at the close of the present academic year, or at such other previous time as the Board of Regents-elect may determine to appoint their successors.

Whereupon the yeas and nays were ordered and resulted in its adoption. . . .

Dr. Pitcher submitted the following resolution:

Resolved, That the example set by this Board in the freedom with which members have commented on the character and conduct of members of the Faculty renders it expedient that its sessions should not hereafter be held with open doors. Laid on the table.

10. George Templeton Strong on the Columbia Trustees and the Gibbs Case, 1853–54

The publication of the diary of George Templeton Strong (1820–75) gave to the world one of the major American personal documents of the nineteenth century. Strong, a well-to-do New Yorker and Columbia College graduate (1838), here reports the inside of the Gibbs case as seen by a liberal-minded member of Columbia's board of trustees. Oliver Wolcott Gibbs (1822–1908) was born in New York City and graduated from Columbia College in 1841. An able chemist from undergraduate days, he entered the College of Physicians and Surgeons and took an M.D., not to practice medicine, but to deepen his acquaintance with chemistry. Subsequently, he studied in Germany and France, and in 1849 he was appointed professor at the Free Academy in New York, which later became the College of the City of New York. His researches had made him a scientist of distinction, and,

Allan Nevins and Milton Halsey Thomas (eds.), *The Diary of George Templeton Strong* (New York, 1952), II, 136–39, 141, 143, 146–48, 150–55, 157, 159, 165–66, 168, 170–72.

upon the vacating of the chair of chemistry at Columbia in 1853, the liberal trustees nominated Gibbs. The board of trustees was predominantly Episcopalian, and six of its members were clergymen. Its conservative faction finally rejected Gibbs, but the issue gave rise to a dispute among the trustees and alumni and in the city of New York that had profound repercussions. The liberal trustees did not relax their intention to improve instruction at Columbia and make of it a true university (see Doc. 11). As for Gibbs, he moved to Harvard to take the Rumford chair in chemistry and went on to many years of distinguished scientific work. See Milton Halsey Thomas, "The Gibbs Affair at Columbia," unpublished M.A. thesis, Columbia University, 1942, and Richard Hofstadter and Walter P. Metzger, *The Development of Academic Freedom in the United States* (New York, 1955), pp. 269-74.

November 21 [1853]. Mr. Ruggles is much exercised at present about a very difficult problem:—viz., the exact part that physical science should play in education.

November 22. . . . At Columbia College last night they hinted Jem Renwick's resignation and appointed a committee to look up a successor. Now we must decide what is to be done about Wolcott Gibbs. Draper will put in for a chance, and then George Anthon will come down on him for his share in putting Anthon out of the University on the ground of his being an alumnus of Columbia College. The election of trustees was postponed. It seems that the two parties, fogy and progressive, are so nearly tied that my election is quite an important matter, and King, Ruggles, Hoffman, and others are straining hard to carry me in; Van Wagenen, Wells, Morris, and the other fossils opposing ponderous inertia to keep me out. I would not have consented to stand if I'd thought I should be battled over in this way like the body of Patroclus. I don't care sixpence how it goes. . . .

December 5. Meeting of the Trustees of Columbia College this afternoon, at which I was elected to one of the three vacancies in the Board, Dr. Wainwright and a certain Presbyterian or Dutch Reformed Dr. Beadle being put into the other two. So I was certified by Ruggles and Ogden Hoffman as I walked uptown this afternoon, and by Professor Anderson tonight at a St. Luke's Hospital meeting. On many accounts much gratified by the result. . . .

December 7. . . . Knox has written to Gibbs, in a candid and fair way, to know whether he holds the "Divine Plenary Inspiration" of the Bible *quoad* physical science, of course, in reference to the Columbia College professorship. Gibbs's reply, which I saw tonight and which will be sent in without change or addition, is excellent in con-

densation of thought and language and in honesty and clearness. The
position he takes is impregnable, viz.: that the material world is itself
a Revelation, and that where it seems in conflict with the other, the
necessary inference is that *one* is misunderstood. . . .

December 15. . . . Much concerned about Gibbs's prospects for Renwick's vacated chair. He will be attacked on the ground of Unitarianism, and certainly with some force. But (1) his duties will not
carry him into contact with *transcendental* physics. And I cannot think
that talking to boys about NO_3 and CHO_2 and Fer Cy Ka has any
connection (for practical purposes) with theological truck. (2) He has,
in fact, no theological position at all. He is a Unitarian from the accident of education. It is not suggested that we should require a truly
religious and devout man for the place, and Gibbs is nothing more
than nine-tenths of those who are not so described, nothing less or
worse, I should have said. (3) A Unitarian is not much if at all farther
from right than a blue Calvinist, and from his belief being simply
negative and his mind blank on religious subjects, is much more likely
to come out *right* and to react into the church, if at any time the religious instinct be developed within him. . . .

December 19. Spent the morning chiefly *in re* Wolcott Gibbs. N.B.
My efforts for him are strictly disinterested. Personal feeling influences
me but little. Gibbs is a cast-iron man who would take little trouble
for me, or any one else, *I think*. But his transcendent abilities and energy must be secured for Columbia College if any exertion of mine can
put him there.

Took my seat in the board at two this afternoon. Session of two
hours. Not much done, save to discuss the arrangements with John C.
Stevens about the lots most improvidently leased to him on the north-
west corner of the Green, where his house is, and to illustrate the
dominion of fogyism in the board, and the necessity of concert among
the progressive people to meet the organized inertia of Betts and his set,
who control the Standing Committee and, through it, everything. . . .

December 27. . . . Anderson tells me that Knox concedes Gibbs's
superiority to Schaeffer, but can't understand his views about "divine
plenary inspiration of the Scriptures" and means, therefore, to vote
against him. If so, it's a bad business as he'll probably carry three votes
at least with him. Gibbs's friends must do their uttermost. I shall despair of the college being ever redeemed from fogyism if Schaeffer is
elected. . . .

About 120 alumni now registered as Gibbsites. Doubt whether they will produce much impression on Clement Moore and G. W. Morris. . . .

January 8. [1854] . . . Of course, the leading idea of the past ten days has been Gibbs. No time to go into particulars, but there will be "a murder grim and great" before his defeat and all the chain of consequences are disposed of. Result of election uncertain and unpromising. We meet tomorrow at two; the committee will report simply the papers in its hands, without recommending anything. And it may be that the *Fossil* party, having a majority (Hoffman can't come down from Albany), will insist on an election at once. If so, we must talk against time or use any other lawless weapon chance may provide. But I don't think they'll be disposed to take that course—and that Schaeffer won't be elected is far less uncertain than that Gibbs will.

Certain resolutions will be offered that will make the fur fly a little, the ayes and noes being called for, and an intimation made of a committee of inquiry from the legislature if they are voted down. . . .

January 9. . . . Now for Columbia College. We met at two P.M. Mr. Ruggles offered his resolutions, and a storm followed such as was foreseen. All the six clerical members of the board pronounced distinctly and expressly against them and *against Gibbs* on the sole ground of his religious belief, and the resolutions were "indefinitely postponed" on motion of Dr. Spring. Election postponed to a week from Tuesday. Gibbs's election no longer to be hoped, but I think Schaeffer may be defeated, who is utterly unfit for the place. Wainwright, Haight, and one or two men of Gibbs's opponents won't vote for Schaeffer, if they can help it. . . .

I am most thoroughly disgusted with the action and language of the clerical members of the board of Columbia College, including the three members of the clerical staff of Trinity. The resolutions offered and objected to by them were, in substance, that inasmuch as the original charter and the subsequent acts of the legislature since the Revolution prohibited any religious qualification for office in the College, members of the board cannot rightfully or lawfully object to any candidate for the vacant professorship on account of his religious creed. One would think it a truism, a mere formal assertion, that men with the enlightened conscience of a professed theologian cannot lawfully do that indirectly by ballot and *sub silentio* which the law of the land and this special contract with the state forbids them to do directly and avowedly; that if it was conceded to be wrong, unlawful, and a breach of trust to adopt a resolution that Unitarianism or Deism or Roman Catholicism should debar a man from office in the College, it was quite as wrong to debar him from that office on that avowed ground without that resolution.

Yet these gentlemen, churchmen and dissenters, all avowed distinctly that they would not vote for any Unitarian candidate, whatever might be his qualifications for the place.

I asked Haight and Wainwright: Suppose Gibbs went to Trinity Church, would you not vote for him? Their answer was *"Yes, most gladly"*—or if he went to the Presbyterian Church. But they say this is *not* establishing a religious test, or violating the provisions under which they hold office. . . .

Wainwright, Spring, and Knox during the meeting of the board, and Haight in talk after the adjournment, were *explicit* on this subject. And the unutterable illogicality of their talk! Confusion of practical immorality with the soundness or error of the tenets in matters of religion to which the enactments in question refer. Confusion between what one *can* do and what one can *lawfully* do. Ignoring of any responsibility except to the Supreme Court on a *quo warranto*. These are thy *priests*, O, Israel!

January 10. . . . Have had Wolcott Gibbs's testimonials copied today for the printer. There is going to be some fight yet, and success not *absolutely* impossible.

If this ground is definitely taken, viz.: the right to make religious belief a test, one good may follow that Knox, Spring, and Fisher don't anticipate. It is competent for us to draw the line at one point as well as another. If we can exclude a man for unsoundness as to the Divine Nature, we can exclude him for denying the existence, supremacy, and organization of the Visible Catholic Church. We can make the College Anglican and Catholic, root and branch.

The reasoning of my astute clerical colleagues is that, although the law forbids a resolution that the act shall be done, it does not forbid the act itself. Very honest casuistry. There are Jesuits outside the pale of Rome and "blacksnakes" unclassified in herpetology.

January 16, Monday. . . . Gibbs must be beat tomorrow, I think. Perhaps the election will be postponed and perhaps indefinitely postponed, by appointing some scrub of a tutor to perform the duties of professor. That will be equivalent to defeat, and then Russel and Cornell and J. W. Beekman may fire away if they like. Dana of the

Tribune and Bryant will be only too happy to raise a storm. I had hard work to persuade Bryant to make no farther row as yet, to hold back his thunders for a few days. . . .

January 17, Tuesday. At Columbia College at two; long meeting without definite result. Mr. Ruggles dined here and at eight Ellie and I went to Gibbs's rooms, where was some nice music with Mrs. Gibbs and Miss Teresa Mauran and Mrs. Isaac Wright.

Columbia College meeting ill tempered and not of good omen. The Schaeffer papers were read and, though they do not in truth amount to much, they will weigh with the two or three undecided men who want a pretext for voting against Gibbs by reason of his Unitarianism, the "outside pressure" generally, and the *Evening Post* article in particular. The outside pressure argument means that whenever any course is so manifestly wise and prudent that all mankind is unanimous in favour of the trustees adopting it, they cannot properly adopt it, and must do the precise opposite, in order to maintain their independence and dignity. . . .

As to the *Evening Post,* I shall see Russel tomorrow and tell him that I withdraw my special request that he do no publishing for the present, that I can be privy to no newspaper war and no petitioner to the legislature, but that the case cannot now be injured thereby, and that if he sees fit to adopt that or any other treatment, to let slip the dogs of war in any form, he may do as he pleases. . . .

January 18. The Gibbs conflict is spreading a little. John C. Spencer's letter received today commits him beyond all recall. Mr. S. B. Ruggles has written a letter to Fish that will tell—exceedingly able, compact, plain-spoken, and Saxon. Russel came here after dinner. He proposes to cross the Danube and commence hostilities, and I can't help it if he does.

The more I see of the way public opinion is shaping, the more plain it is that the Church has made a serious blunder in this matter, a misstep that may lead to very bad results. . . .

Now, waiving all the most weighty considerations of their [the trustees'] duty under their contract with the state to apply no religious test to this case; assuming it to be a church institution, as it is called by Minturn; passing over the presence in the board of Knox and Spring and Fisher and Beadle, brought in avowedly as Dissenters to secure dissenting patronage; taking the highest ground a churchman can take as to its proper management and government, what is it? What is "a church college"?

Not, as I suppose, a hospital for decayed churchmen, an institution created to provide salaries and situations for weak-minded, inefficient presbyters with bronchial afflictions that forbid their venturing on a parochial charge, or most estimable and high-minded laymen who can't take care of themselves and must be provided for somewhere; but an institution in which (1) whatever is done or attempted is done as honestly and thoroughly as its means and opportunities will permit . . . and (2) in which whatever direct or indirect teaching there may be on matters of religion coincides with and enforces the truths held by the Church. . . .

January 24. . . . Columbia College is destined to be a sleepy, third-rate high school for one or two generations more. . . .

I am thoroughly disgusted with Wainwright. The further I trace him in this business the clearer are the signs of double-dealing, want of principle, cowardice, meanness, and humbug.

January 27. There is scarce a possibility of electing Wolcott Gibbs as the case stands now. Knox has come out against him after much wavering. . . .

February 2. Wainwright called on Richard Grant White yesterday at the *Courier* office to deplore and condemn the very decorous and sensible leader that appeared in that paper a day or two since, and to inquire if Mr. King or Mr. Ruggles had not written it? White discussed the question of its deplorability and the justice of its condemnation, and seems to have dodged and chased his Rt. Rev. opponent all round the board (like a king in the last stage of a close game of chess); and by his own account cornered him at last to admit that the dealings of this corporation were legitimate subjects of comment by the newspaper press, and that he, the Rt. Rev. J. M. W. [Wainwright], Provisional Bishop, "had opposed and should oppose" Wolcott Gibbs *on the Unitarian ground.* Wainwright was relieved to learn that the editorial was White's own. "It would have been his duty to have administered a severe rebuke to King" were he an accessory to it.

I think I see him a-doing it! Probably a trustee is entitled to confer with his trust; and for whom are we "Trustees of Columbia College" if not for the community? There is going to be a "general war" before the matter is disposed of; and I think Wainwright will find himself more and more in the wrong place as the conflict thickens and deepens.

Probably he wants to get the presidency as a convenient sinecure after two or three years of an overworked episcopate. Our friend R. B. Minturn seems to back him in this swindle, and I know of no other outsider who does so, lay or cleric. . . .

February 4. The *Herald* had defined its position on the Gibbs question against that gentleman, on the ground that Unitarianism is a stepping-stone to infidelity, and that Spinoza, Socinus, and other unchristian philosophers "of the last century" are shrewdly suspected to have held the same opinion; and because Voltaire had a strong leaning toward it. It regrets the advance of religious dissension from the Five Points to the shades of the College, and is so exactly what I should have wished it that I half suspect some friend of Gibbs's to have smuggled it in surreptitiously in the guise of an editorial. . . . Drafted and sent to Albany a special act which, if we can get it through at this session, will secure us Fish's and Hoffman's vote. It authorizes *proxies* by trustees absent as holding political office. The "parents and guardians" document not as generally signed as I hoped, only some twenty names in at four today.

I think Monday's meeting must be followed by well-marked schism and open war. If so, our clerical brethren will find, perhaps with surprise, that this is not a question of liberality or illiberality, bigotry or enlightenment, but one of good faith or bad faith, honesty or fraud, to which the ordinary truisms of conservative and vigorous theologians are entirely inapplicable. If it were proposed to procure a law excluding Unitarians from all civil rights, and banishing or burning them, their reasoning would be pertinent. But they propose to go further, and to make the enormity of their error a justification for breaking a contract with the state in reference to Unitarianism (or indirectly *with* Unitarians as individuals of the state), and all their statements and arguments are impertinent to that controversy. Unless they are prepared to maintain the proposition that no faith is to be kept with heretics; that the maker of a promissory note endorsed to Peter Cooper or Moses H. Grinnell may lawfully and rightly evade its payment if he believes that the amount there is on it will be applied by the endorsee to the publication of Unitarian tracts or the building of an Unitarian Church; and that it is morally right to do moral wrong for the maintenance of truth or the repression of error—then Wainwright and Berrian and Spring have no logical position at all. They must justify the violation of safe-conduct for the sake of executing justice on a heretic, or admit themselves guilty of dishonesty and immorality for the sake of religious truth, truth which demands many sacrifices but condemns *that*. It's not often that a layman is entitled to the luxury of "sassing" a bishop that a vestryman of Trinity Church stands on moral ground from which he can look down on Rev. William Berrian, D.D., Rector. But I think I'm so privileged at this time.

Hoffman is ill, his confounded larynx being the subject of venous congestion, and his unprincipled uvula morbidly enlarged. Fish writes that he can't come, some caucus having decided that something about the Nebraska bill is to be pushed or to be opposed. So we can't elect Wolcott Gibbs next Monday under any circumstances. . . .

February 11. . . . I've been brought up in an accursed feminine reverence for the White Cravat. Alas, that it should be shaken, for I can afford to spare no safeguards. But this clerical dishonesty is driving me into sympathy with Red Republican Socialist Greeleyan talk about "priests" and ecclesiastical tyranny.

February 21. . . . (Extracts from a letter dated Columbia, S.C., 15 Feby., 1854, to S. B. Ruggles, the joint composition in alternate lines of Francis Lieber and the Astronomical Gould):

> What an unchristian white-cravat is Wainwright
> > To spend his calumnies against Wool Gibbs:
> And can the reverend Knox be in the main right
> > To circulate such anti-Christian fibs?
> Do tell us, who in earth can be Doremus:
> > And who the tenebrists that vote for him?
> Eight votes for Schaeffer too: — O Nicodemus!
> > Against such men poor Wolcott's chance is slim.
> Haste, haste to Washington and fish the Fish up,
> > And snake out Hoffman from his lurking hole,
> To countervail that execrable Bishop
> > And Knox, that reverend benighted soul.
> Hang all the blockheads, fogies, and the Bonzes!
> > They make nine-tenths the mischief that's about,
> And from your College, if there only once is
> > A chance, O thou dear Ruggles, smoke them out. . . .

April 1. . . . Hamilton Fish is in town and will probably be present at the Columbia College meeting Monday afternoon. We are like to have a refreshing season there. Result uncommonly dubious. If Mr.

Ruggles brings Hoffman down from Albany, and if Morris be absent, Gibbs will pretty surely be elected. Whether that be desirable or not desirable, I can't say. Should he be elected, we are only entering on the battle. Our fight has been thus far nothing but a preliminary skirmish. Should he be defeated, we may stand in a better position for the contest as to the strengthening or enlargement of our educational work, the conversion of the second-rate college into a university. And it may be well for us to gain this advantage by the loss of an individual agent clearly the best in his own department.

April 3, Monday. All is lost save our honor. The trustees of Columbia College met at two P.M. . . . the professorship came up. We went into ballot, and the result was as follows, to wit: (I put down names because each is certain and unmistakeable.)

For *Wolcott Gibbs*	*For one* *Richard McCulloh*
Charles King	Rev. Dr. Berrian
S. B. Ruggles	Rev. Dr. Haight
Ogden Hoffman	Rev. G. Spring
H. J. Anderson	Rev. John Knox
Edward Jones	Rev. G. H. Fisher
Robert Ray	William Betts
William H. Hobart	T. L. Wells
Clement C. Moore	G. G. Van Wagenen
G. T. Strong	G. M. Ogden
(9)	G. W. Morris
	Dr. Beadle
	(11)

Hamilton Fish voted for Professor Bache, virtually a blank, as Bache was not in nomination and would not take the place. His expectation no doubt was that the vote would be 10 to 10 and that by this inoperative vote he would keep the question open, retain the balance of power, and after moving for postponement (which he told me he meant to propose after the first ballot) dictate terms to both sides. But the defection of Beadle defeated this very politic purpose. Beadle has no doubt been converted by Knox and Fisher, in whose churches he is a deacon or a ruling elder or something else.

There was no fuss when the result was announced. . . .

April 14. . . . Mr. Ruggles's pamphlet is circulating far and wide, scattered by Moses H. Grinnell, backed by George Cornell and a batch of alumni. It excites attention and almost unanimous approval. The Harvard people (Mr. Ruggles is just back from Cambridge) are enthusiastic about its merits. Only Agassiz says he don't want this battle fought from within the Church. *I do.* If it's wholly without the Church, the field is not worth fighting for.

April 21. . . . As to Columbia College, I hear that the caucus of alumni that has been sitting from day to day through the week has adopted a scheme of action for the meeting tomorrow, and that a string of resolutions will be offered far from complimentary to the trustees. There is room for doubt whether this proposed action can be carried out, though a large majority of the older alumni incline to adopt it. The graduates of the last three or four years will probably be numerously represented, and will be generally in favor of cooperating with the trustees in a celebration. . . .

April 22. . . . It seems that the purport of the [alumni] resolutions is to condemn and censure the policy of the board, to thank the minority, to recommend those members whose conscientious convictions interfere with the execution of their trust to resign their seats, to decline cooperation for the present with the board in any celebration, and to appoint a pretty strong committee of about thirty to ask the board about the programme of the celebration and the policy of its future administration, and report their answer to a future meeting of the alumni. On the whole, a very emphatic rebuke.

April 23. The alumni resolutions in this morning's *Herald* are better than I expected; appear to have been framed with care and accuracy and present no salient points for attack. And a list of the men who adopted them shews an array of very weighty and respectable names, Trinitarian and Unitarian. I think this is a shot that will tell a little. But it won't be as effective as Gould and Peirce and Lovering seem to suppose. . . . I hope for nothing from this demonstration, except a strong skirmish which may move all parties to increased energy and activity in moving uptown and enlarging the usefulness of the College. . . .

11. Samuel B. Ruggles States the Case for the Appointment of Wolcott Gibbs, 1854

Samuel B. Ruggles (1800–1881) was born in Connecticut, graduated from Yale in 1814, and entered the practice of law in New York City in 1821. Eminently successful in the law, he soon devoted much of his time to civic affairs, becoming one of the planners of Gramercy Park and Union Square, as well as one of the early builders of the New York & Erie Railroad. He was one of the most ardent Gibbs partisans and wrote the document represented here with the assistance of George Templeton Strong (Doc. 10). He remained a staunch advocate of the development of a real university at Columbia, an enterprise in which, near the close of his life, he supported John W. Burgess (see Part VII, Doc. 7). On Ruggles see Daniel G. Brinton Thompson, *Ruggles of New York* (New York, 1946), and Doc. 10.

The deliberate opinion of eminent men of science, ought to turn the scale, even if the qualifications of the candidates seemed to us equally balanced.

But the question is not now, between the professional merits of Dr. Gibbs and those of any opposing candidate, for at our last meeting the friends of the candidate most prominent in opposition, withdrew his name or offered to do so, if the name of Dr. Gibbs were withdrawn by his friends. This they did not do, and could not do, believing themselves bound in law and conscience, to vote for the candidate best fitted for the place,—or (to state it in the legal phrase) to select the agent, who would most efficiently execute an important portion of the trust they had assumed.

Of the twenty Trustees, then present, ten had voted for Dr. Gibbs, as abundantly proved to be fit. How could they withdraw his name, and vote for some other candidate whom they considered less fit, and perhaps did not know to be fit at all? That those who had voted for his competitor, not only declined on that occasion, to vote for Dr. Gibbs, whose professional fitness had been so conclusively established, but avowed their intention to look about for some other candidate, shows that his appointment was and is opposed, on other grounds.

Samuel B. Ruggles, *The Duty of Columbia College to the Community and its Right to Exclude Unitarians from its Professorship of Physical Science, Considered by One of its Trustees* (New York, 1854), pp. 6–9, 12–15, 22–23, 26–27, 33–35, 38–39, 46–53.

The first is, that his appointment has been unduly and disrespect-
fully urged by his friends,—that two hundred of our *alumni,* clerical
and lay, have taken the unusual step of petitioning us to appoint him,
—that some of the parents of our present undergraduates have concurred in that petition,—that newspaper paragraphs have appeared, in-
temperately and indecorously asserting the superiority of his claims to
the vacant chair,—and that in these and various other forms, there has
been an "outside pressure" of public opinion in his favor, in which it
does not become us to acquiesce, and which our official dignity requires us to resent, by electing some other candidate.

The second and much graver objection is, that Dr. Gibbs is a "Unitarian." . . .

The question is of our duty,—what is right, and what wrong, in
executing a trust. We do not individually own the endowment of Columbia College. Our title to it is purely fiduciary. We hold it simply
in trust, to promote with it, to our best ability, and with our utmost
diligence, certain definite objects. In accomplishing these objects, is it
not plainly our duty to select the agent, shown to be most competent?
Have we the right to choose any but the most competent, because his
friends or the public have annoyed us, by their too urgent representations of his merits?

Our position, rights and duties, are the same, in principle, with
those of a trustee, under a will or deed of settlement. The only difference is, that the private trustee deals with mere material interests, and
can commit no breach of trust which the law will not at once detect,
while we have a wider range of duties, in which failure and fraud are
practically more difficult to identify. Our discretion is larger, but not
the less a legal discretion.

An austere but salutary course of decisions establishes the responsibility of the private trustee for any unlawful exercise of his power, or
any step beyond the course prescribed by the terms of his trust. What
should we say to the executor or trustee, who asked us if he might
properly invest his trust fund on a second rate security, or commit its
administration to a second rate agent, because his co-trustee, or his
cestui-que-trust, or some unknown person, had unduly and disrespect-
fully urged on him another course? We should advise him that a
breach of trust could not be justified or palliated, by any violation of
decorum in those who disapproved it.

As Trustees of Columbia College, we have nothing, and can have nothing, but duties to perform. Every vote any of us gives on any question, is either the performance of a duty or a breach of trust. We have not, I think, any corporate capacity to receive affronts, or any corporate dignity to be wounded. Our clear duty and office are, calmly and dispassionately to execute our trust, without any of the feelings, preferences or resentment, which modify so much our dealings as individuals. I know it is possible for us, to vote under the influence of offence at "outside pressure," but if we do, we depart as widely from our duty, as if the vote were biassed by personal affection or private interest. . . .

As to the undue urgency of his friends, it may well be, that some of us (including Dr. King, the President of the College) may have expressed an earnest desire for his appointment. Why should we not do so, if we believe his qualifications pre-eminent? Why are we not bound as honest men to do so, if we believe him best qualified of all the candidates? As to the newspaper articles, no member of our Board, to my knowledge or belief, is in any way responsible for them, and were the fact otherwise, it would have no bearing whatever upon the question we have to decide. Their appearance proves only, that public feeling, whether justly or unjustly, is certainly enlisted in the matter, to some extent, and especially in regard to the religious opposition which Dr. Gibbs has encountered. . . .

Can Columbia College, with its little handful of graduates and professors, feel that it has accomplished the object of its creation?

I know it will be said, that we have wanted means,—that we have not shared the bounty of the community,—that few, if any, individual donations or endowments have been added to our original resources. But if we had wisely used the means we had, all this would have been added to us. The millions that have gone to the "New-York University," the Free Academy, the Cooper Institute and the Astor Library, would probably have been ours.

We may console our pride, by claiming that our position has been one of dignified scholarship, too far above the age to be appreciated or encouraged,—but the answer will be, even if the extravagant assumption were founded on fact, that we exist to educate the people, and should have lowered ourselves to a position a little less exalted, that so we might raise them step by step.

The difficulty lies deeper than the want of money. We have wanted Trustees,—more truly and zealously, to carry out the purposes defined by our charter. We have avowedly and perseveringly neglected, undervalued and disparaged "the Liberal Arts and Sciences," and the world has avenged the neglect, by neglecting us.

It is not, and has not been, the want of pecuniary means. Yale College, possessing little else than its buildings, filled her halls for fifty years, with students from every part of the Union, attracted by the fame of her scientific teachers. The annual cost of DAY and SILLIMAN, sitting side by side for half a century, did not exceed four thousand dollars,—but they were constantly and vigorously sustained, cheered and encouraged, by an enlightened and appreciating Board of Trustees.

But if poverty be our excuse, it can avail us no longer. The great wave of commerce has reached our landed estates, and we have but to coin them into revenue, far exceeding our utmost necessities. This flood of pecuniary prosperity, is, in no sense, due to us. It is the work of the busy community around us, and that community has now, more than ever, the right to ask us to come fully up to our duty. It has a right to ask, why the College, surrounded by more than fifty thousand youths, of age suitable for College studies, capable of education, and destined to suffer through life for want of it,—teaches but one hundred and forty?

For I expressly maintain, that we hold a distinct relation to the community and owe it a definite duty. The College is a public, not a private institution. Our Board of Trustees is not a fraternity, nor a religious order, set apart from and independent of the community. It is not a place for personal predilections or partialities, either for men or for subjects beyond the scope of our corporate duties. It belongs wholly to the world around us, and we are bound by every principle of law, equity and honor, to render equal and exact justice to every part and portion, every sect and section alike.

The College is, in no sense, an ecclesiastical body. It is purely a human, secular institution. Founded by a temporal sovereign, it is solely the creature of the State, and to the State alone, does it owe duty and obedience.

And I further contend, that to the community as such, in its aggregate existence, the College owes a peculiarly high and sacred duty,—not only faithfully to discharge its trust, in educating individual students, but to discharge it in such a mode, and with such vigor and intelligence, as to advance the moral and intellectual dignity of the community itself,—to become an element in our social system, felt in all its workings, modifying the culture and elevating the character of all around us. The community has a Right to a great seat of learning in its midst, and is wronged if the College, which it has endowed and enriched with means amply sufficient for such an institution, remain in obscurity or inefficiency. The College should form part of the great living organism of society, giving it tone, vigor, color, growth. But of the million of inhabitants, now assembled in and around this great mart of trade, how many are impressed or improved by our existence? How many know that we exist at all?

By some of the few, who know us, we are regarded, however erroneously, as being, in some peculiar sense, aristocratic in our course of study and administration, as a place for the sons of gentlemen, to whom it is our special office, to give culture, refinement and elegant taste. I will not stop to controvert a notion so unfounded, nor to protest against a construction so narrow, of our duty to the State. I will only ask whether we have fulfilled even that office? Look at the young men crowding the drawing-rooms of our city, condemned to "ornamental idleness," because no proper training has led them up to usefulness to society, the country, or the Church, and tell me, whether Columbia College, with her little yearly *coterie* of five and twenty graduates, has done her duty, even to this small minority of the People?

No thoughtful man can look at the present elements of our society, without forebodings for the future. The utter feebleness of the sons of the rich, and their total inability to combat the misdirected education, the crude theories, that make perilous the growing power of the needy classes, become more and more apparent, with each succeeding generation. If our seats of learning will awake to their responsibilities and their work, they may greatly mitigate, if they cannot entirely remove these evils. If they can do no more, they may at least transmute the holders of wealth, used only for ostentation or self-indulgence, into liberal and intelligent leaders, in every good and generous effort for the common welfare. Benevolence bids us teach the poor,—but it will be a charity indeed, to educate the rich. . . .

It is not to be denied that members of our Board, estimate very differently the necessity, value and dignity of Physical Science. The fact is abundantly manifested, not only in the open disparagement of that branch of human knowledge, but in the utter failure of earnest and repeated efforts to divide the Chair of Chemistry and Physics, now overloaded with duties which would amply employ at least three Professors,—and to provide meanwhile for the single Professor, more adequate and decent apartments. I may be too radical a reformer, but I cannot think it very unreasonable, in the Trustee of a College holding itself out to the public as a seat of science, to remonstrate against its teaching Experimental Philosophy in a dark, damp basement, where its apparatus rusts and perishes, and the health of professor and pupils is endangered,—nor to insist that Optics might better be taught in an apartment, that the light of Heaven can enter.

We all know, and the public knows how we turned away, year after year, from all the entreaties of our late Professor, that his department and the reputation of the College might be relieved from these needless embarrassments, till after thirty years' service, he left us in disgust and despair. . . .

What then was our disappointment and mortification, when WOL-COTT GIBBS,—bearing with him the united voice of all that was commanding in the Scientific world,—a son of our College, winning its highest honors, only to add yet higher testimonials from the ablest masters in the Old World,—rich too, in every moral, mental and social excellence, that could dignify and adorn the place, was called to account by members of our body representing at least three separate religious denominations, for his want of conformity to a theological standard of their own, compounded from incoherent and opposing creeds, and agreeing only in hostility to the denomination to which he belonged!

Before examining the legal and the moral merits of this objection,—let me clear the way, of all idle and senseless suspicions, by declaring distinctly, that I do not seek or wish to weaken the just authority of the Church Catholic, or undervalue any truth it teaches. It might suffice, to point to the members of the Board holding views like my own, in respect to its duty to the community and the Church,—who have voted for DR. GIBBS. But I prefer to purge myself individually. . . .

It is quite as much for their sakes, and that of the Church, as for the College, that I now ask you and every brother Churchman in the Board, to assist in averting the pernicious effects, which an unlawful exercise of power, on the present occasion, must inevitably bring upon her.

Let us then attentively examine the legal and moral nature of the claim, to set aside the best qualified teacher of Physical Science, by reason of his alleged unsoundness on a point of theology.

It is not *prima facie,* a valid or sufficient objection, and the burthen of proof rests on those who assert it. But I contend affirmatively, that the objection is alike unnecessary, impolitic, unjust and unlawful.

In the first place, DR. GIBBS is not an infidel,—and it is to be hoped, we may hear no more of a design to banish religion from the College, and introduce infidelity among the students. Infidelity has nothing to do with the matter, and the application of the term to him, is simply preposterous. An infidel is he who disbelieves the Holy Scriptures, but DR. GIBBS expressly declares, that he believes in them and in their divine inspiration, and moreover adds, that he knows of nothing in any branch of Science, with which he is acquainted, which conflicts with their teaching, or impugns their authority. His written answer to the inquiries of the Chairman of our Board, certainly shows this. But in that answer, he frankly admits that he belongs to that denomination of Christians, known as "Unitarians;" and this is the only tangible objection that is urged against him. He may, therefore, be a heretic, but he certainly is not an infidel. The charge against him is heresy, not infidelity. Now is this heresy?

As I am informed, there are wide differences of opinion among Christians calling themselves "Unitarians," on the doctrine of the Divine Nature. That denomination embraces a school which holds nearly all the fundamental doctrines of the orthodox church,—objecting to nothing in the Nicene Creed itself, except the words "of *one* substance with the Father," for which they substitute the words "of *like* substance with the Father."

We have no evidence of DR. GIBBS' precise position on this question. Very possibly he may never have defined it even to himself, but like too many laymen, has adopted without special examination, the faith which early habit may have taught him to respect. But I know that he is utterly free from any spirit of proselytism, or aggressive hostility to any other faith, and I have reason to believe, that his theological views, so far as he has ever defined them, assimilate to those of the more conservative portion of the Unitarian body.

He was made by baptism at the age of eleven years, a member of the Protestant Episcopal Church, but since his father's death, has attended a Unitarian place of worship. He certainly is one of those "who profess and call themselves Christians," for whom the Church instructs us to pray, but whom she nowhere authorizes us to proscribe. . . .

It is clearly the right of DR. GIBBS to ask those who claim the right

to condemn and punish, to specify which of these widely different offences he has committed,—which of the charges he is bound to answer.
He has the right, and every other candidate, for this or any other Professorship, present or future, has the right, to be distinctly informed
what religious qualifications we require, and how they are to be established.

Should we hereafter become a more conspicuous and authoritative
body that we yet have been, it will be not a little important to the
World of Thought and Letters, to know our standard of orthodoxy,
and to understand from us intelligibly, how we ascertain and identify
those we reject and brand as unfit to teach. The selection of the particular dogmas which are to compose that standard, and the exact definition of each, may possibly task somewhat the industry and acuteness
of some of us. We must define not only the creed, the series of dogmas,
to which we require assent, but also the necessary degree and evidence
of that assent. Shall it be only formal, as in some English institutions,
or must it be *"ex animo?"* and shall the habitual or occasional attendance of the candidate at some prescribed place of worship, be taken as
a sufficient compliance with our standard? Is there no danger that
parents may distrust the College, where theological conformity real
or pretended, wins the professor's chair,—and that students themselves,
of differing faith, may question decisions on academic rank, by teachers who gain by such means the right to decide.

But here it may be said, that exclusion from office is not punishment,
—that a Trustee voting to exclude, only exercises his inherent right to
select whom he thinks fit,—and that if he deem a heretic unfit, because
of his heresy, he may lawfully vote against such heretic, and that this is
not a punishment of heresy.

This common-place of intolerance has long been abandoned. Our
criminal law recognizes exclusion from office as one of the penalties of
crime. If he who would obtain a place of honor or profit but for his
heresy, is lawfully excluded from it by his heresy, the law punishes him
for that heresy. If the law permit a secular College like ours, not created to promote any particular creed, to exclude a heretic from its Professorships, the law in that mode punishes the heretic.

True, we no longer punish by the writ *"de haeretico,"*—for that
went out of the legal world, the very year the Habeas Corpus came into
it,—but we do in fact punish, quite as severely,—in another mode,—
by professional, civil, and social degradation.

But I go further. I claim that even if our Board could agree upon, and could lawfully and safely establish, and could permanently maintain its tripartite theological standard,—and even if WOLCOTT GIBBS, after full information, previous notice, and fair trial, had been duly convicted of non-conformity to its provisions,—it would still be our duty to elect him to the vacant Professorship, as being best qualified to perform an important portion of the duty of education, which we profess to perform. Nay, more, I claim that even if our College existed only as an organ of the Episcopal Church,—were it already and avowedly nothing but a preparatory school for her theological seminaries,—were it created expressly to train up learned men to fight Unitarianism itself, even then it would be our duty and our true policy, to select him, as the best and ablest man to fill the chair of Chemistry, without reference in any way to his views on the Trinity, or any other point of theology.

For surely it is as much the duty of a "Church College," as of any other, to do best whatever it professes to do,—to teach, as thoroughly as any irreligious institution, all it professes to teach. A heretic or an infidel might not be selected, in such a College, to teach Ecclesiastical History or Moral Philosophy, for the reason that his religious belief, or want of belief, might prevent his teaching what the Church holds true; but in the sciences purely physical, the religious creed of the professor would be wholly irrelevant and unimportant.

For what proposition can be stated or imagined, in any department of Physical Science, in which Trinitarians or Unitarians, as such, can possibly disagree? They differ only as to the meaning of Scripture on a single point,—momentous, no doubt, to the individual believer,—but wholly separated from material science. The subjects are wide apart as Earth and Heaven. The united skill of the whole theological world, cannot find a statement, proposition or theory in Chemistry or Natural Philosophy, which conflicts, in any degree, with the teaching of the Church, on any subject whatever,—not one, which, by any possibility, can be called Orthodox, rather than Unitarian. . . .

This, then, is our position. In the middle of this nineteenth century, —in the State of New-York,—under a Constitution guaranteeing equal rights of conscience to all men, a few members of our Board of Trustees assume the right to adjudicate, and do adjudicate, that he who does not believe the Tri-Une Existence of the Supreme Being, is not a Christian, and thereby is disqualified from teaching Chemical Science.

The decision covers, not only WOLCOTT GIBBS, but all his sect,—for if he be not fit to teach, what Unitarian is? and thus, we presume to excommunicate hundreds of thousands of our fellow-men and fellow-scholars, and practically prohibit them from teaching here, or elsewhere, or any where.

Are we quite prepared,—do we really feel strong enough,—to proclaim this decision to the American people and the world? Not to mention the several presidents of these United States, professing the form of Christian faith we now proscribe,—not to point to EVERETT and BANCROFT, on whom orthodox Oxford lavished its highest academic honors, nor to hosts of others, now living, bright among the brightest gems of history, and poetry, and science and art, what shall we do with the deathless works of dead and buried Unitarians? . . .

But we are told, that, after all, the College must be subject to some one governing sect, and that all the American Colleges are, in fact, sectarian. This ought not to be true,—but if it is, it will help to explain their slender success, when compared with the European Institutions not sectarian, and why our sons are obliged to leave our narrow halls, to find adequate instruction in the more catholic and comprehensive institutions of France and Germany.

But it is not true, and certainly not to the severe extent to which sectarian exclusion is now threatened. We know, that many of the American Colleges have selected, and do select professors differing widely, in religious tenets, from the majority of the governing trustees. Presbyterian Princeton placed in one of her scientific chairs a Professor with no religion at all. Episcopalians are tolerated in Congregational Harvard, Yale and Union. Six of the seventeen Professors at Harvard, and three of the Tutors, are of denominations other than Unitarian, some of them, indeed, most earnest in their orthodoxy. An eminent Unitarian divine is associated with clergymen of the Church of England, in the Canadian University, established by the British Crown. A learned and accomplished Jew was trusted by one of the theological Seminaries in this very city, to teach its students the true reading of the Prophets,—and should we ourselves perchance awake to the necessity of qualifying our youth to meet the Asiatic Exodus now pouring in upon our Pacific coast, would we exclude from the Chinese Professorship every follower of CONFUCIUS? . . .

Statistically it may be true, that a majority of our Board may be Episcopalians, but that fact no more makes the College Episcopalian, than a majority being Democrats would make it Democratic. The accidental preponderance of one or another sect or party, would no more authorize a Trustee of that sect or party to gratify his prejudices, religious or political, at the expense of others having rights as sacred as his own, than it would to convert the pecuniary property of the College to his private use.

But the legal prohibition of religious proscription, is by no means confined to this single clause in the charter. On the 22d of March, 1810, the legislature on the petition of the College, incorporated it anew, by a single act consolidating and defining its powers and duties. The Board of Trustees named by that act, again contained a large infusion of members not Episcopalian. Not to mention those eminent divines, Doctor LIVINGSTON, Doctor MASON, and Doctor ROMEYN, whom do we find but OLIVER WOLCOTT, a Unitarian, and grandfather of WOLCOTT GIBBS!—and to him and his associates did the State then commit the care of the College, the direction of its studies and choice of its Professors. The act also condensed and invigorated the anti-sectarian clause of the charter, by directing that none of the ordinances or by-laws of the College should "make the religious tenets of any person, a condition of admission to any privilege or *office* in the said College."

Nor was this all. The State immediately after achieving its independence, passed a general law for regulating Colleges and Academies, which broadly declares that "no President or Professor shall be ineligible for or by reason of any religious tenets that he may or shall profess,"—a practical application only, of that noble provision in its Constitution of 1777, that "the free exercise and enjoyment of religious freedom and worship without discrimination, shall for ever hereafter be allowed within this State, to all mankind." Need we add, that in every successive revision of the laws, this great declaratory provision shines out in living light,—its very diction gaining strength and comprehensiveness, at every step?

It now stands a fundamental portion of the law of the land,—which all good men obey,—summed up in these few but signal words:—

"NO RELIGIOUS QUALIFICATION OR TEST shall be required from any Trustee, President, Principal, or other officer of an incorporated college or academy, or as a *condition of admission* to any privilege in the same."

The constant and uninterrupted current of legislation from 1754 to the present hour, shows conclusively, not only that the law has not made the College exclusively Episcopalian, but has expressly forbidden it to be so, and has guarded the equal rights of every other denomination, by every form of speech known to human law.

Nor has the College by any act or usage of its own, adopted a sectarian character. Not only have all its officers constantly denied the allegation, but the College itself by its own deliberate corporate act has signally disproved it. . . .

Drawing a distinction between the sciences which may be, and those which cannot be connected, directly or indirectly, with religious truth, they [the Trustees] have adopted a Statute, now standing in full force on their records, which provides that,

"*Any religious denomination* who shall endow a Professorship in the Classics, in Political, Mathematical or *Physical Science,* or in the Literature of any of the ancient or modern Languages, to the amount of twenty thousand dollars, shall *for ever have the right of nominating a professor* for the same, subject to the approbation of the Trustees, who shall hold his office by the same tenure as the other Professors of the College."

Now will any one pretend that after an invitation like this, we could reasonably or honorably reject the nominee of a religious denomination, fitted in all other respects for such a Professorship, for the sole reason that he belonged to that very denomination? Who would not exclaim, that we carried toleration on our lips, but intolerance in our hearts? and surely we can not prescribe one rule of faith for Professors thus selected, and another for those we select ourselves.

The arrogant assumption that "Unitarians have no religion at all," and are not entitled to be called a "religious denomination," I must really pass over, as too absurd for grave discussion. The Jews who worship the God of Abraham and Moses and David, and believe in the Old Testament, are surely a "religious denomination,"—and can we deny that title to Unitarians, who worship the same God, and believe both the Old Testament and the New?

But I hear it asserted that even if all this be true,—even if the law and our contract with the State plainly prohibit this religious proscription, both may nevertheless be safely and honorably evaded and nullified,—that if any Trustee conscientiously think a Unitarian unfit as such, to be a Professor, he may lawfully take the fact into account in giving his vote, inasmuch as the vote need not be preceded by any by-law, or any declaration of the motive which governs it,—that because this motive is secret and incapable of proof, it will be presumed to be such as the law allows,—and that no one has any right to say, that the vote was not given exclusively with reference to the fitness of the candidate, apart from any religious test or qualification. Summed up in short, it is that the "higher law" of conscience overrides the obligation of any human law, or the solemnity of any human contract, and justifies their violation,—if the act be known only to him who commits it. But if conscience demand or justify such a vote, it equally demands an ordinance or by-law establishing the qualification which governs the vote,—and if the one would be a violation of law and duty, is not the other still less excusable?

But we have little occasion for these nice distinctions, for we hear it avowed in unmistakeable terms by members of our body, that with their present convictions, they cannot and will not vote for a Unitarian. They further distinctly declare, that they would vote for WOLCOTT GIBBS for the present Professorship, if he were a member of Trinity Church, or of the Dutch Church, but that, as at present advised, they must and will vote against him, because he is a Unitarian.

Now on this state of facts, will any one deny, that he is excluded from the Professorship, in the very words of the charter, "*on account of his particular tenets* in matters of religion?" . . .

I revert then to the fundamental proposition with which I commenced, that as Trustees of Columbia College, we hold our offices and the property committed to us by the State, only in trust, for certain definite objects distinctly defined in our charter, and for none other. Neither the promotion of any creed, nor the suppression of any heresy, is among those objects, and to vote with a view to them, is a breach of trust and an abuse of power.

Rely upon it, the community can be convinced, that if WOLCOTT GIBBS be now rejected, he is not rejected by reason of his religious tenets,—still less that their moral sense can be satisfied, that a mere by-law or resolution to do a wrong, which leaves room for reconsideration until acted on, can be worse than the wrong itself. To maintain that although a by-law excluding a heretic would be unlawful, a direct vote excluding him for heresy would be lawful, will require a casuistry so subtle as to be generally unintelligible.

The fundamental policy of the law in favor of absolute religious freedom, is not lightly to be evaded. Every device, however ingenious, that tends to undermine it, will have to pass the ordeal of a stern and hostile scrutiny, and I fear not only for the College but for the Church, that those, who are ever ready to adopt any outcry against Her and her ministers, will assert in simple Saxon terms, that the present is not a question of tolerance or intolerance, but of Right and Wrong,—of Good Faith and Bad.

I believe the act, if consummated, to be fraught with mischief and danger, not only to the College, but the Church and her most valued interests. I know that a large body of the laity, and many of the most pious and distinguished of the clergy, speak of it with the sternest reprobation, holding that even religion cannot afford to have it matter of discussion, whether the means used to advance it, are not immoral and unlawful. The great community around us sees and can see nothing, but the plain moral obligation of the law,—the ever enduring sanctity of the contract, which none can violate or evade, without becoming a by-word and reproach.

Nor will the evil end here. Science will feel itself persecuted and insulted in one of her purest and noblest votaries, and, however unjustly, will attribute to religion a secret fear of the studies which open the great book of nature. The cause will be deemed weak, that thus seems to shun the light. Men will revert to the history of the Church,—now all but buried,—which records the imprisonment of GALLILEO,—the excommunication of COPERNICUS,—the denunciation, but just withdrawn, of the solar system as heretical,—or looking still further back, to the war upon the Classics themselves, by a short-sighted, half-educated clergy.

The world was rejoicing in the belief, that the Church was growing wiser,—that Science was standing at her side, the chosen champion, the ablest ally of Written Revelation. The concord so happily commenced, was the bright, the distinguishing feature of this our day and time; why rudely dissolve it? Why lead Religion back, into the gloom of by-gone ages? Why not interweave it into the framework of advancing society? Why not consecrate and share with Man, his victories over Nature? With the whole world emancipating its institutions from needless shackles, what infatuation leads us thus to fetter ours? Why blight the College just budding into usefulness, just come to man's estate? . . .

12. Francis Lieber Leaves South Carolina College, 1855

In 1835 Francis Lieber (see Part IV, Doc. 13) was appointed to the chair of history and political economy at South Carolina College as the successor of Thomas Cooper (see Doc. 2). Although he owned slaves, he gained the reputation of being opposed to the South's peculiar institution. In 1855, disappointed at not being elected president, an elevation which his distinguished reputation would have made quite natural, he resigned, attributing his defeat to hard-shell Calvinism and fears of abolitionism. See Frank Freidel, *Francis Lieber: Nineteenth Century Liberal* (Baton Rouge, La., 1947).

TO G. S. HILLARD
SOUTH CAROLINA COLLEGE, DECEMBER 1, 1855

I continue my letter. Next Tuesday the president of this college will be elected. There is a majority of trustees in my favor, and the people outside want me. All the alumni insist on my election; but it is very possible indeed that your friend remains simple professor, because the outgoing president—a regular hard-shell Calvinist, who meanly hates me simply because I am not a bitter Calvinist—has urged another professor, who has been here a year only, as a good president. This professor is Presbyterian. No one thinks that he stands the least chance; but the movement is made to induce the trustees to say, "Since neither of these two will work well under the other, we had better take a third, indifferent person." It is a low election manoeuvre, and may succeed. So be it! . . .

TO S. A. ALLIBONE
SOUTH CAROLINA COLLEGE, DECEMBER 13, 1855

My dear Sir,—I have resigned my professorship in this college. You do not sufficiently know me to be convinced that no irritation at not being elected has been the motive. My reasons are, not that I have been passed over, although a large number of trustees voted for me, and for several ballotings I stood at the head; but because a professor un-

Francis Lieber to George S. Hillard, Columbia, South Carolina, December 1, 1855; Lieber to S. A. Allibone, Columbia, South Carolina, December 13, 1855; printed in Thomas S. Perry (ed.), *The Life and Letters of Francis Lieber* (Boston, 1882), pp. 285–86.

known to the trustees and utterly incapable of ruling this institution, has been elected, and because the college will go to ruin. I am too old to play the college constable for another man. When I see you I shall tell you all about it. Bitter Calvinism,—simply bitter because I do not visit the Presbyterian but the Episcopalian church,—and my "Union" letter, and villanously [sic] hinted suspicion of abolitionism, carried the day. Petigru of Charleston fought strenuously for me. All this is strictly confidential.

I am, then, a mason out of work. Professors here are obliged to give a year's notice of resignation. Next December I shall be a "promenading" workman. For this purpose, I am desirous that my resignation be known all over the Union. It is here in the papers, and will soon make a noise. . . .

13. A Southerner Argues for a "Southern" Education in the Hedrick Case, 1856

Benjamin S. Hedrick (1827–86) was a North Carolinian by birth and a graduate of the University of North Carolina in 1851. After spending some time at Harvard, he returned to his native state and became professor of chemistry at his alma mater. He got into trouble in 1856 when the word got about that he favored the election of John C. Frémont, the Republican candidate. This communication denouncing Hedrick was written by John A. Engelhard of the class of 1854, then a law student at the University of North Carolina. Hedrick's candid reply to this attack (Doc. 14) only increased the outcry against him. Refusing to comply with the demand for his resignation, he was dismissed by the trustees. He went north and served in the government but returned to his native state during Reconstruction days. See J. G. de Roulhac Hamilton, "Benjamin Sherwood Hedrick," *James B. Sprunt Historical Publications,* Vol. X, No. 1 (Chapel Hill, N.C., 1910), and Russel B. Nye, *Fettered Freedom: Civil Liberties and the Slavery Controversy, 1830–1860* (East Lansing, Mich., 1949), pp. 74–76.

Messrs. Editors:—We have noticed with pleasure that Southern fathers are beginning to feel the necessity of educating their sons south of Mason and Dixon's line. The catalogues of Yale and other Northern

An Alumnus [John A. Engelhard], "Fremont in the South," North Carolina *Standard,* September 29, 1856.

armories of Sharpe's rifles, have but few (shame upon those few) Southern names. The importance of emancipating our young men from the baneful influences of the North—and no where is this influence more zealously exerted and powerfully felt than in Northern colleges and under black Republican teachers—has taken firm hold on our people; and we notice, with a high degree of gratitude to Bishop Polk of Louisiana, that the clergy and the church are in a fair way of taking concerted measures for more fully bringing about an object so much desired. We have every reason to believe that unless the course of the North very materially changes—and we are forced to say, we see no immediate chance for such a result—there will be inaugurated at the South a system of education congenial to our institutions.

We are proud of such names as Harvard and Yale; and feel that such benefactors of the human race should be held in everlasting remembrance by a grateful country. But their laudable objects are being frustrated by the fanatics that have obtained possession of the government of the schools their charity has founded, for the benefit equally of the *slave owner* and the *slave hirer*. At the former, the South is insulted by the dismissal of an instructor for performing his constitutional duty as judge; and at the latter the Southern young men see their professors and fellow students, in the name of the college— nay, of the very *class of which they are members*—buying *religious rifles* to shoot their own brothers that may be seeking honorable and profitable employment in Kansas. These colleges have been turned from their legitimate channels and been perverted into strongholds of fanaticism; and from being links of union between all parts of our country, have become hot-houses for the nurture of artificial statesmen of the Garrisonian school and manufactories of "bleeding Kansas" tragedies.

Then, when our fathers and guardians see such a state of things it is not to be wondered at that our Southern colleges are so largely attended, and Southern seminaries of all grades full to overflowing.

The cause is palpable—a determination to free ourselves from Northern thraldom and stop the revenue accruing to their abolition treasuries from the labor of Southern slaves. It is a praiseworthy object; and we glory to see this great reaction in the proportionate numbers of Northern and Southern schools.

But the question occurs, are we entirely rid of Northern influence in the South? Can North Carolina tell the world that her seminaries of

learning are free from the corrupting influences of black Republicanism, and Southerners can receive Southern education unmixed with
instructions hostile to the feelings and opinions their parents have in-
stilled into them? Nay, can the Trustees of our State University invite
pupils to the institution under their charge with the assurance that
this main stream of education contains no deadly poison at its fountain
head? Can boys be taken from Northern colleges and transferred to
our University with perfect security?

We have been led to these considerations, Messrs. Editors, by an
article headed "Fremont in the South" in a late issue of the Standard,
and more particularly the following closing paragraph:

"If there be Fremont men among us, let them be silenced or required
to leave. *The expression of black Republican opinions in our midst is
incompatible with our honor and safety as a people.*

"If at all necessary we shall refer to this matter again. Let our schools
and seminaries of learning be scrutinized; and if black Republicans
be found in them let them be driven out. *That man is neither a fit nor
a safe instructor of our young men, who even inclines to Fremont and
black Republicanism.*" We were very much gratified to notice this
article in your paper at this particular time; for we have been reliably
informed that a professor at our State University is an open and avowed
supporter of Fremont, and declares his willingness—nay, his desire—to
support the black Republican ticket; and the want of a Fremont electoral ticket in North Carolina is the only barrier to this *Southern* professor from carrying out his *patriotic* wishes. *Is he a fit or safe instructor
for our young men?*

If our information be entirely correct in regard to the political tendencies and Fremont bias of this professor, ought he not to be "required to
leave", at least dismissed from a situation where his poisonous influence
is so powerful, and his teachings so antagonistical to the "honor and
safety" of the University and the State? Where is the creative power?
To them we appeal. Have they no restrictive clause in the selection of
instructors or limiting code in regard to their actions?

If the Trustees or Faculty have no powers in regard to the matter in
question, we think it a fit object of early legislation at the next meeting
of our General Assembly. *This ought and must be looked to. We must
have certain security, under existing relations of North with South, that
at State Universities at least we will have no canker worm preying at
the vitals of Southern institutions.*

Upon what ground can a Southern instructor relying for his support upon Southern money, selected to impart healthy instruction to the *sons of Southern slave owners,* and indebted for his situation to a Southern State, *excuse* his support of Fremont, with a platform which eschews the fathers of his pupils and the State from whose University he received his station and from whose treasury he supports his family?

Does he tell the young men that he is in favor of a man for the Presidency, nominated by men whom their fathers *could not* nor *would not* sit in Convention with; placed upon a platform hostile to their every interest; its separate planks put together by the vilest Southern haters of the North, upon which all the isms of Yankeedom find aid and comfort; whose Cabinet, in the event of his election, would be composed of such men as Speaker Banks, who is willing to "let the Union slide"; and Mr. "Niagra" Burlingame, who demands an "anti-slavery Bible and an anti-slavery God"; whose orators belch forth vile slanders upon the South under flags whose venomous folds reveal but sixteen stars, and whose torch-light processions do not "march under the flag nor keep step to the music of the Union"? Does he read the following extract taken from *his* candidate's letter accepting the nomination: *"I am opposed to slavery in the abstract and upon principle, sustained and made habitual by long-settled convictions?"* Are these the doctrines he advocates to young men, two-thirds of whose property consists in slaves?

It cannot be denied by any person cognizant of college influences that each professor has his quota of friends and admirers among the students, and their minds are to a certain degree, upon general subjects, merely daguerrotypes of his opinions. This is natural. The student is young, and the instructors are placed over them, *in loco parentis,* to guide them correctly; and the young graduate leaves with opinions moulded by his instructors that will cling to him through life.

We ask, are we correctly informed concerning the political inclination and expressed opinions of this professor? If not, we hope to be corrected; and if we are we call upon the proper authorities to take action, for the sake of the prosperity of our Alma Mater and the good of the State.

AN ALUMNUS

14. Benjamin Hedrick's "Defense," 1856

See Doc. 13.

For the information of "Alumnus" I will state that he has put himself to unnecessary trouble in blazoning this matter before the public. The whole subject belongs exclusively to the jurisdiction of the Trustees of the University. They are men of integrity and influence, and have at heart the best interests of the University. There is no difficulty in bringing this, or any other question relating to the Faculty or students, before them. "Alumnus" has also made another mistake in supposing that the Faculty take upon themselves to influence the political opinions of the students. The students come to College generally, with their party politics already fixed; and it is exceedingly rare for them to change while here. It has, however, been often remarked that a very violent partizan at College, is pretty sure to "turn over" before he has left College long. I have been connected with our University, as student and Professor, for six years, and am free to say that I know no institution, North or South, from which partizan politics and sectarian religion are so entirely excluded. And yet we are too often attacked by the bigots of both. For my own part, I do not know the politics of more than one in a hundred of the students, except that I might infer to which party they belonged, from a knowledge of the politics of their fathers. And they would not have known my own predilections in the present contest, had not one of their number asked me which one of the candidates I preferred.

But, if "Alumnus" would understand the state of things here correctly, he had better make a visit to the University. He would find each member of the Faculty busy teaching in his own department, whether of science or literature; and that party politics is one of the branches which we leave the student to study at some other place and time. If "Alumnus" does conclude to visit us, there is another matter to which I might direct his attention. The two societies here, to the one or the other of which all the students belong, have each a very good library, and in those libraries are to be found the "complete works" of many of our great statesmen.

Now, for fear that the minds of the students may be "poisoned" by reading some of these staunch old patriots, would it be well for "Alumnus" to exert himself, through the Legislature or otherwise, to "drive" them out of the libraries? It is true the works of Calhoun are in the same case with those of Jefferson; but from appearances, the Virginian seems to be read pretty often, whilst the South Carolinian maintains a posture of "masterly inactivity." When I was a student in College, a few years ago, the young politicians used to debate in the "Halls" of the societies, the same questions which the old politicians were debating in the Halls of Congress. The side which opposed slavery in the abstract, generally had the books in their favor, and as the records of the societies will show, they had quite often "the best of the argument." So that when Col. Fremont said that he was "opposed to slavery in the abstract and upon principle, sustained and made habitual by long-settled convictions," he but uttered the sentiments of four-fifths of the best Southern patriots from the Revolution down to the present day; and I may add of the majority of the people among whom I was born and educated. . . .

15. A Southerner on Northern Attitudes of Educational Superiority in 1860

Francis L. Hawks (1798–1866), Protestant Episcopal clergyman and historian, graduated from the University of North Carolina in 1815. He served northern and southern church and educational posts, including an original trusteeship of the University of Mississippi and the first presidency of the University of Louisiana (1844–49). In 1862 he resigned his rectorate in New York City for a church in Baltimore because of his sympathy with the South.

Compare this statement with Ralph Waldo Emerson's in Doc. 6.

Francis L. Hawks to President David L. Swain of the University of North Carolina, January 3, 1860, Swain Papers, Southern Historical Collection, University of North Carolina Library; and printed in Edgar W. Knight, *A Documentary History of Education in the South Before 1860*, V (Chapel Hill, N.C., 1953), 315.

... The truth is they [the people in the North] looked upon us as *inferiors,* morally, physically, intellectually. They thought our children could not learn to read but for Yankee teachers. Let me give you an illustrative personal incident.—In a mixed company, the question arose, where was I, your correspondent, educated? One affirmed positively that it was at Yale College: another thought otherwise, but somewhere else *at the North.* It was resolved to refer the question to me. I told them that my education had all been in the schools, & the University of No. C.— They cooly asked me how it was *possible* I could have acquired *there,* such an education as they knew me to possess? Some of them did not know we had an university, & were filled with astonishment when I told them that one of our earliest acts after the revolution was to found it, & that it had in it 400 undergraduates with as good a set of professors and instructors as Yale could show.

Especially let us educate our children at home. And to this end we must make our advantages of education quite equal to what they are any where else in the U. States.

16. Nathan Lord's Dismissal from Dartmouth, 1863

Nathan Lord (1792–1870) was born in Maine, graduated from Bowdoin in 1809, trained in theology at Andover, and ordained in 1816. He was elected a trustee of Dartmouth in 1821 and its president seven years later. After the Mexican war he became an outspoken supporter of slavery on the ground that it was supported by Scripture. The Civil War undermined the tolerance of New Hampshire Congregationalists on this issue; and in 1863 the Merrimac County Conference of Congregational Churches adopted resolutions expressing esteem for the "venerable President" of Dartmouth but fear also that the college's welfare was "greatly imperilled by the existence of a popular prejudice against it arising from the publication and use of some of his peculiar views touching public affairs." The Conference urged the trustees of the college to inquire "whether its interests do not demand a change in the Presidency. . . ." The trustees refused to remove Lord but expressed a disapproval of his actions so strong that he felt impelled to resign. This document was his response.

Leon B. Richardson, *History of Dartmouth College* (Hanover, 1932), II, 511–12.

In making this communication to the Hon. & Rev. Bd. of Trustees I take the liberty respectfully to protest against their right to impose any religious, ethical or political test upon any member of their own body or any member of the College Faculty, beyond what is recognized by the Charter of the Institution or express Statutes or stipulations conformed to that instrument, however urged or suggested, directly or indirectly, by individuals or public bodies assuming to be as Visitors of the College, or advisers of the Trustees.

The action of the Trustees on certain resolutions of the Merrimac County Conference of Churches virtually imposes such a test, inasmuch as it implicitly represents and censures me as having become injurious to the college, not on account of my official malfeasance or delinquency —on the contrary its commendations of my personal and official character and conduct during my long term of service far exceed my merit —but for my opinions and publications on questions of Biblical ethics and interpretations which are supposed by the Trustees to bear unfavorably upon one branch of the policy pursued by the present administration of the Government of the Country.

For my opinions and my expressions of opinion on such subjects, I hold myself responsible only to God, and the constitutional tribunals of my country, inasmuch as they are not touched by the Charter of the College or any express Statutes or stipulations. And while my unswerving loyalty to the Government of my fathers, proved and tested by more than seventy years of devotion to its true and fundamental principles, cannot be permanently discredited by the excited passions of the hour, I do not feel obliged, when its exercise is called in question, to surrender my moral and constitutional right and Christian liberty in this respect, nor to submit to any censure nor consent to any conditions such as are implied in the aforesaid action of the Board; which action is made more impressive upon me, in view of the private communications of some of its members.

But not choosing to place myself in any unkind relation to a body having the responsible guardianship of the College—a body from which I have received so many tokens of confidence and regard, and, believing it to be inconsistent with Christian charity and propriety to carry on my administration while holding and expressing opinions injurious, as they imagine, to the interests of the College, and offensive to that party in the country which they professedly represent, I hereby resign my office as President.

I also resign my office as Trustee.

In taking leave of the college with which I have been connected as Trustee or President more than forty years—very happily to myself and as the Trustees often have given me to understand, not without benefit to the College, I beg leave to assure them that I shall ever entertain a grateful sense of the favorable consideration shown to me by themselves and their predecessors in office; and that I shall never cease to desire the peace and prosperity of the College; and that it may be kept true to the principles of its foundation.